GROWING UP:
CHILDHOOD IN ENGLISH CANADA FROM THE GREAT WAR TO THE AGE OF TELEVISION

Childhood is a socially constructed state that can differ significantly from culture to culture and period to period. The history of childhood is rapidly emerging as an important area of study. Neil Sutherland looks at children's lives in modern, industrialized, pre-television Canada, from before the First World War to the 1960s.

Based on adult memories of childhood, this book investigates a wide selection of experiences of growing up. Sutherland lays out the structure of children's lives in such settings as the home, the classroom, the church, the street, and the playground – in short, in the communities of childhood. He explains how children arrived at their gender, class, and other identities, and how they came to adopt the values they did. Sutherland focuses on recurrent, common features of the everyday life of children.

This book offers a unique, child-centred approach developed by a leading expert on the history of Canadian childhood. Written in straightforward, jargon-free language and illustrated with numerous photographs, it will be of special interest to those in the fields of social and educational history. Also, because Sutherland is successful in describing the perceptions and feelings of children, it will intrigue anyone who grew up in this period or who wants to understand the experiences of friends and family who did.

NEIL SUTHERLAND is Professor Emeritus of Educational Studies, University of British Columbia.

NEIL SUTHERLAND

Growing Up:
Childhood in English Canada
from the Great War
to the Age of Television

UNIVERSITY OF TORONTO PRESS
Toronto Buffalo London

© University of Toronto Press Incorporated 1997
Toronto Buffalo London
Printed in Canada

ISBN 0-8020-4136-1 (cloth)
ISBN 0-8020-7983-0 (paper)

Printed on acid-free paper

Canadian Cataloguing in Publication Data

Sutherland, Neil, 1931–
    Growing up : childhood in English Canada from the
    Great War to the age of television

    Includes index.
    ISBN 0-8020-4136-1 (bound)   ISBN 0-8020-7983-0 (pbk.)

    1. Children – Canada – History – 20th century.
    I. Title.

    HQ792.C3S974 1997   305.23'0971   C97-930065-7

University of Toronto Press acknowledges the assistance to its publishing
program of the Canada Council and the Ontario Arts Council

This book has been published with the help of a grant from the Humanities and
Social Sciences Federation of Canada, using funds provided by the Social
Sciences and Humanities Research Council of Canada.

Contents

Preface

In *Children in English-Canadian Society*, published in the 1970s, I explained how English Canadians created a set of social policies to cope with the problems confronting children in a country being transformed by rapid industrialization and urbanization.[1] Between the 1870s and the end of the Great War, I argued, those English Canadians who influenced or made policy affecting children crafted a rough consensus as to which measures they felt would best serve children – and, in the long run, the population as a whole – in their new, 'modern' society.[2]

Sometime after I finished *Children in English-Canadian Society*, I turned to what I thought was a natural second volume, one that would chart the uneven success Canadians actually had in bringing their child-centred programs to bear on the lives of children. I proceeded on two fronts. On one, I began to develop case-studies showing how the new policies were implemented, starting with the 'new education' in the schools of British Columbia. On the other, I examined the work of practitioners – social workers, public-health nurses, probation officers, children's homes' officials, and teachers – who were supposed to change the lives of children. Here I began by looking at how public-health nurses, whose profession was a direct product of the reform movement, actually worked with children.[3] Although I did not see it at first, my study of nurses suggested the book I came to write – the story of the lives of children told from the children's point of view.

In 1928, the British Columbia Board of Health reported that no fewer than 38 out of 130 high-school and 227 out of 703 elementary-school pupils in the city of Fernie suffered from malnutrition. Public-health nurse Jean Dunbar described her campaign against this condition.

After each monthly inspection I now divide the class into three groups ...; all of average weight and over receive white tags, those from over 1 to 7 percent. under-

weight receive blue tags, and those over 7 percent. underweight receive red tags. I explain to the children in the class-room what the different colours mean and have them repeat the following: –
  Cards of white all right,
  Cards of blue won't do,
  Cards of red, danger ahead.
I then urge them to see how quickly they can all receive white cards and so compete with the other rooms in the school.[4]

As I went on with my research, my thoughts kept coming back to that sad little scene. How would I have felt if I had had to hold up a blue or red tag? How had a benignly conceived policy turned into such a travesty of care? Surely here, I concluded, in the actual lives of the children involved, was the most important place to discover, to explain, and to evaluate the effects of public policy directed at them. How did all the new policies in health, welfare, and education touch on or transform the lives of children in their homes, families, congregations, classrooms, and in the total institutions in which some of them were confined? As I continued my investigation of the new education, I began to interview adults about their schooling, asking them to talk about how they experienced various elements in the curriculum and how they later employed what they had learned.

It took only a few interviews, however, to drive home to me the fact that people recall their schooling as a whole. If I had continued to concentrate on my initial list of questions – such as, how did you learn to read? – I might well have been able to discuss such technical matters as the use of the phonetic or look–say methods of teaching reading, the use of reading groups, and oral recitations in the classrooms of British Columbia. I would not, however, have understood much about reading in the life of primary-school children. To my interviewees, learning to read was inextricably tangled together with such matters as the sort of teacher they had, how they got along with other children, and how their parents felt about schooling. They remembered such things as: 'I was physically afraid to go to school on some days, but couldn't get out of it'; or 'With her you knew you learned a thing. The evidence was there because you could repeat the learning accurately, even years later'; or 'I accidentally knocked his book off his desk. He said he would get me at recess. I told the teacher I was sick and she let me stay in over recess, but I wet my pants before lunch. I wanted to die'; or 'Half the fun of school was the walk to and fro, having a friend, going home for lunch, and admiring the flowers in people's gardens.'

Childhood, viewed from its own perspective, is not the generally happy time of sentimental memories. On the contrary, childhood is at least as complex a stage in any life history as is adulthood. Children experience the full range of physical and emotional circumstances that characterize adult lives. Indeed, their acute sense of themselves in their circumstances is frequently exacerbated by their only partially achieved understanding of what is real and what is possible, and by the added fact of their inability to control, or even to comprehend, much of their lives. However, despite the enmeshing powers of parents, teachers, other adults, and even other children, at certain times boys and girls were clearly the subjects of, as well as objects in, their own lives. The ways in which policies affected them for good or ill are embedded in their lives and, if we want to see how such social plans really worked, for good or ill, we must look at them in their everyday surroundings.

I thus came to the writing of this book. I decided that I would deal with the 'implementation' years by carefully describing growing up at that time from the perspective of children themselves.[5] To actually get 'inside' childhood, I would ask adults born between about 1910 and 1950 to tell me about their youthful experiences. From their accounts, I would re-create the routine events – the scripts – that cumulated to form the structures of children's lives. As I described these structures, I would also describe children's experiences within them, and especially their feelings about them. I would investigate these matters as they played themselves out in the home, the classroom, the congregation, and on streets and in playgrounds: in short, in the communities of childhood.[6]

For reasons laid out in chapter 1, I decided to build my work out of the overlapping experiences of children in three British Columbia neighbourhoods. I would find out about these childhoods by asking people to tell me about them. I would test the representativeness or otherwise of what they told me by interviewing some who grew up in other parts of the country and by reading what other Canadians have written about their childhood. Although this book would be very different from its predecessor, I would begin it at the point where the other ended. As the previous book argued, by the end of the Great War, Canadian children were growing up in a modern urban and industrial society. The new policies it outlined were designed to benefit children in that society.[7] Even if I did not discuss them, they would be there in the background, providing some of the context in which my subjects lived through their childhood. One can, for example, see elements of the 'new' education in their schooling, and a preference for foster rather than institutional care for those whose families were unable to care for them. One can also see what a long, complicated, and sometimes unsuccessful journey it is from a statement of public policy, on the one hand, to its positive articulation in the lives for whom it was intended, on the other.

Where was the book to end? For the first time since the end of the Great War, people in the 1950s and 1960s began to question the appropriateness of much of the supposed consensus on child-rearing. These criticisms eventually effected changes in long-lived policies and practices. Parents embraced new forms of child-rearing. Corporal punishment, and the traditional justification for it, sharply declined in home and in school. School curricula shifted from a 'progressive' integration of various fields of study to a concentration on the academic disciplines. In what was probably a more important development, however, the late 1950s and 1960s ushered television into the lives of Canadian children. In March 1950, Canadians owned about 13,500 television sets. By the census of 1961, 82.5 per cent of Canadian households had a set.[8] Parents, teachers, psychologists, and others worried about the long-term effects of sustained television viewing by children. Some research suggested, for example, that television affected the cognitive development of children.[9] Regardless of its effect on them, however, children wholeheartedly welcomed television into their lives. By the 1970s it consumed as much of youngsters' time as did school, and it intruded to a far greater degree than radio, or even the movies, had done in the lives of those who people this book.

One must not overemphasize the differences between childhood at various times. The core dimensions of children's lives – their relationships with their parents, with their teachers, and with other children – showed more continuity than change over most of this century. Indeed, one can see numerous areas of continuity between nineteenth-century and late twentieth-century childhoods. None the less, if many aspects of childhood have a timeless quality, others are rooted in a particular time and place. Although the Great War and the advent of television do not represent major watersheds in the way in which children grew up, they make useful starting and ending points for my study. In the years between them, we can see the shape of 'modern' childhoods that were different both from their nineteenth-century predecessors and from those that characterize the end of the twentieth century.

To whom am I referring when I employ the term 'children'? I must make three prefatory points before responding to this question. First, childhood is a socially constructed rather than a biological state. Even during the period of complete dependency (up to a year or two) and of very considerable dependency (from two years to five or six), what constitutes childhood for any particular society, or group or class or gender in that society, is a matter of human decision rather than biological necessity. Both the historical and the social-science literature provide many examples of children as young as six or seven taking primary responsibility for their own welfare. Second, and mostly a product of the nineteenth-century, the notion of sharply distinguishing people according to age was fully part of our culture by the early part of the twentieth century.[10] This division had led to a heightened consciousness of childhood as a distinctly separate stage of existence. Schoolchildren came to be sorted by age rather than competence, which, in turn, led them to arrange their play along the same lines. By the 1920s, age-sorting had become a central and unquestioned element in Canadians' conventional practices. Third, although much that structures a person's developing sense of self takes place in the first two or three years of life, the governing events are beyond the ability of his or her memory to recall. It is not possible to get a child's perspective on them.

I investigated childhood beginning at the point of earliest memory. The childhoods I discuss thus have no firm beginning age, nor do they have a firm ending one. From their twelfth to their fifteenth birthdays, young people crossed a number of watersheds which, taken together, marked the end of their childhood.[11] Specifically, the onset of puberty, becoming a 'teenager,' earning passing grades in entrance examinations or otherwise completing public (later elementary) schooling, starting high school (later junior high school), being confirmed, reaching one's bar mitzvah, attaining the legal school-leaving age, going to work full-time, combined in a variety of ways for child, family, and society to recognize that youngsters had embarked on a new stage of their lives.[12] People's recollections move back and forth over these boundaries, but it is rarely difficult to sort out when they are talking about their childhood and when about their adolescence. Only very rarely do I comment on that later stage of development; the history of adolescence in these years needs its own study.

Quotations from people's recollections of their childhood make up much of what I report. In what follows, however, most quotations are both brief and unidentified. I eschewed long extracts because, in relation to my goal, they give undue emphasis to the uniqueness of individual lives. Employing brief quotations from many people's accounts enabled me to illustrate the great range of feelings embedded in the same or very similar recurrent scripts. As I explain in chapter 1, my decision to conduct most of my interviews with people whose lives overlapped with each other also meant that the customary code numbers would not protect the anonymity I guaranteed to each informant. While this situation is perhaps unsatisfactory to those of us who feel uneasy in the absence of such detail, it accords, as it must, with the ethical guidelines that framed my study.

At this point I should make four further qualifications to what follows. First, I must note that writing from the perspective of children – to give a collective voice to girls and boys – means that certain adults may be treated unfairly. Clearly, children misconstrue the motives and actions of parents, foster parents, and teachers, and as adults are often still prisoners of what they remember. Second, most of the children who speak here are from the mainstream of English-Canadian society. Those from First Nations or other backgrounds who generally lived outside the mainstream appear but are underrepresented in this book. While some are recorded elsewhere, many more must have their voices heard. Third, while this book is written in a context provided by recent research in such related areas of historical investigation as those on women, education, social class, and public policy, I have cited only research that I have employed directly or referred to in my text. Through the notes, I tied what Canadian children saw and thought to the 'hard' international and comparative data where the latter were central and available. I summarized those data only when they directly related to what I was discussing.

Finally, I must note that my account is not based on a representative cross-section of English-Canadian children of the time. My research assistants and I interviewed about the same number of men and of women, and roughly the same number of each from each decade. One of my neighbourhoods was mostly working class, one was mostly middle class, and the third was made up of agricultural pioneers. Those interviewed in Halifax grew up in a working-class district, and those in Toronto a middle-class one. Since more men than women have published autobiographies, the latter are underrepresented in the examples I read. To make these points, however, provides a spurious objectivity to what is a qualitative study. As I explain in the first chapter, our open-ended interviews varied greatly in both the quantity and the quality of the information they provided. In my view, they also told us an enormous amount about childhood in English Canada, but not in a way that permits reporting it with even the precision that accompanies analysis of an open-ended questionnaire. As they consider what follows – sometimes characterized as 'thick' description – readers will have to judge for themselves if it adds up to anything more than an analysis of the lives of a tiny sample drawn from those who were children in the years surveyed.

This book is organized topically rather than chronologically. The first chapter discusses the problems posed by employing oral evidence about childhood, and outlines how I dealt with them. The fact that my major interest was to lay out the recurrent events – the 'scripts' – common to many childhoods, rather than the unique events peculiar to any particular childhood, sharply diminished problems arising out of the fallibility of memory.

The next three chapters portray childhood as it was experienced in the nuclear family. Chapter 2 describes such aspects of the geography of childhood as neighbourhoods, homes, sleeping arrangements, and patterns of parental work. It also examines the prevalence of lone-parenting, and how the emotional relationships between parents affected the lives of their children. Chapters 3 and 4 lay out the central dimensions of the family life of children. Parents possessed almost unlimited amounts of both authority and power and, in a patriarchal setting, children discovered, developed, and practised their gender, class, ethnic, and religious identities. In the family setting, as well, parents acted as educational strategists for their children, taught children how they expected them to behave, and employed those sanctions, including abusive ones, that followed on failure to conform.

Although still concerned with family life, the next four chapters move beyond their three predecessors' focus on the immediate family. Chapter 5 looks at the family life of children whose circumstances meant they were brought up by grandparents, other members of their extended families, or in foster homes. Chapters 6 and 7 describe the role that children's paid and unpaid work played in the family economies of working- and middle-class urban dwellers, and in those of twentieth-century pioneers. For children, most particularly sad or happy occasions involved their extended as well as their nuclear families, and these are dealt with in chapter 8.

The last three chapters discuss aspects of childhood that were not part of family life. Chapter 9 examines how children experienced the very traditional, very 'formal,' sort of schooling that characterized elementary education in these years. Chapter 10 describes the workings of the 'culture' of childhood: how youngsters learned how to be children, to become members of both the almost timeless world of childhood and their own brief generation within it. The final chapter moves beyond the temporal boundaries of the rest of the book and takes an informal look at continuity and change in the lives of English-Canadian children over the whole of the last century.

I have sometimes been asked about my personal connection to this study, beyond my role of investigator. I was, after all, a child in British Columbia in the 1930s and 1940s. There, I belonged to a family and to peer groups, I attended public schools and Sunday schools, and I participated in many ways in the neighbourhood communities of which I was a part. Sometimes those whom I interviewed made the courteous effort to include me in a discussion about things we may have had in common. Occasionally I would respond, as minimally as possible, and only to the point at which people's urge to tell their own stories took over in the way that I describe in the first chapter. The men my research assistants and I talked to may have had an 'I'-centred story, and the women a 'we'-centred one, but, with one exception, none had a story in which I played any sort of role. In that particular case, I conducted my very first interview with a friend with whom I went to public school for two or three years. I took this step so that I could personally test the merits of overlapping memories as they applied to the sort of research I wanted to do.

As I explain in the first chapter, the life stories people told were in effect crafted at the moment of their telling. As such, they gave coherence to lives as their subjects saw them in the context of both that moment and the particular circumstances of the interview. Only an aggressive intervention on my part could have transformed them into a life story that included me. In this sense, then, whether I shared some or many experiences with those with whom I talked was not an element in what I was told. Further, I did about half of the interviews, and youthful research assistants did the rest. The fact that the texts of their interviews, conducted, as they were, mostly by those whose own childhoods came long after the period I was investigating, displayed similar scripts and structures offered objective evidence to my point that my own childhood was irrelevant to what I was doing.

After noting the major point that my own life had little if any influence on what I have written in this book, I must also say that I see some of my own childhood (and, sometimes, that of my own children) in it. It would be surprising – suspicious even – if I did not. After all, as a child in a lone-parent family, I spent some of my childhood years in two Vancouver neighbourhoods more similar to Cedar Cottage than to Kerrisdale. My schooling in two Vancouver elementary schools was very much like what I have described here. I did reasonably well in school and, like many of my informants, generally enjoyed it. (Later, I also spent a few years as a 'formalistic' teacher.) In the late 1930s, my sister, Joy, and I spent three years in a remote rural area of the province in a setting that was very similar to Evelyn as it was at the time. The children who were our classmates were called upon to play the same major role in their families' economies as were Evelyn youngsters. We ourselves even learned to do some of the same chores, such as fetching the family's water in pails from a creek and cutting what seemed to be unending piles of kindling and firewood. In turn, my own children grew up in the 1960s and 1970s in a middle-class Vancouver neighbourhood.

In consequence, I do recall some but by no means all of the childhood scripts I describe. Even so, my memory of shared experience is only one version of the many ways it manifested itself in people's lives. On the other hand, and of central importance to my narrative, my interviews and other data constantly surprised me with the richness and variety that they told of in the lives of those who were children in the years before, during, and after those of my childhood. This book is their story, not mine.

Acknowledgments

In writing this book I received the help of many people. First, of course, are those women and men who so generously shared their childhoods with me. Readers will soon discover my enormous debt to them, which I gratefully acknowledge. Although they bear no responsibility for what I wrote, clearly they 'made' this book.

Many friends and colleagues gave immeasurable help. My lifelong friends George Meehan and John Calam read the manuscript and made many characteristically wise suggestions. Among the many others to whom I am deeply in debt are Marion Amies, Jean Barman, Roderick Barman, Bill Bruneau, Rebecca Priegert Coulter, Jorgen Dahlie, LeRoi Daniels, R.I.K. Davidson, Donald Fisher, Jane Gaskell, the late Thom Greenfield, Jacqueline Gresko, Norah Lewis, John Murray, Joy Nicolls, Juliet Pollard, Barbara Schrodt, Peter Seixas, Dick Selleck, Nancy Sheehan, Tim Stanley, Frederick Thirkell, the late George Tomkins, Patricia Vertinsky, Rita Watson, Richard T. White, Alan Wieder, and J. Donald Wilson. Although I accepted only some of their suggestions, I did take all of them seriously.

I am grateful for the interviewing and other research assistance provided by Tony Arruda, Brian Bain, Daphnee Butts, Celia Haig-Brown, the late Elizabeth Lees, Bill Maciejko, Indiana Matters, Emilie Montgomery, Denise Newton, Donna Penney, Leanne Purkis, Theresa Richardson, Meira Shem-Tov, Peter van Drongelen, and Tony Varga.

My work in places outside of Vancouver would have been impossible without the help of others. Thom Greenfield put me in touch with some interviewees who had grown up in Toronto. Eric Ricker and 'Greenbank' enthusiast Bill Mont arranged for me to talk to residents of that now-demolished Halifax community. Evelyn pioneer Mollie Ralston introduced me to the community and carefully took me over the ground of the settlement so I could begin to see it as it had been during her childhood. Her fellow pioneer Lynn Lychak provided me with a list of those who might consent to be interviewed.

The staffs of the University of British Columbia Library, the Vancouver Archives, the Provincial Archives of British Columbia, the Provincial Archives of Manitoba, the Archives of Ontario, and the Bulkley Valley Historical and Museum Society were assiduous in providing asked-for assistance. As she supervised the production of the 'Bibliography of Canadian Childhood,' Linda L. Hale directed me to many relevant sources.

Over the whole length of the Canadian Childhood History Project, of which this book is one product, Lily Kuhn typed proposals, notes, and innumerable drafts. Her cheerful and meticulous attention to the detail and volume of this task became a major contribution to its eventual completion. I am very much in her debt.

I tried out many of the notions recorded in this book on my students at the University of British Columbia. They were generous in their suggestions and comments, and helpful with their criticism.

I am grateful for the generous support accorded to the Canadian Childhood History Project by the Social Sciences and Humanities Research Council of Canada and by the Faculty of Education of the University of British Columbia.

Some parts of this book appeared in different forms in *BC Studies*, *The History of Education Review*, *The Newsletter* of the Canadian History of Education Association, *Labour/Le Travail*, *Histoire sociale/Social History*, *Curriculum Inquiry*, and *Our Schools/Ourselves*. I am pleased to thank their editors for their help.

Although they come last in this list of my debts, my family comes first in my affections. Emily, Duff, Frank, and Jessie Sutherland expressed a vigorous, personal, and critical interest in my reflections on all aspects of childhood. When she joined our family, Edena Brown also took part in the frequent family discussions. She and Duff also provided useful editorial assistance. My debt to my wife, Janet Catherine Sutherland, is so immense that it is beyond the power of words to express in any meaningful way.

GROWING UP

1

Listening to the Winds of Childhood

The place to which you go back to listen to the wind you heard in your childhood –
that is your homeland, which is also the place where you have a grave to tend.
Though I chose to live in Quebec partly because of the love for it which my mother
passed on to me, now it is my turn to come back to Manitoba to tend her grave. And
also to listen to the wind of my childhood.
                                        – Gabrielle Roy, *The Fragile Lights of Earth*[1]

A woman born in Vancouver in 1941 recalled that her merchant-seaman
father died during the Second World War, as did her maternal grandfather
a year and a half later. She remembered, 'as a child going to school ... sometimes I would worry ... not sometimes but a lot, that something would
happen to my grandmother. Everybody seemed to be ... leaving.' Since
her widowed mother went out to work, the woman's maternal grandmother
lived with them and looked after the house, staying on even after her
mother remarried. 'If I wanted to talk to anybody I would go to my grandmother and talk with her ... She was always easy to approach.' If the girl or
her brother 'came into the room and sat next to her – there could be a
whole big room with a lot of chairs, but I always came and sat right beside
her on the chesterfield to watch TV ... she would always ... put her hand on
my hand ... or just on my knee, or hold onto my arm. There was always a lot
of physical contact ... it wasn't rushing and hugging and kissing but just very
subtle ... [She did] the same thing with my brother.'

Why take note of this homely little glimpse into the workings of one
Vancouver family as it was in the 1940s and 1950s? In the view of one critic,
what readers gain from 'exotic forays into remote lives' is 'not historical
actuality; it is voyeuristic empathy.' Such 'vivid intimacies promote historical sympathy but attenuate historical understanding' because they under-

score 'universal constants of human feelings' but ignore 'the particular social and cultural trends that both link the past with, and differentiate it from the present.'[2] Although the recollection provided above might serve as an example of 'voyeuristic empathy,' I actually employ it among the evidence for a description in chapter 5 of the complex roles that grandmothers played at a particular period in the history of Canadian families. That topic, in turn, is part of my effort to lay out the structure of children's lives, to understand how they experienced them and what they felt about them in the settings and communities of their childhoods.

Whether they collect memories for voyeuristic purposes or as evidence for serious historical or social-scientific investigations, researchers must confront certain questions about the nature of these data. What is memory? How reliable a guide to the past is it? In particular, how much confidence can one place in memories of childhood? One can perhaps believe that the recollected words of a playground rhyme, once upon a time chanted over and over again, may be reasonably accurate, but what of events that were less discrete but of more moment? These are, of course, not new questions. Psychologists have studied the issue for a century or more, in recent years quite intensively.[3] Historians are now also probing more deeply into the nature of what has always been a central element in their stock-in-trade.[4] Since memories are virtually my only primary source, they give rise to what is this book's most difficult methodological problem: can one use the recollections of adults to re-create the internal worlds of childhood? If so, how? In the remainder of this chapter I outline, mostly in the context of my own work, what I believe to be reasonably satisfactory answers to these questions.

Recollections of childhood are of two sorts, and each sort is produced in two ways. Adults describe how they or others reared children. Adults also recall incidents, feelings, and experiences and the like about their own childhood. In turn, recollections are either self-created, such as those that appear in memoirs, family histories, and autobiographies or novels dealing with childhood or adolescence, or generated deliberately and sometimes systematically by journalists, social investigators, social scientists, and historians. Since adults' memories of how they reared their children do not raise methodological questions about memories of childhood per se, I do not consider them here.

Most adult memories of childhood begin with certain unique events that took place between one's third and fourth birthdays. ('My earliest recollection ... was a very traumatic stay in St Vincent's Hospital at the ripe old age of three, for a tonsillectomy' ; 'I remember the other children in our block had a pin fair, and we played games'; 'I remember my first day at dancing class when I was about three'; 'A mooring line caught around my foot and dragged me overboard. I sank to the bottom. A man pulled me out.') A few people can give connected accounts of certain regular aspects of their lives from about the same age. ('Every Sunday we went to my grandparents' for a big family Sunday dinner'; 'We had our weekly bath on Saturday and put on our clean clothes on Sunday.')

Both sorts of early memories, however, raise questions about what is truly recalled and what is the product of having absorbed family lore and followed family practices over the years. ('My childhood memories were enhanced, of course, each growing year, by repetitious tales my parents told.')[5] Moreover, many of the most important early events in human lives – learning to walk; learning to control bladder and bowels; learning to talk; developing complex relationships with parents, siblings, and other relatives; learning to express (or suppress) certain emotions; learning something about being a boy or being a girl; learning to play complicated physical and mental games; beginning to display qualities that will structure their personalities, their lifelong characteristics, and learning to make connections with other children – take place before the years of either unique or systematic recall.

Psychologists explain the absence of early memories by arguing that forming a memory depends on an initial capacity to interpret what is going on. Since the very young lack this capacity, 'early autobiographical memory is [not] lost in infantile amnesia but ... never existed as such.'[6] We must also note that memory is often multisensory; in their 'mind's eye,' people see, hear, smell, and even taste and touch certain dimensions of what they are recalling. They then transform what they recall into words that are only lightly suggestive of the totality of what they remember. Recorded in some permanent form these words ('texts' in the terminology of recent criticism), rather than a memory itself, become the researcher's stock-in-trade. While most would probably concur with the commonsensical notion that memories of childhood from about four years of age onward tend to be more vivid than those of adulthood, and that we can recollect some of them more easily than we can those of events in our adult lives, we have, despite claims to the contrary, no evidence that these early memories are any less fallible.[7] We must be as sceptical of childhood memories as we are of any others.

Memory is not only fallible; it is also shaped by the circumstances that prompt it. Autobiographies are briefs in advocacy of their subjects; each life story is told or written from the point of view of, and is designed to convey a message to, the present. In autobiographical accounts written years apart, for example, the English novelist Leslie Thomas has given two very different accounts of his life as a Barnardo boy. In his author's note in *In My Wildest Dreams*, published in 1984, Thomas remarked that his first book 'about my days in Barnardo's, and called *This Time Next Week*, was written twenty-one years ago. It was a fragment of autobiography but I have not re-read it ... After all an autobiography is how you remember things now.'[8]

Further, autobiographies display an overall coherence and sense of unity that does not characterize life itself. As prisoners of the chaos of living, of circumstances they did not make and over which they have little or no control (what Alexsander Solzhenitsyn calls 'the pitiless crowbar of events'), most people live lives that are an agglomeration of chance, choices, contradictions, false starts, accidents, and lucky and unlucky breaks. After each major change in personal circumstances – triggered by such events as moving from one school to another, being promoted from elementary to high school, joining the workforce, leaving home, getting married or divorced, undergoing an intense religious experience, losing a job, suffering a serious illness, or the death of a child, a parent, or a spouse – people establish new priorities and personal continuities. Each time life 'happens' to them, they adopt a new structure (or what Craig Barclay calls a 'self-schema') that frames the new phase of their lives.[9]

At each of these stages of their lives, people also see the accumulation of their experiences as adding up to a coherent whole. This unity, however, is accomplished by a generally unconscious but none the less thorough reordering and editing of the past. Further, while men and women tend to tell or write their life stories chronologically, they approach them from very different socially conditioned stances. Both my own experience and that of others who conduct oral histories show that men's stories tend to revolve around their systematic activities, their games, their work, their sequence of occupations, displaying their narrator as the central subject. Women's stories are less individualistic, usually focusing on their relationships to such significant others as parents, spouses, children, fellow workers, and friends.[10] Recollections or novels that deal extensively with childhood are often written by those whose early lives were unhappy ones.[11] Most life stories also contain mythical elements, such as those French historian Jean Peneff noted were the 'most frequently found – the self-made man, the unhappy childhood, the modest social origin, the successful militant life ...'[12]

Taken together, then, these characteristics of life stories indicate that, whether we think that earlier events in our lives are significant, or whether we even remark on them at all, depends on how we currently structure our lives and how we describe, explain, and justify them. The skills, therefore, that produce a coherent life story or readable autobiography, and one that will perhaps provide historians with sharp insights into events that took place when the autobiographer was an adult, may actually take us away from the realities of childhood. Alternatively, a series of unconnected but vivid vignettes suggests a childhood as yet not reflected upon or put in a final perspective and comes closer to the events of childhood, with all of their sensual and emotional freight, which are the subject of the anecdotes.

Psychologists provide support for this position. I have already noted that, for an event to impinge on our consciousness, we must have some capacity to interpret or understand it. From this position psychologists go on to explain that the shape a memory takes is as much the product of the process of remembering as of the actual characteristics of whatever it is that is being recalled. They argue, therefore, that a memory is really a reconstruction of what is being recalled rather than a reproduction of it and, further, that a succession of reconstructions of the same event form themselves into a chain that tends to diverge more and more from the original.[13] Consider an oversimplified example. When she is four, a girl is joined in her family by a baby brother. Since she is old enough to understand this event, she will also have the capacity to recall it. When prompted by some event in her adult life – say, the birth of her own child – she will reconstruct it in light of her current circumstances. When she recalls it at another time – say, when her brother also becomes a father – she will then reconstruct it in the light of both the original event itself and her previous reconstruction of it, and so on.

The fact that people tend to write their autobiographies or tell their life stories during or after that stage which psychologists call the 'life review' strengthens reservations about life stories and autobiographies. At this point people feel the necessity to look back over their whole existence in order to justify themselves to themselves, to make the self-edited sum of their lives to have been worth living. At this stage, Paul Thompson notes, people are more willing to remember and are less concerned than those who are younger about fitting their stories to social norms.[14] On the other hand, as Robert Roberts discovered, at this stage people tend to look 'through a golden haze' at events they once viewed objectively.[15] Both circumstances may contribute to a coherent life story or autobiography that satisfies the teller's or writer's need for a life that he or she can look back upon as being worthwhile. Unhappy, embarrassing, shameful, or unpleasant events can be transformed or omitted as the narrator moves towards his or her 'happy ending.' Coherence may, as well, be a product of the cumulative effects of the extending chain of reconstructions of the past that accompany a life review.[16]

Social scientists and historians have tried in a number of ways to reduce, or even eliminate, the subjectivity of unstructured recollections. They employ questionnaires, or ask a series of narrowly focused questions. None the less, interviews, and even the collection of questionnaires, take place in a social relationship, however fleeting it may be. Historian Paul Thompson explains that the form recollections take varies because of differences in style among interviewers; the sex, race, and 'social presence' of the interviewer; whether the interview is conducted anonymously, privately, or in a group setting; and whether the interviews take place in an office, home, or tavern.[17] Those whose recollections are deliberately solicited may set out to make a strong, positive impression of themselves on the interviewer. Moreover, reports of interviews or conversations involving both women and men, or different social classes, are usually transformed into writing by those who possess hegemony over the others.[18]

Even if they do not consciously or unconsciously tailor their recollections to what they think the interviewer wants to hear, or what they want to hear about themselves, those who had unhappy childhoods or unhappy lives may suppress details, or refuse to be interviewed at all because their memories may be too painful to summon up. When some of those I interviewed talked about their schooling, they made their first negative remark either assertively or tentatively, as if they were expecting someone from the educational establishment to take issue with any criticisms of schools or teachers. Other reticences are more deeply rooted. When I asked one middle-aged woman, 'Would you mind talking to me about your childhood?,' she replied, 'My childhood was so awful I don't even want to think about it. Even your asking the question has upset me.' Until recently, those who were sexually or otherwise abused as children have been particularly silent on the topic.[19]

If the fallibility and subjectivity of recollections pose such problems, then why use them at all? My response has three parts. First, memories are more similar to other historical sources than may at first appear to be the case. Many written sources begin in an oral form – the mother of an injured child describes an automobile accident to a police officer; the 'head of the household' gives details about it to a census taker; a newspaper reporter talks to children lined up to see Santa Claus; the diarist overhears the conversation of her youngsters; the letter writer proudly tells relatives of the clever sayings of his sons and daughters. As such they can be less 'objective' than we customarily believe.[20]

Consider this not-unusual situation. A fifteen-year-old became pregnant. Her parents decided to bring up their grandchild as their own, ostensibly a sibling to its natural mother. Although family, friends, and neighbours probably know what took place, the state does not. In the case described to me – one I was asked not to record or note down – the grandfather placed his name and that of his wife rather than the real parents' names on the birth registration form. Consequently, the child's 'long' British Columbia birth certificate is inaccurate. The grandmother as 'mother' received the family allowance cheque. I surmise, as well, that, over the years, census takers were told of one fewer ever-born-to child by one woman, and one more by the other. A decision taken in the supposed best interest of both children meant that at least five official, 'objective' records are less objective than they appear to be.

None the less, the problems of oral evidence are mostly posed by the recollections themselves rather than by any particular mode of collecting them. From the very beginnings of their discipline, historians have applied the canons of their craft in ways that enabled them to use recollections (and all other sources) to good effect.[21] As Thucydides himself wrote in the preface to his *History of the Peloponnesian War*:

As regards the material facts of the war, I have not been content to follow casual informants, or my own imagination. Where I have not been an eye witness myself, I have investigated with utmost accuracy attainable every detail that I have taken at second hand. The task has been laborious, for witnesses of the same particular events have given versions that have varied according to their sympathies or retentive powers.[22]

Historians can also employ their traditional procedures in their investigations of childhood.

As they utilize memories, historians are helped by the fact that certain types of recollections are more reliable than others. Our lives are mostly organized around what psychologists sometimes describe as 'schemata' and 'scripts,' or what oral historians label 'recurrent events.' Schema theorists argue that we develop mental representations of the general characteristics of events, activities, and even places to which we are repeatedly exposed. All of us, for example, develop a sense of the age-old structure that stories assume.[23] Scripts, or recurrent events, are a particular kind of schema. They are the way in which our memories organize those events and activities ('episodes') in our lives that are very similar to each other. Since many 'episodes' in life display such similarities, we remember them 'in terms of a standardized generalized episode,' or 'script.'[24] Indeed, recent research suggests that, from their very earliest years, children employ scripts as the framework around which to organize most of their experience and perhaps develop a sense that they are gaining some control over what they do.[25]

We have learned, too, that people can remember with reasonable accuracy the 'schemata' and 'scripts' of their childhood. Our schemata of house, yard, school, and neighbourhood, for example, provide the stages on which we recall the enactment of the scripts of our childhood. As we become socialized, we gradually take on the routines, beliefs, and related rituals embedded in the scripts of our lives. In turn, scripts become tremendous engines in the development of our gender and other identities. Further, and of major importance to this study, as adults remember the scripts of their childhoods, they also remember the feelings and emotions that were embedded in these scripts.

There are two sorts of 'scripts' – situational and personal. The daily routine of family life in the 1930s, for example, was made up of numerous situational scripts. Family members arose in the same sequence each weekday morning, and certain people were charged with such regular tasks as lighting fires, preparing breakfast, feeding siblings, clearing the table, washing the dishes, and filling the woodbox. Thus, although people cannot recall any particular morning, they find it easy to remember the breakfast routines and other family scripts of their childhood. They can describe how Saturday and Sunday scripts differed from weekday ones. They can describe the family scripts that took place every Christmas. They can remember phrases and sentences that recurred in the speech of parents and teachers. 'The words of my mother were heard so often that they too became part of my memory,' wrote Mildred Young Hubbert, including such comments as 'Life's tough so toughen up. If you don't like it you shouldn't have got born.' Jim Caplette's mother often said, 'Hard work never killed anybody.'[26]

Personal scripts take place within situational ones. For example, each and every day they went to school, and in all the classrooms they entered, certain children behaved in such a way as to draw as little attention to themselves as possible. They dropped their eyes if the teacher scanned the room, they held back when teachers or pupil leaders were picking members of teams, they stayed away from noisy or extroverted children. They had a whole series of personal, self-effacing scripts that they acted out in the context of the many situational scripts that characterized their schooling. Of both First Nations and Japanese-Canadian children, Joy Kogawa observed: 'There's something in the animal-like shyness I recognize in the dark eyes [of Native pupils]. A quickness to look away. I remember, when I was a child in Slocan, seeing the same swift flick-of-a-cat's-tail look in the eyes of my friends.'[27]

The same script may be played out in different families cheerfully or in an atmosphere of hostility and tension. Mothers and daughters doing dishes together used to be one of the most common scripts of family life. In some families that followed it, the 'dishes' script was a pleasant occasion. Daughters told mothers about the day's events at school and gossiped about their friends and their friends' families. At this time, mothers passed on the oral traditions of the family, and this is why women tend to know these traditions better than men, and why they know more about their mother's family than they do about their father's. Dishes were sometimes done with the radio on, and mother and daughter shared in an aspect of the popular culture of the day. ('Mom even came to like Elvis!')

In other families, the same script took place in an atmosphere of hostility and resentment. In an intimate setting from which the child could not escape, mothers criticized the behaviour of their youngsters or the quality of their work, and made other judgmental or derogatory remarks. Thus, while both versions of this script have the same job as their core, done in almost the same way, and are therefore recollected similarly, they also had very different emotional dimensions that are also well remembered. When in later chapters I describe the central scripts of childhood, I also describe individual examples of them to show the range of feelings embedded in each.

Two characteristics of recurrent events, or scripts, are especially important. First, children spent most of their time in situations that were highly structured. The components of the life of a primary-grade child – the time before school each morning, the trip to school, the time in the classroom, recesses, and so on – embedded themselves in a complex of everyday routines. In turn, personal and situational scripts comprised the central elements in the pattern of daily, weekly, and seasonal routines that, when added together, formed the structures of each child's life. Families followed a pattern of days – Monday, washday; Tuesday, ironing day; and so on – that laid out what parents, and especially mothers, had to do. Children had to fit into this pattern. When they were small, they were to keep under the eye but out of the way of their mothers. As they got older, they began to help. On washdays, older children kept younger siblings out of the way. When children started school, they entered another world, one tightly structured by the clock, and in which they played a central role but had no part in framing.

Further, each stage of a child's life had a structural unity; those of preschoolers possessed a different unity from those of primary-grade children, and so on. This unity varied from family to family – children in large families had different structures from those in small ones; those with one parent from those with two; those from working-class backgrounds from those in the middle class; and those of Salish origin from those of Scottish. While each aspect or stage of childhood must be understood as much as possible in its own enclosed context, it is also part of a chronological sequence. Further, human structures are organic; they change over time. In stable family and school environments, change is both gradual and predictable. Indeed, predictability itself becomes an important part of changing childhood. By observing their own families and those of their peers, children learned when it was appropriate for certain changes – a later bedtime, the right to play outside after supper, and so on – to take place, and they actively pressed for them. Children were unable to influence other predictable changes, but they could ready themselves for them. They knew, for example, when they would start school or be old enough to be confirmed.

The second important characteristic of scripts is that people share them. While each human life is unique, containing both events and scripts that are distinctive to it, each person also shares with others scripts that are virtually the same. Even those whose childhoods differed considerably along class, gender, religious, and ethnic lines recalled scripts displaying many common patterns. Lives that share many similar scripts have enough common structure to enable us to generalize about them. Thus older children grew up into similar routines of chores and duties involving the care of their younger brothers and sisters. Youthful child-minders shared with each other not only the scripts of infant and child care, but also the same ambivalent feelings about their siblings.

In turn, common patterns prevailing across the country and across many groups enable one to put together the history of childhood in a particular era. My interviews showed that the classroom and other scripts of Halifax children were virtually identical to those described by their Vancouver counterparts. Hence, while each person we interviewed had an interesting – sometimes fascinating – life story, it is not my purpose to relate any of them here. Instead, I analysed the life stories of my subjects for their common patterns. I then put these together, not into a generic history of childhood, but into one that displays as fully as possible the range of experiences represented in common scripts. Thus chapter 3 describes corporal punishment as a disciplinary measure employed in some families by one parent or by both. It took the form of a mild swat in some families and a bare-buttocked thrashing in others. On the other hand, my data did not permit me to make any but the most tentative of statements as to the actual incidence of either corporal punishment itself or any particular form of it.

Finally, there is a practical as well as an historiographic argument for using recollections in writing history. Oral and other life histories are the principal sources that can take us across those barriers, such as class, that separate the few who might write down their memories from the vast majority who do not. More important, if we are ever to get 'inside' childhood experiences, then we must ask adults to recall how they thought about, felt, and experienced their growing up. Childhood is suffused by periods of joy, happiness, exuberance, intense physical well-being, sadness, embarrassment, shame, hatred, and fear. 'As a child,' Judith Finlayson wrote, 'I found the story [Hans Christian Andersen's 'The Little Match Girl'] terrifying. And even now, it sends a shudder down my spine. The fears that story conveys are the fears that go hand in hand with being a child. Because children are so powerless and dependent, they live with a constant ... fear that they will be abandoned. What, for instance, will happen to them if their parents die?'[28]

Children and adults have a different relationship with their physical selves, with animals, with aspects of the physical world; children must acquire what Northrop Frye calls the 'social skin' that marks the boundary between people and their environment.[29] They learn only over a long period of time the difference between the real world and imaginary ones; between figurative and literal meanings in the discourse of adults; and between appropriate and inappropriate behaviour for their gender, class, religious, and ethnic group.[30]

The following examples demonstrate how some adults recalled an event from their childhoods, reconstructed – usually for the first time – into words what they saw, heard, and felt, but in these reconstructions appear not to have greatly distorted the image that triggered their description. 'I was ten or twelve,' reported one woman. 'I was coming home from Uncle Cory's house. It was just beginning to get dark in the winter; cold, crisp snow. I was watching the sky and it turned sort of green. A star tumbled out of the greenness and went back in and came out again. Other stars came out.' A Toronto resident related, 'When I was in Grade Four I got scarlet fever and had to be taken to the hospital. We went down Parliament Street in an ambulance; I was so sick and so excited on the way to the Isolation Hospital.' One woman cautiously recounted, 'I had an unhappy experience with 'Mary's' stepfather; I knew it was wrong, but I was too afraid to say anything; but I finally did.' On a lighter note, one woman said, 'I can remember once my sister reading the paper and saying these people had been arrested for keeping a disorderly house, and Betty and I decided we had better keep our house cleaner than we did.'

In one account, a woman reported, 'One of the things I can remember ... is when I was around five ... coming home really late at night on the street-car ... falling asleep ... my father carrying me ... and just loving being carried ... and I was in that drowsy, wonderfully drowsy place where I wanted to be held ... then to be put down into bed and the covers pulled up over me and just left to sleep. But ... in well-brought-up families the children don't go to bed ... with your outside clothes on ...; I had to have all the dirt of the day scrubbed off me ... and of course by that time I was thoroughly awake and that wonderful feeling I had wanted so much to hold onto was gone, long gone, and ... I don't recall an instance before and ... since, at any time, that I was ever held.'

Novelist David Ireland neatly captures a sense of the process of collecting the oral history of childhood: 'Kids have plenty of thoughts, but not always the words to dress them up in. They stay, the undressed ones, in you some-where, then maybe you remember them later.'[31] Or, one might add, histori-ans may prod people into putting their childhood thoughts and feelings into the words of adults, something they could not have done even if they had been interviewed during their childhood. Indeed, even if they are articulate enough to put their most intimate thoughts and feelings into words, many children feel compelled to hide them. (Rose 'was building up the first store of things she could never tell.')[32] Like slaves and prisoners, children conceal events that seem beyond explaining to parents and teachers, or they conceal the physical or psychological oppression that they feel.[33] One man, reported to his school for saying 'fart' on the streetcar, and strapped because he wouldn't tell the principal what the word was, explained, 'You couldn't actually say that word to the principal.' As adults, no longer subject to sanc-tion by parents, teachers, or peers, they can now tell us what happened to them at home and elsewhere and what they really felt about these events (but note the characteristic euphemisms – 'unhappy experience,' 'that word' – appearing in two of the examples above).

In each of the examples cited, the factual core – walking home at night, going to the hospital, being abused – is encapsulated in the feelings that it aroused. As David Vincent argues, their very subjectivity is a merit that autobiographies have for historians.[34] The attendance register for Mrs Hall's Grade One class in General James Wolfe School in Vancouver shows that I started in September 1937, a snapshot shows how I was dressed, but only my adult recollection of it enables me to articulate the combination of joy, excitement, and fear, terror even, that the event triggered.

Within the structures of their lives, what brought children great joy or excitement? What made them feel ashamed, humiliated, self-hating? What aroused feelings of love, of a sense of well-being, of hatred, of jealousy, of despair? What strategies did youngsters adopt to deal with both their feelings and the events or situations that occasioned them? How did their experiences and their reactions to them help them create their gender identity? How did their feelings affect their developing sense of being a girl or a boy; belonging to their family, their 'gang,' their school or Sunday-school class; their emerging sense of being, say, both English and middle class or working class, or 'pot-lickers' or 'cat-lickers'? Since I am dealing with the preadolescent phase of young lives, these latter sorts of identities were at a rudimentary stage, but many children saw that some of the differences between them were rooted in more than their own personal characteristics.

From the general case for employing recollections as a source for the history of childhood, let us turn to an examination of their use in this study. First, what sorts of recollections did I examine? The only form of recollection available to historians for the years before the memories of those still living are autobiography, fiction, and responses made to earlier investigators. Those of us dealing with the fairly recent past are more fortunate in that we are also able to select our own subjects. In this book my core set of data, that which I analysed to identify the scripts of children's lives, came from the memories of people born between about 1910 and 1950. With the help of research assistants, I conducted more than 200 extensive interviews.[35] These produced segments of life histories, detailed looks at one part of the life courses of my subjects.[36] I stopped at that point for two reasons. First, time and resources had run out. Second, and for this I was very thankful, most of the content of the more recent interviews enriched my fund of examples within common scripts rather than adding new ones to those I had already identified.

I supplemented my interviews with two other sorts of recollections. In the category of those that people themselves decide to record, I examined a useful collection of autobiographic and less formally put together recollections. Most of these were written by non-professional writers, and many as part of a 'life review.' As well, I have made sparing use of accounts of children appearing in Canadian short stories and novels set in the years between the 1910s and the 1960s. That writers of fiction sometimes create their characters, and especially those in their early writings, out of their own youthful experiences is, of course, a truism of literature. That writers also re-form what they experienced into something that is artistically but not necessarily historically authentic is also obvious. Can one make any use of such material in which fallibility is, as it were, built in – in which the writer sets down experiences that may be 'true' artistically but not necessarily 'true' historically?

In response, I would argue that the subjectivity of autobiography is so similar to that of realistic fiction that we must treat both as though they were a single kind of source; that however well-intentioned autobiographers are, what they write about their childhoods may be close to being fiction. Whether, at the point of the 'life review,' people distort the experiences of their childhood more than they do other events in their lives is an open question. On the other hand, writers of short stories and novels often utilize events from their childhood long before they embark on a life review, which may circumvent the problem of the 'golden haze,' whatever other difficulties it may also raise. I found that there is considerable truth in John Updike's observation that fiction 'is nothing less than the subtlest instrument for self-examination and self-display that mankind has invented.'[37]

I will now to turn to two of the three major methodological questions that this sort of research poses: How does one select one's subjects? How does one interview them? How does one analyse the data that emerge from the interviews? While the answer to this last question is, as I have already noted, infinitely complex, it is really no different from that posed by other historical research. I will therefore explain here only how I identified the scripts in each of the major parts of my study: family life, the extended family, children's work, special occasions, the culture of childhood, and schooling. I read and annotated each transcript right after each interview took place. A female research assistant also read and annotated the transcripts and some of the other autobiographical material.[38] As I came to write each section, I began by rereading all of the interview transcripts and all the notes on other recollections.

One can follow a number of procedures in selecting interviewees for research into social history. If one wants to generalize from the data, then the least satisfactory way is to pick one's subjects at random. In conducting the research that led to *The Edwardians*, Thompson selected a 'quota sample' according to such variables as sex, region, and occupation, and in proportion to their members in the whole British population as revealed by the British census of 1911.[39] While the merits of quota sampling are obvious, as a method it shares with random recruiting the major flaw that it is not possible, except in the most general sort of way, to follow Thucydides' practice of testing what one is told in one interview against what is disclosed in another.[40]

To put together sets of subjects whose lives share similar structures and whose accounts could be tested one against the other, both within and between the sets, I decided to focus on three small localities. I chose two neighbourhoods in Vancouver to examine childhood in urban English Canada. I chose Evelyn, a small community in the Bulkley Valley area of north-central British Columbia, as an exemplar of those areas of rural Canada that, in the years following the Great War, were still in the pioneering stage of development. I describe these communities in chapter 2.

It is important to underline a central effect of this practice. Given the realities of research costs, the practicality of time, and so on, to decide to investigate those whose experiences overlap with each other is also to decide not to employ quota samples. Some sorts of childhoods are necessarily left out. I do not, for example, discuss the work of children in mining towns, although there is evidence of children in these places developing sets of complex occupational skills at precociously early ages.[41] As I indicate below, I have endeavoured to take into account such variables as gender, class, ethnicity, religious denomination, and geographic region that have the most important effect on the structure of children's lives. Only time, and the research of others, will tell whether my three communities are representative of anything more than themselves.

Those interviewed spent all, or nearly all, their childhoods in Canada. Although some spoke other languages at home, they attended public or parochial schools in which English was the language of instruction and, as adults, they speak it with complete fluency. I selected my pioneer subjects from among the fifty-nine pupils who attended the Evelyn one-room school between its opening in 1920 and its closing in 1946. I also interviewed some of those from the area who later attended the 'consolidated' school that replaced the one-room one. Most of my Vancouver interviewees came from cohorts who grew up in one east-side and one west-side neighbourhood. Although both neighbourhoods displayed the mix of classes characteristic of much of Vancouver at the time, middle-class families predominated in west-side Kerrisdale and 'respectable' (their term) working-class ones predominated in east-side Cedar Cottage.[42] In each neighbourhood, children played together in the street and in the playgrounds, belonged to various organizations for girls and boys, and attended local churches and schools. I used a local elementary school as a focal point for each of my neighbourhoods.

Once I selected a neighbourhood, I moved from one person to another, sometimes by means of lists of those who turned up at school reunions, and sometimes along a 'chain of acquaintanceship.' In some instances this latter

practice merely meant that people were in a school classroom or neighbourhood group at the same time and identified as such from class photographs or other documentary evidence. In others we talked to people with
closer ties, such as siblings and those who were best friends. In each case, we
interviewed about the same number of men and women, and the same number from each decade.

Overlapping memories enable one to explore common schema, events,
scripts, rituals, and structures through more than a single memory. Overlapping memories also help overcome another factor that psychologists
have noted – namely, that we tend to remember the good things about ourselves and forget the bad. More important, they enable the historian to
compensate for what one psychologist calls a 'superiority complex' which
manifests itself in overestimating our own contribution to tasks or events,
and seeing ourselves in a better light than we see others.[43] As one man said
to me, 'That is the way I remember myself, being helpful.'

The principal problem with overlapping memories is that they make it
impossible for one to follow the usual scholarly practice of both footnoting
sources and protecting the anonymity of those interviewed.[44] I had originally intended to identify each person by a code number. I soon discovered,
however, that these identifiers undermined my promise of absolute anonymity to those I interviewed. After I had written an early version of the
chapter on schooling and coded (using a table of random numbers) and
footnoted the respondents, I gave the draft to others who had also grown up
in the same area. To my naïve surprise, the readers connected up the separate quotations from, say, 'M-8127' and 'F-3621' and put correct names to
the code numbers. Since I had no reason to doubt that those in the other
Vancouver neighbourhood could do the same thing, I removed the code
numbers (keeping them, however, on one copy of the text). Even without
code numbers I found it very difficult to disguise identities in the Evelyn
data. (Books such as Thompson's *Edwardians* are able to use codes because
the interviewees were drawn from the whole nation and did not know one
another.)

For each of my communities or neighbourhoods, therefore, I put
together an informal sample that had a great deal of overlap in the lives of
the subjects built into it. My research assistants and I interviewed working-
class and middle-class men and women. I organized the interviews in such a
way that about half were conducted by members of the same sex as the
interviewee. We made a special effort to interview those who, at least by
external standards, may not have led successful or happy lives. Such people
are difficult to locate. They lead harder lives than most, physically and emo-

tionally, and many die far short of a full life span. Many are naturally reluctant to talk about their lives. Others have so creatively employed their life histories in order to make a case to a truant officer or parole board that their narratives, however plausible, must be treated with more than usual caution. We therefore collected fewer such life stories than I would like, but this lack is perhaps partly compensated for by the fact that the records of social agencies and the courts sometimes provide insights into the lives of certain children, particularly at moments of personal or family crisis. I found some Vancouver and rural British Columbia childhoods described in a series of University of British Columbia social-work theses written in the 1940s, 1950s, and early 1960s.[45] Although perhaps only occasionally were the children discussed known to one another, the lives described in these documents overlapped inasmuch as they came from similar environments, met the same social workers, and stayed in the same hostels, and sometimes with the same foster parents. Useful as they are, however, such records lack the children's own perspective on their lives.

I tested the representativeness of my samples in a number of ways. I interviewed people in other parts of Canada. I was able to interview chains of acquaintances who grew up in Toronto and in Halifax. I interviewed some individuals who grew up on the prairies at the same time as my British Columbia groups. In Vancouver itself, we interviewed people from neighbourhoods that were both better off and worse off than those in my sample. We interviewed some who attended parochial or ethnic schools. I read transcripts of interviews housed in museums and archives.

Finally, I tested what our interviewees said against what I learned from the many written formal and informal autobiographical items and the fiction that I read. Did Vancouver boys treasure comic books in the way Mordecai Richler says Montreal ones did? Did girls put the same value on them as did boys?[46] Did other youngsters share religious experiences with the intensity of those described by poet and professor Roy Daniells?[47] Did Bulkley Valley girls and boys share in the farm work the way Elizabeth Varley did in nearby Kitimat Valley? ('After the horse cultivation came the real work: every row had to be weeded by hand. We kids had to kneel and shuffle along the rows, pulling the weeds from around the vegetables. We enjoyed shuffling along in our bare legs and feet in the soft, warm, brown earth, but sometimes we had to endure the work for three hours at a stretch.')[48]

My second methodological question was, how should we actually conduct our interviews? Considerable experience in other investigations that involved interviewing suggested two characteristics that I framed into this

research.[49] First, only long interviews build in the interviewee a commitment to its outcome, and create a sense of intimacy and trust that brings
people to talk about things they have rarely, if ever, shared before. Second,
open-ended, relatively unstructured interviews often lead people, eventually, to talk about those things that really mattered to them.[50] We mailed
potential interviewees a two-page summary of the project, and answered
questions when we telephoned to see if they were willing to be interviewed
and to arrange time and place if they were. We began each interview by
again describing and answering questions about the project. These prelimi-
naries usually took very little time because people had primed themselves to
talk about themselves and not about the research or the researchers. We
had a short, informal list of topics that we hoped to cover, and our initial
questions grew directly out of this list. ('What is your earliest memory?'
'What happened in your house before you went to school in the morning?'
'What do you remember about your early days in school?') My instructions
to the interviewers were to use as few of these questions as possible; our
goal was to have people construct their own narratives.

In confirmation of research showing that people's memories range across
the senses, we found that people recollect childhood scripts through all of
them.[51] Thus adults recalled the smells and sounds of their classrooms, the
taste of iodine pills, and the pain of the pinched ear. ('As I begin to think
about it, two dominant things stand out; the smells of the room – Plasticine,
the smell of rubber erasers ... the sour paste – and the sounds – crackling of
radiators'; '... it never really twigged until you asked about what kind of furnace, and then it brought back the smell of sawdust and the hopper and you
know ... you need a little trigger to bring those remembrances back'; 'Do
you remember the sound of a bike on a street that has been watered? I can
just hear the flicker of water coming off the wheels.') As Betty Bell wrote:
'Whenever a hint of a sound or a drift of scent related closely with those
[childhood] years comes my way, the magic of some moment of the past at
Saanich can be instantly recaptured, and it seems certain that ... it will always
be possible to summon back those nostalgic impressions ...'[52] Although we
were unable to provide people with their own versions of a madeleine and
tea, or their 'Rosebud,' we did find that we could trigger memory with such
artefacts as class photographs, staff lists, or copies of prescribed textbooks,
or from asking for comments on words – 'Double Dutch,' 'conkers,'
'sinkers,' 'alery' – that were once part of the vocabulary of children.

In many ways, ideal interviewees are those who claim not to remember
much about their childhood. In such cases, memories flow slowly, and initially need prompting through questions or the further display of artefacts

(but not through hypnosis or drugs).[53] Such a beginning is more reassuring than an initial outpouring of recollections. One senses in the former case that one is getting the past 'fresh,' as it were; that the items have not been drawn out before and refurbished, or honed into a good story or anecdote.

One must be particularly wary of the well-used anecdote about childhood or a well-crafted school story. One begins to recognize those items that have become part of a person's regular lore, told to amuse, or to make a point about the 'good old days,' or to emphasize to today's youngsters 'did I ever have it tough as a kid.' Each has been told many times to its narrator's family and friends. These stories are perhaps true in essence, but the fine honing that comes from constant reconstructing, retelling, and polishing also removes them farther and farther away from the reality that they are supposedly portraying. One story that recurs in rural areas, for example, involves the farmer who moves his privy on Hallowe'en in such a way that boys intent on pushing it over end up falling into the pit. I heard it myself as a child, was told it in three different interviews by men whose lives did not overlap, and found it in four autobiographies.[54]

I must emphasize that we employed questions or artefacts only at the beginning of an interview. Since it was their lives as they saw them that we were interested in, we shifted responsibility for the agenda over to our interviewees as soon as we could. We wanted to have a minimal effect on their reconstruction of the past. Thus we worked hard to get people into the right mood, one in which their memories were stimulated. Mostly this meant letting silences go on until the interviewee felt the need to fill them. We found that, as a good interview proceeds, people get more and more involved in their own life story. One memory triggers another, which in turn uncovers other scenes, other events, other feelings, all of which begin to crowd in on one another, and rapidly tumble out.[55]

A critical point occurs when people shift from describing the events themselves to their feelings about them. They become more articulate, less diffident about revealing themselves. At first they are polite, holding back, waiting for comments or questions; at the beginning they view the interview as a conversation in which the interviewer, as well as the interviewee, has a right to a certain say. We discovered that the longer a good interview goes on, the less tolerant people become of any intervention; they show impatience at distractions that break into the flow of their narrative, and especially so when they are in the midst of a recollection that has a strong emotional dimension.

People pause occasionally, gaze into the distance, not seeing the interviewer but perhaps events or people that the questions or narrative have triggered in their memories. At this point the wise interviewer greets this silence with silence and not a question. After they have finished describing certain – often intimate – events, some people give out signals that they do not want to go back to the subject again; that one is lucky that they opened up on the particular point and should be grateful for whatever form of response they chose to give. To ask too many questions, to follow a schedule, leads to a series of discrete responses that may or may not tell us very much about what someone feels is the reality of his or her childhood. I cannot overstress the importance of this point. Open-ended interviews may be disconnected, and may contain items that are not closely related one to another, or do not fit into a temporal sequence. They also produce material that is very intimate and personal, material that people are sometimes surprised that they recall, and even more surprised that they would tell to someone else. ('I've never even told that to my husband!')

More often than not, subjects decide when the interview is over. Especially when they have revealed more than they thought they would, they come to decide that you have taken enough from them, and their responses to questions become very perfunctory. Whether you have completed your agenda or not, you clearly understand that the interview is, in effect, at its end. This point may come before or after the interviewer's notion of an appropriate point to close. In a set of interviews in which I focused primarily on schooling, people talked to me for between two and six hours. In some cases when I had to stop before the interviewee was finished, I tried scheduling a second session. These were not very fruitful, and we avoided the practice as much as possible. Most people seem not to want to be reminded that they talked so intimately to a stranger. I eventually concluded that it was unethical to ask further questions, to continue to probe after a point when only the good manners of the subject was the basis of our continuing the discussion.

Sociological theorist Howard Becker observed that studies of research on research methodology have shown that interviewers get the answers they expect, that most of the data they gather tend to confirm whatever hypothesis they are investigating. This happens, Becker explains, because the interviewee generally has no real stake in the outcome of the interview, and therefore tries to please the questioner.[56] I have no objective evidence to show that this finding is any less true of our interviews than of those of any other researcher using this technique. However, when our interviews followed the pattern generalized above, I think that those to whom we talked had come to assume a stake in the outcome. In Becker's terms, the most important element in the interview shifted away from the interviewer and became the life of the interviewee and his or her need to make sure that this story was correctly heard and accurately recorded.

I want to close this chapter by returning to the story with which I opened it, that of the woman in her forties talking about her grandmother. Let us suppose that someone had studied her and her family when she was about ten years old, someone who possessed the full panoply of modern research devices and observational or participant-observational techniques.[57] Undoubtedly that person could have described the family's scripts more fully and accurately than I or any other historian could reconstruct them from oral evidence collected a generation later. The researcher would have learned how the grandmother felt about her grandchildren and would have learned some things and inferred more about the granddaughter's feelings about her grandmother.

None the less, a point would have been reached beyond which the investigator was unable to go. Only as an adult did the woman have the vocabulary and, indeed, the conceptual and contextual structure that enabled her to put her childhood emotions into words. What is clear, too, from what we know about memory is that, if the child had been pushed too hard, too persistently, to describe her feelings at the time, the effect would have been to make any later effort at accurate re-creation even more difficult to accomplish. The more thoroughly she had been probed by my notional social scientist during her childhood, the more likely it would be that that discussion, rather than the inchoate but complex underlying emotions, would have framed any later reconstructions.

Indeed, the paradox is that the closer in time you try to probe the rich complexities of childhood, the farther away they may go. In this regard, Gabrielle Roy, who provided the title and epigraph for this chapter, also posed its concluding question. 'Is it possible,' she asked, 'to record in a book the spellbinding powers of childhood, which can put the whole world inside the tiniest locket of happiness?'[58] My answer is, of course, 'yes,' but only if a pensive adult looks back on and tries to capture his or her 'lockets of happiness,' and, of course, lockets of unhappiness as well.

2

Children in Their Families:
Contexts and Settings

The men and women who people this book lived their childhoods in the context of the great events of their times. They also lived them in the physical settings of their homes and neighbourhoods, and the emotional setting provided by their parents. Some grew up in the aftermath of the Great War and the influenza epidemic, and the unevenly distributed prosperity of the 1920s. Others spent childhoods menaced by the Depression or the Second World War. Still others began their lives in the era of relative affluence that followed that war. Since this book focuses on a decade or a little more of their lives – from ages three or four to thirteen or fourteen – people saw both contexts and settings in a foreshortened and intensely personal way. As they grew older they certainly acquired an increasing awareness of the wider world. However, since they also took their circumstances, no matter how harsh, as a given in life, and focused on the immediate aspects of their lives, many children had little sense of the wider world, of depression or war as major events that affected, or might affect, their lives. As Betty Bell wrote of her childhood in rural Vancouver Island during the Great War, 'the sense of permanence which permeated my early childhood now turns out to be rooted in an illusion' that grew up 'when every day of those long years of childhood the same faces were seen and every detail of the surrounding landscape grew more familiar.'[1]

Three brief vignettes of the Depression and four of the Second World War underline the immediate and unreflective nature of youngsters' experience of these events. Thus, of Depression-era footwear: 'I have an image of a child standing in the snow with a different shoe on each foot,' remembered a woman who grew up in Glace Bay, Nova Scotia. 'One shoe was black with the buckle missing from the strap, the other was a brown laceless oxford, both too large! She had red-knuckled hands without mittens and no buttons on a frayed coat.' A man who grew up in Cedar Cottage recalled 'a pair of hand-me-down boots worn in all seasons. Dad got them from the Infants' Hospital (from some dead infant, I now imagine) and for the first half-year or so they were too big, then for another half-year or so they were okay, and then for another interminable while they were too small.' Another man, also from Vancouver's east side, explained, 'At least I had running shoes, although not socks ... our school would supply shoes, with a note from our parents.'

Of the war, a Halifax woman remembered her 'father returning home in a soldier's uniform. I went hysterical. Everybody I knew who was in uniform had gone away.' A Cedar Cottage woman remembered 'blackouts at night and the air-raid sirens. They were awful ... My stomach tightens even now when I hear sirens ... My dad was in the army ... I knew it was a real threat.' Except for one or two major events that particularly upset his parents – the collapse of France in 1940 was one, the bombing of Pearl Harbor in 1941 another – one man's major remembrances of the war are of the way it shaped his games: 'We roared about with our arms out as Spitfires shooting down Stukas, and used sticks as tommy-guns when we played commando. When my uncle came home on leave once, I paraded around in his tunic, proudly pointing out the "GS" on his sleeve; there were no Zombies in our family!' Another man reported, 'The neighbourhood was drastically touched. A lot of families lost their sons.'[2] Although, as both Norah Lewis and Emilie Montgomery have demonstrated, Canadian youngsters were well aware of the Second World War, discussed it in school, and took part in various civilian activities associated with it, only when it affected them personally, through internment, or the enlistment, wounding, or even death of a close relative, did it assume a real immediacy for them.[3]

Only in adolescence and adulthood did people begin to comprehend how their particular situation fitted in with general ones. One man, for example, came to conclude, of the effects of the Depression on his family, that 'times, they were damn tough,' and another now surmises that his parents 'went without so I could have things to eat.' Thus while, as this and later chapters show, the 'big' events in Canadian history clearly structured many of the patterns and scripts of the lives of young people, and their effects are evident in what they tell about their childhood, these events are discussed only when they impinged directly on it.[4]

To children, the wider economic and social environment in which they lived manifested itself most immediately and most obviously in the general scarcity of family resources. Scarcity was a given throughout most of the era, and of nearly all childhoods. Although they lived through times that

Two east-side Vancouver girls demonstrate their competence with a stirrup pump in 1943.

saw a significant shift in attitudes towards the disposability of goods, both working- and middle-class youngsters of these years, even of the prosperous 1950s, grew up in an atmosphere that saw careful frugality as the norm. Much of their early life was characterized by 'making, making over, making do.' Their parents knew from observation, and often bitter experience, that whatever a family had by way of property or savings had been acquired laboriously, over a very long period of time. These assets were vulnerable to such vagaries of life as unemployment, injury, and illness.[5]

All but the most prosperous of middle-class families lived close to narrow margins and had to manage their resources cautiously. 'We couldn't skip too much,' stated one Halifax woman, 'because it wore out our shoes.' Indeed, many families believed in frugality – defined by one person as 'plain living and high thinking' – as not merely a necessary but a desirable quality in life. 'Jeez,' one man exclaimed, 'Mom and Dad took real pride when they could save a buck by making do.' Childhood resentment of frugality sometimes lingered on into adulthood: 'My mother,' reported one woman, 'was an extremely careful housekeeper, and watched every penny ... The family never went anywhere, they never did anything for fun, they just worked and scrimped ... Mother's idea of a big treat was to go down to the Hudson's Bay cafeteria and get a bowl of tomato soup and a piece of apple pie for a quarter.'

For many children their clothing formed the most personal aspect of making do. Since what they wore was central both to their concept of themselves and to the role they would assume in the culture of childhood, recollections of childhood are permeated with discussions of clothing. As both photographs and recollections make clear, children of the 1920s to the 1950s appear a drab lot indeed to eyes accustomed to present-day children's clothing, with its rich array of materials and styles and its relative abundance. Children then had fewer clothes and changed them far less frequently. None the less, there were differences in garb, and children then were as acutely aware of them as are children today. Children in each neighbourhood or community had a concept of the ideal outfit, to which all aspired and to which as many as possible adhered. Children's aspirations, however, were tightly circumscribed, with the current style expressed through the use of such minor accessories as caps, gloves, and hair ornaments. When she moved to a new school in 1947, Elizabeth Gordon wore 'the baggy sweater, tight skirt and saddle shoes popular at that time. I didn't have a large wardrobe, but I compensated by wearing a different coloured barette in my hair each day.'[6]

Most parents considered durability rather than fashion as the most important quality in good clothing. Further, schools tended to set fairly restricted dress codes for their pupils; not until the 1960s were girls permitted to wear slacks, and many schools frowned on boys wearing jeans or coveralls. Indeed, in some parts of the country, parochial, and even public schools suggested, or even demanded, that pupils wear a school uniform. For girls, these uniforms usually consisted of a white blouse, navy tunic, black stockings, and black shoes. Such schools asked boys to wear navy or grey flannel pants; a buttoned shirt, sometimes with a tie; and black shoes or boots. Generally, boys were more often permitted to deviate from the norm than were girls. As one parochial-school boy of the 1940s explained, 'In September you could more or less tell that most of us had at least some part of the uniform, but that didn't last. In our neighbourhood, those who bought their kids' clothes at St Vincent's, or even the Sally Ann, didn't have much to choose from. The nuns sometimes made critical remarks, but they knew how poor we were.'

Much more then than now, as one person explained, most families 'used hand-me-downs. They went through our family, and then to cousins' families.' Mildred Young Hubbert 'happily' wore her cousin Harry's 'cast-off clothing as he outgrew it. He wore leather jackets and scratchy wool sweaters, and especially a leather airman's helmet complete with chin strap and goggles ... my favourite item of clothing in the era when Amelia Earhart was winging around the world.'[7] 'My sister and I,' explained one Evelyn woman, 'were well dressed in those days. Our cousin was a year older. We got all her clothes at Christmas.'

Mothers (and grandmothers) also made or remade much of the clothing that their children wore. In most homes, as in Robert Collins's, there 'was always a ragbag ... a bleached flour sack ... stuffed with clean ragged socks, shirts, dresses, and underwear – an Oriental bazaar of tattered silks, satins, denim, polka dots, stripes, floral reds and royal purples, all tumbled together awaiting further duty. They served interim roles as costumes for plays or ribbons for cats, until reassigned as patches for elbows and knees, or as hooked and braided rugs.'[8] Many mothers, like Mary Cook's, used flour sacks to make 'underwear, pinnies and sheets.' When her mother 'found one with scant writing on it, we would all rejoice' because 'the job of bleaching out all the printing was tedious.'[9] Some girls even wore dresses made out of flour sacks. Circumstances compelled other parents to insist that their children make do with what they could buy at second-hand stores or rummage sales. Still others clothed their children with items from charitable agencies.

When parents made or bought new clothes – sometimes referred to as their new 'duds' – they often included 'room to grow.' Mothers who were good seamstresses could partially conceal this characteristic, but some children had to wear outfits as they were. A man who 'hated' his clothes reported being teased about their size. Kids would pull his oversized trousers out at the waist and say, 'Can I climb in, too?' Many rural families 'used to get – once or twice a year – a big order from Eaton's,' including 'lace-up, ankle-high rubber boots.' In some families children 'could help decide on clothes' to be bought or ordered. And, whether it came from Eaton's or relatives, 'it was always exciting when the box came.'

In urban areas, until the end of the 1950s reasonably well-off middle- and working-class children had three basic outfits: their 'Sunday best,' their school clothes, and their chore and play clothes. Girls' best clothes consisted of an overcoat, white gloves, a dress, their newest stockings – 'white were best' – or ankle socks, and perhaps special patent-leather, white, or other shoes that were clearly for 'dress' occasions. Their school clothes were a coat or jacket, a dress, or skirt and blouse (the latter often a white 'middy' and a pleated, navy blue skirt), a sweater, stockings or ankle socks, and oxford-style shoes. In a typical example, the daughter of a Canadian National Railways switchman 'had one special Sunday dress which I wore to church ... [and] a darker-coloured dress for school. My mother made both dresses using the same pattern. They were my only dresses.' Another woman explained, 'I had one new outfit every year that I wore every day; this was quite common then,' and a third reported, 'My father took my blouse and skirt to a dressmaker and said "Make three of these for this girl."' Other middle-class parents dressed their daughters with greater variety. The daughter of a professional man in a small town 'always had nice dresses. I was the best dressed in the school because of my mother's attitude. My skirt and blouse or dress was usually made by my mother but sometimes bought.' For many girls, however, their hair ribbons had to serve to provide day-to-day variety.

The winter climate, together with school and community dress codes, forced girls in most parts of Canada to wear long cotton stockings for much of the year. 'I had to wear long stockings for months at a time and ... how I hated them!' reported one woman. Ellen Davignon vividly described what she wore every day: 'Cotton underpants. Rib-knit undershirt ... Over that, a grey flannel vest with long dangling garters. A white rayon slip. And over all, a practical brown cotton dress patterned with small red and yellow flowers ... long brown cotton stockings ... How I hated them! Ribbed and formless, they hung on my legs like wrinkled tubes, corrugated at the knee and ankle no matter how tightly I pulled them up, and gaping down below

my hemline ... despite the carefully set metal garters.'[10] With the onset of
spring, girls could shift from stockings to ankle socks, from woollen clothes
to cotton ones, and from oxfords to a pair of T-strap sandals.

For middle-class and some working-class boys, Sunday clothes consisted
of shirt and tie; woollen suit, generally serge but sometimes flannel; and
oxford shoes. For Hugh Palmer's 'Sunday best,' his father 'bought me a pair
of black Oxfords to go with my blue serge suit. How I hated that suit. The
short trousers, or "stovepipes," were unlined, and the serge was a particlarly
rough sort – no doubt designed to cause maximum chafing just above a
boy's knees.'[11] In Cedar Cottage, one man explained, boys' Sunday outfits
'weren't suits, you know ... odd pants and some gloves, a shirt or something ... but they weren't too fancy clothes at that, because, when I got too
big for them, my brother ... he had to wear them, and when he got too big,
my [other] brother had to wear them.' To school, boys wore shirts, sweaters,
buttoned or zippered jackets, and woollen or cotton long trousers. In the
early 1920s, some boys still wore 'bloomers' or 'knickers,' that is, pants that
came to just below the knee, 'with long ribbed black cotton stockings held
up by half-inch garter elastic just above our knees, over which the bloomers
draped in a fold.'[12] Some boys with English parents had to wear the hated
short pants to school as well as for dress. On their heads boys wore toques,
visored caps, or, if fashionable, 'either a Lindbergh helmet or Skeezix hat,'
the former having plastic goggles and straps that did up under the chin, the
latter a man's hat with a turned-up, scalloped brim, not unlike the cap worn
by Jughead in the perennial comic strip *Archie*. In the 1940s 'gauntlet gloves
were very popular with the kids; they had a fringe on them.'

To most boys in Vancouver, the ideal winter footwear was a widely available hard-toe-capped boot modelled on a man's work boot. Parents valued
its durability; with luck one pair would last the whole winter. To this the
most envied boys affixed a metal toe protector, and steel 'blakeys' (or pro-
tectors) on the soles and heels. As one man explained, boots were 'made by
lots of manufacturers, but in Vancouver pride of place went to the locally
made Leckie boots.' When he started school in suburban Burnaby in 1955,
Allan Safarik's mother 'bought me my first pair of Leckie boots. They had
metal clasps along the laces so they could be cinched up ... They were
nearly indestructible.'[13]

Many children, of course, could not begin to approach the ideal outfit for
their neighbourhood. 'I dressed funny in inexpensive clothes' was a conclusion shared by many girls and boys. Some wore clean but threadbare clothing. But even clean clothing, and especially the woollens of winter, often
exuded a musty smell. Harsh circumstances kept other children unkempt,

and even dirty. Despite the admonitions of teachers and school nurses, many girls and boys wore only cheap 'runners' in the summer and when it was dry, and 'gumboots' when it was wet or snowy. A few wore runners or gumboots whatever the weather. Classmates noticed that such children, unlike those of the employed working class or middle classes, 'had nothing new ... after Woodward's 95-cent day.' At the beginning of the era described in this book, many children – and especially boys – went barefoot in the summer, but at the end the practice had almost died out. In the 1920s in Saskatchewan, Lloyd Person reported, their neighbour 'Mr. Kaschl worked with the section gang, and his salary only sufficed to buy his large family the absolute necessities of life ... The Kaschl boys, like Huckleberry Finn, were the first ones ... to shed shoes and stockings in the spring and the last ones to put them on in the fall.'[14] Although the practice was rooted in economic necessity, those whose parents permitted or enforced bare-footedness gave status to their youngsters.

Except that they often wore boots, the clothing of rural girls resembled that of their urban sisters: dresses, skirts and blouses, sweaters, and ribbons in their hair. As later chapters show, this garb was not really appropriate for the lives girls actually led. Many rural boys, however, wore coveralls to school as well as for working in at home. In rural Ontario in the 1930s, Roy Bonisteel reported, 'the boys at school wore bib overalls, flannelette shirts, wool socks and black leather work boots ... Everything we wore was patched, darned or resoled ... To a farm kid underwear meant long johns worn in the cold weather. To have anything between you and your overalls in July seemed ludicrous.'[15] In the late 1920s, and newly arrived from southern Ukraine, John Friesen and his brother Henry each 'begged for and received a pair of genuine denim farmer overalls' for Christmas. 'Nothing helped more to break the chill betweeen us and the local children than these overalls. We were at last accepted!'[16]

Postwar prosperity brought some changes in children's clothing. More wore appropriate footwear, a trend encouraged by the widespread use of X-ray machines in shoe stores. Parents cautiously indulged some of their youngsters' requests for greater variety and a closer adherence to fashion in their other clothes. Girls began to covet, and a few to wear, the saddle shoes and 'twin sets' – the best of cashmere wool – that were the peak of high-school fashion of the 1950s. Urban and rural boys began to wear cotton underpants in the summer in place of woollen drawers or longjohns. Corduroy pants in a wide variety of shades became popular, and boys had more than one pair for school. 'Sunday' clothes became more sharply differentiated from those worn to school. Eaton's catalogues of the late 1940s and

1950s devoted considerably more space to children's clothes than did their pre-war predecessors.

As their clothing provided one way in which children came to apprehend how political, social, and economic events affected their lives, so the settings in which they lived provided another. Their community formed the central point of the geography of parents working at home or going to work, and of children doing their chores, going to school, and participating in the culture of childhood. While Cedar Cottage and Kerrisdale were physically quite similar to each other, Evelyn provided children with a very different setting in which to grow up.

Cedar Cottage and Kerrisdale derived their geographical identities from the communities themselves rather than from sharply delineated political boundaries.[17] Initially taking their names from stops on interurban lines, they came into being during the very rapid growth of greater Vancouver in the early years of the twentieth century.[18] Large tracts of cheap land available for housing made it possible for many middle- and working-class families in Vancouver to live in detached houses on fairly large lots. Although by the 1920s each neighbourhood contained enough people to have an urban rather than a rural character, each also enclosed vacant lots, empty blocks, and larger tracts of pasture and the second-growth 'bush' that figured so largely in the local culture of childhood. One man said, 'In the middle '20s my [Kerrisdale] bedroom faced west, and I passed some time looking out the window. Cows were lowing in the distance, chickens were clucking ... My parents owned the lot to the west of the house, and it was used as an orchard.' In Cedar Cottage in the 1930s, 'there used to be lots of open spaces ... there were fields ... they were old farms ... down below us there was a great huge field.'

Although the amount of vacant land diminished sharply over time, enough of it remained even by the end of the 1950s for it to figure in the recollections of those who grew up then. A Cedar Cottage man reported, 'They used to graze cows in the yard over from me. People would bring their cows down to Trout Lake, and that was pretty late. The interurban just stopped running in 1957 or '58, and there was a cow pasture and there was our chicken farm. Then things started becoming more urbanized.'[19]

Both Kerrisdale and Cedar Cottage possessed a commercial centre within walking distance of most homes. There, families could buy most necessities in terms of food and clothing, and consult such professionals as pharmacists, physicians, and dentists. Both neighbourhoods contained churches of many denominations to meet social as well as religious needs. The main buildings of both Lord Selkirk School in Cedar Cottage and Kerrisdale

School were imposing brick-faced structures on extensive grounds. The lack of any public funding for them ensured that the Roman Catholic parochial schools, serving much larger territories than their public counterparts, were housed in modest frame structures. Cedar Cottage Catholic youngsters attended St Joseph's, for much of time housed in the church basement. Their west-side counterparts went to Our Lady of Perpetual Help, or to such private schools as Vancouver College or Little Flower Academy.

As noted in chapter 1, both Cedar Cottage and Kerrisdale possessed the mix of social classes then characteristic of most Vancouver neighbourhoods.[20] As one man who grew up in a west-side neighbourhood recalled, it was 'mix of wealthy and poor, with some kids well off and others not.' None the less, middle-class families predominated in Kerrisdale, and working-class ones in Cedar Cottage. Kerrisdale fathers earned their living in commercial, managerial, professional, educational, clerical, and other 'white collar' occupations.[21] Cedar Cottage fathers earned their living as artisans or as skilled or unskilled labourers. However, Cedar Cottage contained the middle-class families of local merchants, teachers, and those in other clerical, professional, and business occupations, while the families of postal employees, policemen, streetcar conductors, mechanics, carpenters, fishermen, and school janitors made their homes in Kerrisdale. Thus one woman reported, 'My father worked at the American Can Company. I always thought we were poor, but my folks saved enough to build the house' in Cedar Cottage in 1926. In another typical example, a business executive established his wife and two children in a home in the heart of Kerrisdale in the late 1920s or early 1930s. The son of a clothing merchant reported, 'My father built us a new house in Cedar Cottage' between the wars. In turn, a father who 'was a very hard-working mechanic, so not wealthy at all,' built the family home in middle-class Kerrisdale in the 1940s.

My third community, Evelyn, was very different from Kerrisdale and Cedar Cottage. By the 1920s, much of the best agricultural land in British Columbia was already under cultivation, but some parts of the province, most notably along the Grand Trunk Pacific (GTP) line of the Canadian National Railways between Prince George and Prince Rupert, and in the Peace River district, still awaited many of their agricultural settlers. Those moving into these areas extended settlement farther into what Isaiah Bowman called the 'pioneer fringe' of North America, and which Cole Harris harshly characterized as a 'last, if terribly minimal, agricultural opportunity.'[22] As one woman proudly recalled of Evelyn in the 1920s, 'We went to the bush and started a settlement!' These agricultural frontiers closely resembled their predecessors of the pre-war and nineteenth-century world.

For those with only enough capital to buy their land, or their need to 'prove up' their pre-emptions through their own labours, the pressure of work to be done always exceeded the time available to do it; in this environment, children retained their traditional value as integral members of the family economy. As the woman quoted above put it, 'people survived by their children.'

Evelyn itself is a small community in the Bulkley Valley, eleven miles northwest of Smithers on the GTP line.[23] Its public buildings in the 1920s consisted of a one-room school and a community hall. It is located just below the glacier on Hudson Bay Mountain, which shaded the community in winter, making the days very short. In summer, on the other hand, 'it was very light, even at 10:00 P.M.' Its climate was severe, characterized by long, cold winters, with temperatures often dropping to −40°F, and short, warm, and generally dry summers. Although white settlers had begun to come into the area even before the GTP was completed, Evelyn really became a community with the establishment of its school in 1920 or 1921.[24]

Most Evelyn settlers aspired to economic self-sufficiency and a better life for their children. Their family farms would produce much of their own food needs through their crops and livestock. They would sell or sometimes barter their surplus crops and livestock for the food, clothing, equipment, and other necessities that they did not themselves produce. The long-term goal of many was to acquire and clear enough of the still readily available land for their children, and especially their sons, to have farms as well. By the 1920s, one especially industrious Valley family had already assembled three mostly uncleared properties, one measuring 640 acres, all in a row: 'Grandfather's, my uncle's, and Dad's.' However, as pioneer Nan Bourgon accurately observed, the Bulkley Valley was 'a hard, cruel country, where it had been so hard to get a start, so hard to make a living in those early days.'[25] For this reason, most men had to supplement their farm income by such off-farm work as trapping, logging, sawmilling, clearing land for others, hauling, cutting ice, doing railway maintenance and road work, and, probably of greatest importance, 'tie-hacking,' that is, hand-cutting wooden ties for the railway.

To children, the core of all three communities was their family home. Together with whatever yard or grounds surrounded it, their home formed the stage on which youngsters' families played out their routine scripts and participated in major and minor events. However, since pioneer housing was so intertwined with family work, I describe housing in Evelyn in a later chapter.

In the 1920s, homes in Vancouver came many different forms.[26] Families lived in tents, rooming-houses, floathouses, 'boathouses' (built on pilings along undeveloped parts of the harbour), cabins, tenements, apartments, and the crowded-together houses of Yaletown or the east end; in the one-, two-, and three-storey homes of the west end and inner east side; and in the small and large houses of the new suburbs.[27] The detached houses surrounded by their own grounds of Cedar Cottage and Kerrisdale generally represented neither the meanest nor the most lavish of this range.

Working-class homes in both neighbourhoods displayed a wide range of styles, quality of workmanship, and degree of completion. Newcomers to the city often stayed with friends or relatives while their homes were being built. An immigrant family from Scotland, who arrived just before the Great War, 'stayed in Grandview – my Aunt Liza's in Grandview – for about six months ... and, that fall, my father bought a lot ... just a long block off Kingsway ... and he got a couple of fellows to build this four-room bungalow and ... we moved in. I think it was March.' Some of those who couldn't afford to have a house built did it themselves. One woman remembered making a summer-long visit to relatives in Cedar Cottage just before the Great War. 'My uncle was building their house himself and, in the meantime, the family was living in a big tent with a lean-to shack and a privy out back ... One thing only was firmly impressed on me: if I heard the cry "Timber" ... I was to run for my life. Clearing was going on all around and "Timber" was heard constantly.'[28]

Working-class families often put up a 'starter' house, or even lived for a time in shacks, cabins, or sheds that they would eventually turn into workshops, chicken houses, woodsheds, or garages. In time, and doing much of the work themselves, families gradually improved their starter homes. They replaced wooden footings with concrete ones, and dug out partial or full basements in which they installed a furnace to replace their space heater. On the main floor they added rooms, in the early years often first a bathroom to replace the privy. A brother and sister reported that, by the early 1920s in their part of Cedar Cottage, 'there were only two houses without inside plumbing,' one of which was their aunt's. 'We never visited there when it was cold.' Next came more rooms, sometimes in the form of outward extensions or an upstairs, which often included a sleeping porch. In one typical example, a Cedar Cottage woman explained that, in the early 1920s, 'we moved into a three-room house. My mother got enough money together by cashing in an insurance policy to buy the lot and lumber. My baby sister would be in a cot, and I would share the room with her. My brothers would have been in another room, and my parents in the third ... The outhouse was in the yard ... Then we gradually added on to our house with a bathroom, two more bedrooms, and an upstairs, but there was no running water.'

Middle-class families went through fewer stages in arranging their generally more extensive shelter. In the 1920s and 1930s, they often had themselves built, or bought from a builder, a bungalow above a full basement. In the basement the builder installed a pair of washtubs and a wood and coal hot-air furnace. The main floor of 850 to 1,200 square feet contained a kitchen, bathroom, living-room, dining-room or -alcove, and two bedrooms. In some, a staircase led from the main floor to an unfinished, generally low-ceilinged attic. As their families grew, some parents, often doing the work themselves, installed bedrooms on the upper floor or in the basement. Second bathrooms, however, did not become common in most middle-class homes until the late 1950s and 1960s.

Rather than remodel, other middle-class families moved to better quarters. Between 1919 and 1927, for example, a successful salesman built no fewer than six different Kerrisdale homes. Thus 'Dad had his eye on 100 feet of property across from our house ... and had a house built on 50 feet of it, and he put in a lovely garden there – fruit trees and vegetables too. My mother used to worry because my young brother ... helped remove heavy stones.' The rich lived in even larger houses. Lawrence Freiman recalled that, in Ottawa, when he was four, just before the Great War, 'we moved to the house on Somerset Street ... Three drawing rooms, the jungle-like conservatory, the seemingly millions of tropical and other plants, the billiard room off the large library downstairs – all marvellously vast places for a boy to run, to hide, and to play.'[29]

Although land for home building remained readily available over all of these years, other circumstances made great differences in how Vancouver families housed themselves. The Depression had a paradoxical effect. For those of both classes who had assured, continued employment, even at reduced rates of pay, homes were both in good supply and cheap to buy.[30] These lower house prices were accompanied by low rents.[31] On the other hand, the underemployed and unemployed, who already lived in the least satisfactory of Vancouver's housing stock, found that their already dismal situation deteriorated. Families moved from rental houses to tenements and other inferior forms of housing, or crowded in with relatives or friends. 'We left a small apartment for a time to live in a vacant store,' explained one man. 'Mom pasted old newspapers over the front windows. When Dad eventually got a job, we moved into a tiny little house just down from Selkirk School.' A regularly employed divorced woman with two small children had, according to her son, 'fortunately been left some money from

England.' Accordingly, in 1931, she 'used it as a down payment on a house' in Kerrisdale. Later, 'she had some old friends ... who were not having an economic time as good as we were, so she asked them ... to come and stay with us ... They lived upstairs and we lived downstairs.' Their rent helped with the expenses of maintaining the house. Those home-owners of both classes who became unemployed for long periods of time often fell so far behind in their mortgage and tax payments that they lost their homes and the life savings that these represented.

The Second World War and postwar prosperity strained the city's ability to house its residents. Despite house construction that continued almost throughout the war, working-class families arriving to work in war indus- tries found they had to double up, or to live in empty stores, auto courts, basements, garages, and even converted woodsheds. Discharged veterans and their families exacerbated the situation in the immediate postwar years. As early as 1941, and before the housing shortage in Vancouver became really acute, 8.3 per cent of households had lodgers, and 8.5 per cent of city households had one or more 'lodging and sub-tenant families.'[32] As late as 1949, a study of Canadian renters undertaken by the Canadian Welfare Council showed that 'a real housing emergency exists among middle and low income Canadian tenant families.'[33]

After the war, a rising standard of living enabled many of both classes to increase their expectations in terms of what they considered to be minimum quality in a home. In turn, ever-tightening local building codes and the stip- ulations laid out in the National Housing Act (NHA) led to greater stan- dardization in house design and construction. None the less, families continued to transform 'the monotony and modesty' of the original NHA plans with 'vivacious individuality.'[34] When compared with the size of their households, postwar houses tended to be larger than their predecessors, with basic houses containing three rather than two bedrooms, and larger living-rooms.[35] In the 1950s, recalled one child of a two-child family, 'my dad built the extension ... and my brother and I didn't share the same bed- room anymore. And I can remember helping him. I had to hold the lumber and do this and that.' Nevertheless, families on welfare and many of the working poor continued to live in housing that fell further and further behind rising standards. The federal government did not include housing in the emerging social-welfare system. Thus the small stock of public housing constructed in the 1950s did little to alleviate the conditions of the very poor.[36]

Far fewer working- or middle-class children then than now had the personal space represented by their own bed, or even their own room.

Although the years between the end of the Great War and the 1960s saw some increase in the average size of houses, over all of these years many homes of both classes were small enough that children often shared rooms, and even beds. A survey of pupil nutrition, conducted by the Vancouver School Board's medical health officer in 1920 and summarized in table 2.1, provides some rough statistical data as to room and bed sharing at the time. In addition to the figures for the city as a whole, the table shows what was reported in four representative elementary schools. Each contained children from a mix of classes, with Strathcona School the most working class, and Tennyson the most middle class. Secord was likely more working than middle class, and Bayview the reverse.

Since I conclude, as did the school medical health officer, that the sleeping conditions of underweight pupils reasonably approximates those of all pupils, then about three-quarters of school-aged Vancouver children shared a bedroom. Given the size of bedrooms at the time, it is probable that many of those who shared a room with one other child also shared a bed. It is almost certain that most of those who shared with two or more children also shared a bed. In the early 1920s, their Cedar Cottage house 'was just a four-room bungalow, shingles on the outside,' explained one man. 'Three of us [boys] slept in the front bedroom, and then my mother and father in the back bedroom, and my sister [who] was young then ... They packed a lot of people in one bed in those days. None of this individual room for each guy. Gosh no.' Max Braithwaite, the sixth of the eight children of a not very prosperous Saskatchewan lawyer, had to share a bed with two of his brothers. 'All the mattresses in our house ... sagged in the middle. This meant that the two bodies on either side rolled towards the middle, and on top of whoever was lying there. There is no torture in the world to compare with the feeling of two heavy, sweaty, snoring bodies of top of you.'[37] In another home at the same time, the one girl in her family 'had her own room,' but her two older and one younger brothers 'were all in one room.' Brothers and sisters sometimes shared, as did a Kerrisdale girl who slept in the same bedroom with 'my brother until I was about eleven.' In another home, and for reasons perhaps only partly to do with the space available, 'the girls and Mom slept upstairs [in an undivided loft], and Dad and my brother downstairs.'

Sharing with siblings remained common right through the 1950s. In the late 1940s, the daughter of a small businessman lived in a 'big white house' in Cedar Cottage. Despite the size of the house, she complained that 'I shared my room and my bed with my sister. There was a great deal of hostility with that arrangement.' 'It was great when it got warm enough for me

Table 2.1
Sleeping Conditions of Underweight Vancouver Elementary School Pupils, 1920

| | Number underweighed | Number 10% or more underweight | Number of children in family | | | | | | | | | | | | Sleeping conditions | | | | | | |
			1	2	3	4	5	6	7	8	9	10	11	12	Alone	With 1 other	With 2 others	With 3 others	With 4 others	Alone figure minus lone children	Total of those with others
City as a whole	14,282	3,587	395	838	801	563	340	204	105	67	30	25	8	2	677	2,082	323	122	70	282	2,597
Secord	410	101	13	23	25	21	7	3	4	1	0	0	0	0	49	45	1	0	1	36	47
Strathcona	839	167	11	22	19	26	29	14	8	3	4	6	0	0	21	52	34	14	20	10	120
Tennyson	548	103	11	20	38	17	5	4	5	2	0	0	0	0	41	46	9	0	3	30	58
Bayview	375	107	10	22	20	22	14	6	1	4	2	0	0	0	0	100	2	0	0	0	102

Note 1: Five schools – Bayview, Gordon, Hudson, Kitsilano, and Roberts – reported no children sleeping alone.

Note 2: Since data were recorded only for children underweight by 10 per cent or more, there is no way of computing exactly how accurately the data also sample the sleeping arrangements of pupils. None the less, since all elementary pupils were surveyed, and the school medical officer also concluded that 'poverty forms but a small portion of the cause of under-weightedness,' it seems reasonable to conclude that the data provide a reasonably close approximation of the sleeping arrangement of all pupils.

Source: Vancouver School Board, Report, 1920, 39–4; table

to move out onto the sleeping porch,' stated one Kerrisdale man. 'My sister moved into my closet-sized room from Mom's bed. I guess Mom was glad to have space to herself, too.' Another pair of sisters who also shared a bedroom 'argued all the time.' On the other hand, for one woman born in the early 1950s, the intimacy as well as the tension brought about by sharing a small room with one of her sisters created between them 'a closeness, a warmth, a sense of being able to communicate almost wordlessly' which has lasted throughout life, and which did not exist between them and a much-loved but more remote older sister.

From the Second World War to the present, many families lived in housing initially built for war workers in and around Vancouver, including in Burkeville, near the Vancouver airport. One style of house in these neighbourhoods, described as a 'small four,' consisted of 'two 10-by-12 foot bedrooms, a kitchen, a living-room, a single bathroom with claw-footed tub and a utility room – all on one floor. There was no basement, no garage, no furnace ... no insulation.' Bonnie Hamilton was one of five children who grew up in a 'small four.' 'The three girls slept in one bedroom, the two boys slept in the converted utility shed.' She had a friend 'who grew up with five kids in one bedroom; mattresses from one side to another. Privacy just wasn't possible. And you know what? Every weekend we'd have friends sleep over. It's all we ever really knew.'[38]

The fact that the public-health sample from the reasonably representative Bayview School showed ten pupils without siblings but none of them not sharing a room emphasizes the fact that members of their extended family, and even roomers or boarders, competed for space in small – but not the smallest - family homes.[39] When, during the 1920s, his mother's sister came to help with the five children – three boys and two girls – one man noted that 'all the children shared one room.' When the aunt left, 'then the three boys had one bedroom, and their sisters the other.' In 1949, the family of a Winnipeg plumber moved to a new, prefabricated house which the father had finished. 'When we moved,' the son reported, 'my grandmother's heart began to fail and she came to live in our two-bedroom house. My grandmother slept with my mother, my father in the living-room, and I was on my own in my own room.' At about the same time the family of a Kerrisdale woman had five children.' And we had, Nan, of course, my stepmother's mother. She lived with us, too. So we had a houseful.'

Robert Thomas Allen gave a child's perspective on his family's roomers. They were 'shadowy, elusive characters ... They came up the street at suppertime with long, springy strides, holding tightly rolled evening papers

under their arms, or, later in the evening, passed the living-room door looking straight ahead and went silently up to their rooms trailing cigarette
smoke or the smell of chlorine from the YMCA pool.'[40] During the desperate housing shortage in Halifax during Second World War, a family with
three boys and two girls also took in two boarders. As one of the daughters
reported, 'They took over my brother's bedroom ... I think the dining-room
was turned into another bedroom.' In the 1950s, and after eleven years
away from his family, Mary Burma's father had earned enough to bring his
family from Yugoslavia to Vancouver. 'My father was a fisherman at the
time and he bought a house at 655 East Pender for $650 [on credit] and we
took in eight boarders ... We were broke but happy.'[41]

Family homes were the heart of the family economy. What is called the
'family consumer economy' constituted the most common pattern of family
work.[42] By the 1920s, most middle- and many working-class families had
come to the arrangement whereby fathers – 'the breadwinner' – earned the
family income, and mothers worked full-time at housekeeping and caring
for the children. As one man explained, 'My mother never worked outside
the home after she married my dad in 1920.' A Cedar Cottage woman
pointed out, 'Our life was very ordered. Mom stayed home, Dad went to
work, and kids did "kids" things.' One man noted, however, 'Mother had to
quit teaching when she got married. She worked in a café in the shipyards
and loved it. Father made her stop. She'd sneak out and work anyways.' A
woman from a middle-class family explained: 'My mom was very regi-
mented. On Monday she washed, on Tuesday she shopped, on Wednesday
she did something, on Thursday she went downtown ... to a show, to do her
shopping.'

When one adds travelling time to their working day, fathers in such families were away for at least ten hours, and often up to twelve or more. Until
the 1950s, most male and female wage-earners worked more than forty
hours a week, usually over five and a half, or even six days.[43] The son of an
unskilled labourer noted that, in the 1920s, 'they worked a ten-hour day ...
six days a week – sixty hours, that was the normal work week.' The son of a
retail merchant reported that 'Dad left at 7:00 o'clock on the interurban
and came home at six.' A working-class woman explained that her father's
'working hours were from seven in the evening until three in the morning.
In the Depression he would walk home from downtown.' In one upper-
middle-class family, said one woman, 'my mother had the idea that when
Father came home everything should be calm and pleasant, and probably he
didn't need two little children at the dinner table ... We'd have this little
playtime when he came home, and then we would go into the kitchen [with

the maid] and we'd have dinner there. And my parents would have dinner in peace and quiet in the dining-room.'

While the working lives of the adults in a majority of Canadian families followed what children generally looked upon as this 'regular' or normal pattern, a substantial minority did not. In pioneering families in Evelyn, and in families that kept small shops in Vancouver, both parents were equally available to share in the tasks of parenting. Divorce, or the desertion, illness, unemployment, underemployment, improvidence, or death of the father, forced some mothers to work away from home at full- or part-time jobs. 'When dad was out of work in the Depression,' a Cedar Cottage man reported, 'Mom worked in Shaughnessy as a cleaning lady. She used to complain about the petty meanness of some of those she worked for.' She kept up the work, however, even during and after the war. 'She like to have her own money, see, independent of the old man.'

Further, a substantial though declining proportion of families over the whole of this period were, to employ present terminology, 'lone parent' ones. In 1931, no fewer than 13.6 per cent of Canadian families were headed by one parent, in most cases the mother. The proportion declined to 12.1 per cent in 1941, 9.9 per cent in 1951, and 8.4 per cent in 1961.[44] Recollections put flesh on these figures. A woman explained, 'My father became quite ill when I was about seven ... and he died when I was four-teen ... He sort of slipped away.' Another woman explained that her father died in 1923, leaving her mother 'a widow with nine children ... who lived on the earnings of the two oldest boys.' Another woman was the youngest of her widowed mother's seven surviving children (out of nine). Since her father died when she was four, she had only 'spotty memories of being with him' and of him 'sick in bed.' To support her large family, her mother rented a house and took in roomers, mostly nurses who worked at a nearby hospital. A '"prim and proper" woman, Victorian, strict, and school-marmish,' this mother ran a 'very structured ... very well-disciplined house-hold.' Although the household was 'very loving,' there was 'not the time for individual attention.' Her older siblings ensured that 'she need never feel alone in the world' but 'at times she also felt constricted' by her family.

Other stories illustrate other responses to lone-parenthood. A widow with two children left them during the day in their grandmother's care while she went out to work. Although she was, her daughter reported, 'often tired, she was never too tired' to give her children attention. After her divorce, reported another woman of her mother, she worked as a nurse, had 'what I think was a nervous breakdown ... left nursing, and then what she used to do was housekeep for people.' Before her mother eventually

remarried, this daughter spent some time living with her grandmother. Jack
Munro remembers the 'relief' farm near Calgary on which he, his sister,
and his mother lived after his father entered the sanitarium. Munro particularly resented the petty tyrannies of the supervisor, the humiliation he felt
when his mother had to make her monthly trip to the relief office, and the
patronizing attitudes of neighbours towards those on relief.[45] None the less,
relief, mothers' pensions, and workers' compensation, for all their harass-
ments, kept some children together with one or both parents instead of in
foster homes or in institutions. As a later chapter will reveal, however,
family disruption took some children into the care of relatives or welfare
agencies.

Although they did not show up in the social statistics, many other British
Columbia and Canadian families were also female-headed lone-parent ones
for much of the time. Prospectors, those put out of work by the Depression,
and unskilled, and thus often itinerant, labourers went off, leaving their
families behind. A Kerrisdale woman explained that her father, who had
formerly worked in a steady job as a stationery engineer, 'in the '30s was
away a lot. He would go for three-month stretches to various places to
work, so Mother had a lot to do.' Construction workers, loggers, and miners often worked in camps that made no provision for wives and families.[46]
Those who worked on the railway, in local, coastal, and deep-sea shipping,
or on whalers – officers, engineers, deckhands, stokers, oilers, and the like –
worked for short or long stretches away from home. An Evelyn man
reported, 'My mother was always there, whereas my father was always
away,' working as a pump man 'keeping the railway water towers full of
water.' While some fishermen worked mostly in local waters, others made
long trips as they followed the various salmon runs or as they ventured after
halibut far out into the ocean, north and west of the Queen Charlotte
Islands. Since fish canneries scattered up and down the coast needed the
work of men, women, and children, and therefore provided rudimentary
housing, whole families moved to cannery sites for the fishing season.[47]

In describing his father's working life in the 1940s, Rudy Wiebe lays out
one of the classic patterns:

In the spring, he would [travel to] ... where the big farmers hired laborers for their
huge War Effort crops. By the middle of summer, he would be working his way
north with the harvest, pitching bundles onto the hayracks ... for hauling to the
giant threshing machines, and as he approached home he would sometimes return
for a Sunday and leave immediately after with his own rack and team (he could earn
up to $3.50 a day that way) ... [He] would remain home only until the winter settled

in; by early November he would harness our two best horses to the heaviest working sleigh, heap it with hay and oat bundles, and drive north to the sawmills ... He would skid logs out of the bush with the team, and always be home for Christmas, but after New Year's he would be gone again to the mills if there was any work; during the war there always was ... My mother and brother (beginning in his teens) farmed our homestead ...[48]

One woman explained how a variety of working situations played themselves out in the life of her family. Before the Depression her father, 'an operating engineer in construction,' worked locally, bought their house, and ran a car. In the early part of the Depression, he worked away in a gold mine in the summer months, then for two or three years got 'the odd job now and then, but it was a case of relief' providing the family's main support. In consequence, they lost their house, and 'he used to get pretty down at times.' Next, her father 'got this job up in Atlin in a gold mine and he worked five months of the year.' By the time he died suddenly in the early years of the Second World War, he was back working in Vancouver, and the family had managed to buy a small house, but not life insurance; so her mother, who had once been a telephone operator, 'went back to work at BC Tel.'

Chronic ill-health of parents, and especially the dreaded tuberculosis, had a devastating effect on some families. Fraser Miles's father contracted the disease after being gassed in the Great War. Miles wrote that the year he was twelve – 1924 – 'was probably the worst one in Mom's whole life.' She had 'no money at all, two kids to feed and keep in school, and a husband she knew was never going to work again.' After two years of extreme poverty, she was awarded a small war pension, but her husband never returned home from hospital.[49] Ray Perrault's father, who also had tuberculosis, worked away from home 'to avoid ... the sanitarium.' Until he died at age forty-two, when Ray was nine, he 'sent money home to his wife.'[50] Jack Munro's father, a butcher, also contracted tuberculosis, when Jack was six. At first, his father 'was in and out of the san,' and then, until just before he died when Jack was eleven, 'confined to the san permanently.' During most of these years, the Munro family lived on 'relief.'[51] Alec Lucas's father had to stop working because he contracted silicosis at Britannia Mines. His mother not only took in boarders, but also 'converted the downstairs part of the house to a store so she had an ice-cream parlour and a store, and this is how she earned our keep.'[52]

While working away was more characteristic of working-class fathers than middle-class ones, the latter were by no means exempt. Surveyors, foresters, timber cruisers, logging camp and cannery managers, engineers, ships' officers, salesmen, and others in similar occupations spent long periods away from home. One man's father 'made money in the business world ... did a lot of roaming with his business,' mostly in the Prince Rupert area, and became 'a millionaire by thirty, mostly in real estate.' When the children reached school age, the family settled in Vancouver because his mother 'appreciated the advantages of Vancouver; the children could stay in the same schools, and not move around.'

Service in the armed forces during the Second World War and the Korean conflict took both working- and middle-class fathers away from their families for long periods of time. Some officers and men of the First Division, who went to Britain in December 1939, did not return to Canada until after the war.[53] Of his father, who was initially skipper of an RCMP patrol vessel, and then of a series of Royal Canadian Navy vessels, Robert MacNeil reported that, from 'the time I was three, in 1934, until the war ended in 1945, he was home only for brief periods and my mother was effectively the parent.'[54] Billie Housego, whose father was in the services, looked forward to the end of the war, when 'my dad would be home to stay, there to sit down at the table with us morning and night, day in and day out.'[55]

For children, the family home was the centre of their emotional as well as their physical geography. In their relationships with each other, and collectively and individually with their children, parents set the emotional environment within which their children grew up. Similarities and differences in temperament and personality, rooted in gender, ethnicity, religious denomination, and class, structured the outward expressions of the bond; indeed, these were sometimes all that the children apprehended about it. None the less, an openly expressed or concealed animosity between parents had a major effect on all the other relationships within the family. These similarities and differences also affected children's relationships with their parents, their siblings, and members of their extended families.

In many families a reasonable equanimity between parents constituted the norm. One woman explained she was 'very thankful that I came from a home with loving parents, a home with a warm and loving extended family. These helped to make my childhood a wonderful experience.' A man who grew up in Cedar Cottage during and after the Great War, and was the oldest of the four children of Scottish immigrants, explained that his parents were affectionate, 'everyone got along with one another. But my mother ruled the house, you know. She ruled him, too. Scottish women are like that, you know.' In discussing his parents and his relationship with them, a man who grew up in Halifax reported his working-class family 'was fairly strict. Dad was "boss" of the house, but my parents generally did things together; they talked it out.' Joan Michener Rohr offered some objective evidence of the warmth of the relationship between her parents. 'My parents were affectionate, in fact very physically affectionate. It's not so much that I remember, but I've frequently seen these early family movies, and my mother's very affectionate and cuddly,' as was her father.[56]

Other parents had cold, or even hostile relationships. A man, an only child, reported that his parents 'hated each other but stayed together because of him.' Because he wet his bed, he 'got waled [on] with a stick by his mother' with the result that he had 'no great love for his mother.' Another man, who had five sisters, explained that his family was 'not close; ... most of the interaction was on a negative basis.' His parents expected them to be 'perfect little slaves, not to talk back or question.' A third man noted that 'Mom, Dad always fought. She pretended to be dying and would lie down on the floor and play dead. This was terrifying.' A woman, whose father was 'a compulsive gambler,' would 'lie in bed and hear my parents arguing.' These quarrels sometimes 'ended in physical violence towards Mother.' Since she 'adored them both,' she was 'very upset and anxious.' Iris Allan wrote of her parents that 'constant battles took place, even about trivialities; a spot on the tablecloth, someone who arrived at the table with unwashed hands, simply anything could set off the spark of explosion from my father. Money ... headed the list of the quarrels between my parents and went on throughout their entire life together.'[57]

Two brothers, interviewed separately, demonstrated the complexity of parental relationships. They told of how they and their two sisters, the children of European immigrants, grew up in a series of settings in rural and urban British Columbia during the 1930s and 1940s. Their 'relatively well-educated' father came from a middle-class family from whom he was completely estranged; their mother, who 'always felt that she should have had an education,' from 'quite a close farming family.' In the view of one son, 'the only thing they [his parents] had in common was the intellectual stimulation of each other; otherwise they had different ideas as to what they should accomplish in the world.' The other son reported that 'they came out to make a fortune and go back.' When 'faced with a family and the Depression,' his mother sometimes became moody, irritable; her goals in life suppressed.' These differences, however, 'didn't affect us as children; they kept their differences separate' from their relationships with their children. None the less, one son reported about his childhood: 'I don't remember it too fondly, as people do today, but I don't remember it with bitterness either.'

Children also judged how closely their own families measured up to social norms. In situations in which, say, the mother dominated, they saw these as exceptional ones, worthy even now of special comment. 'I was never one to take kids to my home,' reported one man. 'I always wanted to go to their houses. Since my mother was always working, I was embarrassed that mine was not a "normal" situation to go to.' In the 1910s and 1920s, Jim Spilsbury's mother had her hair 'all clipped off boy-style ... and she always wore pants. Sometimes knickers, with puttees or high leather boots ... Everybody we knew admired the hell out of her, but I hated to be around her. I would get so embarrassed.'[58]

As they grew through their childhood years, children gradually acquired some sense of the larger circumstances of the world in which they lived. Even as they moved into adolescence, however, concepts such as depression, war, even prosperity, merely formed the background to the day-to-day immediacy of their lives. On the other hand, throughout their childhood they acquired both an emotional and an intellectual grasp of those dimensions of their environment that enveloped them. As adults, they can still recall the tastes of what they ate; the feel, shape, sounds, and smells of their clothes and their homes; their immediate neighbourhood; and the coming and going of the adults in their lives. They can, as well, recall how the nature of the bond between their parents set the boundaries for their relationships with them and with their siblings. The next two chapters discuss what form and shape their lives took in the family setting.

3

Children in Their Families: Relationships and Identities

In a recent essay summarizing three decades of research on the history of the family, American historian Tamara K. Hareven explained 'that the modern family is privatized, nuclear, domestic, and based on the emotional bonding between husband and wife and between parents and children.'[1] The families of those who described their childhoods for this study also fulfilled the objective characteristics – 'privatized, nuclear, domestic' – laid out in this description.

One must emphasize, however, that the 'emotional bonding' of families ranged along a spectrum from love to hate. The family of the man who reported that 'I accepted what my parents did. You didn't go along asking for the moon. You just – you were family. You lived together, you played together. You sat around the piano, sang together, that sort of thing' clearly came from the loving end of the spectrum. A middle-class man, an only child of the 1920s and early 1930s, came from the middle. He described his parents as 'cold.' They 'weren't affectionate towards each other or me.' His mother 'constantly told me I spoiled her figure.' She 'ran the family and made every decision; she had total control over [him and his father].' She 'used to beat me. All I had to do was oppose her.' She was, he concluded, 'sneaky and deceitful and would do anything and hurt anybody to do what she wanted to do.'[2] At the other extreme, Jeanise Davis, born in the early 1950s, 'felt her father's anger with belts, hairbrushes and tree branches. He made his children choose their own willow branches ... "I was so stupid, I always picked the thin ones ... but man, those thin ones wrapped around your legs ... I was so ashamed that I was bad enough my dad had to beat me."'[3] Accordingly, if their family served as a 'haven in a heartless world' for some, for others their families were a heartless centre from which they moved out into a hostile world.[4]

Family members interwove their lives in both physical and emotional contexts, and within a structure of power and authority. As this and other chapters make clear, a family's particular economic circumstances placed sharply defined boundaries around its options along most dimensions of family life. In turn, the nature of the bond between the parents constituted the emotional stage on which other family relationships developed and changed. Parents held both authority and power, and set the boundaries that governed their relationships with their children, and of their children with each other. In these circumstances, the individual qualities of some children were suppressed, and youngsters had to hold themselves in tight check in order to survive in their families.

Given all the varying and individualizing effects of the differences among them, can one say anything meaningful about what some families have in common? In fact, my interviews and other data suggest that characteristic scripts appeared frequently enough to permit considerable generalization. In this chapter, I lay out those characteristics of English-Canadian family life that grew out of youngsters' relationships with their parents and siblings, and those that grew out of their emerging sense of their gender, class, ethnic, and religious identities. In the next chapter, I explore how parents used their unlimited power over their children in both legitimate and illegitimate ways.

Power and authority within families flowed from notions embedded in a patriarchal social order as it expressed itself in twentieth-century Canada.[5] One woman's comment subtly and neatly epitomized the pattern: 'If I was with Father, if he bumped into someone he wanted to talk to, we'd move away. Women and children had their place.' A man echoed this report: 'Dad would go downtown to the Stanley Hotel to drink beer, and leave me outside.' Parents exercised their powers in ways that ranged from tender to severe. The choice, however, lay entirely with parents; children had no right to fair and equitable treatment. As one man aptly put it, in his family children were to 'do as you're told when spoken to; be seen and not heard.' Canadians, even children, looked benignly on the exercise of the power that flowed from the legitimate authority that parents and teachers had over the young. On the other hand, most objected to any exercise of power over their children or pupils by those such as bullies, or neighbours or other adults who did not possess legitimate authority. One man recalled his father's anger when the son, after lighting a fire that damaged a neighbour's fence, 'got a good tanning' from the irate owner. When Ignatia Lanigan Grams's uncle spanked her and her sister Agnes because he thought they had left his car lights on, 'Daddy was furious with him, and Mother was pretty angry too ...'[6]

For Canadians with British or European roots, notions and practices related to authority and power were expressed in terms of what some believed to be traditional Judaeo-Christian doctrine. Even those who had no connection with any religious denomination, or held a Marxist or other hostility to religion, customarily behaved as if patriarchy was the natural order of humanity. In its baldest form, this notion held that God had ordained society in such a way that husbands were subject directly to his authority, that wives were subject to God's authority through that of their husbands, and children subject to God's authority through that of their parents.[7] In fact, of course, a patriarchal order is as bound by time and place as is any other social condition. Most parents and children, however, had no sense of historical subtleties. As Melinda McCracken explained in her memoir of her 1950s childhood: 'In the world we lived in things were generally seen as being hierarchical. God was the supreme authority ... Parents were strong, responsible, mature people. The people they had power over were their children. However generous in other ways, parents assumed they knew best, that they had the right to control their children's lives and tell them what to do. Kids obeyed.'[8]

Kids also observed that their mothers obeyed.[9] Once, when one farm wife wanted to go to town, recounted her daughter, her father 'wouldn't let her. He was the boss. He started to unhitch the horses.' Another woman remarked that 'Father could be sharp and intolerant.' Her mildly rebellious mother would 'be easygoing in some ways, but it had to be done right for Father, so she would say, "I won't do it! It wouldn't suit him anyway."' Sometimes authority, or children's perception of where it lay, shifted in families. A woman reported that 'Father at first seemed to make all the important decisions, but ... Mother always had an important influence' and, later on, when she was in her teens, her mother 'became the chief decision maker.'

Children often had very different relationships with each parent. Family work patterns generally dictated that they would have far more to do with their mothers than with their fathers. One man said, 'Mother was a bigger figure in our family life than Father,' and another that he 'had most contact with Mother ... in the city, Father was [only] around at night.' For this reason the emotional relationship between mothers and children, whether warm and loving or cold and hostile, was usually a closer one than between fathers and children, which were often, as Robert MacNeil records, 'paralysed by the silence between generations.'[10] In his survey of 200 fourteen- to eighteen-year-old Kerrisdale boys over the 1951–2 school year, Allan Hare discovered that 40.5 per cent preferred to discuss their problems with their mothers, 23 per cent with their fathers, 3.5 per cent with both parents, and 22 per cent with siblings and friends.[11]

A warm intimacy between mother and child often involved touching, hugging, kissing. A man reported, 'My mother was especially affectionate. She would like to hug, she liked to caress. She liked to cuddle, and, you know, smile at you, and could be very sympathetic and supportive.' A woman told of a time when she and her brother were playing away from home that they heard their mother call them and they 'ran all the way ... Mummy stood there with her arms out and when we got there we ran right into her arms and she swung us around and around.' Another recalled that 'Mother would sit and brush out my hair and tell stories.' On the other hand, another woman reported that her 'childhood was really horrible. Mother was a sick woman. I was terrified of her.' A social worker reported that, over a series of eight interviews at which eight-year-old 'Billy' was in attendance, his mother employed such 'denunciations as "he's been a miserable kid since the day he was born," "I certainly didn't plan on having a boy," and "if I'd given in to him I would have killed him," [and] "I sometimes wonder and worry what I am doing to Billy."'[12]

Children also recall their mother's active role at the centre of the household. Fredelle Bruser Maynard, who grew up in various Prairie towns between the wars, wrote: 'when I look back on my beginnings ... what I remember is home. My mother was, in the truest sense of a now debased word, a homemaker.'[13] A man explained, 'Mother kept the household together. Dad handed his paycheque over to her: "she can stretch it further than anyone I know."' After being deserted by her husband, and the failure of 'a disastrous common-law union,' Hugh Garner's mother supported him, his brother, and their two half-sisters in the late 1920s and 1930s by 'many unskilled little jobs, and when these failed she worked by day scrubbing floors and cleaning house ... on the days she could get the jobs.' He remembered 'lying awake long after midnight and hearing her in the kitchen ... scrubbing our laundry on a scrubbing board or ironing it on the kitchen table.'[14] Recollections of meals are often central to this aspect of the relations between mothers and children. His mother 'was a good cook,' noted one man. 'It was just plain cooking you got – nothing fancy, let me tell you. And there would be enough supper made for the six of us, and you got put on the plate what it [was].'

The relationship between mothers and children could be particularly close when children were ill.[15] 'I looked forward to getting sick,' explained one man. 'It meant staying home and ... having my food brought to me.' When she was sick, one woman reported, her mother would keep her home from school, 'probably longer than she should, in an excess of care.' 'When I had pneumonia, before penicillin,' said another man, 'Mom sat beside my bed all night – for weeks, it seemed. I can still feel her cool hand on my hot forehead.' When Helen Sigurdson 'began to menstruate, I was put to bed with a hot water bottle for the first day.' Her mother's 'comfort food for me was oatmeal cooked in milk or a scrambled egg sandwich.'[16]

Evelyn and other rural children also recalled how arduous were the lives of their mothers. As one Evelyn woman explained, 'Our life was hard, ... hardest on Mom.' Another woman gave much of the reason for this situation when she noted that 'Mom did real well with very little.' A third expressed regret that her mother 'died before I showed her any appreciation.' Looking back on his mother's life in a long-settled farming area of Ontario, Roy Bonisteel wrote: 'I would like to say it was a good life, but certainly her married years were hard and often disappointing. Ten children, back-breaking work on a farm with no modern conveniences ... For her, one day was very much like the last – the months, seasons and years a continuum of work, obligations and survival.' None the less, she possessed 'an indomitable spirit, open generosity and joyous humour.'[17]

As the primary caregivers, mothers helped create children's attitudes towards their other parent. 'My mother,' reported one man, 'believed in Father first, then the kids.' One woman recalled that 'Mom respected Dad and insisted that we kids do so as well. His grumpiness, Mom said, came from the long, hard hours he put in at the foundry. When he came home after that, and then an hour standing on the streetcar, he was entitled to a little peace and quiet.' Another woman explained that, 'when I got to be an age to listen ... to my mother rant and rave about my father ... I hated him very thoroughly.' A third woman explained of her mother that, 'unfortunately, I took after, looked like my father, and every time she got mad ... she would take her anger on my dad out on me.' A fourth woman's mother encouraged her 'to be positive about life. I was told not to think about my father and not to dwell on the past, which could not be altered, and not to expect life to be fair.'

When compared with their memories of their mothers, people's memories of their fathers often display two differences. First, and in a way analagous to the aura that school principals cast over their schools, many fathers, as the ultimate authority and source of power in their households, projected a strong, sometimes remote, although not necessarily negative presence over family activities and relationships. Upon hearing an anecdote about his father's childhood, MacDonald Coleman was, he wrote, surprised to discover that 'once upon a time he had been a real person.'[18] Rick Ouston noted that his adoptive father's death 'weakened the ties binding the family ... The family was my father, my father the family. Without him at the head of the table, the kitchen felt empty, populated but leaderless.'[19] A woman explained that generally her mother was responsible for family discipline: 'We would have to be pretty bad before Dad spoke up ... Dad was the final authority.'

Second, except at moments of crisis, some fathers had a more relaxed, if not necessarily more intimate, relationship with their children than did mothers. This situation was possible because fathers were spared the unending demands of family and home care, and were away from the wearying, day-long interaction with children that characterized mothers' diurnal round. 'I remember my father,' stated one woman, 'as this nice, warm man who just loved me and I wanted him to be there ... I used to drink ginger beer and cream soda with him ... I just remember he was big and brown and round and bald and warm.' A Vancouver man recalled of his working-class father that 'we had lots of fun. I used to go with him whenever I could ... He used to deliver wood.' A woman who grew up in Powell River remembered 'going to dances at New Year's ... when I was twelve ... My father always took me ... His crew knew better than not to ask me ... It was a marvellous thing to go through because you're very happy, and you know everybody and you're very safe.' In an affectionate memoir of his Baptist minister father, Arthur Mayse wrote, on 'the river we were comrades, equal in our desire to catch the biggest possible trout. In town we reverted to the standard father-and-son relationship.'[20]

The two later chapters on children's work (chapters 6 and 7) make clear that fathers as well as mothers trained both girls and boys in their 'outdoor' tasks. However, in those mostly rural and pioneering families in which sons grew up expecting to follow into the work of their fathers, boys sometimes had a specially close relationship with their fathers. For Horace Goudie, growing up on the Labrador coast in the 1920s and 1930s, at ten 'my biggest dream came true. Dad had to go back to his trapline to strike up his traps and I pestered him so much to go he took me ...' Goudie's father built boats in the summer, and if 'Dad had to build two boats one summer, it took the two of us most of the fine summer days to finish the jobs.' As chapter 7 makes clear, a close working relationship between parent and child is not necessarily a harmonious one, but a warm and affectionate bond between his father and Goudie permeates the latter's autobiography.[21]

As the discussion of family discipline in the next chapter also indicates, some children distrusted, disliked, and even hated their fathers. A man explained that he 'resented Dad's discipline and authority ... He was always a bit of an authoritarian.' Her father, reported a woman who grew up in Cedar Cottage between the wars, 'wanted to put the fear of God and the devil into everyone, not as a religion but as a way of life. He had had a hard life ... brought up by foster parents in England.' A woman explained that her 'relationship with Father was okay' while she was young, but 'from Grade Seven onward he'd go into my bedroom and I felt awkward.' Another woman, who was born about 1930, and who grew up in Vancouver's east end, was the oldest of five girls. Her memories are laced with recollections of certain happy times, especially musical ones. Her father was twenty years older than her mother. However, her father had been brought up by 'a very domineering' mother, and 'my Dad took after her, I guess.' He 'was very violent in his reaction to things he didn't like. No matter what we did, we didn't deserve his reaction ... My mother thought he would kill me a couple of times.'

Alcohol contributed to or exacerbated unhappiness in families. In the words of one woman, 'her [her mother] and my dad didn't get along, then. He took to drinking, then. He beat her up, so it was rather sad. She finally had to leave him for – save her life, I guess.' Stuart Keate's father was a 'bat' drinker. After seven or eight months 'abjuring drink altogether,' he 'would take off, hole up in a hotel, club, or some nearby city, and drink himself into a state of senselessness for weeks at a time.' And in 'spite of threats, cajoling and endless tears,' Keate's 'mother would always take him back, dry him out, and put him together again.'[22]

Memories focus especially on how alcohol affected children's relations with parents. 'Martha,' born in the 1940s, said of her father that sometimes 'things didn't make sense. He'd fall asleep or fall down. We never ate meals together as a family ... I couldn't understand why he didn't want to play with us ... Were we not good kids?'[23] Another woman explained that 'Dad was a drunk; he used to beat me up. I wanted out of that.' Fourteen-year-old 'Sally' told Margaret Cork that 'I hate both of them [her parents]. They're not happy and neither are we, even when he isn't drinking. We kids all fight just like Mom and Dad.'[24] 'Keith,' who by seventeen had already served six months in a correctional institution and had shown 'disturbed behaviour at least since [of] school age,' started on his career of delinquency when he was ten. His alcoholic parents quarrelled frequently and 'Keith was the particular butt of his father's anger, receiving both verbal and physical abuse from him.' Although 'open in stating his hatred of his father,' Keith 'seemed to retain a feeling of closeness for his mother.'[25]

Although a far higher proportion of fathers than mothers were alcoholics – Margaret Cork's sample included fifty-three alcoholic fathers and nineteen alcoholic mothers – the children of the latter sometimes felt even more dismayed than the former. Sixteen-year-old Scott told Cork, 'Mom is different when she is drinking – not rational – sort of sentimental and less organized. We never get any regular meals. You can't talk to her. She never minds what you do or where you are, so long as you are on her side.'[26] A Kerrisdale woman reported, 'I came to hate my mother' after she developed 'a drinking problem,' one exacerbated by the difficulty of getting liquor during the Second World War.

Children's relationships with sisters and brothers were as complex as those between children and parents. In the conventional wisdom of family life – often reiterated by parents and others in authority – siblings were enjoined with the duty to love, take care of, and protect one another. At their best, however, relationships might resemble those of the woman who explained, 'My brother and I used to have gorgeous fights. Even though we used to fight in the home, we stood up for each other when we were with our friends.' Her brother reported 'a bit of sibling rivalry ... but not major confrontations.' Of his older brother, Trevor Lautens wrote, 'I can still hear Mother's voice: "Now, take your brother with you." Gary protested, but not much. We went together.'[27] When their father came upon two sisters fighting, one of them reported, 'he made us sit on a stool and hold hands and repeat "You are my sister" for one hour. We hated each other at the end of that hour.'

As these examples suggest, realities of family life often undercut the ideal. Children were rivals for the affection of their parents, for the scarce resources possessed by the family, for the very space in which to sleep, to do their chores and school work, or to amuse themselves in quiet or vigorous ways.[28] To one woman, her sister, who was fourteen months younger, was 'the "sandwich" person ... between my brother and me ... I got all the attention and she never got any and was jealous and mean ... She'd hold things against you and tattle to my mother.' 'My sister,' noted another woman, 'was just two years younger ... She was a brat and she used to tell tales to Mother about things ... We used to fight all the time because ... we didn't agree about anything. If she wanted something, I wanted it.' In a rare admission - usually siblings are reported as the ones who behaved badly – Olive O'Brien asked: 'Why was I often so mean to my sister Betty although I loved her? I think the cause of my jealousy was her looks. To me she was beautiful.'[29] 'My dad,' explained one woman, 'bought my older sister and me a bike to share. We had more fights as to whose turn it was for the favoured afternoon shift.'

Boys shared these rivalries. One man, who had both learning and related behavioural problems at school, explained that, when his younger sister had to admit to a teacher that they were related, she 'cried because I put her to shame.' As a youngster, Lew Duddridge 'often felt hard done by. From day one it seemed that [younger brother] Len could twist his mother around his little finger ... There is more than a slight chance that I never quite recovered from the setbacks I received' when he was blamed and punished for his brother's misdemeanours. On the other hand, their younger sister, 'the baby of the family, with all the attendant rights and privileges that seem to go with that position ... seemed to be aware of the clout she had about the place. About the only times that Len and I ever teamed up occurred ... when, beyond a shadow of a doubt, our sister was the culprit ...'[30]

The intensity of feelings among siblings was related to whether or not they were of the same sex and how close they were in age. Thus, to a man who was ten when his sister was born, 'the relationship with my sister was distant. The age difference meant that we had different friends and led separate lives.' Another man reported, 'I never saw my sisters,' who were three and eight years younger than him. 'They went a different way than I did.' A woman who had one brother two years older and one three years younger 'didn't have much to do with my brothers ... [but] was closer to the younger one when we were growing up. He was the "baby," the "sweetheart" [who was] thin and rather frail.' One man explained that he and his brothers 'once got really mad at the girls [their three sisters], but most of the time we left them alone. We didn't tease them. We didn't play together.' A man whose sister was a year older and brother a year younger explained that he and his brother 'were always together. We were kind of inseparable ... [but] we were really bratty boys in the sense that we always agitated [their sister]. She agitated us ... [and] she would probably agree with me today that she had a bit of a temperament I think we exasperated.'

In a way that mirrored parental control over children, older siblings sometimes exerted, or tried to exert, their power over younger ones. Charles Dougan, the sixth child in a family of eight, observed: 'In a bigger family the younger ones were pared and trimmed by the older ones and generally no "sass" was vented from a lesser to the older ones.'[31] 'My older brother,' declared one woman, 'was a rotten kid! He'd lock me in the bedroom and tie the door to the hot-water pipe if I didn't do what he said.' Another woman, the youngest of four, 'was always being told what to do ... and it's one thing for Mother to tell you what to do, but when you've got ... two big sisters telling you what to do ... you go around just sort of fighting this ... being very independent of what you want for yourself; ... I wasn't going to be pushed around.' There were six years between a third woman and her older sister,' and as we were both determined children, there were many quarrels. She felt she could order me around. I threw things at her.' According to one man, he 'wasn't that good a brother to my two younger brothers, especially the one who is four years younger than me ... I was just trying to show myself ... to prove that I was bigger and stronger and could push him around if he bothered me.' On the other hand, reported one woman whose home life was a very unhappy one, her stepbrother 'looked after me a lot, doted on me ... [there was] a void in my life when he left. He was the only bright spot in my life at home.'

While most children were able to work out short- or long-term accords, others, especially those who felt that they were unfairly treated in relation to their siblings, carried a sense of grievance for much or all of their lives. A man, the eldest of six, reported of the next child, a brother five years younger, that 'he was favoured, protected by Mother. It was not right.' Another man described the 'rivalry between me and my younger brother for Mom ... My younger brother was the baby and got privileges as a result.' A woman, who through her skipping a grade and his failing one, at first caught up to, and then passed, her brother in school, 'couldn't resist taunting and teasing him. After all, he'd always picked on me ... and now I finally had something on him. I was relentless in my jeers, and boasts, and he countered by destroying my toys, stealing my books ... name calling and other "sibling rivalries."' Sour relations prevailed between them until they were mature adults. In another example, the upshot of events between him, his parents, and his siblings meant to one elderly man that 'I hate my two older brothers to this day.'

As they grew up children learned who they were. They learned that who they were depended on an ever-changing set of circumstances. They discovered that they were children, that they were boys or that they were girls, that they were grandchildren, nieces, nephews; that they were pupils; that they were Catholic, or Baptist, or Jewish, or Mennonite, or Sikh; that they were Canadian, or English, or Ukrainian, or Cree; that they were 'respectable working people' or members of the middle class. How youngsters actually began the process of acquiring the various strands of identity is inaccessible by means of the memory-centred evidence employed in this study. None the less, it is clear that, soon after they were born, children discovered and took on many of the characteristics by which they came to know themselves. By the end of childhood, most youngsters had built into themselves beliefs, roles, and practices that manifested a not always articulable but complex inner sense of who they were.

While we can sort out various elements in identities for description and analysis, it is important to note that they fluctuated, often from moment to moment. Which element or elements came to the fore at any particular moment depended on circumstances. Boys playing soccer by themselves with no girls nearby were less conscious of their gender than when they played in mixed games of scrub. Japanese-Canadian children were less conscious of their 'Japaneseness' at a family gathering than on the school playgound. As they changed into their street clothes after a volleyball game at a west-side Vancouver school, girls from an east-side one were much more aware of such external trappings of class and status as hairstyle, clothing, accessories, and shoes than when they played against another east-side school.

From almost their earliest moments, children began to acquire a dynamic sense of their 'gender identity,' their sense of themselves as girls who were growing into women, or as boys who were growing into men.[32] Gender identities grew out of the interaction among the ways in which parents and other members of families provided role models; family discourse on appropriate behaviour, rules, and the like; and their tasks in their household and family economies. Thus most family activities were conducted in gender-specific ways, ways that mirrored the power relationships between adults. Moreover, gender, as with other forms of identity, is much more than knowing; it is also very much a matter of daily doing and living.[33] Within the family, the sexes separately constructed the behaviours and skills, and constantly practised the roles that their parents and society assigned to and modelled for them. As well, youngsters took on the 'body language' appropriate to their gender and class.

In many families both boys and girls learned that boys were more important than girls, that male heirs came first in family priorities. A woman explained that her father 'was terribly disappointed that we were girls instead of boys. He always called us boys when he would come into the bedroom and say "It's time to get up, boys" or "What will you have for breakfast, boys?"' As one woman born in the 1950s put it, 'Boys did and girls watched. The whole family went to the rink to see [her brother] play hockey. I did nothing that anyone could come and watch.' Iris Allan explained that her brother, 'Frank, as the only son, was the apple of Mother's eye' and also revealed that she and her sisters went along with this evaluation. Frank was, she continued, 'full of antics at home, luckily having three girls as an audience.'[34] Six-year-old Pierre Berton started the 'Be-a-Boy Club.' However, as an associate member – there were no other boys to join – his younger sister, Lucy, 'was permitted to engage in daredevil feats, just like a boy ...'[35] In 1932, when she was twelve years old and living in

Two brothers taking tea with their sister in a west-side Vancouver garden in 1932.

Vancouver, Jean Lumb's parents said, 'Jean, we have to talk to you about school ... We need another person to go to work in the store. It has to be you because your brother, Robert, is a boy and he has to have a little more education to get on in the world" ... I cried. I remember that.'[36]

Boys and girls learned that 'it was a man's world.' They heard that that certain difficult jobs were 'man's work,' or, when fathers went away to work, they were 'the man of the family now,' that they must 'take care of' their mothers and sisters. One woman reported that, at ten years of age, her much younger brother became 'the big man of the family when Father was away,' undertaking such tasks as using a 'shotgun with a cushion on his shoulder to shoot the hawk' that was after their chickens. In a man's world, men's needs or wishes, ranging from the best or only piece of meat on the dinner table through new clothes, new tools, new farm equipment, new cars, new shotguns, and most other paraphernalia of male life, took precedence over the needs and wants of women and children. Middle-class parents taught girls to expect and boys to provide appropriate mannerly deference to the 'weaker' sex: to tip or doff hats and caps in their presence ('Mom insisted I tip my lid to ladies'), to hold doors open for them, to stand when they entered a room, to walk on the outside, to help them on and off streetcars and buses, and so on.

Children were encouraged to take on gendered emotional stances. Small children of both sexes cried, but as they grew older boys discovered that it was unmanly to be a 'crybaby': 'boys don't cry!' As girls discovered that 'women don't fight – they're supposed to be understanding,' boys learned to 'be tough,' to 'take it,' to stand up for their rights and, if necessary, to employ violence in doing so. As boys were encouraged to compete vigorously and physically in all aspects of their lives, girls learned that most competition was unladylike. (It was, however, fine if girls came 'first' in school work and music festivals, activities that had a female aura about them). As boys learned to put their needs above those of others, to think and talk and act in terms of 'I' and 'me,' girls learned to subsume their needs, feelings, ambitions, and goals, to think and talk and act in terms of 'we' and 'us.' Girls learned to be passive, to hide displeasure, and to smile whatever their real mood. Indeed, learning to be submissive made them vulnerable to abuse.[37]

Boys and girls learned both to visualize and to use their bodies in very different ways.[38] For boys, to be tall, strong, and sturdy was better than to be short, and especially to be soft and fat. Boys discovered that peers and adults encouraged them to use their bodies to the limits of prowess and with a casually insouciant style. They celebrated their bodies, showing off the developing muscles in their arms, and all their athletic and other physical achievements. They took pride in the sweat they gave off as they worked or played. Boys soon sensed that society set broader norms on their behaviour than on their sisters and would indulge certain actions as the product of youthful exuberance, of incipient 'manliness,' or of the 'sowing of wild oats.'

Girls learned that their bodies were an inferior form of the male one. Only a few were encouraged to pursue athletic or other forms of physical prowess. ('I liked to skate and Dad took me to lessons.') Most learned to value softness rather than muscles, to avoid looking and smelling sweaty. Tall, slim bodies were valued more than short, dumpy ones. ('I was pudgy, but my sister was not. Mom said she was the pretty one, but I'd have to really work on my personality.') Constrained both by clothing and precept, girls learned to walk, to run, and to throw a ball in the style of other girls or risk being labelled a 'tomboy.' Girls were enjoined to place and move their bodies only in socially appropriate ways: to cross their ankles, to keep their knees covered and together, and their underwear concealed. ('My mother rarely yelled at me, but she yelled at me about keeping my knees together.')

Both boys and girls learned to make their clothing and other aspects of their appearance accord with their gender and their class. Until the Second World War, girls wore dresses for all their activities. Even after they began to wear slacks in the 1940s and 1950s, they did so only for chores or for play. Although at certain stages youthful gender and class fashions ran contrary to parental preferences – 'No make-up until high school, young lady,' and 'No, you can't have a crew cut and look like some Yank soldier!' – these fashions were gender-specific. Since girls were encouraged to give more attention to their appearance than boys, they role-played through 'dressing up' more than did boys. The boyhood code that labelled such behaviour 'sissy' may also have prevented some boys from taking part in an activity they might have enjoyed.

Both girls and boys learned how the world was divided into a private, or domestic sphere, and a public one. In the context of the overall authority of the breadwinner, women predominated in the domestic sphere, men in the public. Notions of the gendered division of the spheres permeated popular culture, and were reiterated in movies and in radio and television programs. The very language children were learning – *milkman, mailman, policeman, draftsman, tomboy,* – confirmed the public sphere as primarily male territory.

As boys began 'boys'' work within the family economy, they were at one end of a continuum whose other end was full-time membership in the workforce. If they did chores identified as belonging to girls, they worried that their friends would label them 'sissies.' Boys discovered that the core of their adult identity would come from the work that they did; that they would eventually move relatively freely from one sphere to another; that their destiny in the public sphere was that of 'breadwinner.' As such, they would acquire the economic resources, and consequently the authority and power, to establish and control their own domestic sphere. Boys and girls saw that fathers earned, and therefore usually controlled the family's income, often giving mothers a 'housekeeping' allowance. In his well-off middle-class family, Hugh Palmer explained, his mother received 'an amount each month to cover the normal housekeeping expenses ... For any special item she required she had to approach Father. She found this a difficult business since his initial reaction was always explosive.'[39]

Girls heard sentences including such phrases as 'when you have your own home,' '... own children,' '... own kitchen,' or were admonished, 'Be ladylike!' They heard their fathers and brothers speak patronizingly of their mothers and their own competence with mechanical processes. In turn, they patronized boys, although to far less effect, for their inability to sew on a button or prepare a meal, even for themselves. Compared with what her father taught her brother, claimed one woman, 'the things my mother taught me – cleaning silver properly, even baking a cake from scratch – never seemed as important.' They learned that their clothes, their adornments, and their language – 'A lady doesn't say that!' – had to fit within the narrow boundaries society laid out for 'nice' girls. They learned to smile even when they had no reason to, and not to laugh too loudly or to shout.

As girls did both 'girls'' and 'boys' tasks in the household, they began to see that they were rehearsing their role as a worker in and 'supervisor' of their own domestic sphere. Girls learned that their public movements must be more circumspect than that of their brothers, that between school and marriage they would work in the public sphere in one of the jobs – a waitress, a telephone operator, on the 'woman's line' in a factory, a stenographer, a nurse, an elementary-school teacher – that permitted, even encouraged, short-term stays there.[40] They learned that they were destined to return to the domestic sphere as a full-time housewife or, to use the later term, 'homemaker'; that the core of their adult identity was likely to be a dependent one. As Margaret Fulton reported, 'I think there was an assumption in my family that the boys would grow up to be farmers and the girls would grow up to be teachers and then become farmers' wives.'[41] In order that their transition from childhood dependency to eventual adult dependency be an easy one, girls learned that they should defer to and please fathers, brothers, and other male figures on their way eventually to deferring and pleasing a husband.

Parents initiated children in the gendered rituals and practices of adults. Fathers took their sons fishing, hunting, and to sporting events; 'Dad used to box, 'reported one man, 'so he got me to, too.' Some fathers modelled stoical behaviour in the face of pain or adversity, as did the miner who came home from work and 'collapsed still wearing his cap and light' from the pain of a shoulder blade broken by a rock fall. Since there was 'no compensation, [he] worked anyway.' Mothers and daughters went shopping together, they prepared for and attended bridal showers, and helped out at church suppers and bazaars. In their 'putting up' with pain, adversity, and even violence, some women modelled a form of feminine stoicism for their daughters. Some boys learned from fathers and other males that men could treat women violently, and some girls learned to expect violence from males. Jeanise Davis reported that, when she was growing up, violence 'was totally accepted. I saw it in my father. So when I saw it in other men, I thought ... "he's normal."'[42]

As later chapters show, when children moved outside their homes into the culture of childhood and into the ambience of congregation and school, they found that teachers, friends, acquaintances, even enemies, reinforced what they had learned in the family. Jean McKay reported that 'Mrs. Hardy sometimes minded me in the afternoons [and] ... taught me how to play Chinese checkers. A nice girl, she told me, doesn't make distracting clicking noises with her tongue while her opponent is deciding on a move. Nice girls also keep their feet on the floor, and off the furniture. And they don't complain that the noodles in their soup are too soggy.'[43]

Connie Kuhns, a child of the 1950s, summarized what girls learned about themselves: 'Nothing in my upbringing ... prepared me to view the opposite sex as equal. I was taught to be ignorant of my feelings, my body parts and to defer to men.'[44] Although notions of male pre-eminence permeated what they said or wrote, none of the men we interviewed or whom I read expressed any parallel insight into what he learned about male identity. Not surprisingly, the cumulative effect of the constraints on them led some girls, such as Ellen Davignon when she was about ten, to wish many times to be a boy. 'By summer's end,' however, 'I was still a girl and Mom was still refusing to buy me overalls, like [her brother] Aksel's.'[45]

Although class often played a major role in determining family attitudes and behaviours, many people only came to comprehend this dimension of their identity when they became adolescents or even adults. As one woman put it, 'Looking back I guess we were lower middle class [and] most of my girlfriends ... had similar backgrounds.' In their interviews, those who grew up in Kerrisdale from either middle- or working-class families rarely made specific reference to class, but they did mention status. One woman noted that her mother had 'an aversion to the thought of me working in a store.' Another explained that, when teachers 'asked kids what their fathers did for a living, ... you felt like ducking under the desk if your father wasn't a doctor, or a lawyer, or a big shot.' Others shared the stance of the man who still feels 'very attached to Kerrisdale, where I grew up, worked, and lived all my life; ... it gave me a good outlet on values and respect.'

None the less, some Kerrisdale youngsters probably developed an attitude similar to that of the son of a merchant who grew up in another mostly middle-class Vancouver neighbourhood, who in the 1920s 'didn't know any poor people as a child. The kids who lived below Broadway on False Creek had poorer homes. We disdained them. Orientals lived there and half-assimilated Europeans.'[46] Charles Ritchie also learned to 'disdain' the poor of Halifax, who 'lived in squat, bug-ridden wooden boxes, the windows sealed tight, winter and summer. A charnel whiff of ancient dirt issued from the doorways where the children thronged.'[47] An east-side middle-class family 'looked down on people who rented rather than owned their own home,' and a girl from the same area remembered the poor, 'and the cultural differences between their families and mine ... they were dirty, unkempt, used bad language, were rough, so rough.'

Cedar Cottage and east-side families generally had a sharper sense of class identity. 'We were all working class in that area, you know,' reported one former resident and was echoed by another: '[Cedar Cottage] was a working-class community.' As in Kerrisdale, neighbourhood identity in Cedar Cottage could be affectionate and non-ideological. One man said warmly, 'I've been here ever since I was born and I'm still here,' and his wife added, 'I like the east end, I always have.' Another former resident explained, 'Maybe the area was poor, but it was respectable, with lots of families and churches.'

Although few informants reported that their parents passed on to them sense of the ideology of class, or the need to participate in politics that challenged social relations, I suspect that this reticence sometimes represented their own adult conservatism. None the less, one woman from a working-class family there explained that 'some of my father's beliefs certainly rubbed off on me, because he was a socialist.' Thom Greenfield explained that he grew up 'in an environment of protest, a generally left-wing ideology. I was raised by my mother. She had a vivid sense of social outrage at the social injustices she suffered.'[48] Certainly from the Cooperative Commonwealth Federation's founding during the Depression, Cedar Cottage's constuencies elected CCF members to represent them in both the provincial and the federal legislatures. 'I was brought up to admire – even revere – Harold Winch and Arthur Turner,' said one man.[49] On the other hand, some working-class youngsters came to aspire to move up in the world. Of her childhood in Montreal, Maureen Forrester wrote, 'I knew that I didn't want to be working class. I was tired of hand-me-downs and frayed edges and I longed for my own things, brand new from the store.'[50]

Those who grew up in Evelyn made even less mention of class and status than did those in Kerrisdale. Most came from families that wanted to make an economic success of their own lives and provide a better one for their children. As the later chapter on their work makes abundantly clear, the children themselves grew up feeling proud of the acres and the crops that their families had wrested from the bush. Those families which failed in the task, and therefore generally left the community, seemingly revealed their own inadequacies as pioneers rather than flaws in the economic system. For the local Native population in nearby Moricetown, Evelyn residents felt

Vancouver children taking part in a labour demonstration in 1937.

either contempt or pity. 'Indians had it a lot tougher than we did,' said one man. 'They were treated tough at school; they were looked down on. They lived in one-room shacks and didn't have nothing.'

In contrast to notions of class, both rural and urban children began at an early age to acquire some conscious sense of their ethnic identities. Since the process is both complex and in many ways particular to each ethnic group, I shall merely suggest certain of the central characteristics of it that people have described in their interviews and elsewhere. As with the acquisition of notions of gender, children began to learn who they were in an ethnic sense soon after they were born. They heard their mothers sing traditional lullabies to them. They began to take part in family devotional activities such as sabbath observations in Jewish homes. Some learned to speak a language other than, or as well as, English. Mary Trocell Veljacic spoke Croatian at home 'but not when we were out ... and I used to resent that.'[51] Verna Kirkness doesn't 'ever remember only speaking one language. I seem to have learned both of them [Cree and English] at the same time.'[52] Myer Freedman attended 'Hebrew School, an after-hours type of school for extra-curricular learning of language ... 2 hours in the late afternoon, 5 days a week and Sunday.'[53]

Some families appeared to reject some or all of their background. The child of Danish immigrants said that, because his 'parents didn't expect to go home,' they 'didn't speak Danish at home.' Another man from the same background reported that he was 'English-speaking when he went to

Sikh boys on parade in East Vancouver in the late 1930s.

school,' but now 'I really regret not learning Danish.' Gertrude Story 'never ever felt very German. My mother would never permit it. To be German in any country but Germany led only to pain ... And she wanted to spare us that.'[54] In a deeper form of rejection, a woman reported that her father 'was ashamed that his father was from Poland.'

Other families proudly affirmed who they were. A woman reported that her mother and aunt spoke Welsh to each other, and the Welsh Society 'was a large part of our lives ... , the children's parties and the picnics and everything like that.' Another woman's parents 'sent me to the German language school held Saturday mornings at the church.' While she spoke English with her parents, she 'was required to speak German in her grandparents' home.' Another family spoke German in the home, and the son proudly reported that he had 'learned to read the Luther Bible.' Of Low German, Harold Ratzlaff reported, 'this was the vernacular among our parents socially and I remember sitting in the corner and listening. This was entertainment enough just to listen to this talk swirl through the living room, to sense the verve of low German, to sense the passion behind it, the earthiness of it.'[55]

What children learned about themselves at home interplayed with what took place at school and in the culture of childhood. Thus one man of English descent found that family, school, and community worked together to make him feel 'proud of myself as British first, as Canadian second, and as a British Columbian third.'[56] In sharp contrast to an identity in which the parts interwove into a whole, Canadians of Asian origin felt a particularly strong sense of what Denise Chong described as 'the claustrophobic exist-ence of being excluded from the larger white society.'[57] Thus a man explained that his parents wanted 'their children to learn some Chinese cul-ture because they felt discriminated against ... so my parents took me and my sister back to China to study Chinese.' Sing Lim 'was not allowed to speak English at home or with other children. Our parents suffered so much racial intolerance, they did not want to be part of Canadian culture.' In addition to day school, Sing Lim attended Chinese school for ten hours each week.[58]

Many families initiated children into religious practices and beliefs, and ensured that they would begin to take on a religious and denominational identity. Indeed, in some families much of what they did centred on reli-gious observances and congregational affairs. In R.F. Sparkes's Newfound-land village, life 'revolved around the Church and its customs. The secular calendar merely told us the day of the month; it was the Church calendar which set for us the "season and the time for every purpose."'[59] Jimmy Pat-tison told a reporter that his family life in Vancouver 'centred around a Pen-tecostal church and mission, on East Hastings. 'Father sang, mother played the accordion and [my] life-long love of music was established.'[60]

Religious observances usually began in the home. 'Growing up in an Orthodox Jewish home,' reported one man, 'there were a million rules and these had to be enforced.' In another family 'Mother was the religious per-son ... , a fundamentalist ... who said prayers before bed,' told her son Bible stories, and to whom death was 'a very big deal ... an obsession.' In one fam-ily 'the Bible and Mary Baker Eddy was read every day before school.' Many people particularly recall giving thanks at meals, and other occasions for family prayers. 'We took turns saying grace at mealtime. I remember how I longed to be old enough to take my turn, and what a joyous day it was when I finally was.' A woman, whose mother 'was fairly religious,' and as a little girl was herself 'quite religious ... enjoyed the Sunday school, and I loved the stories ... and I always said prayers at night before I went to sleep.' Isabelle Daley wrote that, when she was a child in Prince Edward Island in the 1920s, her 'brothers liked to pretend they were priests saying Mass. Although [her sister] and I were too young to understand well what they were playing, they asked us to act as their congregation. They gave sermons and distributed white paper hosts at Communion time.'[61] Another woman remarked, 'We'd play "church" on the back porch. Once thunder started and we thought God was angry because we were making fun of the priests.'

Crossing a watershed: a bar mitzvah lad preparing to be called for Torah in the 1930s.

The sabbath was generally treated as a special day. In one Roman Catholic family, 'on Sundays we got up early and attended church as a family. Afterwards we would go home and all have breakfast of bacon and eggs, a treat for the children.' They also 'had family prayers every day after supper, when we would say the rosary.' For the Loder family on the Labrador coast, 'Sunday was different from every other day ... Some time during the day Ma (or Pa if he was home) would read from the Bible and we would sing hymns ... It seems as though Sundays would drag a bit, as we were not allowed to check the snares, ride or play games.'[62] Such restrictions on Sunday behaviour were quite common, especially in Protestant denominations. 'No games or cards,' said one woman, 'and reading material was supposed to be appropriate – Sunday school papers and *Pilgrim's Progress*. We envied the Catholic kids; their Sunday seemed to be over at noon.' Of the restrictions on Sundays and other holy days, Sparkes reported, 'the stern rule of no play pressed rather heavily on youthful spirits ... It was not difficult to find other urchins ready to take a chance on provoking the Divine wrath ... [but we] discovered early in our young lives that God was a good deal more tolerant than most grown-ups ... He knew very well what we were doing – He knew everything – but He never seemed to take offence.'[63]

Congregational activities stand out in many family memories. In one, the Presbyterian church was 'where the social life was. There were plays and Sunday school parties, the Christmas parties, the Christmas plays, strawberry ice cream socials in summer, your meals, your banquets for Robbie Burns ... and Sunday was a very special day. You know, we all wore special shoes, dressed up, had hair ribbons.' Ignatia Lanigan Grams recalled, 'what joy when Mother came up with the new white dresses' for First Communion. 'Nothing could dampen our spirits; our faith was strong ...'[64] One man particularly recalls 'the missions held once a year by Jesuit priests with a special session for kids.' It was 'more than just going to mass; the fire and brimstone talk made more impression.'[65] The 'social life of the Jewish community [in Sault Ste Marie] revolved around a suite of two rooms,' of which the smaller 'was occupied as chedar for the children as well as a place for memorial services.'[66] For some children in families in which 'the church was the centre,' it was also where they made their friends; 'you played with kids you met at church.' Others had a 'whole other set of friends at Sunday school.'

For many youngsters, their religious identity had an inner as well as an outer dimension. Long before they could articulate it, children absorbed the sense of piety that was at the heart of the devotions and observances in many families. Harry Boyle wrote: 'There had been stirrings in me from time to time about the priesthood. They came usually in association with reading about faraway missions, the simple grandeur of Benediction, or the overwhelming assault on the senses of midnight Mass.'[67] In another Catholic family, a girl 'enjoyed prayer in the morning. Say you got punched around by Mom and Dad, the psychology of prayer did wonders.' 'As a child of 10,' wrote Dawn Ward, 'I discovered religion and became judgemental. Mother was not receptive to my newly found ideas of purity ... I tried to show her the ways of the Lord. She drank liquor and smoked cigarettes. She often said that being forcibly overdosed on church as a child had provided the adult cure.' None the less, Ward, 'with my insufferable righteousness,' persisted in trying to reform both her mother and her brother.[68]

On the negative side, one man recalled how frightening it was to recite: 'And should I die before I wake, / I pray the Lord my soul to take.' For Roy Daniells, brought up a Brethren in Victoria, 'instant and everlasting destruction hung over me like the sword of Damocles ... I have come home from school ... and found no one in the house ... Christ has come; they're all gone; I'm left for judgment ... From this ultimate terror, the fear of eternal fire and torment, one never recovers. It is the extreme and final terror to which the mind and body, the heart and soul, the whole crushed and dismembered personality of a child can be subjected.'[69]

For some, the effects of family religious observances were lifelong. 'From my mother,' said one man, I picked up a sense of – what would you call it, respect, maybe piety? I don't know what to call it, but it has been a sheet anchor in my life.' In his eleventh year, about 1910, Pentecostalist Eugene Vaters recalled, cottage meetings were held in individual homes. 'People were coming forward ... and, amid great jubilation, professing to be saved.' After he made his own commitment, Vaters reported, 'I felt so light and full of life. I had, in the presence of God and man, made a commitment of my life to God.'[70] John Norris was sent rather than taken to his local Anglican church in Nelson. He attended Sunday school, and then became a member of the choir. 'It was the music and the language of the church that I most loved,' Norris wrote. 'My uncritical child's soul responded wholeheartedly to whatever mood the hymns conveyed, from the gentle happiness of "God sees the little sparrow fall ..." to the martial vigour of "Onward Christian Soldiers."' Writing in his sixties, Norris observed that he now felt 'greatly enriched' by his years in the congregation, and that, 'whatever creed or lack of creed' he now professed, 'the values that guide me through life are essentially the ones I learned at the Church of the Redeemer.' [71]

In some families, religious practice seems to have been more educational or social than spiritual. Many parents insisted that their children attend

Vancouver children attending Sunday school in a heated tent in the 1920s.

Sunday school, emphasizing that the religious knowledge purveyed there was almost as important as the learning at school. When neither parent attended church regularly or when both parents did, then both conveyed the message that church-going was or was not an important part of the lives of adults. When, as was frequently the case, mothers attended and fathers did not, youngsters learned that churches and religious experiences were for women and children but that boys would eventually grow out of them. 'My family weren't religious at all,' explained one woman, 'but my parents thought it was good to go ... to Sunday school, and we went faithfully.' A man whose 'parents were not attenders' remembers from about four or five years of age 'trudging off' every Sunday with five siblings to Sunday school. Another man, whose mother also sent him to Sunday school, recalled it as 'social not spiritual, fun things ... I have little medals for nine years perfect attendance!' A girl 'went to Sunday school with one of the neighbourhood children ... which my family did not mind. I liked listening to Bible stories and what the minister said.' A boy 'attended [Sunday school] regularly, but I didn't think about it much. It was just a place to socialize and a chance to wear good clothes.' Another boy 'switched to a Baptist Sunday school because they had a gymnasium where we could play.'

Some parents were indifferent to or expressed hostility to religion or religious organizations. A Jewish woman stated, 'My religious education was neglected. I had more non-Jewish than Jewish friends.' 'My father didn't believe in [religion],' reported another woman. 'That was one thing he was very definite about.' Another father, himself the son of a Presbyterian minister, 'wanted nothing to do with [religion]; you could see it in his behaviour.' In another family, there was 'no question of us being baptised; Mother wouldn't have heard of that idea.' And some children in even devout families developed their own hostility to religion. After a long preparation for it, Lloyd Person was delighted by his First Communion, but not for the appropriate reason. As a full member of the church, he would be now free of youthful obligations to it. 'I knew when Reverend Kreuz brought the cup to my lips that I was drinking "unworthily" ... but since I didn't believe I couldn't have cared less. All I could think of was, "Thank God, it's soon over. I can get these duds off and go out to the garage!"'[72]

At sentimental moments, many adults claim to have had a happy family life when they were children. They loved and respected their parents and siblings; their parents loved and respected them. In more reflective moments, however, adults can recall their life in their families more accurately. What they really felt about their parents and brothers and sisters was, of course, much more complex than suggested by the simple formula. The previous chapter showed how homes and neighbourhoods provided the setting for family life. It also showed how the bond between their parents set the emotional climate in which children lived their lives. This chapter showed how children's relationships with mothers, fathers, brothers, and sisters framed much of their growing up. It also showed how their families began to give them a sense of who they were.

Families, however, are much more than a collection of relationships and identities; they are also active, dynamic organizations. The next chapter describes how parents employed their almost unlimited power over their youngsters to help them find their way into their adult occupations and to govern how they behaved. It also shows how some parents employed their power to abuse their children physically and emotionally.

4

Children in Their Families:
Using and Abusing Parental Powers

As dynamic entities, families actively undertook important as well as trivial activities for and with their youngsters. This chapter explores the children's perspective as to how their families carried out two important tasks that social convention assigned to them. First, families directed or helped their children to set life goals for themselves and to acquire the appropriate training and education necessary to achieve them. Second, families taught their children the behaviours they (and the community) considered appropriate to their age and status. Although siblings and the extended family played some role in each activity, parents assumed the primary responsibility.

As they went about these tasks, parents used their almost unlimited power over their youngsters in ways that more or less accorded with the norms of the time. However, some parents, and others with the status of parents, employed their powers in dark, abusive ways that greatly exceeded these norms, in ways that had a malign effect on the whole life course of its victims. In turn, children both cooperated in and resisted the parental power and authority exercised over them.

Much formal and informal family discourse and activity focused on the future. Central to this process was the role parents played in ensuring that their youngsters had the appropriate amount of training and education to function as adults. Parents' own experiences and the earlier ones of their families, together with their observations of friends and neighbours, had demonstrated that the difference between succeeding and not succeeding in life could be a narrow one. 'I think,' observed one woman, 'my mother just wanted her children to be everything she didn't have the opportunity for herself. She wanted to give her daughters as much as she possibly could.'

With the substantial exception of families severely affected by drought on the prairies or by the Depression, the living standards of Canadians rose slowly during the first half of the century, and then more sharply after the Second World War. Although pleased to benefit from this expanding economy, prudent families continued to be wary. Prosperous times had come and gone before; this current phase could also come to an end soon. Families were therefore vigilant to ensure the future of their children. Robert MacNeil wrote: 'my mother exhorted me to do things to "make something" of myself ... "to get on in life." Every child of Depression parents knew that advice better than his prayers.'[1] The daughters of immigrants from Germany, who grew up in the 1930s, described an attitude common to many parents: they 'wanted the best for their children, better than what they had had in the old country.' Another woman reported that her mother – before the war a housewife, during the war a worker at Boeing, after the war a widowed telephone operator – 'just wanted her children to be everything ... to give her daughters as much as she possibly could ... ; certainly my mother was determined that I was going to go through university.' For urban youngsters and those rural ones who wanted, or whose parents wanted them, to work other than in the woods or on the farm, increasing amounts of formal schooling became necessary.

In consequence, parents acted as educational and vocational strategists for their children, weighing short-term and long-term economic goals against family resources. Up until the Second World War, most working-class parents and many rural ones viewed the completion of 'entrance' – that is, completing the requirements for entry into secondary school – as the minimum necessary formal education.[2] In the 1940s and 1950s, such people's sense of what constituted an appropriate minimum inched up to include Grades Nine and Ten. From this starting-point, children could move into an apprenticeship, or at least a steady job, preferably one that 'had a future.'

As these youngsters reached the school-leaving age, they and their parents began the search for a job. Mitchell Sharp wrote, 'Like those of my generation living in ... a working-class district, in a small frame house without indoor plumbing or running water, I was expected to contribute to the family income as soon as I reached the minimum school leaving age ... When I was fourteen, my mother through a friend found me a full-time job (8:00 A.M. to 5:00 P.M. and to 1:00 P.M. on Saturdays) as a delivery boy at the Grain Trade Press ...'[3] A Cedar Cottage man explained, 'I went to work for $6 in 1927, when I was fifteen.' When she was sixteen, noted one woman, her father said: "Well, you've had a year of high school, that's enough. Off you go to work, you go and get a job."' When Charles Dougan's father learned that, at age fourteen, he was regularly skipping his Grade Eight classes, 'Dad simply said

Full-time delivery boys in Vancouver in 1943.

to me, "Well, Big Fella, you don't want to go to school, so I'll put you to work,' and found him a job as a blacksmith's helper.[4] Of the eight Dougan children, only one went, for a year, beyond Grade Eight.

Behind this attitude towards the appropriateness of eight, nine, and eventually ten years of formal schooling lay the belief that only practical, 'hands-on' training provided the knowledge and skills needed to make a living. Such training, in turn, led to some control over one's life and work that many working people thought was missing in white collar jobs. To Rolf Knight and his teenage friends, for example, logging 'was real work, work that dealt with things more than with people ... It was work in which there was some variety, some challenge and maybe even a little danger.'[5] Further, working-class children often came to believe that to be fully a person was to work, that to avoid going to work was a form of avoiding adulthood and responsibility. Parents had gone to work at about puberty, and so should their children. Although Tommy Hunter left school in the middle of Grade Ten for a career very different from those of most who grew up in working-class families, his attitude to the need to leave was the same as theirs. His parents knew he 'wasn't quitting school to run away from responsibility but to accept it in the work I had chosen so many years earlier.'[6]

And, whenever schooling ended, working-class parents often encouraged their children to enter 'practical' occupations.[7] 'My father was a carpenter,' said one Cedar Cottage man, 'and he encouraged me to apprentice to the trade. "There's always work for carpenters," he said.' A woman from the same neighbourhood reported that, in the 1950s, 'both Mom and Dad made me take the commercial program in high school. When I was hired right out of Grade Ten into an office, they pointed out how right they had been to insist on a practical education.'

Some working-class parents and their youngsters clearly wanted more than the legal or fashionable minimum of formal schooling. Many had absorbed a sense of potential mobility, the opportunity to move from working- to middle-class. Consequently, some working-class and rural parents also wanted their children to reap the benefits of junior matriculation, and urged their children to aspire to reach it, not always with community approval. As one woman from the working-class reported, 'I graduated from the twelfth-grade university course. Everyone thought it was ridiculous to have a girl go to [high] school.' The son of a Victoria delivery man, born in the early 1920s, reported that his mother always insisted that he plan to attend university, which he indeed did. As school-leaving data – discussed in greater detail in chapter 9, on schooling – suggest, however, even by the end of the 1950s only a minority of working-class children completed their university entrance.[8]

Parents had to balance family resources against educational and vocational aspirations. 'Although I longed to be a teacher,' reported one woman whose father was a skilled craftsman, 'my parents said I had to be a steno like my sister.' In the 1920s one could complete basic stenography training in two years of high school (or in an even shorter period of time at a private business college) in contrast to the matriculation, and then Normal school, that was required for teaching. Even as the commercial program lengthened to a full twelve years, many young women used what they had already learned to enter the workforce a year or two earlier. Until they were abolished in most parts of Canada in the 1920s, high-school fees constituted another deterrent for families with limited resources.[9] After her mother died when she was fourteen, reported one woman, 'I had to graduate before I was sixteen' in order to avoid paying tuition.

The cost of sending their children away for further schooling deterred many rural parents. As one man explained, 'Public school was about all you could think of because ... [you] would have to board with someone ... Well, this was kind of prohibitive.' A Powell River woman 'passed to high school when I was fourteen and there was no high school here then, and my mom and dad didn't have any money to send me to Vancouver, so I just had to quit school.' Although Robert Small of Grand Manan, New Brunswick, could afford to send his daughter away for high school, he argued that she 'only needs grade 8. We both know she will be comfortable ... can settle down here, marry, and live quite happily. She'll want for nothing.' None the less, Ina, Maureen's mother and herself a Normal school graduate, took Maureen to Saint John and stayed there until she also graduated from Normal school.[10]

Both working- and middle-class parents saw other ways of getting ahead. They encouraged their sons to complete matriculation, and then to enter apprenticeships in accounting or pharmacy, or to join one of the banks. In banks, mobility, while generally slow, looked to be inevitable. One example showing that this strategy worked even until fairly recently is the fact current or recent senior executives of at least two of the big five banks of Canada entered banking right after high school.[11] Still other parents saw small business as the route upward, and encouraged their boys to go to work for one at school-leaving, with a view to saving money and eventually setting up a business themselves. 'Dad was a meat-cutter at Woodward's,' said one man, 'and persuaded me to become one, too. "When you're done, perhaps we can open our own shop," but he got sick and died before we did anything about it.'

By the end of the Great War, middle-class families expected their children to complete at least their junior matriculation. 'There was,' reported one woman, 'a Kerrisdale tradition of a lot of high-school graduates [and] about a quarter going on to university.' Even during their early childhood, middle-class boys and girls were encouraged to think of the longer term; to see schooling as extending through, and even beyond, their adolescence. They came to look upon junior matriculation as the stepping-stone to entering the workforce or, in a minority of cases, to attendance at university. 'Mom always talked about me becoming a doctor,' reported one man, who is in fact a teacher, and a woman regularly heard the message from both parents that 'you should train as a nurse or a teacher, so you always have something to fall back on.' Norman Lidster, son of a New Westminster lawyer and schoolteacher, noted that his mother 'believed that all four of her children should have a good academic grounding and insisted that we have Normal School training, after which she left us free to choose careers for ourselves.'[12]

Many parents gave practical reinforcement to their educational aspirations for their children. One woman remembered 'that my mother used to help me study for exams by asking me questions,' while another explained that 'we had a great big blackboard at home. My father would give us things to do.' A rural woman reported that she 'took correspondence courses, and my step-dad taught me, and Mother taught me a bit.' A man explained that 'my parents attached a great importance to education,' so much so that his mother 'taught him to read and write' with the effect that, on starting school, he was 'pushed forward two grades.' Some families moved in order to improve their children's educational opportunities. 'At Mom's insistence,' one woman's family moved from rural Alberta 'to Calgary so the kids could attend school regularly,' and another to Dominion City, Manitoba, for the same reason. The latter's six children 'began school with the understanding that we would finish,' and five of them did complete high school. Not all children willingly received this help, and some rebelled. One middle-class woman, who did not finish high school, recalled that 'it was a constant battle between myself and my parents with regard to studying.'

In some families, parents' interest in their children's education went beyond its practical aspects. Many parents read to their children and encouraged them to read for themselves. One Evelyn woman recalled, 'Mother read to us a lot ... We'd say, "One more chapter!"' Another from the same area explained, 'Dad read to us sometimes – *Swiss Family Robinson* – as did Grandmother when she visited.' These and other rural parents ordered books by mail from the provincial library. Many parents subscribed to newspapers and, as their own letters to them eloquently testify, their youngsters carefully read the children's sections.[13] Writer and broadcaster Robert MacNeil explained that his interest in words began with his mother reading to him: 'She read with enthusiasm and delight' and 'sounded as enthralled, as full of wonder and close-rivetted attention as I was.'[14] A man who grew up in the Eastern Townships in the 1920s had a less positive view of being read to: 'although my mother read to us at great length in the evenings, perhaps it would have been more valuable' if instead he had been able to practise his own reading. Some families, of course, did both. One woman, whose 'mother and grandmother read to us at night,' also 'would read aloud at night' and they would 'help me with the "s" sounds.'

Oral tradition was particularly important for those whose families came from other cultures. A woman of Swiss descent recalled that 'Dad was always a great storyteller and I delighted in hearing him repeat the legend of William Tell.' Playwright Ted Galay, of Ukrainian descent, explained that his mother 'was a storyteller ... she was always urging that things not be forgotten. Her stories had a ballad-like quality. They were short on form but strong on details and images.'[15]

Many parents also provided a musical education for their children. Many

An elder of the Squamish nation shares his knowledge with a girl of a later generation in the 1950s.

families sang together. Oscar Peterson's father began music with his children earlier than they can remember. Peterson recalled, 'There's a good way and a bad way to expose children to music ... Fortunately we were introduced to it in a good way, and we all learned to play.'[16] Peterson himself was playing both trumpet and piano by the time he was five. While both girls and boys took piano lessons, the former greatly outnumbered the latter on the rolls of music teachers. Robert Thomas Allen's music teacher 'was always one of my favourite adults, a short, chunky, pale-faced, pop-eyed, excitable man ... [who] sang along with me off-key.'[17] Another man, whose father started him on the violin at six, went on to play in 'three levels of school student orchestra as I moved through the school system.' A woman explained that she 'loved to tickle the ivories but was not great at it,' to the disappointment of her father 'who had an illusion that his voice was similar to Caruso's and he wanted me to accompany him.' Other parents took their children to concerts or had the family radio tuned to the Metropolitan Opera on Saturday and the symphony on Sunday. As a result, some found lifelong pleasure in music.

Not all children took enthusiastically to music lessons. Although he came from a musical family ('Mother played the piano, Dad the mandolin and clarinet'), one man reported, 'I took very expensive piano lessons, which I detested. I once ran away ... to avoid piano lessons.' Morley Torgov re-created what was likely a common scene: '"Lots and lots of good solid practice, that's what does the trick," the teacher says. Father and teacher nod solemnly. The rapport between them, established only minutes ago, is now centuries old.'[18] Diana Michener's cello teacher would ask her to repeat something until 'at one point he would stamp his foot and say, "Goddamn it! That's all I can take" ... and would storm out of the house.'[19] However, even those who disliked music lessons noted that they could sometimes employ 'practising' as a device to avoid chores and other less pleasant activities.

Other children took dancing lessons. Lynn Seymour started lessons when she was six. Her natural talent was accompanied by what her biographer calls her 'ambition, the passionate desire to succeed that lay beneath her carefree exterior.'[20]

Families followed an informal as well as a formal educational agenda for their children. Thus they instructed children in behaviours and beliefs that were an inextricable mix of morality, on the one hand, and politeness and gentility, on the other. They 'made it clear that parents were the authority at home and teachers at school.' Thus, 'you obeyed your parents'; you 'did as you were told'; you didn't talk back ('we would be given a smack for talking back'); 'you solved problems on your own'; you understood that 'children should be seen and not heard'; you didn't 'listen to adult conversation'; you 'stayed out of the way when there were visitors'; you 'didn't swear' or smoke ('no profanity and no smoking tolerated'); you 'always washed your hands before touching a book'; you didn't lie; and you were 'good losers and good sports' (because 'Father would not tolerate cheaters'). Through the whole of your life, 'you were to do the right thing by all people.'

Her parents (and many others), one woman stated, were strict 'about manners, like chewing gum, and vocabulary ... "a lady doesn't say that."' Others were told, 'Don't wipe your nose on your sleeve. Use your handker- chief!' and 'Don't chew gum in public, don't run in the house, don't say "What?" or "Huh!"' George Dorman reported that, when 'I started going around with my hands in my pockets, my dad had my mother sew the pock- ets up.'[21] Other family requirements, such as individual or family prayers, learning the commandments or other codes of belief and practice, and ask- ing the forgiveness of parents or siblings for transgressions, were more explicitly religious and moral.

Many parental demands centred around family routines and rituals within the regularly repeated scripts of daily life. Parents set the times that children were to rise and to go to bed, to go to school and return from school, and to do their routine chores. In the years before television, for example, families tended to enforce fairly early bedtimes. When a woman later asked her mother, 'How did you survive?,' she replied, 'You went to bed early.'

Many parents made a particular point about behaviour involving meals, including an insistence that children learn the rituals associated with them.[22] In consequence, 'it was important to be on time for lunch and sup- per'; 'I had to be home by six for dinner'; you 'were made to eat stuff you didn't like (I can still smell cabbage cooking)'; 'if you don't want to eat something, don't put it on your plate; if you put it on your plate, eat it.' Middle-class families, such as the Micheners, their daughter reported, were 'very finickety about table manners. If you didn't handle your knife and fork correctly, and use your dessert spoon and fork correctly, you'd get corrected – not usually when company was there, but afterwards.'[23] Other families insisted that 'you don't talk with your mouth full'; you 'keep your mouth closed when you chew'; you 'don't put so much in your mouth at once'; you 'hold your knife and fork properly'; 'you don't slurp your soup or tea (although Daddy sometimes did)'; and 'you don't reach across the table, (although it was years before I knew what Mom meant by "No boarding- house manners here").' In some families, meal times were when 'you talked a bit about what happened during the day.' In others, and particularly in working-class ones, 'we said grace and didn't talk again except "please" and "thank you", and "may I leave the table, please"'; we 'didn't talk unless spoken to; if we opened our mouths too much, we were swatted and sent to bed without food.'

Other rules governed behaviour when children were away from home. Accordingly, 'my brother and I had to say where we were going when we went out'; 'we didn't play on the waterfront [because] a kid who had a three-wheel bike went off the wharf and drowned, which really upset Mom'; 'the railway "flats" and Trout Lake were strictly verboten'; and 'we didn't go down to the mill site; the sidewalk was the boundary.' Rolf Knight wrote: 'Log booms and rail cars were taboo. "Stay off them, period! No ifs, buts, or maybes. Just stay off. Or else!"'[24] After more than fifty years, Lloyd Person could 'still hear my parents warning ... my older brother and sister never to venture down to that part of town, they were to stay on *this* side of the tracks, *this* side of Main Street. The same warnings were repeated to me when I got old enough, and to my younger sisters and brothers after me.'[25] Play with certain other children was discouraged: 'the lady two doors down ... had a sleazy background and Mother didn't like me playing with her kids.' Others reported that they were 'not allowed to play on the block where the Italians lived' and 'I was not allowed to associate with the Japanese or the Italians.'

Parental expectations for their children extended beyond behaviour into such matters as appearance. Most families believed, with the Roddans, that 'cleanliness was next to godliness.'[26] As children came in for supper or prepared for bed, parents enjoined them to 'have a good wash' and 'make sure you wash your neck and behind your ears,' and inspected to ensure the task was done, completing it themselves if it was not. Until after the Second World War, baths tended to be weekly rather than daily affairs, and to have certain rituals attached to them; such activities as shoe polishing, laying out the Sunday clothes, rehearsing memorized prayers or biblical verses, and listening to a story in front of the fire accompanied the weekly bath. One man recalled that 'we bathed every Saturday night. My sister was first, then me, and then my brother.' Another man recalled, 'I got to use the water last because I was the youngest.' In both rural and urban homes, this part of the weekly 'ordeal' or 'ritual' often took place in a small round tub in the kitchen, 'beside the stove, where it was warm.' In the 1950s, one woman recalled, 'I loved my bath at the end of each day. Mom let us play as long as we liked. Later, [her brother] and I bathed separately, and that was not as much fun.'

Only the most chaotic of families, those for economic, health, or other reasons near or at the point of disintegration, made few or no behavioural demands on their children. Hence one man whose family was overwhelmed and demoralized by the Depression explained that his parents 'didn't use physical force. It was more neglect, but they were gentle.' His experiences outside the home made him 'well mannered. I learned a lot by myself, dealing with [delivery route] customers, people.' In 1923, a public-health nurse in Arnprior, Ontario, wrote that she had found 'a woman with tuberculosis, an advanced case, in bed most of the time.' She had 'three children, aged eleven, seven and two years,' had 'no neighbours nor relatives who ever call to see her, and the children are just running wild.'[27] In another example, 'Dick' was born in 1940, his younger brother a year later, and his sister two years after that. Their parents separated after the father returned from war service overseas. According to Vancouver Children's Aid Society (CAS) records, 'both parents consistently refused to accept responsibility for their children, who often were left alone at night, and forced to beg for food from passers-by in the street.' In addition, 'Dick had seen his mother in bed with different men, and he himself engaged in "sex play" at an early age.' The children came into the care of the CAS in 1947.[28]

Although some parents acknowledged, or even actively rewarded good behaviour, others expected it as the norm. In turn, most children aspired to comply with the wishes and demands of their parents, even those which, to an outsider, might seem to have been excessive, or even cruel. 'I always wanted to please my mother and grandmother, as did my brother,' reported one woman of a 'very loving family.' A brother and sister were, according to the latter, 'good kids; neither was ever a member of the wrong crowd at school, and my brother was heavily involved in sports.' Even, or perhaps especially, a sister who was told by her father that 'it was unfortunate that you were not born a boy ... tried hard to please Dad.' One woman, however, felt that her sister 'did a lot of things for which she was punished not by design but because of a lack of coordination. It took her longer to absorb things than other children.'

Patterns of parental control over their children changed but slightly and very gradually over these years.[29] In the 1920s, child-care advisers tended to advocate a 'rigid, systematic approach to infant care.'[30] By the 1930s, they suggested, as Dr W.E. Blatz of the University of Toronto's St George's School for Child Study put it, a 'learning process by which the child is coming to rule himself.'[31] Child-rearing advice in the 1940s and 1950s went further in recommending that children develop self-control. As another widely quoted and respected Canadian expert, Dr S.R. Laycock, explained, 'the child needs to be subjected to experiences of both receiving and exercising authority in such a way that he will be ... helped to grow in self-control and self-direction.'[32]

These new notions, however, did not penetrate deeply into popular culture until after the Second World War. While many parents may have heard of the new ideas about child-rearing – Laycock broadcast regularly – it was not until then that many internalized them in such a way that they began to affect their actual behaviour towards their offspring. In the inter-war years, most middle- and working-class parents continued to employ traditional physical means in their discipline. In contrast, those who grew up after the Second World War told about corporal punishment that was often less severe and less frequent than that experienced by earlier cohorts. Although my data are not quantifiable, I judge that this shift to an ever-increasing reliance on non-physical means began earlier in middle-class than in working-class households. However, it was not until the 1960s or later that even in the middle-class community norms changed enough to bring about a sharp decline in the incidence of both corporal punishment and community attitudes towards its appropriateness.[33]

Two further general points about discipline in these years need to be made. First, one must remember that, at a time when the standard of living for nearly all people was very much lower than currently prevails, living within the family consumer economy placed enormous, almost claustro-phobic burdens on mothers. Further, the smaller homes characteristic of these years exacerbated family tensions. Just being in the way, or squabbling with siblings, could trigger a parental response ranging from a mild rebuke, or a shout, to being sent elsewhere. The mother whose 'favourite saying' was 'go away and play' spoke a line that surely was repeated in countless other households every day. In these circumstances, the absence or long-term unemployment of many fathers added to maternal burdens.

Second, one must remember that many working-class men put in long hours in jobs that were noisy, dirty, and physically exhausting.[34] Such men found no locus of power in their work and were therefore perhaps more inclined to use their power in the family harshly. For some fathers, severity appeared to be rooted in work or health. Accordingly, one father, on a partial pension for 'nerves' from the Great War, and who therefore abhorred noise, made his children 'scared stiff' of him. They were 'not allowed to yell or throw stuff ... and couldn't drop anything' or 'he'd holler and bellow.'

Given these circumstances, one should not be surprised that parents sometimes lashed out at their children or that, in the long run, many children did not think that their parents were overly severe with them. As one woman explained, 'My parents were quite strict in the sense that they expected good behaviour. Both spanked the children, and hard, if they were late for supper or did not do their garden chores.' However, 'this form of discipline was common in the neighbourhood,' and she 'did not and does not think of it as unjust.'

Clearly, some parents were relaxed and tolerant in their discipline. In one home, the son noted, 'Mother was never angry. She was a cool customer. Dad didn't get angry much either. We didn't give them much trouble.' In another home, where 'both parents were more or less the authority,' their daughter could 'not remember being punished or whipped.' One woman explained that she had 'no recollection of either Mom or Dad raising their voices at the kids,' or of having been punished, but also noted that her mother now reports that she used to slap hands on occasion. Another woman reported that her 'very strict' mother 'had a little piece of kindling wood but never hit with it; the threat was enough.' Other mothers employed wooden spoons in the same way.

Mothers tended to be less severe than fathers. As one recalled, 'Father was too hard' on his two children, both daughters. 'Mother was different, a very gentle soul. She'd teach you right from wrong ... If you did something wrong, you knew it.' Another woman recounted that 'Mother was short, small, not over one hundred pounds. She could hurt your feelings to keep children in line. Mostly, we avoided disappointing her.' A man explained of his mother that, if he did 'something bad, she would sulk and not speak to you for some time. You should feel guilty for offending your mother.' Another woman said that she 'never had physical punishment. Mother could always tell when I was lying.' In another family, in which 'Father would strap girls and boys,' the mother 'never punished the kids physically. If they behaved badly she would warn them of the consequences and demand an apology.' 'My mother was the one who disciplined in our family,' explained another woman. 'We always had to say we were sorry. I remember staying in my room because I couldn't bring myself to go out and say I was sorry.'

The contrasting severity of some fathers grew out of their sense of themselves as their families' supreme arbiter, its final authority. One woman described being made to take a swim test when she didn't want to, 'also being very frightened, but doing it. I didn't have any choice ... because my father wouldn't give me any choice, such was his power over my life.' In another example from the late 1950s, the father of a ten-month-old boy who had been apprehended because of severe physical abuse 'stoutly defended his right, as master in his own home, to discipline his child as he saw fit, and by his standards physical discipline was the only way to teach the child.'[35]

Parents dealt with inappropriate or bad behaviour with techniques that ranged along a continuum from non-verbal signals and mild rebukes at one end, through various psychological mechanisms, to extreme forms of corporal punishment at the other. Few parents utilized the whole spectrum. Some parents selected punishments as they judged them to be relative to the seriousness of an offence; others moved with great rapidity from mild to severe; and still others treated all breaches of the family code with severity.

Children learned to interpret nods, and facial and other non-verbal messages. 'My father only had to look at me in a certain way,' said one woman, 'and I would go to my bedroom.' Roy Bonisteel's father 'never hit or spanked his children ... A steely, penetrating gaze from his pale blue eyes would have you jumping to obey or confessing to any number of misdemeanours.'[36] 'I can remember,' explained another woman, 'getting the cold treatment from my mother ... you'd get "the look."' When Haldor Beebe's mother overheard him swearing, she stopped him in mid-stride. 'Mother never said one word then or later; she just looked at me, and then walked calmly back to the house.'[37]

From grimaces, parents moved to such verbal means as a 'bawling out,' some shouting, or playing on their children's feelings to express their displeasure. Verbal chastisement sometimes took the form of a rhetorical question, as Ellen Davignon reported of her mother ('Would anyone like to go to bed? Now? Without supper?').[38] Parents also sent children to their rooms for short or long periods of time. Some parents even employed frightening stories – of the 'bogeyman,' for example – as a means of keeping their children in line.[39]

Non-physical punishment often meant the loss of privileges. 'I remember,' said one woman, 'if you got into trouble you couldn't go out of the yard. That was it! Talk about punishment! Because the whole gang was outside. Oh, you had to stay in there for a week or three days, whatever the case may be.' Her brother recalls that 'a good smack on the behind was administered when I really messed up, but this didn't very often happen. Most disciplining was grounding, taking away privileges. I was pretty good at playing within the rules.' Other people report being kept home from the weekly Saturday matinée for bad behaviour: 'It was mortifying! What could you tell your friends? Mom sometimes even told the other kids why!'

Parents sometimes supported moral suasion by appeal to higher authority. Thus one woman, who 'would take one of the cookies and shake the box' so that her transgression would not be noticed, got a 'lecture on God seeing what you do.' One man reported briefly feeling divine intervention when 'I stole a couple of doughnuts. My grandmother saw me, grabbed me, and pulled me back, and at that instant, the [Halifax 1917] explosion took place.'

Some parents employed bizarre forms of punishment. A woman noted that her father ordered her sister to 'eat that vegetable soup.' When she refused, 'Dad took his bowl of soup and dumped it upside down on her head.' In one family, 'Dad would go to the granary and get a whole sack of [mixed grains] and so kids would have to pick all the oats out of the grain ... It might take a week or even two weeks.' Maara Haas had 'to kneel on dried peas for five hours holding a 28-ounce tin of tomatoes over my head' for a particularly bad bit of behaviour.[40] When a Powell River lad 'got a bit lippy,' his father picked him up and hung him on a hook. When his father realized 'he couldn't breathe, he let him down.' In a family where the father was responsible for discipline, his daughter reported that, 'whenever I did anything bad, I never got a spanking, I got a dose of castor oil.'

Over all of these years, probably a majority of families employed some form of corporal punishment.[41] Most of this disciplining was of the 'warm-blooded' sort, delivered in the heat of the moment. As one man laconically put it, 'I was paddled at home and at school.' Another remarked, 'Your parents kept a pretty strict rule on you. They weren't afraid to wallop you in those days either ... You'd get a bang over the head. Christ, yes, you got lots of that.' A third man remembers that he would 'get a slap on the side of the head' from a father who was 'cranky, growled, but not one to dish it out.' His punishment came 'mostly from Mom ... She would give a slap on the head, and you went off bawling.' In another family, 'both parents believed in the razor strop, but seldom used it.' One son explained that 'Mother had a strap in the pantry, and would use it on boys and girls, always across the legs. They were not love taps ... The strap became a symbol and "wait till Dad gets home" became the threat.' 'I remember,' explained one man, 'one time my mom just pulled back and gave me one across the side of the head with an open hand and I remember thinking ... I'll learn to put a zipper on my mouth. She said, "You can think it, whatever you want to think, but don't you say it!"'

In some families fathers administered all corporal punishment. One woman reported that 'Mom couldn't handle' her children; 'she was too easy, too kind.' On the other hand, 'Dad just had to holler "children" and we stopped.' If they didn't, 'he gave a tug in the hair, and then the razor strop.' A man reported that, in his family, 'Dad was the disciplinarian.' He spanked rarely, for, 'if he said something, you listened. He was not cruel to us.' Another man explained, 'My father was responsible for discipline. We would be swatted once in a while for not doing our chores ... [and] for talking back.' Once the boy was swatted for breaking his father's hacksaw cutting a rock, and once for saying 'hell.'

Cold-blooded punishments followed a fairly standard ritual. One man had to go out to the woodshed, bare his buttocks, and wait for his father to appear. After what he described as a 'thrashing,' another man had to apologize formally first to Father, and then to Mother, for the transgression that had led to it. After punishment, E.H. Cayford's father 'would reinstate us in the bosom of the family by a little excess of joviality on his part, a little praise, a little nonsense, or a wrestle. If I got a spanking on Tuesday, he would be my partner at horseshoes on Wednesday.'[42]

Although girls were not immune from corporal punishment, interview data suggest that their parents beat them less frequently and less severely than they did boys. In contrast to his elder sister, reported one man, 'you hit boys more. You were supposed to hit boys a lot more than girls, you know.' So between them, he and his brother 'absorbed I don't know how many spankings ... [but] it does not leave what I call a real bitter memory.' In another family, the mother did most of the disciplining, including spankings, and the father intervened only for 'something very major.' His daughter remembers 'being strapped by my father ... because I lied ... that was a no-no in our family ... He didn't put much of an effort into it ... but I mean you did not lie, that was all there was to it.' In this regard it is also clear from their reports of corporal punishment at home and at school that boys came to regard being able to 'take it,' without crying if they could manage it, as evidence of their growing 'manhood.'

In some families, parents whipped or beat their children so severely that charges of child abuse should have been laid. 'Every once in a while,' wrote Fraser Miles of his 1920s childhood, 'one kid or another would show up, when we went swimming, with black and blue welts all over his back.'[43] A woman reported that, when she was quite young, 'she enjoyed being near her father and enjoyed the physical nearness of him.' He was, however, 'unable to deal with the reality of ... adolescence.' She came to think of him as cruel but 'never dared to defy him ... He spanked her a lot and kept her in her room a lot,' upsetting her mother. One man, who looked back without apparent rancour on his working-class childhood, declared that 'my father was handy with a strap [razor strop] and not afraid to use it.' If his son 'got into trouble out of the house, then [he] got more at home than anywhere else.' Accordingly, when he and a couple of other boys broke into a clothing store, 'I got caught and the police took me home. I got whipped with a belt so bad that I was not able to go to school for three or four days.'

For some, excessive physical punishment led to lifelong difficulties. A man who attributed his serious emotional problems to events in his middle-class childhood, explained, 'I was raised in fear ... Mother was very physical with her punishment ... We would dodge, or try to, now and then. She would connect a lot, though ... My father did a lot of beating, too,' as did a maid/nanny and his two older brothers. His mother's physical punishment was 'constant,' while that of his father 'occasional but very severe.' Although he now believes his punishment was clearly abuse, 'I couldn't tell anyone then. There was no place to go.' He concludes that 'it was not so much the beatings and constant physical abuse that I feared; it was the humiliation and being embarrassed.' Born in 1949, Pat Capponi 'learned fear long before I learned anything else. In our family home, we breathed it, ate it and slept with it alive in our beds. We were six victims – a mother and five children – totally dependent and viciously controlled ... Beatings were the most consistent feature of our lives.' Like many vicious parents, Capponi's father made his youngsters blame themselves: 'Guilt always with me, always on the verge of being found out, deserving of punishment.' [44]

In some cases, parents who had difficulty controlling their children arranged for them to be cared for in residential institutions. Those who could afford them employed private schools.[45] When 'Olga's' adoptive parents found themselves unable to deal with her 'nail-biting, nose-picking, [and] masturbation,' they sent her to a private school.[46] A Cedar Cottage boy, the oldest of three brothers, was the 'most difficult' for his ailing mother to handle, 'so off they packed me to private school ... in North Vancouver. I'd get home-sick, terribly home-sick. I ran away once ... ran home ... Mother and Dad were pretty upset. Dad scooped me up ... and I was packed off again, ... well after midnight. I got a caning the next day for good measure.' The parents of another boy sent him to private school because, as he reported, 'my mother thought I was incorrigible because I didn't do as she wanted.'

Parents who could not afford private schools sometimes called on the help of public institutions. By the time that he was arrested at twelve for stealing a car, 'Donald' had already acquired 'a long history of truancy, petty thievery and lying.' Two years later, in 1949, his mother laid a complaint of incorrigibility, and Donald went for a time to the Boys' Industrial School.[47] After 'Reggie' rebelled at what a social worker described as 'the suffocating restrictions of his own home,' his mother charged him as 'incorrigible' under the Juvenile Delinquents Act. Reggie spent six months in the Boys' Industrial School before going into a foster home, where his behaviour improved.[48] In 1952, when 'Bobby' was twelve, his father placed him in the Juvenile Detention Home because he was 'incorrigible.' He continued there for some months. His father and stepmother refused to take him back because, they said, they were 'unable to control him and unwilling to have him in their home,' and the CAS had some difficulty in finding a suitable foster home.[49]

Of all forms of the misuse of parental and adult power over children, sexual abuse was surely the most pernicious. Of those interviewed for this study, only a few reported, sometimes obliquely, experiencing direct sexual abuse.[50] One woman reported that she 'had an unhappy experience with [another person's] stepfather; I knew it was wrong, but I was too afraid to say anything, but I finally did.' A woman told that their neighbour, a teacher, 'would put us on his knee and play with us. We'd just sit there and never tell. We were afraid to tell. We didn't know what to do ... I'm sixty-six and still ashamed.' Another woman said that, during the 1930s, a neighbour girl, then ten or eleven, 'would talk of her grandfather taking her to bed ... but if we had told our mom that, she'd never have believed it.' A man stated that he had been sexually assaulted during a medical examination by a school physician. Another man was sent to an industrial school at age nine, where, he reported, he was subjected to 'the usual thing that happens in those places,' which, he continued, 'sex-wise was an awful way to start a kid off.'

Although few women reported exposure and other offences against them, the fact that two of them each reported more than one instance suggests how widespread the practice may have been. During the 1920s, a Cedar Cottage woman recalled, 'a man exposed himself to me one day when I was on my way to school.' Another time, 'another girl and I were approached by the milkman, who asked us to come into the bushes with him because he had candy for us. I ran home and told my mother, who telephoned the police. They caught the man in the bushes with the other girl and arrested him.' Another east-side woman told that, when she was about nine in the early 1920s, 'a man tried to lure us into the bushes to look for a lost parrot. I remember telling my parents.' Another time, as she cut across the school grounds on an errand, 'a man stopped me and I was terrified.' Some girls 'didn't tell' because they feared the abuser, because they wouldn't be believed, or because they 'rightly divined,' as did Patricia Graham's friend who was 'groped' by a man at the riding stables, 'that her freedom, not his, would have been curtailed.'[51]

If evidence of sexual abuse was rarely provided by those we interviewed, other data certainly suggest that sexual abuse was much more widespread in these years than many then thought. Considerable evidence of abuse can be found in case reports prepared by social agencies, by reports of court cases, by survey data such as those collected by the Committee on Sexual Offences

Against Children and Youth (the Badgeley Committee), and as revealed in autobiographical items.[52]

'Joyce' was born in 1936. Children's Aid Society records described her father as a diligent and successful fisherman who was also belligerent and a heavy drinker. Her mother was 'an alcoholic and promiscuous.' For her first five years, Joyce lived in a house 'where she was subjected to total rejection by her mother and ... extreme marital strife existed.' None the less, Joyce and her father had 'a strong bond of affection.' Her father then deserted her mother, taking Joyce with him. Over the next seven years, the two moved from one fishing port to another, and, during that time, CAS workers believed, her father 'had incestuous relations with Joyce.' Subsequently Joyce spent some time in a convent, a year in the provincial mental hospital, in many foster placements, and with her aunts. Eventually Joyce became pregnant and remained only two days in her final foster home before she 'disappeared with her father.'[53]

In another case, in 1938, 'Dorothy's' father took her to the United Church Home for 'medical care and confinement.' Eventually Dorothy admitted to a Children's Aid Society worker that 'she had been having intercourse with her own father and brother over a period of years' and that her child was probably 'the result of an incestuous contact.'[54]

A woman, born in the early 1950s, testified in court in Vancouver, in April 1989, that her grandfather, convicted on other counts of sexual assault, 'repeatedly molested her in the family barn when she was between three and seven years old.' She believed 'that being an incest victim prompted her violent teenage rebellion and escalating pattern of drug abuse.'[55]

A man wrote to the Badgeley Committee, telling for the first time a story that 'has been a source of shame and despair all my life.' He continued: 'As a boy of six I was sexually assaulted over a period of months by a male member of the family in whose keeping I'd been placed by my father. I didn't know it was wrong. No one had taken the time or trouble to inform me. Whenever I protested, the threats of a beating kept me docile. One particularly severe beating just before the initial encounter left me dreading others.'[56] He continued with an account of brutal treatment in a series of foster homes, and eventually of a life that included petty crime. He concluded that he was 'so ashamed of what was done to me that the words just won't come, and when they do, I still stammer badly.'

In another letter to the committee, a woman explained:

My father committed incest on me when I was a child. It started when I was about eight or nine until my late teenage years. It was devastating. My childhood was ruined. I always felt people could see and tell what was happening ... To this day, every day, I think about it. It is something that can never recede to the back of my mind. I stopped drinking four years ago. With the help of A.A. (Alcoholics Anonymous) and reading all the books I can on incest, it is getting better. Ever since I can remember, I thought of suicide. It is a viable alternative. But my two sons are what kept me alive and a husband who went through hell with me and stuck by me.[57]

These accounts of sexual and other forms of abuse indicate that those who survived the experience often suffered lifelong physical and emotional consequences. Abusers infected some of their victims with venereal diseases. A survey of clinics and physicians conducted in Toronto in 1937, for example, reported 178 cases of syphilis and 45 cases of gonorrhoea being treated in girls and boys under the age of fourteen.[58] Some of those who were abused in the years after the Second World War may, later in life, have been helped by increasingly available social, psychological, and self-help services.[59] For many others, and likely for nearly all victims of earlier years, abuse cast a dark, destructive shadow over the whole of their lives and, as recent widely publicized evidence suggests, perhaps over the lives of their children and grandchildren as well.

One thread that runs through accounts of both physical and sexual abuse is that children could not define or sometimes even understand what was happening to them. One woman remembered 'one horror story when I was a little kid ... my Mom and I were hitchhiking and I got in the car first and a man bared himself.' Her mother 'let a holler out of her and told him to stop the car ... I didn't know what it was, I mean I was six or seven, so I didn't understand what it was.' In describing the father of one of his friends, a man born in the late 1930s explained that 'his [friend's] father would have a short temper and would rely on taking the belt off and whacking somebody ... or shaking the hell out of somebody, I mean that today is what could be called a mild form of abuse but ... we wouldn't have the words for it, you know.'

Clearly, many children lacked the words to describe what happened or was happening to them, or the understanding that it might be wrong. After his mother told John Norris that his Cubmaster was 'a bad man, that he's been doing nasty things to the boys ... I lay on the bed, my whole body sick with shame and misery ... I hadn't known these things were so terrible.'[60] With limited, inaccurate, or no sense of the processes of growth in their bodies, for example, they might well be dismayed and frightened by the changes brought by the onset of puberty. Sexually abused youngsters learned from the threats made by their abusers, and from the guilt that they tried to project onto their victims, that what was happening to them was wrong. Such children, however, often had little or no sense of the sexual dimensions of what they were compelled to conceal.[61] Indeed, not knowing 'the words' prevented them from articulating their anguish, and perhaps bringing it to an end.

In these years parents had the sole responsibility to teach their youngsters about 'the facts of life,' as they were then described.[62] None the less, although children came to sense that sex was this 'very big powerful thing,' their parents were often very reluctant to teach them anything about it.[63] A woman's report that 'we didn't know anything about having children or sex; our parents never talked about it' was echoed in a man's statement that 'no one would answer' his questions; 'everyone would get quiet and my brother would squirm.' 'I remember,' said one woman, 'filling out a form when I was about thirteen and not knowing what to put in the space marked "sex." I had no idea.' 'I wondered why I shouldn't take candy from a stranger,' reported one man. 'Finally, a friend told me it would be poisoned.'

Some parents gave mythical information to their children. When his sister was born at home during a blackout in wartime Halifax, one man recalled 'looking up through the searchlights to see if the stork was coming.' Millicent Blake Loder's mother served as midwife in Labrador. 'Ma told us, when we were little, that she found the babies she brought to people in rotten stumps, but my sisters and I searched in all the stumps we could find without seeing one baby.'[64] Such stories sometimes led to later disbelief. Even when her mother finally told her 'where babies came from,' one woman still believed that she actually 'saw the doctor carry her brother in a blanket.' When told some of the truth at age nine, another woman 'just couldn't believe that's how I came into the world ... and ... your parents, there's no way that they would do that.'

Out of necessity mothers taught their daughters at least some of the 'facts of life.' 'I can remember my mother telling me about my period,' said one woman. 'It was a secret ... what would happen to me and it was very embarrassing to her, and consequently to me.' When, sometime later, she was with a group of girls and boys openly discussing periods, she was asked if she had had one yet. She was 'very upset and said, "This is a secret and you're not supposed to talk about it."' Another woman recalled, 'My mother called me into the bathroom one day and told me the facts of life and ... that she had written away for a little booklet.' When a ten- or eleven-year-old girl asked her aunt, 'What's a ——, I can hear her saying ... "O Nan" to my mother to come up and have a little chat about the birds and the bees.' Other mothers either passed on only partial information such as the one who explained 'about menstruation ... [but] did not tell me about childbirth or sexual intercourse' or were tardy with the information: 'I was out in the backyard raking the leaves,' one woman explained. 'I went into the house and this had happened. I nearly had a fit.' Later, 'my mother was kind of smiling, telling me all the things that probably I should have known before. And I remember my grandmother started to cry and said, "Oh my goodness, now you're a lady."' At this point some girls began to really comprehend that they, too, could really become mothers some day.

Parents often provided their sons with little or no information at all. Some boys were given pamphlets to read.[65] One man reported, 'It was my grandfather who explained to me about the birds and the bees ... so from a very young age he told me ... this flower is female and this is male ... and the chickens and the cows and the calf being born and fertile chicken eggs, what the rooster's role was, so that I got an understanding of what the mechanics were ...' Another was sent by his lone-parent mother to the family doctor, 'who gave me a mysterious and completely incomprehensible talk that only years later I finally figured was meant to be my sex education. That, of course, I had long since picked up from the gang.' Too often, such characteristics of the onset of puberty as erections and 'wet dreams' came as a surprise that boys felt they had to keep secret. Indeed, the experience of many boys was summed up by the man who reported that 'neither Dad nor Mom would discuss it,' and another who said, 'Our parents never discussed sexual matters. We learned the facts from brothers and peers.' But these informants often did not know or deliberately misled: 'I was terrified that hair would grow on the palms of my hands and everyone would know what I had done.'

The previous chapter opened with the suggestion that children could situate their family life along a continuum from happy to unhappy. What in fact the evidence shows is that children experienced their family along many continuums, such as those involving the relationships with each parent, with their sisters and brothers, and modes of family discipline. Autobiographies and autobiographical novels show that each life involves a unique mix of youngsters' experiences of the scripts of their lives. Hugh Garner admired his mother's 'strength, intractability, and self-reliance' while despising his father, and later his stepfather.[66] Fredelle Bruser Maynard initially described an unusually warm relationship with her mother and father. Only much later did she reveal that they favoured her in all sorts of seemingly unfair ways over her sister.[67] Those I interviewed also experienced their own particular mix of elements, but my pledge of confidentiality and anonymity to them does not permit me to lay out any single person's experience in great detail.

Two other concluding points must be made. First, when one accumulates all the central elements that make up family life, one sees that, while clearly this era was certainly not a 'dark age' of childhood, neither was it the golden age of popular mythology, an era during which children basked in a perpetual sunshine of family love. Further, those whose lives are described in this chapter, living, as most did, with their own parents, had the best chance for a stable childhood. In the next chapter, I describe the lives of those whose circumstances led them to live with relatives other than their parents, or with foster families. Second, these chapters have only touched lightly on the special, particularly happy, and even joyful, occasions of childhood. Since many people recall these in the context of their extended as well as their nuclear families, they are also discussed in a later chapter.

5

Children in a Wider Environment of Care

Children lived in extended as well as nuclear families. Indeed, many people's most cherished memories – discussed in a later chapter – are of events that took place in their extended families. Especially at times of crisis, many children also found in step-parents or in other relatives an additional measure of the sort of physical and emotional nourishment customarily provided by their parents. Other youngsters had to look for support to neighbours, to foster parents, or to fellow inmates and staff members of the institutions in which they spent some or much of their lives. In this regard, recent autobiographical accounts, evidence submitted at public inquiries, and other reports have emphasized what truly grim alternatives to family care institutions sometimes were.[1] Even though they did serve as a 'family' for some children, the 'closed' culture of 'total' institutions for children is beyond the scope of this study. The social history of the institutional care of children in Canada needs its own investigation.[2]

Although the odds were longer that children would find themselves appropriately nourished by parents other than their natural ones, some certainly did. The father of a woman whose mother died of cancer when she was about five, 'remarried on my seventh birthday.' The new couple came back from their honeymoon 'on my brother's third birthday. She was very beautiful and dressed well. She gave me a hand-made doll. I liked her from the beginning.' The mother of a woman whose father died during the Second World War, when she was three, remarried when the daughter was nine: 'I always got along well with my stepfather ... He had been friendly with Mother for a long time, so we [she and her older brother] had time to get used to him ... He bought me a little dog ... [and] always went to the sporting events my brother took part in.' Although her father 'was very cold,' reported another woman, her stepmother 'was very good. We had one fight though ... I told her the only reason ... my father married her ... was because I needed a mother, and she slapped me. So, of course, I reported her to my father right away. But I apologized and we made up, and we're very, very good friends. She is my mother.' When 'Dude' Lavington's widowed father remarried, his two sons 'were doomed to a stricter upbringing ... Our happiest memories have to do with our neighbours ... Mary Burnstad was the nearest to a mother we ever had and she seemed to be a mother to many other boys and girls as well as her own two sons and three daughters.'[3]

Other children, who in these instances we see through the eyes of social workers, experienced the reality that lies behind the long tradition of 'wicked' step-parent stories.[4] On entering Alexandra Cottage, a Vancouver home for the study and treatment of 'problem' children, 'Case 18,' four years and nine months old, suffered from 'persistent enuresis; fears and nervousness.' Of his stepmother he said: '"Will you spank me if I have wet underpants" - "Mummy says I won't go to heaven if I don't get cured, will you cure me?"'[5] 'Charles,' who the Vancouver Child Guidance Clinic diagnosed as a 'severely disturbed boy,' had suffered 'many brutal beatings' by his stepfather. 'Once he was beaten until unconscious – resulting in a permanent injury to his eye from the whip used,' and another time his stepfather 'seems to have tried to kill him by dumping bales of hay on him.'[6]

'Joan' was equally unfortunate. Born in 1941, she 'was the illegitimate child of a thirty-four-year-old woman who was badly crippled with arthritis.' Until Joan was about five, she and her mother lived with the maternal grandparents. Her mother then married a seventy-five-year-old, who, it turned out, had been accused of molesting children. Case records express 'some doubt' as to whether Joan herself was molested. In any case, after her mother died in 1947, her stepfather 'completely ignored her,' and she came into care. By March 1949, Joan was in her fourth foster home. In each case, she appeared to 'settle down quite well,' but then began to have severe 'crying spells.' Although a psychiatrist diagnosed Joan as 'a very disturbed child with an obsessive-compulsive pattern, and a deep neurotic fixation on her dead mother,' it seems more reasonable to suggest that sexual abuse was the cause of her difficulties.[7]

Some children were adopted as infants. Except for their sense of a stigma associated with being adopted and a natural curiosity about their origins, their childhoods were similar to, although not identical with, those described in the previous two chapters.[8] Born in Vancouver in January 1928, Dorothy Jean Morrow was put up for adoption. As her natural mother later explained, 'in those days to be pregnant and unmarried was such a disgrace that you didn't tell a soul. My father would never have spoken to me again or let me into the house.' Morrow's adoptive parents, her '"real" parents, the ones who raised me and made sacrifices for me ... gave me a loving home.' At eight years of age, Morrow accidentally learned that she had been adopted. Whenever she tried to find out more about herself, however, 'Mother became upset, wondering why, if I loved her, I would want to know about the woman who gave birth to me.' Only after her mother died did Morrow initiate the search that led her to a happy reunion with her natural mother.[9]

Other youngsters also had happy adoptions. The hockey player, and later coach, Barry Long, born in the 1940s, was adopted at birth by a Red Deer couple. When he was five, his adoptive father deserted the family. His mother, 'a heroine to him,' rented a house and took in boarders, many of whom became substitute fathers. 'They'd take me fishing and to ball games, things like that.' Though she couldn't afford it, his adoptive mother encouraged him to participate in hockey.[10]

To many children, their grandparents significantly enlarged the circle of those who both loved and looked after them. The grandparents of a Melville, Saskatchewan, girl lived 'less than three blocks away. I saw them daily. I went there after school, [and] frequently stayed for dinner and overnight.' When one boy was about five, his father had to work out of town a lot, so 'I stayed with my grandparents ... My grandfather taught me to read.' Another man, son of a particularly harsh father, 'liked Grandpa because he was a little more congenial, not so harsh or strict as Father ... He told me many different stories about the old country.' When she was six, a girl went with her parents to Britain to meet relatives. 'I met my paternal grandfather for the first time. It was a wondrous experience ... [We] walked on the beach and he always held my hand ... For the first time I loved and was loved by an adult other than my parents ... I will always cherish the time I spent with my grandfather.'

People talk more often of their grandmothers than of their grandfathers. A woman, born in the late 1920s, would 'pedal my bike' from Kerrisdale right across the city to Hastings Park 'to Grandmother's on Sundays.' Later, 'Grandmother got older ... and took turns living with all [of her children] ... I liked my Grandmother a lot; I thought she was a neat lady ... She had cards and I loved playing with her.' To a Kerrisdale woman, 'my mom's mom was a very important part' of her life. 'She lived in West Vancouver ... [and] if my parents would go away ... we might get to stay at her house. It was wonderful. It was great.' 'My maternal grandmother lived in Vancouver,' reported another Kerrisdale woman, 'and we would visit once a week

Two children visit their maternal grandmother in West Vancouver in 1942.

... My father's family lived on Vancouver Island.' Since this paternal grandmother 'wanted to have all her grandchildren visit during the summer ... my older sister and I used to spend between two weeks and a month ... Those summers were idyllic.' Bill Maciejko, who was born in the early 1950s, explained, 'All of us kids would end up under Baba's care for the whole summer, which ... freed our mothers and gave us a lot of free time and a lot of play and at the same time a lot of work. It was a really big deal to be able to participate in the work on the farm.'[11]

Over all of these years, even after old-age pensions became universal in 1952, widowed grandmothers and sometimes other elderly relatives joined the household of one of their children or that of a niece or nephew. When they did so they usually played a major role in family affairs. In some homes they did the chores that children did in other households. In one family in Burnaby in the 1950s, for example, the daughter never had to make her bed and never helped in the kitchen or learned how to cook: 'Grandma did all the cooking.' To a Kerrisdale woman, her maternal grandmother who lived with them was 'an important figure in my life. If I wanted to talk to anybody I would go to my grandmother and talk with her ... She was always easy to approach ... If either of us [the woman or her brother] came into the room and sat next to her – there could be a whole big room of a lot of chairs, but I always came and sat right beside her ... and she would always put her hand on my hand ... or just on my knee, or hold onto my arm. There was always a lot of physical contact ... it wasn't rushing and hugging and kissing but just very subtle.' Mary Cook's unmarried great-aunt visited her family's Renfrew County, Ontario, home every winter in the 1930s. While there, she made it 'her task ... to get us caught up with the mending,' as well as telling the children 'wonderful German fairy tales that kept us entertained for hours.'[12]

When grandparents became infirm, their children and grandchildren helped to care for them. When his eighty-four-year-old grandmother came to live with his family, an Evelyn man 'had to look after her,' as he euphemistically put it, whenever his mother made day-long trips to town. Until she died, in the 1930s, at age ninety, another family had to deal with the problem that 'Grandmother drank. She would sneak to the neighbour's house next door. They would give her a little whisky.' A Halifax grandmother 'was getting so old and feeble my aunt couldn't look after her and they moved in with us. Nine people in the house – four teenagers – and only one bathroom ... My grandmother was there eight or nine years before she died. She didn't understand the children of the family.' In another family, the grandmother who moved in with her son, daughter-in-law, and their four children at first did much of the housework and caring for the children.

But by the time the children were entering adolescence, however, her increasing senility 'made all of us kids embarrassed to have her around. It was sad, really.'

At time of tension, crisis, or disaster, families naturally turned to relatives for short- or long-term help. Some families – perhaps a higher proportion than represented among those interviewed – lacked relatives or friends who could or would help them out in difficult times.[13] They had no extended families, or such relatives were dead, or very poor, or lived far away, many in the 'old country,' or were estranged from them. A man whose childhood was 'not happy,' who because 'there were too many kids, and no funds,' reported 'there were no family outings.' Within his extended family 'no one had anything' so they 'couldn't help each other out.' 'The war cut us off from all our relatives,' one woman lamented, 'and when Mom came down with cancer, there was no one to turn to.'

Others did tell of receiving family help. Just before their younger brother was born in the mid-1920s, two boys were sent to stay with their mother's sister in Seattle 'to be out of the way.' In Cedar Cottage in the early 1920s, a man reported, 'my oldest sister had diphtheria. My dad and I moved in with my grandmother, who lived a block away, while she was sick' and quarantined in the family home with her mother. When she was in Grade Two in the early 1930s, a Kerrisdale girl and some of her cousins caught scarlet fever. While her father stayed elsewhere, both she and her cousins were quarantined in their house under the care of her mother. However, when 'Father eventually returned home, he got it too, and we were quarantined again.' When the mother of another woman became extremely ill with bronchial pneumonia during the 1930s (and before sulpha, penicillin, and later drugs greatly reduced the dangers posed by this ailment), a girl's uncle moved in 'to take turns staying up with mother.' Mildred Young Hubbert's widowed mother regularly fed the children of a neighbouring family hard hit by both the Depression and illness: 'Nearly every night one or another of them ate at our place.' [14]

Some families needed more long-term help. When children had to go elsewhere for schooling, they customarily stayed with relatives or friends. A Powell River girl 'went to school in Victoria, to stay with my grandmother. I looked forward to it. She used to spoil me. Once my brother was born, he was the one.' A boy from the same community went to Vancouver, 'way up Kingsway. I stayed with my grandmother for the year or so I went to school there.' When consolidation closed a rural school near Prince George in 1950, a woman reported that 'Mom thought the long walk and then a long bus ride – even in good weather I travelled [each way] for nearly two hours – it was too much. So I went in on the bus on Monday, stayed with my aunt in town, and came home on the bus on Friday. It was okay, but I really missed Mom and Dad.' When after his father died, Silver Donald Cameron adopted what he described as 'punk habits' in a Vancouver high school, he joined, in a process he described as 'informal adoption,' the family of Nelson Allen, one of his father's friends, 'someone I cared for and admired deeply.'[15]

Other long-term family help was more a product of necessity. In one family who were 'always hard up' during the Depression, the mother regularly 'wrote to her family' in England. Her six unmarried sisters 'sent wonderful parcels ... clothes, books – lots of books – for both boys and girls. English books were different.' In 1935, Pete Loudon's father lost his job when the Depression closed the smelter in Anyox. The family moved to Vancouver, where his father had great difficulty getting any work, and then his mother died. The family moved to Toronto, where twelve-year-old Pete stayed with his mother's family while his father looked for work. After a year, he moved to Kirkland Lake to live with his newly married sister and her husband. 'The world became brighter. We were all on our way to new happiness despite the approaching war.'[16] 'Joan,' abandoned in infancy by her mother, was left in the care of her sometimes 'sexually promiscuous' grandmother, who was 'harsh and cruel,' making her 'work long hours on the farm.' The only person Joan 'showed any affection for was her deaf-mute uncle, who gave her candies and sometimes bought her new clothes.' Joan eventually ended up in the provincial Industrial School for Girls.[17]

Ferne Nelson described the mixed reception with which she and her family greeted the permanent addition to it of her mother's twelve-year-old brother, Lester. 'Papa hoped he would be some help around the farm. Mama loved him, of course, and tried hard to make up for his unhappy childhood. Ve [Nelson's sister] wasn't pleased; he would now take her place as the eldest. He established his relationship with me right away when he called me Fatty. Rus was delighted to have another boy in the family, and he and Lester quickly became pals.'[18]

Failing parental health was a major cause of family disruption. A woman told of an event that took place when she was about eight: 'I remember the time of [Mother] just going right out of her mind ... the people from upstairs took her and she went off somewhere and I didn't see her for a long time ... I lived with my grandmother ... I had her [grandmother's] room and she ... had the chesterfield. She spoiled me. She was just a doting grandmother.' Robert H. Thompson's father died six weeks before he was born, probably as a result of damage done to his health by service in the Great

War. His mother took him, his sister, and his brother to stay with her parents in Richlea, Saskatchewan. A couple of years later, they moved into a house owned by the grandparents.[19] A man, born in Edmonton in the early 1920s, moved with his widowed mother when she 'came to Vancouver for treatment' of her tuberculosis. When she died of the disease when he was seven, he 'went to live in Burnaby with my grandparents ... for a couple of years.' He then moved back to Vancouver to live with a maternal aunt and uncle: 'they were the ones that raised me ... They were like a mother and father to me.' After he moved away from his grandparents, however, 'I'd visit them to do their chores.'

When, after a long hospital stay (and before hospital insurance and medicare), the father of seven children died in the early 1940s, three different sets of aunts and uncles helped out by taking almost permanent care of three of the youngsters. Their mother, 'who lived for her children [and] who loved everyone of us' (reported one daughter), was most distressed by the necessity of taking this step and 'prayed we would all know who she was.' Although well cared for in their new homes, the children also regretted the partial break-up of their family. At least one, to the distress of the aunt whose family she had joined, 'moved home to be married.' Others visited frequently.

When family or friends proved unable or unwilling to help, children in distress came for short or long periods into the care of social agencies. In June 1925, when William Holmes was about two weeks old, he was left, with a warm bottle of milk, a five-dollar bill, and a note, in a basket outside the Protestant Orphans' Home in Victoria. The note read: 'Please, please keep my dear little baby for me. I can't support him now for I have to earn my own living but as soon as I am able to keep him I will come for him.'[20] When he was ten days old, in December 1932, Peter Kornelson was left on the doorstep of a Winnipeg hospital with a note reading 'Please Missus take him in. I have nine others and have got to have an operation so cannot look after him. Got no money and husband can't work.'[21] Both Holmes and Kornelson were eventually adopted. Not so for 'Stompin' Tom' Connors, who had a really grim childhood in institutions and foster homes after his mother went to jail.[22]

Other children returned to their families or stayed in institutions until old enough to leave on their own. J.F. (Sandy) Carmichael entered the Protestant Orphanage in Victoria in 1938 because his 'parents could no longer care for me due to the ravages of the Depression.' While 'my folks reorganized themselves,' Carmichael spent a year there, looked after 'by two very caring people.'[23] When, in the early 1940s, the previously prosperous

Four children at a Vancouver Children's Aid Society foster home in the 1920s.

middle-class de Montezuma family became destitute, the five children entered the Loyal Protestant Home for Children in New Westminster. One recalls being 'delighted that we were given three meals a day and each our own clean bed; clothes that fit and regular baths.'[24] Each of the de Montezuma youngsters stayed in the Home until age sixteen.

Most children taken into care found themselves placed out into foster families. Some families took in children out of a sense of social and religious duty, or because they liked to have children in their homes. More took foster children out of necessity; deserted or widowed women, for example, took in children as a way of supporting themselves and their own youngsters. Others looked to foster children for the unpaid work they could get out of them. Some children settled with reasonable comfort into foster homes. Particularly if they stayed in one place for a long period, the lives of foster children came, in some senses, to resemble those of the girls and boys described in previous chapters. Other children – particularly those who had been neglected or abused over a long period of time – were much less likely to end up in a long-term relationship with foster families.

As the examples described below make clear, there were two reasons for the generally dismal record of the placement of severely troubled children. On the one hand, no matter how socially essential their work was seen to be, foster parents were very poorly paid. Foster mothers had heavy loads to bear in looking after their own as well as foster children. Not all were able or willing to give that extra measure of care that troublesome or deeply disturbed youngsters required. On the other hand, foster children became wary of foster parents. Often, they were unwilling to commit themselves emotionally to situations that might prove to be temporary. Sometimes they behaved in ways that severely tested the dispositions of foster siblings and parents.

Although it is clear that child-welfare agencies selected some unsuitable foster homes, available data made it difficult to identify them. The social-work theses that I examined were based on confidential records. Their writers did not meet the children whose lives they described, but built their studies out of files prepared by agency workers. I was not therefore surprised to find that the blame for problems arising from a fostering relationship was usually laid on the children themselves or on their natural parents.

Sometimes, however, these theses give glimpses of foster parents behaving in inappropriate ways. The Child Guidance Clinic concluded that 'Mickey's' foster parents 'were not able to recognize his needs and therefore he was not able to relate to them.'[25] 'George' left his third unhappy foster home because 'immature foster parents' would not accept him. They complained that 'he was unable to demonstrate affection and gratitude to them for "giving him a home."'[26] 'Betty' entered her foster home as an infant. At four years of age, reported her social worker, Betty was 'unsocial, disobedient, highly excitable and uncooperative ... She sucks all four fingers of either hand.' Her foster mother 'lunges at her and threatens "a good spanking."' None the less, 'Betty runs like a hare as soon as she catches sight of a CAS car or the worker.'[27] 'Tom,' at about age eight, 'was strapped or locked in the cellar' for disobedience by his foster mother, but the Children's Aid Society left him in the home so he could be with his sister.[28] While his social worker wrote that thirteen-year-old 'Eddie' seemed to be happy in his farming-family foster home, the worker also noted 'there were difficulties arising' between Eddie and his foster father; 'perhaps the foster parents expected him to do far too much work.'[29] In her foster home, Maggie MacDonald wrote, 'I had many beatings. With a broom in particular – the handle – on my back, or anywhere it would hit. "You are bad!" I was always told. "You're bad, you're bad!"'[30]

From these general comments about fostering, let us turn first to four examples of successful placement, although the last one ends on a sad note. After his widowed mother proved no longer able to care for him, 'John,' the seventh child in a family of eight, entered a foster home when he was eleven. His foster parents had two sons, and 'took a keen interest' in all the boys' activities. John became 'an integral part of the foster family and ... identified completely with their standards and goals.' He stayed with them until after he left school and became financially independent.[31] 'Florence,' the product of a marriage broken up by her father's service overseas in the Second World War, came into care at eleven. According to her social worker, the atmosphere of her foster home was not 'particularly warm,' with a foster mother who expressed 'high and inflexible expectations.' Florence often felt 'some real or imagined discrimination on the part of the foster parents compared to ... their own children.' None the less, she remained with the family through high school and her training as a practical nurse.[32] After 'Lorrie's' mother died and her father was unable to care for her and her four siblings, she came into care at age eight. After two brief placements, Lorrie entered a foster home, where she stayed until old enough to move to Vancouver to work. Over these years she also maintained 'a positive interest in her brothers and sisters to whom she was attached.'[33]

Finally, another 'Florence.' Considered non-adoptable because of her mother's apparent low intelligence, this child joined a foster family when she was six months old. In 1947, when she was ten, her foster mother died. Because her foster father was 'so fond of her' (and, apparently, of his other foster children), he tried, with a succession of 'rather unsuccessful' housekeepers, to keep the family going. After a year, however, he decided to remarry and give up the children. He then reported that Florence 'had a very nasty temper if she did not get her own way.' None the less, the case worker reported that she was 'an appealing child but seems quite immature.' She enjoyed 'reading a great deal and changes her [library] books faithfully every week.' The worker 'took Florence out for a drive and ... asked ... whether she had any idea she would be leaving her foster home. She said 'No' and started to cry. Then I explained the situation to her ... She continued to sob but she controlled herself quite well and asked about where she would be going ...' The following week the worker collected Florence to take her to the Receiving Home. 'She seemed quite happy today and had numerous toys, clothing, doll's furniture, etc., all ready to take. She said good-bye to her foster father ... and there were no tears. The foster father seemed more upset than she was.'[34]

Some children entered foster homes soon after birth because they were, in the opinion of Children's Aid Societies, not adoptable. An analysis of the files of the ninety-six illegitimate children so judged in 1941 by the two Vancouver Children's Aid Societies, conducted by a social-work student, showed that these agencies employed, either alone or in combination, twenty-five factors in making this decision. They concluded that infants were not adoptable if the identities of their fathers could not be established; if the fathers displayed such 'features' as asthma, tuberculosis, epilepsy, or Negroid blood; if a psychiatrist or social worker concluded that the mother displayed 'low mentality' or 'inadequate personality,' or was promiscuous; if other relatives possessed these or other undesirable characteristics; or if the babies themselves appeared to physically or in some other way to be abnormal.[35]

The stories of 'Roy' and 'Gerry' suggest some of the effects of such decisions. Sometime during the 1940s, 'Roy,' the illegitimate child of a seventeen-year-old mother, came into care at his birth. The Children's Aid Society placed him in a home 'where the foster parents had three children of their own, as well as caring for two children of relatives, and two CAS children.' By the time he was five, Roy was a 'severe' bedwetter and later developed 'nightmares, sleepwalking, and destructive behaviour such as head banging, destroying his clothes and killing chickens.' Since it was 'the only home he has known,' the Child Guidance Clinic was reluctant to suggest he be moved. Although his symptoms gradually decreased over the next two years, a family emergency forced the CAS to move Roy to another home the agency hoped might prove to be a permanent one. There, his problems recurred and he asked 'to return to his former home.' Although the CAS agreed to this request, a social worker noted that, while 'no longer destructive,' Roy 'tends to be apathetic, and is unable to form permanent relationships.'[36]

After 'Gerry' was born in May 1945, her mother asked the Vancouver Children's Aid Society to arrange an adoption. However, although Gerry was in good health, the CAS 'reserved' her from adoption because of her mother's 'lack of moral sense (this was her third illegitimate child).' The mother then decided to try to 'make her own plans for the baby' and, while she did so, the CAS placed Gerry in a 'temporary boarding home for babies.' Late in 1945, and in the face of the mother's continued inability to arrange care, the CAS placed the now six-month-old infant with a couple who were 'anxious to keep Gerry permanently.' In September 1946, these foster parents returned her, probably because the CAS had told them that their 'chances for adopting were slim.' The CAS then placed Gerry with another couple 'anxious to proceed with adoption' and, in February 1947, sent her to the Child Guidance Clinic for evaluation. Although the clinic found that Gerry was developing satisfactorily, its psychiatrist concluded that 'because of background adoption still could not be recommended.' In the following June, the foster mother became pregnant and asked the CAS to remove the child from the home.

At two years of age, Gerry moved to her fourth and final placement. There, after some months, her new foster mother stated, 'it would break my heart' if Gerry left. Whenever a social worker visited the home, Gerry became apprehensive 'in case she was going to be moved again.' The foster mother exacerbated Gerry's fears when, until coming to see the practice was wrong, she occasionally greeted naughty behaviour by threatening that 'the worker will take you when she comes.' In July 1948, the Child Guidance Clinic retested Gerry and now agreed that she could be adopted. Although the foster family wanted to keep her permanently – they were 'devoted' to her – they were for some time reluctant to give up the board money. In July 1951, however, Gerry's placement became one of 'permanent free board,' although the foster mother did ask the CAS to pay some medical bills when Gerry contracted whooping cough. Meanwhile, her natural mother had married, moved to the country, and, anxious to conceal the fact that she had an illegitimate child, 'took almost two years to ... sign the consent for adoption.' She eventually did so in April 1953. Gerry was thus ten years old when her adoption was finally completed in 1955.[37]

Children who entered foster homes later in their lives often found themselves frequently on the move.[38] One girl 'learned to call every woman "Mom" and every man "Daddy."'[39] Don Scott, fostered many times as a youngster and now working for World Vision, recalled that 'I don't know how many people I've called "Mom."'[40] In such circumstances agencies tried, often unsuccessfully, to keep siblings together. When, after several years of marital disagreement, their parents separated, 'Harry,' 'Alice,' and 'Joan' came into care in the late 1930s. The CAS placed them all in a home 'where the foster father was a very kindly man, interested in his home and very fond of children.' There 'Joan, the younger sister, was very well liked ... in spite of her bed-wetting habits.' Alice, also a bed-wetter, 'was considered to be "cheeky" and disobedient, and the foster mother felt she could not keep her.' In any case, illness in the foster family intervened, and all three children had to move. When it was unable to place all three together, the CAS separated Harry from his sisters.

Over the next few years each of the children went through no fewer than five more placements. In their next home, the girls 'seemed to get along quite well' but had to move when the foster parents left British Columbia. Their 'enuretic difficulties' led to further moves and, in the seventh home, the social worker reported 'enuresis still persists.' The foster mother in this particular placement found ' Alice a very sweet child who likes to help about the house,' but 'Joan's problems are increasing. She lies, steals food and is very high strung.'

Meanwhile, Harry also moved through a series of foster homes. In the fourth, the foster father had 'fallen for the child,' and everyone 'loved him and they wished to keep him.' Unfortunately, the foster father died suddenly and Harry moved on to another 'superior' foster home. There, although he seemed to settle in well, he had to move again when it appeared the foster mother was developing tuberculosis. In this next home Harry, now six, began to wet the bed, much to the annoyance of the foster father. Eventually, Harry himself 'asked to be taken away.' In his next home he continued to wet his bed but was 'loved by both foster parents' and said himself that he 'wishes to marry' his new foster mother. Since the oldest of these three children was only about twelve when this record was compiled, their own and other case histories suggest it is unlikely that they were in their final placement.[41]

'Dave' also lived in many homes. The second of four boys, he was born in 1941. His father died in 1948. Soon thereafter provincial child-welfare authorities investigated the family, describing Dave's mother as subject to epileptic seizures, as 'selfish, boastful, and not very interested in her children,' and as 'living with another man reputed to be a bootlegger.' Since she 'was not giving the children the proper care,' they were apprehended. Over the next few years, and because of behaviour problems at home and at school, Dave spent short periods of time in three foster homes; a total of two years in a receiving home; and, when he was nine, 'was placed temporarily in the Vancouver Detention Home.' In the summer of 1952, however, Dave entered a foster home where, 'for once, he felt that perhaps he was wanted and needed.' His foster father, a farmer who had lost both legs in the Second World War, called on Dave for help with farm chores, and Dave 'was very proud of himself when allowed to drive the tractor.' In 1953, when he was twelve, welfare records reported that Dave had 'proudly' prepared a calf for the fall stock show and, despite continued problems at school, was 'settling down nicely in his home,' so much so that another boy was placed in the same home.[42]

Their persistent longing for their 'real' family is surely one of the most poignant signals that foster children gave of their dismay.[43] 'Dick,' taken into care at age seven, constantly 'worried over his parents.'[44] At six years of age, and in his fourth foster home, 'Jim' wanted to know 'why I cannot stay with one mamma like other boys do.'[45] Born in 1937, 'Donald' came into care in 1942, when his mother deserted his father. Over the next twelve years, Donald lived in at least six foster homes, spent three sessions in the Receiving Home, and returned at least twice to live with his reunited parents. On one of these occasions, he turned up, 'very disturbed,' at the CAS and announced that 'Mother and Father don't want me any more.' However, after he was placed in a new foster home, he soon returned again to his parents, telling the CAS that 'kids should be with their parents, and Mother and Father want me.'[46] 'Evelyn's' father had probably abused her sexually; she told a foster mother that her mother would not let her stay alone with her father because 'he played dirty with me, like men do in the street.' None the less, she told a social worker that 'she did not think children should be taken away from their parents even though ... "it was for their own good."'[47] 'Larry' spent his first year in an infants' home and his second in four foster homes. He then stayed with the fourth set of foster parents throughout his childhood and youth and 'considered them as his parents.' At age fifteen, however, he demanded to meet his natural mother. The CAS eventually located her in prison, and a worker took Larry there to visit her. After embracing her, Larry exclaimed, 'Gee whiz, my own mom. I finally found you.'[48]

The foregoing accounts provide only slight evidence of the feelings of foster children. However, two cases do permit us a more intimate glimpse. First, the example of another 'Joan.' After she was born illegitimately, Joan lived until she was five with her maternal grandparents and their young children. A 'close family' that got into 'very desperate straits,' it had to give Joan up when she was five years old. She was placed with a family with whom she stayed until she was an adult. Her case file reported, 'Joan had been prepared somewhat for placement, and on the drive to the foster home the worker tried to explain placement further and why she was in care.' However, she 'seemed quite confused ... [and] asked numerous questions ... was very quiet and did not smile or laugh ...' Years later, as an adult, Joan wrote, 'I remember asking why I had to leave and these were the words spoken, "There are too many in the family now, and one has to leave, and you being the youngest are chosen." That is stamped on my mind forever! How cruel and absurd!' Throughout her years with the foster family, Joan persisted in wondering about herself, 'but when I would even mention the subject [her foster parents] would freeze up, like everything in my past was a bad sin and should not be revealed to me.' Although now happily married, 'deep down I have this awful pain. The pain of not knowing who, what or where I am ...' Fortunately, the Children's Aid Society enabled Joan to be reunited with her extended family.[49]

Next, the case of James Hale. Born in the late 1950s, James was given up by his mother for adoption when he was two. His first foster parents, with whom he stayed three years, either initiated or continued the practice of giving him the tranquillizer phenobarbital. When provincial child-welfare services eventually moved him to a new foster home, he asked the social worker, 'Do they really want a little boy just like me?' While in this home what appears to have been an entirely suitable couple tried to adopt Hale but were rejected by the authorities. Over the next few years, he was placed in a number of institutions, including the Vancouver Children's Foundation, Brannan Lake (supposedly a place for adolescent juvenile delinquents), and the New Denver Youth Centre, described by a teacher as 'a warehouse for up to 30 males aged 12 to 15 ... [who] brutally enforced a pecking order among themselves through violence and sexual assaults.' While Hale was at New Denver, this teacher and his wife tried to adopt him but were rejected.

New Denver then sent Hale to the Vancouver General Hospital for psychiatric evaluation. There, while he was 'on Haloperidol (Haldol), a tranquillizer and antipsychotic, and Congentin, used to control the Parkin-sonian-type side effects of Haloperidol,' he was diagnosed as suffering from 'mild mental retardation due to minimal brain dysfunction.' In consequence, Hale was sent to Woodlands School for the mentally retarded, where he remained for three and a half years. A report from the school at the time explained that Hale, 'who at least has food and lodging, is not a "squeaky wheel" in the system and, therefore, tends to be low on the priority for placement in the already overloaded resources.' When he was seventeen, Hale ran away from Woodlands. When Hale was in his late thirties, his psychologist reported him as suffering from 'sleep disturbances, outbursts of rage, periods of confusion and poor concentration, anxiety attacks and suffers from social isolation.' Of his childhood and youth, Hales said, 'I get outraged. It leaves a real emptiness in my heart when I see the sad state of affairs that I was put through as a child and as an adolescent.'[50]

One wonders just how many children grew into adults with a 'deep ... awful pain' or with a 'real emptiness' that they would never be able to relieve. Certainly many tried for solace by seaching for their birth relatives and their roots. Organizations such as Parent Finders, provincial reunion registers, and legislative changes permitting adults to learn more of the information contained in adoption and other social-welfare files has undoubtedly given some the 'feeling of inner peace' that writer Rick Ouston found when, 'for the first time in my life, I met the woman who gave me life.'[51]

Some life stories do not round themselves off with a happy ending. This and the previous two chapters on the family life of children show how many families raised their own and their foster children to the reasonable satisfaction of the children themselves and of the community. These chapters also showed how physically and emotionally destructive some families could be. Those who grew up in a series of foster homes and in institutions had even less chance for a reasonable start in life than those who grew up in their own natural or adoptive families. For many youthful victims of their own or foster families, the malign effects were lifelong. Recent accounts of trials for sexual and other forms of physical abuse testify to patterns whereby some of those severely mistreated as youngsters repeat what was done to them on the next generation. And, despite education and a more vigorous search for abuse, and prosecution of abusers, only the most unrealistic of observers could conclude that the future will be much better than the past. Some children will, of course, benefit from such social action. Others will experience and then go on to perpetuate the cycle of mistreatment and abuse.

6

The Paid and Unpaid Work of Urban Children

Whatever else they did as they grew up, most children spent some of their waking hours working. However, historians examining the topic of children at work focused on efforts to control or prevent the most visibly exploitive forms of child labour. Traditional accounts of child labour give little attention to the place that work itself played in the life course of boys and girls in all social classes. This chapter and the next examine how work crafted much of the lives of both urban and rural youngsters.

Recently some historians have looked at the ways in which families interwove the work and education of their young in practical and long-term apprenticeships for adulthood. In preindustrial times, learning by doing, mostly in the family setting, the work at which they would spend their lives formed the core of youthful education. Industrialization and urbanization added to the locations in which child labour took place. Instead of working on family farms or in small (often family) workshops, boys and girls found work in mines or large factories. Others were exploited in family sweatshops as their homes became outposts of large enterprises.[1] As members of the family wage-unit, they continued to make an important and sometimes essential contribution to the economic survival of their families.[2] Such children also continued to work in and around their homes.[3]

By the 1890s a major restructuring of manufacturing led to a decline in the demand for full-time child labour. An accompanying rise in the purchasing power of workers permitted an increasing proportion of working-class families to withhold their children from the labour force. Only then were many children able to take full advantage of formal schooling. In a closely connected development, new ideas about child-rearing and about the kind of schooling necessary to produce an efficient workforce effected a major transformation in schooling. Nevertheless, conflict persisted between some families' need for the full-time labour of their children and the modern state's demand that all children attend school.[4] By the 1920s, however, the state had triumphed; most children enrolled in school and, when compared with their predecessors of a generation before, they attended more regularly and stayed in school longer.[5]

Full-time schooling absorbed less time than full-time work. Adults devised activities that contributed to the family economy to fill those hours that were available before and after school, on weekends, and during the school-vacation periods.[6] Relative prosperity in the 1920s brought larger houses and yards that, in turn, gave rise to more household tasks for which children could be called on to help. The Depression forced parents to incorporate children's work into the 'make-do' requirements of the time. Although growing prosperity in the 1940s and 1950s began to change the working lives of children, not until the 1960s did social and economic changes transform deeply rooted patterns of children's work.

Since children's work was grounded in ideology as well as necessity, it was as important in the upbringing of middle-class children as it was in that of their working-class counterparts. This chapter describes the work of children as they themselves saw it, and distinguishes between the unpaid work that they did within households and the paid work that they did outside the family. In both working-class and middle-class families, boys and girls alike made their greatest contribution through household work. None the less, in many working-class families the paid work of girls and boys also helped provide basic necessities. Within the middle class – and, after the Second World War, in an increasing proportion of working-class families as well – the paid work of boys and girls also contributed in a less direct but still important way. Finally, since it played a central role in shaping adult identities, children's work had much more than merely economic consequences.

The preface noted that young people crossed a number of watersheds in their lives which, taken together, marked the end of their childhood. For the topic of this chapter, children's age when they left school is the most appropriate of these indicators. It and child-labour legislation set legal limits to the full-time work of children and young people. In 1921, British Columbia passed legislation that provided free education to all children from ages six to sixteen years, and compelled all children 'from over seven to under fifteen' to attend school.[7] Although as late as 1930 the federal Department of Labour noted that child labour usually meant 'the work for pay of children under 14,' these conditions in British Columbia make age fifteen the appropriate dividing line. In this chapter 'child labour' refers to that work undertaken by boys and girls before their fifteenth birthdays.[8]

Custom and ideology mandated that families should divide household duties into one set for women and girls and another set for men and boys.[9] In practice, however, families divided work into two different categories. In one category was work done mostly by girls, and in the other work done by both girls and boys. As one Cedar Cottage woman explained, because her separated mother worked 'there were certain chores I had to do. I had to have the wood in and the wood split. I was the boy, eh, in the family, so it seemed to me all my life was splitting wood, and bringing in wood, and I had the fire going, the vegetables on cooking when my mother came in the door.' Only children's paid work discloses a set of activities engaged in exclusively by boys. In most families the cumulative effect of this division of labour meant that parents, and especially the more heavily burdened mothers, demanded a greater proportion of their daughters' time than of their sons'.

Most of the duties custom assigned women and girls took place inside the home. These included all the tasks involved in rearing children; in buying, storing, and preparing food; in caring for the sick and elderly; and in cleaning clothing, house, and furnishings.[10] As two brothers, speaking matter-of-factly of their three sisters, reported, 'The girls worked around the house a lot, cleaned, cooked, and stayed with Ma.' A Kerrisdale woman reported that, by the primary grades, 'I was responsible for myself after school and to prepare vegetables for dinner before my mom came home from work.' She also made her bed, tidied up the house, and helped with the other housework.

'Our family had five girls,' reported a working-class woman. 'I was the oldest ... I was a mother hen with the other kids.' Certainly, being a 'mother hen' to other children is so central in the memories of many women that child-minding and being a girl are bound inextricably together. Thus a Kerrisdale woman reported that, 'when I got older, I could take my brothers and sisters to the beach ... that was really good because I didn't have to do chores if I took them.' Very young girls helped to care for their even younger siblings; they fetched and carried, they watched over them in the bath or as they played. As they got older, their responsibilities increased proportionately. By the time they were ten or eleven years old, girls often found themselves in full charge of younger brothers and sisters for long periods, changing, bathing, dressing, feeding, and amusing them. One woman 'had a younger sister who never walked. She died when she was seven ... I looked after her ... She was just like a baby.' Another, whose single-parenting mother worked, 'had to look after my younger brother' unassisted by her older brother. As one woman, third in a family of ten children, lamented, 'There were so many children, so much to do, and so little to do it with.'[11]

In large families, older sisters gradually shared the duties with younger ones, but seldom escaped completely until they left home. If their mother became serously ill or died, the oldest might be called upon to take her place. After her mother died when she was twelve, Maria Campbell took care of her six younger siblings, including cooking, gardening, canning, laundering, and mending.[12] When the widowed mother of twelve rural Manitoba children died, 'the older members of the family ... remained and helped bring up the brothers and sisters ... One of the girls ... took over care of the house and the Mothers' Allowance paid for her services.'[13] While girls who cared for siblings must sometimes have resented their tasks, most reported this duty matter-of-factly, and seem to have shared with girls of earlier generations the notion that child care was a "given" of female childhood.

Mealtime activities probably comprised the most frequent of 'inside' chores. Women reported setting the table; preparing food; washing and drying dishes; emptying the drip pan under the icebox; filling the stove's hot-water reservoir; fetching apples, potatoes, and other items from storage bins in the basement or root cellars; canning fruit and vegetables and making jams and pickles; and, for a time after the Second World War, working colouring into margarine. A Kerrisdale woman reported that, following her after-school play-hour, she 'would help her grandmother with the vegetables and set the table.' A middle-class woman stated that, as a preschool child, she helped with the dishes. By the time she was in the primary grades, she 'did the dishes without help,' and later learned to cook. Another woman explained that her mother, who went out to work, 'left supper ready, and I was expected to cook it.'

Many girls probably shared the sentiments of one middle-class informant who reported that 'I enjoyed cooking but hated housework.' One can easily understand such distaste. Although Vancouver became cleaner over the years, even in 1960 it remained a dirty city. Grime entered houses borne by smoky, soot-laden air, dusty and dirty fuels, and family shoes and clothing. Only constant effort kept it at bay. Girls of both classes usually made their own beds, and sometimes those of other family members as well, and tidied and dusted their rooms. Weekly chores tended to be more elaborate and time-consuming. A Kerrisdale woman explained that 'every Saturday was a whole house clean-up ... vacuuming, dusting, windows.' An east-side woman remarked that, 'while Mother ironed on Saturdays, it was my responsibility to scrub floors and bake bread. It was an all-day chore for a week's supply of eight to ten loaves.'

Women's recollections of the heavy labours of washday and its follow-up are especially vivid. A Cedar Cottage woman explained that 'washing was a big chore since we had no washtubs. It involved three stages, a round tub on two chairs, an oval boiler, and "blueing" in the sink.' Then she 'ironed it all with flat-irons when I came home from school. I hated those things. They were always getting cold.' Another working-class woman reported that 'many a time, I'd come home [from school] and do a tub full of laundry. You had no washing machine; you'd use a scrub board.' A Kerrisdale woman could remember no time when she 'didn't help with the washing and ironing. Washday was always Monday ... [and was] a complicated and strenuous procedure' employing a wooden tub, a hand-wringer, and big copper tins for blueing and rinsing. 'It was nothing,' she concluded, 'to iron twenty-four shirts on a Monday night.' Gradually, electric washing machines and irons took over some of these tasks and reduced the drudgery of others. However, until the introduction of the modern washer, washing still involved feeding everything through a hand-turned or electric wringer after each of the three stages.[14]

Before refrigerators and automobiles became commonplace, shopping for groceries and other household needs was a frequent and time-consuming affair. Families could buy bread, milk, and produce from vans; those with telephones could order groceries for home delivery. In order to ensure that limited finances went as far as possible, however, many families shopped daily or every other day. Mothers who worked full-time at home did this task, travelling on foot, and often pushing a baby buggy or pulling a wagon. Their preschool children accompanied them, carrying parcels, watching siblings, and helping in other ways. 'I can remember,' a woman recalled, 'walking into Kerrisdale when I was six and helping her bring home groceries.'

School-aged children also shopped after school. Girls in large families, or whose mothers worked outside of the home or were ill, found themselves at surprisingly early ages conducting most or all of the shopping. One woman recalled: 'I did the shopping every day, and would buy the meat for supper.' Such girls set out regularly with baby buggy, wagon, sled, or bicycle in which they stowed their purchases and, sometimes, a younger sibling or two. 'I had a wagon,' explained one woman, 'and my brother was only little, but I can remember taking him by the hand, and ... we used to go down to the ice place and get your block of ice and bring it home.' Another vividly recalled 'one trip when the bag broke and all the cans went rolling down the street.'

A few mothers were able to employ 'girls' to assist with housework.[15] A

Kerrisdale woman recalled, 'I don't know whether I was asked to do it, or whether I just liked to wipe the dishes for the maid ... We'd talk.' Another family 'brought out two Scottish maids that were sisters; first one, then the other. These girls were anxious to come to this country, and were nice to have.'

Mothers assigned housework to their sons only if they had no daughters available, and not always even then. As the youngest son in a family of three boys noted: 'We didn't do that much in the kitchen, I must say. I think Scottish mothers generally spoiled their sons, anyway.'[16] However, some male informants from both classes reported that they had helped around the house. One family of three Cedar Cottage sons reported that 'each week one of us would be doing dishes.' Another man explained that, 'after school, I'd start the fire, boil potatoes, and prepare ahead of time anything that needed to be done for dinner.' A middle-class woman said that she and her brother 'took turns getting up ... getting Daddy's breakfast, our own, and [their ailing] Mother's on a tray ... [They also] took turns setting the table, clearing the table, and washing and drying dishes.' Some shopped. 'My grandmother was very fussy; she sent me to the butcher shop on Broadway and would tell me to order two steaks, the butcher was to trim off the fat, and then he was to grind them into hamburger for Grandfather's favourite shepherd's pie,' reported a working-class Vancouver man. 'On Saturday morning,' said a Halifax man, 'I would take my cart and list of groceries, pick them up, and bring them home [which was] a fair distance.' A few cared for younger siblings. A boy, son of a deeply disturbed mother, not only learned in his early years to fend for himself, but also 'carefully protected his younger sister as best he could.'[17]

The fact that some boys did housework and shopped should not, however, mask the real differences between the sexes. First, and despite some contrary examples, most boys did little or no work in the traditional female sphere. Second, when parents did call on sons to do housework, they rarely expected the same standard of performance required of daughters. (A man recalled his father telling his sister that 'I want the toilet and tub immaculate!') Third, housework contributed to the different 'gender identities' of each sex. Since parents and sons alike looked on boys' housework merely as a chore, boys saw it as but a temporary phenomenon in their lives. Parents and daughters, on the other hand, looked on girls' housework as very much more than a chore. For them, housework was both an essential part of their practical education and an introduction to the culture of women. In other words, both girls and boys learned in one patriarchal setting how they would be expected to behave in another.[18]

Custom assigned men and boys the tasks involved in heating and maintaining the house, and looking after the grounds and garden. Although sometimes very time-consuming, this work was generally less demanding than the constant round of inside duties. In families with no daughters, and in families with a range of both boys and girls of appropriate ages, boys assumed the major responsibility in these areas. In families of both classes, however, parents generally asked daughters and sons alike to help with the 'outside' chores. Thus, 'inside' chores belonged to girls, but 'outside' ones to all the children.

Providing heat for warmth and cooking were the most important and time-consuming of 'outside' chores. Middle-class and working-class Vancouverites alike lived in uninsulated wood-frame houses. Until after the Second World War, most stoves, hot-water heaters, space heaters, and furnaces burned wood, wood and coal, coke, or sawdust. Since wood and sawdust were much cheaper than coal, the latter was used sparingly. Space heaters warmed houses without basements; hot-air furnaces heated those with partial or full basements. People recall that they 'didn't have a furnace, only a pot-bellied stove in the only warm room in the house,' and remember 'huddling around the stove,' especially in the morning. Except for the scrounging for coke or coal, most fuel-related chores undertaken by Vancouver children involved wood in one form or another.

In the late spring or early summer, families began to organize their wood supply for the following winter. Wood was sold by the cord, in wagon or, later, truck loads. Vancouverites recall that 'East Indian people would come around selling wood. We bought it by the cord'; that 'Father bought seven or eight cords of wood in the summer'; and that 'it took six double cords to heat our house in the winter.'

Families bought some dry wood, but most loads of fir 'edgings' and 'slabs,' only a day or two out of the water, arrived soaking wet. Sawdust adhered to each piece. 'I remember the pungent, sometimes sweet odour of the wood,' recalled one man. 'You could smell the difference between fir and cedar, for instance.' As a matter of course, both boys and girls helped store this wood, and many soon found themselves with the primary responsibility for it. By the time a family had put away a full winter's supply, tidy piles of drying wood traced their way along back and side fences, and the outside walls of woodsheds, garages, and the house itself. So that woodpiles would not rot what was behind them, parents demanded that they be free-standing. Most children found this work 'tedious.' There 'were splinters in it.' If one had gloves, they soon became soaking wet. As one man concluded, 'It was a good thing to get out of, but there was no getting out of it.'

For those families who could not afford a full year's supply of wood or who lacked storage space, procuring fuel proved considerably more oner-ous. Small loads of wet wood arrived intermittently over the winter. Chil-dren stacked it as best as they could out of the weather. They moved it from yard to spaces under porches, onto porches, and right inside the house in hallways or under beds. It was common for such families to run completely out of dry wood, and both heating and cooking became very difficult tasks for parents and children.

Sawdust - a fuel used in British Columbia from the mid-1930s onward - called for a different set of initial chores. Fuel companies delivered wet sawdust in bulk, by the sack, and, later, by blowing it through a flexible tube into basement sawdust bins. Since bulk-delivered sawdust cost less than sacked sawdust, many families bought their fuel in this form. A Cedar Cottage man reported: 'They used to sell sawdust in bulk ... We used to organize [other youngsters] to help us move it into the basement.' A middle-class Kerrisdale woman spoke for many children of both classes when she reported that she 'hated bringing in the sawdust. You used to get it in your fingers and I didn't like that.'

Tasks associated with the delivery of fuel merely initiated year-round duties. As soon as wood had dried sufficiently, families cut as much of it as could be stored in the woodshed or basement. One man reported, 'In sum-mer time ... I cut a hell of a pile of wood'; another that 'me and my brother would split the wood and bring it into the basement to dry.' Next, children did the daily and weekly chores that accompanied its use. Before leaving for school in the morning, when they came home at lunch-time and after school, before and after supper, and before they went to bed, children cut wood and kindling, and filled woodboxes, coal scuttles, and sawdust storage boxes.

People vividly recall all phases of these routines. 'You had to cut fire-wood,' reported one man, 'and you had to cut kindling for lighting the fire in the morning.' Another explained: 'I had to make sure that there was paper, kindling wood, and a scuttle of coal for the morning before I went to bed.' 'On an average day,' another reported, 'I would get up, stoke the coal and wood furnace ... [and] bring up three five-gallon pails [of sawdust] on each arm for the [kitchen stove].' 'On Saturday,' stated a fourth, 'we'd go out and split wood. Then you'd take a wheelbarrow and wheel the wood into the basement ... woodbin. Every morning before school you'd take out an armful and put it in the woodbox behind the stove.'

Sawdust plagued its child attendants with special problems. Since it was a dusty fuel, children cautiously moved it from storage bin to furnaces or to kitchen storage boxes, and then to the stove. Sawdust stoves and furnaces had a tendency to 'blow back,' shooting out smoke and burning bits of wood – especially when someone was adjusting the flow, pushing down blockages, or peering in to find out why it was not burning properly. Speaking for many, a middle-class woman reported, 'I was scared to death of it.' Another woman reported that 'a blow-out burned off both my eyebrows and eyelashes. I was scorched and frightened.' A third 'purposely' never learned to deal with the sawdust furnace, leaving it to her brother, because 'you only need to get one back-fire in the sawdust burner and you've got soot absolutely everywhere ... so just one of those and they never trusted me again; I hated that hopper.'

Changing technology in house heating gradually reduced children's seasonal and daily fuel chores. During the 1930s, some middle-class families installed coal stokers or stoves, space heaters, or furnaces that burned oil, but none of these expedients became common until after the Second World War.[19] Increased use of gas, oil, or electricity for cooking purposes cut sharply into the need for children to cut kindling and to keep fuel boxes and buckets filled; it also reduced the amount of nagging that mothers had to do. As home-heating sources shifted away from wood and coal to oil, gas, and electricity, the summer routines of moving, cutting, and piling wood began to disappear. By the late 1950s, only a minority of children would have understood the old saw about wood's ability to warm one twice.[20]

Parents (especially working-class parents) called on their children to help with all phases of the family gardening and other agricultural activities. Until well after the Second World War, most Vancouver neighbourhoods contained empty lots and even larger tracts of vacant land. 'Our house,' reported one east-side man, 'had a double lot. We grew our own potatoes and cabbage for all year. We also had fruit trees.' On the east side of the city in South Vancouver, many working-class families conducted intensive agriculture on a substantial scale.[21] They often raised chickens, pigeons, rabbits, turkeys, ducks, and even cows. A Cedar Cottage family operated a small dairy, had two barns, and also had 'chickens and ducks and a henhouse.' A woman from the same district noted that 'Dad had a chicken coop that took up the whole backyard,' and another explained that 'our backyard was big, so we had a small chicken farm, and rabbits.' Across town, in Kerrisdale, even in the 1950s a working-class family 'grew pretty much all of what we ate. We had turkeys once, geese and rabbits.' Families also grew vegetables, berries, fruit, and some annual and perennial flowers. One mother, for example, 'grew peas, beans, beets, carrots, Swiss chard, spinach, corn, and squash ... With five people in one house we went through a lot of fruit and vegetables.'

Middle-class families generally confined themselves to gardening and rarely raised animals. One Kerrisdale salesman developed two lots, building a house on one and, on the other, putting in 'a lovely garden with fruit trees and vegetables'; another Kerrisdale father 'took up the whole of the back yard with his garden, but the front yard was for us.' During the Second World War, families who were not regular gardeners planted 'Victory' gardens, both as a matter of patriotism and to provide vegetables that might be in short supply.

'I hated weeding,' a lament uttered by a middle-class man, was echoed by his working-class counterpart who 'never volunteered to work in the garden. I hated gardening.' On the other hand, one working-class Halifax boy had a backyard garden – 'my kingdom' – where he grew potatoes, carrots, and other vegetables, and kept hens 'for their fresh eggs.' Each spring, vegetable gardens had to be dug and raked, and old plants and roots removed. 'It was,' reported one man, 'hard work getting the ground ready because we did all the work by hand.' During the late spring and summer, children found themselves hilling potatoes, killing insects, and endlessly weeding. In the words of one, 'It was up to me to weed, hill the potatoes, do the watering, and things like that.' One woman did not mind hoeing, weeding, or harvesting so much as 'when we planted we had to go between the lumps of manure and put the seeds in.'

Summer and fall brought the harvest of both the 'free' crop of berries which grew abundantly in and around Vancouver, and family-grown fruit and vegetables. Children would 'go and get blueberries and huckleberries,' would 'pick blackberries in Foxy's field' or 'cranberries at Burnaby Lake.' One woman has 'vivid memories of hay cutting, piling it and carting it to the barn,' and a man recalls that 'we used to dig up the potatoes and bring them home [from the allotment] sack by sack in a wagon.' Animals involved chores all year round. One girl 'fed the chickens before school [and] collected the eggs at night'; another 'would pluck [the chickens] but wouldn't watch them being killed.'

Through activities that were often described as 'scrounging,' many working-class children made an accepted, even required, and sometimes essential contribution to family economies.[22] Recourse to such practice was certainly not confined to improvident families. Although the father of a working-class Cedar Cottage family 'felt that respectability was very important,' his daughter reported that, when fir logs were unloaded from the train, 'there'd be pieces of bark left behind [and] we'd go with sacks and take bark to burn in the stove.' Other children collected and sold wood for pocket money. A man from a self-described 'respectable' working-class

Halifax family would scour the lanes for wood, cut it into kindling, and sell it for five cents a bag.

Scrounging children made their most important contribution by supplementing the family fuel supply. In cities and towns across the country, families with limited means or storage space searched for free fuel. Children looked along lanes and around building sites for wooden packing cases and other scrap wood, around the coal gas plant for partially burned coal, and along railway tracks for coal or old railway ties. People reported that the 'boys went to the train tracks for coal all summer long. They would get enough for the winter'; that 'we'd torment firemen so they would throw coal at us'; and 'we used to bring old railway ties and cut them up for firewood.' In and around Vancouver, driftwood provided abundant fuel for families living near the river or the sea. Some families also cut cord-wood from second-growth timber in the city's large tracts of 'bush.'

Children also scrounged for their families' animals and gardens. They cut grass on boulevards, in vacant lots, and in neighbours' yards to get feed for rabbits, cows, or horses. In Vancouver's east end in the 1920s, Elisa Martini Negrin gathered hay from vacant lots, boulevards, and the railway yards. 'We would,' she reported, 'start at 6 o'clock in the morning and we'd go on until 8 or 9 at night, until it got dark.'[23] Since no urban informants reported that their family or neighbours kept pigs, health authorities had probably succeeded in eliminating this traditional budget supplement in Vancouver's suburban neighbourhoods. Although trucks gradually replaced horse-drawn drays in transporting large goods, until the 1950s horse-drawn carts carried milk and bread and collected junk on residential neighbourhoods' streets and back lanes. Gardening parents valued the droppings from delivery-van horses, and their children 'had to go out with a shovel and get the manure.' Many youngsters found this an embarrassing chore. It was 'awful, really awful' to go up and down the streets with a wagon and shovel searching for it.

Children also disliked scrounging that virtually cast them into the role of beggars or thieves. Some parents sent their youngsters to ask the green grocer for stale vegetables for 'our rabbits,' or to the baker to offer a penny or two for stale loaves, or to the butcher for a bone 'for our dog.' In this way, explained one person, 'we could get a bag of bones free for soup.' In Vancouver, 'kids collected gleanings from ships at the docks, bananas and stuff. Some we sold, some we took home.' In Halifax men 'unloading mackerel kept count by setting aside one fish out of each bucket. Kids would steal their "counts."' At Hallowe'en, in Lethbridge during the Depression, some children 'came round to the doors with large sacks hoping, not for candies, but for donations of food which they could take home to their families.' In

Vancouver in the 1940s, the Children's Aid Society took six-year-old 'Evelyn' into care because her father encouraged her and three older siblings to beg on the streets. In the 1950s, the five children of a single-parent family on welfare 'would steal from a local supermarket ... [and] Mother would just have to not acknowledge it at all.'[24]

Children also patrolled lanes, vacant lots, and dumps for scrap metal, car batteries (for lead), and other items they could sell. Some 'collected junk for a cent a pound. Brass, copper, and lead were worth more.' Since junk dealers rarely asked for the source of the goods they were offered, scrounging children sometimes stole rather than found their wares. Others would collect 'old medicine bottles, bring them home and wash them, and take them back to the druggist. You would get a dime for a dozen of them.' Others collected cigarette butts for the tobacco they contained. Those who lived near golf courses, explained a Kerrisdale man, 'would go to look for lost golf balls late Thursday afternoon. The doctors always played on Thursday.'

Children whose parents owned small businesses put in long hours working in them. Their unpaid, or virtually unpaid, labour often provided the margin that kept such enterprises afloat. A Cedar Cottage woman, whose mother had a small grocery, 'had to deliver groceries after school ... In those little stores, you're there all the time. And so us kids learned to do all the housework and cook and everything else before we were knee-high to a grasshopper.' A man from the same neighbourhood reported that, from age six, 'I delivered bread every day [from his father's bakery] after school and on Saturdays ... I was given a dollar every week but was expected to use it to buy my clothes. I saved enough money to buy my own bike.' Another baker's son reported, 'I was the delivery boy, Father baked, and Mother worked up front.' A west-side woman reported that, after her father, a banker, died, her mother opened a nursing home. As well as attending school, she 'helped with the cooking, washing, ironing, and supper trays. At age thirteen I was considered a full adult with adult responsibilities.'

In addition to assigning them common chores, parents of both classes set children to many other tasks. If a job needed doing that was within their capabilities, girls and boys generally found themselves undertaking it. They washed walls and automobiles; they swept or cleaned basements, especially around coal and sawdust bins. They took fathers' and boarders' lunches to workplaces. 'My dad,' said one Powell River woman, 'worked in the Sulphite ... My mom used to make hot meals for him, and I would run down and up the stairs and into the mill and give him his hot meal. Just a lid on a plate.' A developer's son helped clear land and build a house for their family. Boys and girls helped in home decorating and prepared the family's home-made toilet paper from catalogues and other sources. One father raised birds for a hobby, and his children 'used to have to clean the cages and feed the birds.' One boy regularly accompanied his father on fishing expeditions to places that could be reached by streetcar. They fished for a wide variety of fish – rock cod, tommy cod, lingcod, and even sturgeon: 'It all helped financially since Dad didn't work too much.' During the Depression, while his father was laid off, a Kerrisdale boy sold eggs laid by the family's chickens, from door to door: 'We not only lived on eggs, we sold them.'

Middle-class children, as some of them explained, 'had to mow the lawn ... rake leaves' and 'help in the garden.' Postwar affluence, with its ever-proliferating packaging, and the ever-thickening newspapers that were no longer needed for lighting stoves and furnaces, combined into enough waste material to make wrapping and carrying out the daily garbage, and care of the area around garbage cans, into a regular chore.

As they grew older, boys and girls of both classes began to work at regular and irregular part-time, paying jobs as child-minders, delivery boys, sales clerks, and labourers in other forms of unskilled work. Boys, who usually had more time to devote to work outside the household, found a much wider range of opportunities to work, higher wages, and considerably more jobs in total than their sisters. Consequently, boys' affluence relative to their sisters' sometimes sparked jealousy and acrimony in families.

In those days when most householders expected 'free delivery,' boys began work as delivery or errand boys as early as their eighth or ninth year. One man explained that he 'worked from the time I was nine years old delivering groceries for a grocery store'; another noted that 'from age eleven I always had a job.' They worked for grocery and produce stores, butcher shops, hardware stores, drugstores, and fish and chip shops. Employers generally paid delivery boys on a piece-work basis. Many boys in east-side Vancouver, for example, worked at one time for one of the small chain of Curry's grocery stores.[25] Clerks packed grocery orders into boxes of a size that would fit into a bicycle carrier. Right after school, Curry's delivery boys rushed in to work, with the first arrival taking the box with the shortest distance to go, or one bound for a customer known to tip. Later arrivals 'sometimes ... had to go a mile or more.' Some older or bigger boys insisted that prize deliveries belonged to them by right, but usually the grocer enforced a first-come, first-pick rule. After collecting his 'change,' which usually contained at least one nickel or dime to encourage tipping, the boy rushed off with his box. If he was lucky, he might get in two more deliveries before all the boxes were gone, but most made only two deliveries each day. When Saturday's rush was over, the manager paid out the week's earnings at a rate of ten cents per delivery. With an average of fifteen deliveries a week, a boy earned $1.50 to add to whatever he had already collected in tips. Thus one lad, in addition to tips, regularly 'made about $2.00 per week ... $1.50 for delivering groceries [for Curry's] and 50 cents for delivering handbills.' By the late 1940s, the rate of pay for deliveries had increased to twenty or twenty-five cents an hour, and rose again in the 1950s, before the practice faded away.

In other shops, boys' jobs tended to include inside work as well as deliveries. In one hardware store, 'the worst thing was unpacking china from barrels in which it had been packed in wood shavings and washing the shavings off in cold water.' An eleven-year-old who 'had to go to work in a butcher shop' reported: 'I tried to clean out chicken guts, which I didn't like and wasn't good at, so I made sausages instead.' Another man explained: 'if I was lucky I could get a job on Saturday with [the breadman]; I would get to feed the horses, hold the reins, and got all the leftover bread free.' Another boy 'worked [in a drugstore] after school, sweeping up and stocking shelves.' One boy even stole 'some pencils ... but [the druggist] let me back to work even after that.' Unlike most stores, drugstores stayed open in the evening, and their delivery boys often worked until 9:00 P.M. or later.

Most delivery jobs required youngsters to provide their own bicycles. As one man noted, for a delivery job, 'all you had to have was a bicycle,' and a typical newspaper advertisement called for 'Boy with wheel for meat market; good wages.'[26] A Toronto boy bought his balloon-tired delivery bike 'for a dollar down and a dollar a week.' Parents often made, or helped their sons make, this capital purchase so that they could take such jobs. One father, employed as a longshoreman, bought his son 'this bike; he wanted me to earn some money.'

The market provided a hierarchy of jobs in magazine and newspaper sales and delivery. Young boys – and a few girls – distributed handbills, and sold seeds, Christmas cards, or magazines, especially *Liberty* and *The Saturday Evening Post*, to friends, neighbours, and door-to-door. 'During the Depression,' reported one man, 'I used to deliver *Liberty*. ... You were lucky if you made two dollars a month.' Some were paid to deliver weekly community newspapers. Most boys, however, wanted to become regular sellers or 'carriers' for a daily newspaper. In the 1920s, some still sold papers in the traditional way. 'When I was about nine years old,' one man reported, 'I had a corner where I sold the morning paper ... I was there at five every morning. The fog was terrible. The cold air went right through me.' Since such boys were more likely to be late for school, or to skip it altogether, than those who had regular delivery routes, they were the particular targets of those trying to get children out of the street trades. By the end of the 1920s, school-attendance regulations and attendance officers had sharply reduced the ranks of those newsboys and other youthful street pedlars who worked full-time. Others continued selling on corners after school. In the 1930s in Victoria, Malcolm Harper reported, downtown corners were 'owned by a newsboy until 6 P.M., and he controlled halfway up the block in both directions ... For $7 I purchased the southwest corner of View and Douglas.'[27] In Vancouver in 1945, Danny Flick sold up to 150 papers a day in the downtown area after school, 'hitting restaurants and hotels.'[28]

In these circumstances newspapers shifted to a 'route' method of circulating their product. In cities with more than one newspaper, most boys aspired to deliver the one with the greatest circulation. Until the long, bitter battle between the Vancouver *Daily Province* and the International Typographers Union began in 1946, this newspaper had the largest circulation, and thus Vancouver boys wanted *Province* routes. After the *Vancouver Sun* achieved permanent dominance of the Vancouver market in the 1950s, it naturally became the most popular paper with delivery boys. As a morning paper over part of this period, the *Vancouver News-Herald* provided both the advantages and disadvantages that came to boys who delivered morning papers anywhere in Canada. Those who so wished could deliver their papers before going to school, then take other part-time work after school or participate in sports or other recreational activities. However, since the *News-Herald* had the smallest circulation in the city, its routes covered fairly long distances. Its carriers also had to rise early and do much of their work in the dark. As one reported, 'to deliver the *News-Herald*, I used to get up at 4:30 in the morning.'

In Vancouver, the newspapers trucked their papers to the local newspaper 'shack.' Here boys picked up their 'daily draw,' and on Saturday 'stuffed' them with the weekly 'funny papers' and other supplements, and headed out on their rounds. Boys who wanted routes turned up regularly at the shack, helped other boys, delivered the routes of those who were ill or away, and gradually worked themselves to the top of the waiting list. Particularly during the Depression, some never made it there. Shacks often provided a rough initiation. As one victim explained, 'They gave me a rough time ... and the shack manager wasn't much better ... he would hit out at times ... [and] was very loud-mouthed.' A Chinese-Canadian boy so suffered at the hands of companion paper boys that 'he and another boy [went] early to the supply hut so that they avoid the bigger boys who intimidate them' and took their papers home to fold.[29] Throughout these years, once paperboys acquired good routes, they tended to hold onto them until they left school.

Newsboys gather at a 'shack' in New Westminster in 1933.

Newspaper routes ranged in size from about forty papers to just over a hundred. One boy 'got up at 4:00 A.M. and had forty papers to deliver'; another 'had about 80 to 90'; a third 'delivered in apartments, with approximately 100 subscribers.' In fine weather, boys found their task a pleasant one, with opportunities to chat with friends and customers. When it rained or snowed, however, they 'wrapped their papers in brown waxed paper' and worked through their routes as quickly as possible, often returning home soaked to the skin.

Newspapers companies did not actually employ their paperboys. Instead, they treated them as independent 'businessmen' who bought their newspapers wholesale and retailed them to their subscribers. At the end of the weekly or monthly circulation period, the newspapers presented a bill to each carrier, which he had to pay within a few days. The carriers, in turn, collected subscription payments from their customers. The difference between what a boy owed and what he could rightfully collect constituted his profit. Even in areas where most people had regular jobs, boys found it difficult to collect all that they were owed. One boy 'delivered along a good route with well-to-do people, but these people were hard to collect from.' Boys had to call at some homes many times before they collected what was owed to them. If the subscriber went two or three months in arrears, or 'skipped,' the manager was supposed to help collect the money, but not always to any effect. As one man lamented, 'lots of people skipped out and the money came out of your pocket!'[30]

Newspapers obliged carriers to take part in efforts to increase circulation. They gave out cash awards or prizes to carriers who secured certain number of new subscriptions, and sometimes penalized those who failed to do so. One carrier 'was fired because the rule was that paperboys had to get two new subscribers a month and [I] failed to do so.' Newspapers also conducted subscription 'drives' in which all the carriers in a shack turned out to call on every non-subscribing home in a selected area. As one reported, 'we had drives on Wednesday and Friday nights. I neglected my homework [but] won some campaigns ... I got a trip to Keats Island.'

Although most boys earned their money in delivery jobs, some found other forms of employment. 'When I was fourteen,' said one man, 'my uncle got me a job in Melrose Dairy.' In Brandon, Manitoba, twelve-year-old Grant MacEwan 'sold vegetables nearly all summer and, what was particularly remunerative, the sale of mushrooms. A few of these lowly plants grew on our lot, but other carefully guarded beds were located and visited with maximum secrecy.'[31] A Powell River boy 'used to go and cut wood and kindling for a person and pack it in the house every day after school. For that, I got a dollar a week.' In the 1920s, a Vancouver boy stacked wood for neighbours for fifty cents a load. Boys also found work as pin-setters, as caddies, and as helpers on milk and bread wagons. In the late 1940s, a working-class Cedar Cottage boy 'earned good money. I worked from 7:00 to 10:30 four nights a week [in a bowling alley] and earned between $60 and $70 a month!'

Snow provided an irregular but welcome source of income. When it fell, many boys headed out with shovels to clear sidewalks and driveways. After a big snow, one man reported, 'I got up, [but] nothing for breakfast was in the house, so went off without anything to eat ... As I was shovelling snow I got weak and passed out. Another kid came along, brought me to, and finished shovelling for me. He wouldn't take any of the money.' Some enterprising boys even created work with the snow. 'We would,' reported one, 'pile up snow at points where cars got stuck, and help dig them out and be tipped, and then put the snow back again.'

During summer holidays, some boys, most nearing school-leaving age, found full-time work in factories or canneries, or on farms. In 1927, for example, the provincial Department of Labour 'found four boys, one in a boiler shop, two in a cold storage plant and one in a woodworking plant.'[32] In 1928, the department permitted seventeen children under age fifteen to work in canneries; in 1929, twenty-four children; and, in 1930, eighteen children.[33] When he was nine years old, Sing Lim began to spend his summers working full-time on a farm owned by a friend of his father's. 'I was probably more a nuisance than a real help that first summer,' he reported. 'We worked from 6:30 in the morning to 7:30 at night every day except Sunday, when we finished at noon.'[34] As a 'fourteen-year-old officially passing for sixteen,' Rolf Knight's first full-time job 'was as a messboy and spare hand on a coastal passenger-freight ship in the summer of 1950.'[35]

Most girls who found part-time work did so in caring for other families' children. Some began by working without pay, partly because they liked babies or young children (or felt they were expected to like them), and partly to gain experience. After completing her own chores, a Kerrisdale girl, from age eight onward, helped the mother of three who lived next door: 'When I got to be about eleven, I would bath them and take them out for a walk while their mother prepared supper.' Another reported that, before she started paid babysitting, she 'had pushed babies out in their carriages for free.' As such girls got older, they moved on to more regular work as 'child-minders' or 'mothers' helpers,' as they were customarily called until after the Second World War. In working-class neighbourhoods, families employed child-minders only out of absolute necessity, to enable mothers to go out to work, to shop, or to deal with sickness or some other family emergency. One Cedar Cottage woman explained that 'people didn't go out in that neighbourhood much' and another noted that 'nobody had any money for babysitting; I never heard of babysitting' of the sort that came of parents going out for recreational purposes. One girl there made lunch for a little girl and took another 'for a walk for fifteen cents an hour.'

Increasing prosperity after 1945 enabled more families in both classes to employ babysitters as a matter of choice rather than as a matter of necessity. The greater availability of this work coincided with the shift in terminology from 'child-minding' to 'babysitting.' A Kerrisdale woman outlined the pattern of a babysitting career as it was towards the end of the 1950s: 'I started about ten ... being a mother's helper ... I remember taking the neighbour's kids for a walk so the mother could be free ... I was not left alone at night. [Later, at about age fourteen] I babysat ... for five boys and I'd go away with them in the summertime ... [and] I babysat for another family.' Like other child workers, babysitters could be exploited by their employers. One woman explained that 'the woman I sat for was known for not paying regularly. Often she would say she hadn't enough change, [but] the next time I babysat I didn't have the courage to ask for the money owed me.' Another remembered one family with 'about six or seven kids that I used to have an endless fight with, but I think I got what was equivalent to twelve and a half cents an hour' when the prevailing rate was twenty-five cents.

Girls found other sorts of part-time work. To one, 'the selling of Christmas cards was indeed a source of revenue. Scavenging bottles was not beneath my dignity, when the lure of "cherry strides" pictured in Eaton's catalogue became too strong.' During the summer holidays, many girls (and some boys) could find work picking berries and hops on farms near Vancouver. Thus, in June 1930, Lakeshore Farm of Hatzic wanted 'girls for raspberry picking': and, in June 1940, a Burnaby farm wanted '10 girls to pick raspberries.'[36] While some advertisements for pickers specified 'girls over 15,' most did not mention age.[37] If employers checked ages at all, they did so perfunctorily. In turn, the children told them what they wanted to hear – that they were, indeed, 'over fifteen.' A Cedar Cottage girl no more than thirteen years old 'used to go out picking berries. And we'd start off with strawberries ... and we'd pick raspberries, loganberries, and we'd end up picking hops. So I was always two weeks late coming back to school.' Picking was piece-work, and the really nimble and persistent could make more money this way than in many other summer jobs.

Older girls clerked part-time in neighbourhood or downtown stores. A Kerrisdale girl got 'my first job at "Sweet Sixteen," when I was just thirteen.' An east-side girl, whose father was a small merchant, worked from age fifteen onward at part-time jobs at Woodward's, Famous, and the Sally Shop: 'I had to put myself through [school].' At Christmas in the late 1940s, one Grade Eight girl worked in a 'fifteen-cent store' and 'quite enjoyed the experience,' so from then on 'worked on Saturdays.' One enterprising Kitsilano girl at age fourteen or fifteen used to beachcomb for logs from a rowboat. 'I used to bring the logs back to Barnacle Bill ... He gave me $3.00 a log.'[38]

Especially in the 1920s and 1930s, children's part-time earnings formed an important and sometimes an essential part of family economies. The earnings of working-class children often stood between their families and real hardship, and occasionally helped avert complete economic collapse. As Charles Dougan reported, it was 'expected in our house and others that the money earned by the older boys would go to keeping the house and it is doubtful if my parents could have kept their heads above water financially if this principle hadn't been applied.'[39] And, whatever the family circumstances, until after the Second World War, most working-class children turned their earnings over to their parents. As one put it, 'our money was pooled in the family pot, not kept for personal use.' In the 1920s, a Cedar Cottage boy 'delivered papers for four years but didn't get to keep the money. I had to turn it over to Mother and got an allowance of twenty-five cents.' In the mid-1930s an east-side boy worked from age twelve to fourteen as a delivery boy from 4:00 to 6:00 P.M. on weekdays and 10:00 A.M. to 6:00 P.M. on Saturdays, kept 25 cents of his $1.75 weekly earnings, and gave the rest to the family. In the Depression, a Powell River girl sold daffodils: 'We'd stand on a street corner or go door-to-door. That's how we got our shoes to start school with in September.' In 1934, the Depression drove a family from Winnipeg to Vancouver. The father, a bookkeeper, found only occasional work to support his wife and five children. The eldest, then twelve years old, found himself 'thrust into responsibility very young in life ... I had two sometimes three [paper] routes, 70 papers in one, 112 in another ... I gave $10.00 a month to Mom; $8.00 for rent, $1.50 for light ... I kept what was made above $10.00.'

After the Second World War, high levels of employment and a rising standard of living permitted many working-class families to allow their children to keep some or all of their earnings. In the early 1950s, a Cedar Cottage boy, earning about twenty dollars a month on his paper route, 'spent most of my money on junk; pop, ice cream, etc.' Another, a millwright's son, found a job, on his own, at age twelve as a drugstore delivery boy: 'It was totally my own decision that I should look for a job ... and I could keep the job ... as long as my marks and grades didn't get into trouble ... Economically I was somebody ... and it gave me a great sense of independence and freedom to have ten or fifteen dollars ... to go and say I'm going to buy a shirt or whatever.' In the late 1940s, a Cedar Cottage girl held two part-time jobs from age fourteen onward and 'was the only one in the family with a bank account ... [which she held] to save to go to Europe.'

As middle-class youngsters bought some or all of their clothes, school supplies, and entertainment, their earnings also reduced pressures on tight family budgets. However, except for a few families in the worst part of the Depression, children's income rarely made the difference between a family having, or not having, enough money to provide themselves with the bare essentials of food, clothing, and shelter. However, one boy, whose father had been laid off during the Depression but got work again in wartime, 'worked all day on Saturday delivering [meat] all over the Kerrisdale area ... I gave all my money to my parents, except a dollar for pocket money,' to help pay off the mortgage. His two brothers and two sisters also contributed from their part-time work.

More representative was the Kerrisdale girl who babysat ('not on school nights') and then worked part-time at Woodward's in the late 1940s, 'didn't save any money, I spent it [often on] things I was forbidden to have' such as 'high-heel shoes, make-up, and even cigarettes.' Another Kerrisdale girl 'made lots of money babysitting.' She saved most of it for clothing. Her father (employing a very common middle-class practice) would pay for 'the standard [jacket] and if I wanted to make up the difference I could have the other one.' A middle-class Kerrisdale man, who received a small allowance, reported that 'if I wanted anything extra special I worked for it. My sister had polio and needed many operations.' Another delivered the *Province*, 'which sold for $1.00 a month, with 30 cents for myself ... Thirty dollars was big money.' In the 1940s, an east-side minister's daughter spent her babysitting and other money on clothes because, otherwise, as 'was fairly common then,' she had 'had one new outfit a year that I wore every day.'

Contrary to legal constraints, and usually with the conivance of parents, some children entered the full-time workforce before their fifteenth birthdays.[40] In 1918, thirteen-year-old Joe Olson became a full-time deckhand on the Vancouver harbour tug of which his father was the master.[41] Particularly in the 1920s and 1930s, a few employers even advertised for children of legal school age.[42] Census takers in 1921 reported only 117 Vancouver children under age fifteen in full-time work, while their successors in 1931 found a mere 48.[43] Although other evidence suggests that there were more children in full-time work than the census takers discovered, it does not indicate that the number was large.[44] In a study of the 1929–30 school year, the Vancouver School Board found 'that over four hundred pupils of compulsory age withdrew, and that most of these were not granted exemption in the usual way.' The 'chief reasons ... were economic, lack of ability to do and of interest in school work, and a desire to go to work.'[45] Most, indeed, appear to have been almost old enough to leave school legally. George Johnston was perhaps one of those the board investigated. 'Proficiency in hookey forced him out of school, so at fourteen he began working at Woodward's in the meat department.'[46]

What sorts of full-time work did these children do? To authorities like the truant officers, those in the street trades, especially newsboys, were the most conspicuous group.[47] In the 1920s, provincial factory inspectors 'found an occasional child under the age of 14 working in a factory,' but, by 1932, the labour department claimed that child labour was 'almost unknown' in British Columbia.[48] In 1931, among the children aged fourteen and under in full-time work, thirteen of the thirty-two boys were messengers, and ten of the sixteen girls were in service.[49] One man explained that, in February of his Grade Eight year, at age fourteen, he went to work in a rope factory, where his first job was to 'spool up wire onto bobbins.'[50] A Cedar Cottage man reported that, in 1920, 'at the start of the summer holidays, my mother ... heard that [a downtown company] ... wanted a delivery boy. It was ten dollars a week for a forty-five-hour week ... I gave my mother the ten dollars every Saturday and she'd give me fifty cents spending money ... and she bought my car tickets ... Well, at the end of August ... that ten dollars was such a big help to my parents that I was told to keep the job.' The school authorities took no action in his case, probably because he turned fifteen towards the end of October.[51] In the early 1930s, when Phyllis McMillan of Aiyansh was twelve years old, she joined her family in seasonal work at the North Pacific Cannery at Port Edward. Under the 'Chinese contract system,' she was hired to 'shoot cans' from the can runway into baskets and take them to the 'hand fillers.' She worked twelve 'very boring' hours every day. 'Our pay was eight cents an hour.'[52]

Although census figures report that more boys than girls entered full-time work before they legally were old enough to do so, the actual situation was probably the reverse. Both because of their superior home-making skills and the fact that boys could get paid work more easily and earn more than their sisters, girls rather than boys stayed home full-time in cases of domestic necessity. These working girls tended to be invisible to census takers and truant officers. The census of 1941, for example, classified boys working full-time on a family farm or in a parent's business as 'no pay' workers, but such girls were 'not classified as being gainfully employed at all.'[53] Older daughters of large families sometimes missed much or all of their schooling to help their busy or ailing mothers. Agatha Raso, born in Italy in 1911, came to Canada in 1921, the oldest of six children, and 'started to go to school a little bit.' Soon, however, she 'had to stay home and help my mother with the boarders. Believe me, I had only two years of education ... I wanted to go to school, but I couldn't go.'[54] A Powell River woman explained: 'My mother was sick so I took over the house about, well, when my brother was born I was twelve. She was sick for quite a while ... I more or less took on the house.' A First Nations woman, born in the 1920s, reported that she had 'no education except how to look after my mother's babies, and housework.'[55]

Young girls whose families could not afford to care for them, or whose potential earnings were needed, often went into domestic service. A Cedar Cottage girl, who had skipped one grade and thus finished Grade Eight at age thirteen, went to work for 'five dollars a month and my board as a mother's helper ... you just worked in the house and you were there all the time ... It was wonderful, three months later, I got eight dollars a month ... I got married about seventeen and kept on working till I was nineteen ... I worked for four or five different families.' Newspaper 'help wanted' columns contained many advertisements for girls for 'general housework' or to 'assist with children.'[56] Some specified that the girls would 'sleep out,' while others, such as one for a 'strong girl for scrubbing,' would 'sleep in.'[57] Of more than forty such advertisements appearing in the Vancouver Province on six different days during September and October 1935, twenty did not specify a rate of pay.[58] Of the rest, one offered $5.00 a month for a 'young girl, mother's help; room and board,' two others offered $8.00 a month for the same services, three offered $10.00 for 'housework,' five offered $12.00 or $12.50, seven offered $15.00, and one offered $20.00 a month. Given this range of rates, it is likely that only the most inexperienced and underaged would work for five to eight dollars a month.

Girls placed in foster homes by the Children's Aid Society or those by agencies that gave assistance to pregnant girls often found themselves working especially hard. One man reported that his parents had acquired a thirteen-year-old 'foster sister' for himself and his two brothers – aged five, three, and one – who in fact became a full-time house servant and nanny. 'She had an awful life, with real chores, hard work. My father never spoke to her and wouldn't even look at her.' After she had given up her baby, a thirteen-year-old was placed in a home where the foster parents needed a lot of help, 'which at first she willingly gave. But as time went on [she] resented the household chores.'[59] In another case, in her twelfth foster home, and one in which the pregnant foster mother had a seven-year-old stepchild, a five-year-old stepchild, and a year-old infant of her own, the foster mother wanted the thirteen-year-old girl to be a 'mother's helper,' but the youngster 'just did not see the work to be done.'[60]

The Second World War brought something of a boom to those children old enough to work outside the home, whether full- or part-time. In the words of one, 'you could always get a job in the 1940s.' Men and women moved out of the most menial and low-paid of full-time jobs and were, in turn, replaced by those who had just left school, and by underaged youngsters. As the labour shortage intensified, governments began to ease legislative restriction on child labour.[61] Thus, in the early 1940s, a twelve-year-old Cedar Cottage girl started full-time work in a laundry. 'I was the oldest, so I went to help the family. We needed the money; twelve dollars went a long way. I liked the idea that I could help my dad [a soldier who owned a car] if I wanted to.' She was not alone; the women who customarily worked in laundries and similar occupations had gone to the shipyards, 'so the companies turned to kids.' At about the same time in Halifax, a boy aged twelve or thirteen went to work one summer as a boiler chipper, scaler, and bilge cleaner. 'In one of the little compartments just big enough to squat in, with a bucket and clean rags, I would mop up oil and water off the floor, fill the bucket, and pass it back via the crew behind. The smaller you were, the closer to the front you worked. I worried about a short circuit in the [power] line. It was very hard on the nerves.' At the end of the summer, his family insisted he continue work, and he did so cleaning up the railway yard, sweeping out boxcars and other 'dirty work.'

The end of the war, which also saw the introduction of family allowances, marked the end of full-time child labour as a widely perceived social problem in Canada. In July 1945, the federal government sent out the first family allowance cheques to mothers whose children were fifteen years old and younger. Since children working for wages or improperly absent from school were ineligible for family allowances, school attendance among older children improved markedly.[62] In all of British Columbia, the 1951 census found only 437 boys and 70 girls under fifteen in full-time work.[63] The attention of society and school authorities shifted to school 'drop-outs,' a group made up of those who went to work, legally, before they completed high school.[64]

None the less, school-attendance officers and social workers discovered a few children who still worked virtually full-time, especially in domestic situations. A financially hard-up family in which both parents worked for wages often kept one of its three sons home from school to care for his four-year-old sister.[65] In another case, a twelve-year-old boy worked twenty-five to thirty hours a week helping his widowed mother with her small street-vending candy business.[66] After being reported for frequent absences from her Grade Six classroom, one girl poignantly described her family situation: 'There was a new baby at Christmas time and three-year-old twins. Her mother had been ill and she had to stay with the children while her mother went to the doctor ... and did her shopping.' When she did go to school she found 'a lot of work to do' when she came home. 'She would like to go to bed at 8:30, but it is often 10:00 or 10:30 before she does ... [and] she has the responsibility of waking the family in the morning.'[67] By the 1940s and 1950s attending school for the required number of years had become so much a matter of social custom as well as of law that children themselves felt that attending school was a necessary part of their lives. This 'pale, thin, and worried-looking' girl, for example, didn't 'want to fail as all her relatives have passed.'[68]

Why did children work? The answer to this question is more complex than might initially be apparent. First, obviously, they worked because families, and especially mothers, needed their help. Most working-class and many middle-class families functioned within extremely tight budgets. Continued solvency demanded a very cautious creating and husbanding of resources by means of the domestic labour of all family members. As well, in all but the richest households, which could hire help, domestic comfort also required a lot of work; inevitably, parents insisted that their children share in this labour. Children accepted their household duties as a 'given' of their lives. As one woman put it: 'We always had things to do,' a sentiment echoed by the man who reported, 'Whatever there was to do, you did it.' 'Really,' reported Tadao Wakabayashi, 'we had no time to play, because Dad was in business and any spare moments we had to work. And after we finished work, then we sat down and tried to do our homework, two homeworks, the Japanese and the English.'[69]

Second, parents of both classes distrusted idleness in their children and were keen to keep them busy. 'It was like an unwritten eleventh commandment,' wrote David Weale, '"Thou shalt work hard," and was supported by a popular proverb, ... "The devil finds work for idle hands."'[70] Many children heard the refrain: 'There is nothing for nothing.' Parents' own experience gave substance to the cultural ideology: in their own childhoods they themselves had worked both inside and outside their homes.[71] Child-care experts and others in authority supported the conventional wisdom on the merits of chores. As one of the 'Little Blue Books' argued, 'Children ... want to "Help Mother" and "Help Father" ... Let them help, and let them keep right on all through life ... The useful people begin young!'[72] A mental-hygiene clinic blamed 'spoiling' at home for the poor performance of a Grade One pupil. 'He has received no training at home in jobs and responsibility which indicates that he has had little encouragement to grow.'[73] When an 'incorrigible' fourteen-year-old boy's therapy sessions conflicted with his paper route, social workers 'decided that the paper route was of more value than continued play therapy.'[74]

John Calam's account of how, as a new arrival to Canada from England in the early 1940s, he took on a paper route and bought the necessary bicycle on credit amusingly highlights a common national attitude. His Canadian uncle had to intercede with his father, who argued that 'no son of mine is going to make it appear I don't support him.'[75] To the uncle (and Canadian parents generally) to take on such a task showed that a child was sensitive to family needs and was helping out. It also showed to parents (and their friends and neighbours) that their children had the required amount of 'get up and go.' As well, many working-class parents believed that their children had a duty to contribute to the family economy as a partial repayment of the costs the family incurred by rearing them. The matter-of-fact way in which children turned over most or all of their earnings to their parents perhaps suggests that they, too, accepted the legitimacy of this notion.[76]

If children worked because they had to, they also worked because they wanted to. A Halifax woman reported picking blueberries 'all day' and feeling 'pretty bedraggled by the end,' but 'you felt you were doing your part.' Talking of her work helping her mother in the garden, and in canning, one woman explained that 'I really appreciated that cooperative spirit of doing something together. I really liked the family togetherness.' A ten-year-old foster child, 'exceeding anxious to please,' insisted 'on chopping wood and digging in the garden, etc.'[77] Adults who expressed resentment over burdens placed on them as children were usually those who believed that their parents treated them unfairly by demanding contributions of time and effort that greatly exceeded family needs or community norms. One man reported that he and his brother had to spend all their after-school, weekend, and summer-vacation time working in their father's extensive garden. 'We used to see the other kids go by, and really hated our father for the way he kept us from ever playing with them.'

Making a contribution also added to children's sense of self-worth and gave them the feeling that they were moving towards independence. Children who earned money could view their activities as a step in the process of freeing themselves from their parents.[78] The income of the boy who supported his family during the Depression with two, and sometimes three, newspaper routes, for example, made him an important authority figure in the family, contemptuous of his unemployed father and, although fond of his mother, not above small displays of power over her as well. In a less extreme way, those girls who did not have bicycles when their delivery-boy brothers did were acutely conscious of their relative lack of power and the measure of freedom that came to those with a 'wheel.' As one reported, 'I threw the first tantrum I ever had when my brother got a bike when he became a delivery boy.'

Finally, children worked in the household and family economies because of the role that this work played in making them into women or men of their times. As we have already seen, girls absorbed a domestic ideology as they went about domestic activities. If by doing (or not doing) housework, boys began to develop notions of what they would not do as adults, their employed work reinforced what they had begun to learn through their outside chores about what men in a patriarchial society do. They could see themselves taking a major step on the road to becoming a 'breadwinner.'

When, in 1931, fourteen-year-old Mennonite immigrant John Friesen quit school to work on his father's farm, he 'was so happy I could have jumped for joy ... the ability to work and do a job well was what it took to be a man! ... I was now doing a man's job; I was now worth something.'[79] Homer Stevens started 'fishing on my own during the summer holidays of 1936, when I was thirteen years old. I fished with an old boat of my father's, gill-netting on the stretch of river near our house ... I'm trying to think back on how I felt at the time. Part of the feeling was that I was now – A Man. It was pretty hard work but you had to prove that you were able to do something like that to be accepted by your peers, those who were a bit older than you.'[80]

As boys took what they believed to be major steps towards manhood, they also entered into its culture. As it was in the newspaper shack, so it was also at the pin-setting end of bowling alleys, on the shop floor, and in other all-male working environments. There boys learned and began to practise the sexist, racist, and other vulgar and obscene elements of the behaviour and language employed in such environments.

Between the end of the Second World War and the 1960s, traditional patterns of children's work underwent a cluster of changes. Interviews and other evidence shows that some children of the 1950s – especially among the severely disadvantaged and immigrants from areas devastated by the war – worked as hard as had their predecessors, and at similar tasks. None the less, such children formed a decreasing proportion of the total. Changes in Canada's demographic profile, and a rising standard of living, combined to reduce the role of children in the domestic economy and transformed their role in the family.

As it had throughout the twentieth century, family size continued to decline in the postwar era.[81] With fewer children to look after, mothers could devote more attention to the upbringing of each individual child, with less need to call on older siblings to look after younger ones. Smaller families, with children born more closely together in time, also meant a shorter period of responsibility for the care of children. Especially in working-class families, as their children reached late childhood or adolescence, many women entered the part-time workforce, and their earnings replaced, to a degree, those lost to the family when it allowed children to spend their part-time earnings on themselves.[82]

A rising standard of living in both middle-class and working-class families permitted them to take advantage of technological changes that only the well-to-do had previously been able to afford. As families adopted electricity or gas for cooking, and gas or oil for home heating, the long connection between children and the provision of fuel came to an end. As the means of cleaning homes and clothing changed, children's work diminished much more than did that of mothers. For the latter, new 'labour-saving' gadgets often encouraged them to set ever-higher standards for themselves. New standards in clothing cleanliness, however, did not call for daughters to carry water from stove to washtub, or to turn wringers. Refrigeration, both in the home and in the store, sharply reduced the number of shopping trips a family needed to make.

The consolidation of shops into larger units that were farther away from home shifted shopping duties from children to parents, and again especially to mothers. The automobile was central to this change, for families gradually came to convey the week's groceries home in the family car rather than in the baby buggy, wagon, or bicycle carrier. Increasing affluence, together with stricter enforcement of municipal by-laws, also cut back on family agricultural activities. Many families replaced the produce of their vegetable garden with the relatively inexpensive and more varied items from local and California farms. New housing on previously vacant land, together with a more vigorous enforcement of municipal health and zoning regulations, effectively eliminated all domestic animals except pets from the city.

A rising standard of living also reduced the family's need for the part-time income of their children. Most boys continued to find part-time work outside their home and, with a reduced load of domestic duties, more and more girls also worked at part-time jobs. The 'consumption revolution' affected children as well as parents, expressing itself in an increasing need to conform to standards set by peers. While few youngsters achieved absolute freedom as to how to dispose of their earnings, as they took financial responsibility for some of their increasingly varied and more expensive clothing, sports equipment, school supplies, and entertainment, their parents allowed them considerable choice in these matters.

Such changes, in turn, provide some evidence about a broader dimension of social change. Bryan Palmer has argued that, in the 1920s and 1930s, mass culture, consumerism, and such other classless concerns as 'individualized family-centred activity' dissolved what had been a distinctive working-class culture in anglophone Canada. After the Great War, the experiences of working-class and middle-class children alike in the school classroom and in the culture of childhood had much in common, and what they had in common came mostly from the new, classless elements Palmer has identified. None the less, such practices as scrounging, intensive urban agriculture (including the keeping of animals), together with parents collecting the earnings of their children, point to the persistence of distinctive elements of working-class culture until after the Second World War.[83]

In both classes some of the characteristics of traditional child labour persisted into the new era. Parents continued to need their children's help with many household tasks. Indeed, as fewer grandparents – especially widowed grandmothers – and other relatives joined households, and more single adults with full-time jobs set up their own, some younger children may have had more rather than less domestic work to do. Parents continued to believe that idleness was dangerous and that work built character. Mothers continued to find more for their daughters to do than for their sons. With the encouragement of their parents, both sexes found part-time work. Finally, both boys and girls continued to construct their adult identities in part through their work. Like their rural counterparts described in the next chapter, children of the 1950s and even beyond still found they 'had things to do.'

7

The Working Lives of the Children of Modern Pioneers

From the time the apothecary Louis Hébert, his wife, Marie Rollet, and their three children began to cultivate land in New France until the present day, children have played a central role in pioneering in Canada.[1] This chapter describes how work permeated the lives of children growing up in a modern pioneering community. It shows how, like their urban counterparts, rural families tried to integrate new notions with traditional practices. It begins by outlining the daily round of chores, moves on to discuss 'the greater circle of the seasons' tasks,' and then considers two sorts of work – house and barn building and land clearing – that were so central to pioneering. The chapter concludes with general observations on the role of work in the lives of the rural young, including its place in the development of their adult identities.

As what follows clearly demonstrates, the differences between a pioneering and a long-settled agricultural community is mostly a matter of degree rather than kind. Indeed, there were broad continuities across most Canadian childhoods of the time, whatever their individual settings. None the less, a community in the throes of creating itself reveals with particular clarity the tensions between the demands placed on children by their families, on the one hand, and an increasingly intrusive state, on the other.

Although childhood in newly settled areas in the twentieth century closely resembled pioneer childhood of earlier times, the years between the end of the First World War and the end of the 1950s had characteristics that made the period unique.[2] Arduous, endless, and generally mindless work remained a central element in the lives of all pioneering children. Like predecessor generations, they treaded, as Robert Collins put it, 'two endless wheels of labour ... one within the other: a daily round of chores spinning inside the greater circle of seasons' tasks.'[3] A transforming society added to customary burdens. On the one hand, urban popularizers of new notions of childhood and of child health, welfare, and education tried to bring children in the remotest areas under the sway of their ideas. Schoolteachers and school inspectors, outpost nurses, public-health nurses, travelling physicians and dentists, mothers' allowance investigators, and missionaries brought new ideas and practices, together with the apparatus of the modern state, to pioneering areas.[4] In particular, the state incorporated nearly all school-aged children into the laddered school system. It, rather than parents, now held the major responsibility for when and how children would learn their literary and cultural tradition. Much more schooling and school work had to be fitted into the 'two endless wheels of labour.'

On the other hand, twentieth-century pioneers interested themselves in the effects that social, medical, technological, and scientific changes might bring to their lives. They came from motorized communities, and expected roads and railways to follow them.[5] They expected eventually to employ mechanized farm and other equipment, and to own automobiles. Since they were always short of cash, and with the demands of farm and family competing for their meagre supply of it, pioneering families were extremely sceptical of anything they regarded as a 'frill.' As one woman explained, 'We didn't have the cash to buy these things [such as a new coat for school] ... because every time there was cash in our family there was a threshing machine to buy ... Always on a ranch it's always machinery and equipment.' None the less, most settlers wanted the benefits of recent advances in medicine and an up-to-date education for their families.

Women demonstrated their commitment to modern medicine for themselves and their families by their enthusiasm to bear their babies in hospitals. From the late nineteenth century on, social reformers and medical practitioners campaigned to reduce extremely high rates of infant and maternal mortality. Pregnant women were exhorted to bear their infants in hospitals rather than at home. Although the shift from home to hospital was eventually accompanied by decline in maternal mortality, historians do not agree as to whether these events were causally linked.[6] Interviews and other data show, however, that most rural and pioneer women welcomed the shift to the hospital.[7] Before the railway was completed, one Evelyn woman 'walked forty miles to the hospital ... where her first child was born.' Later, and despite the presence of a trained midwife in their midst (the 'lady who helped when babies were born,' as one child thought of her at the time), many Evelyn women chose to go to the hospital in Smithers. One woman, who had an exciting race with time getting to Smithers for the birth of one child, for the next went early to Smithers and 'stayed with a friend ... for

three whole weeks before the baby decided to come.'[8] Some children continued to be born at home, even after the Smithers hospital opened. One
man reported that he had been 'born in the farmhouse. No midwife was
present. Since my father had been an amateur vet, he may have helped.'

Most Evelyn parents wanted a modern education for their children. After
initiating formal schooling in a private home, the community soon built a
log schoolhouse.[9] In Canada in the half-century before the Great War, state
and community together had lengthened the school year, increased the
number of years children spent there, and given a more urban cast to standardized curricula. In consequence, twentieth-century rural schools such as
Evelyn's were less able than their nineteenth-century predecessors to fit
themselves tightly into local mores and work patterns.[10] In the past, rural
school trustees set the dates for opening and closing schools so that they
accorded with the needs and rhythms of community life. By the 1920s, Evelyn's schools opened and closed on province-wide dates set by the Department of Education in far-away Victoria.[11] Fewer families followed the time-
honoured rural practice of sending their children to school only at those
times when they were not needed at home.

As passing high-school entrance examinations became the goal for city
children, so it did for their rural counterparts. Eight whole years of ten
months' attendance became the norm. Attendance records provide some
objective evidence of what Evelyn parents and children accomplished in
meeting it. In 1921–2, the average daily attendance in graded elementary
schools in British Columbia was 87 per cent; by 1931–2, it was 90 per cent;
and, in 1941–2, it was 89 per cent. Average daily attendance of all pupils in
British Columbia first exceeded 90 per cent in 1939–40. By then, Evelyn
School had *exceeded* that figure in thirteen of its first eighteen years.[12]

For Evelyn families needing their children's work, the new educational
norm added an enormous burden to all the others. Some families came
closer than others to meeting the goal. As one man reported, 'Some kids
couldn't attend school regularly; they had to stay at home for work.' This
was especially so at seed time and at harvest. 'I did not attend school during
threshing time,' explained one woman. Although the man quoted above,
the son of a particularly demanding father, did not complete his entrance,
he none the less spent much of each of eight years at school. Another
youngster, whose day started at 6:00 A.M. and who sometimes did not complete his chores until 9:00 P.M., 'studied to 12:00 at night.' In his last year, in
the entrance class, he had a 'teacher who was determined I would not fail
[the entrance examinations],' so she had him 'at school at 8:30 until 4:30.'
He 'would have continued' beyond Grade Eight if there had been school

buses into Smithers. To board there would both take him away from his round of chores and put a heavy burden on family finances. Other Evelyn youngsters did go on to complete their high school, often taking part of it by correspondence. Coming, as they did, later in the settling process, some younger children had more time than their older siblings to attend school regularly.

The 'ideal' division of labour for pioneering families was similar to those of their urban and long-settled rural counterparts. The work of pioneering families differed from both in the much greater demands that it placed on all members of the family. Mothers' work centred on the household. Fathers' work centred on the land. Mothers' and fathers' duties met in the farmyard, 'middle ground, fair for either boys or girls to do.' Since pioneer families always had more to do than time to complete it, children began working very early in their lives – in the words of one: 'I can't recall when I didn't help.' In normal circumstances, daughters helped with their mothers' duties, and sons helped with their fathers'. Boys who were called upon to do 'inside' chores did so because, as one Evelyn man explained, 'my mother had no daughters.'

When it came to 'outside' chores, however, there was, as one woman explained, 'no such thing as boys' work; as soon as you could walk you worked.' In concurring with this view, one man also revealed the fairly common male attitude that the 'real' work of farming lay in the male domain. There was, he reported, 'no sex difference in chores,' and his sisters could 'handle chores like a man.' When a father had to work away, the rest of the family had to do his work as well as their own.

Children and adults started early on their daily rounds, all made more arduous by primitive settings. As one woman put it, 'lots of things had to be done every day, and they had to be done at a certain time.' First, someone lit the kitchen stove and other fires, sometimes using curls of wood or a shaved stick – 'paper was precious' – to ignite the kindling. 'My father got up first,' reported one woman, 'lit the kitchen stove, and stirred up the heater,' while another told that her mother 'was up first and lit the fire.' Soon, the whole family was up, the younger children to dress by the fire, the older ones, after having something hot to drink or eat, on their way to the first of the morning's chores. 'We would have coffee with Father,' noted one man, 'and then went to the barn to milk the cows, to feed the calves, to feed the pigs.' A woman had 'fond memories of mornings with cattle bawling and horses whinnying.' Until she was herself old enough to help with the milking, she 'threw hay down from the hay barn.' One lad, whose family homesteaded near Powell River at this time, 'had to milk eight head morning and night.'

Meanwhile, mothers and other youthful helpers worked inside. They tended the youngest children. They emptied the contents of chamber pots into the 'honey pail' to dispose of in the privy. They prepared a hot breakfast, usually a porridge made from grain grown on the farm, together with bacon, eggs, toast, or pancakes. They made lunches for those going to school and packed them in each child's lard, toffee, or Rogers' syrup pail. 'After breakfast we rushed to school,' explained one man, and another noted that he was 'up no later than 6:00 and started to school just after 8:00.' A third man noted that 'we always liked to go to school, in the sense that it was a relief from ... farming.'

Pupils attending Evelyn School also had a round of chores to do there. In winter, after a walk of from a half-mile to over three miles, sometimes through deep snow, the children were cold when they got to school. As soon as he arrived, one of the older boys lighted the 'drum-type stove in which the logs were loaded from the front.' He and the other boys chopped the wood, brought it in from the woodshed, and kept the fire going. Children took 'turns bringing milk, cocoa, and sugar. The first thing you'd do is make a big kettle of hot chocolate. Everybody would have a drink.' Both men and women recalled going, usually in pairs, with a pail to get water from glacier-fed Toboggan Creek, which was a quarter of a mile away. Since it was 'a good big creek,' children had to be careful, especially in the winter, when the boys 'used an old axe' to cut holes in the ice. They often came back, as one man reported, 'with icicles on my pants.' The older children also took weekly turns as school janitor, sweeping, cleaning the wash-basin, washing blackboards, and cleaning brushes. Eventually the school board paid one boy to light the fire, and another to fetch the water. Towards the end of the summer, and at other times in the year as well, children helped their mothers give the school a thorough cleaning, and their fathers bring in or add to the winter's wood supply and repair the school, barn, woodshed, privies, and fences.

Children hurried home from school; as one put it, 'work was there waiting for us.' Among the most important tasks was caring for animals, of which 'choring with cattle' took the greatest amount of time. Except in the winter, cows remained outside, sometimes in pastures, but in the early years of settlement they often 'roamed free' as widely as they liked. Children hunted out the cattle to bring them home to the night pasture or barn. Fortunate youngsters would 'go on horses for them, sometimes [as many as] four miles.' Others, who put in 'hours of walking' as they brought home the cows, would 'love to have had a pony.' When Gertrude Story proved incapable of this task on her Saskatchewan farm, 'I got moved up the ladder of farm chores ... and the boys got set to fetching the cows home.'[13]

Once the cows were in the night pasture or barn, in some families 'Mom and the kids did the milking,' while in others fathers took charge. Some families were 'before-supper milkers,' while others were 'after-supper milkers.' Children eagerly acquired the skill, and the woman who reported that she 'learned to milk at six years of age' was not unusual. However, she may have, like a male contemporary, also soon 'wished I hadn't started it, because it became a regular chore!'

After the morning or evening milking, mothers and children ran much of the day's milk through the cream separator. One woman explained that, when she was small, 'it took two children to turn the handle.' After each use the separator had to be taken apart and thoroughly washed with water as hot as the hands could bear it, and then reassembled.[14] Since no soap could be used, separators had a characteristic odour that people can still summon up in their minds. Children then fed the skim milk to chickens, calves, and pigs, and helped to make butter with the hand churn, and then 'to mould it on the wooden "butter table."' As Ferne Nelson recalled of churning: 'The action of the heavy handle made my little arms ache, and it seemed as though the cream would never turn to butter.'[15]

In winter, cattle also had to be fed and watered. Families grew much of their turnip crop for cattle feed. While families eventually came to own a turnip pulper, in the early days parents and children chopped them up by hand. One man reported, 'I didn't do a very good job; [the too-large pieces] got stuck in the cattle's throats.' As another man reported, this could 'kill the cow, because cows don't chew, they just swallow.' On some farms, children took the cattle from the barn to drink at spot in a creek where holes had been cut in the ice for them, and on others they filled drinking troughs. 'In the very coldest weather,' one woman explained, 'the water had to be slightly warmed by pouring a kettle of boiling water into each troughful, or the milk production went down.' Cleaning the barn was also a major daily chore for both boys and girls. One 'escaped the mundane jobs of milking cows by offering to do the "dunging out," the "mucking out" that had to be done on a daily basis.'

Evelyn farms also kept horses, pigs, and chickens, all of which required daily care. In addition to her daily milking and wood carrying, one woman 'fed the chickens, looked after the young chicks, gathered the eggs, and cleaned out the chicken houses ... Dad killed the roosters, Mother scalded them, and the kids plucked them.' Another, in a family that kept about 100 chickens, recalls 'gathering the eggs, cleaning them for the store, and cleaning the henhouse.' In another family, the daughter whose job it was to look after the chickens selected the older one destined for the supper table, 'got the axe, put it on the chopping block, cut its head off, got the hot water, [and took] the feathers off, but Mom would clean it.' This woman also had the job of finding the barn cats' litters, 'just leave one and the rest I had to drown ... to make sure we weren't overrun with cats.'

Girls and boys also had regular meal-time duties. Before supper, they filled coal-oil lamps and lanterns, cleaned their chimneys, and trimmed their wicks. Helping with supper often took one to the root cellar or root house. As one woman explained, 'you had to put on ... your boots and your heavy clothes because, usually in the wintertime, that was quite a chore to go to the root house and make sure you got everything ... Usually you had to light a lantern to take with you ... because you couldn't leave the door open for light ... [You would get] three or four days' supply' at one time. Another woman noted that 'the fruit and vegetables in the cellar had to be picked over carefully,' and 'any that had started to rot had to be culled out.' One woman 'had to do the vegetables for supper, then all the dishes after the meal.'

Mothers rarely delegated much cooking to their youngsters. As one woman explained, her mother would not let her bake because the mother had 'lived through the hard times' and thus was 'afraid I would waste.' When the mother baked 'she would use her fingers to scrape out the bowl so there would be nothing left to lick, ... not a thing!' A man remembers, 'My brother and I took turns washing and drying dishes every night. We did that for years.' In another, perhaps more representative family, however, neither father nor brother 'ever did dishes, or even put the dirty ones in the sink.' Elizabeth Varley, whose family pioneered in the Kitimat Valley, explained that dishwashing was the worst chore 'because of insufficient water' and the fact that, in order not to scratch it, the 'enamel porridge pot ... had to be scraped with a wooden chip from the woodshed.'[16]

Most Evelyn pioneers built their homes close to creeks, from which they took most of their water. Some also had a 'rain barrel' in which they collected soft rainwater for 'washing hair and white clothes.' Others 'melted snow for washing; ... it took more and more buckets of snow.' A few had the pump for their well right inside the house, beside the sink. Most families used buckets to bring their water to the house. Once at the house, children would 'bail water into the reservoir on the stove, or stored it in pails in the kitchen.' For youngsters 'carrying water from the creek was an endless chore, winter and summer.' One 'household used four buckets every day ... [and] the butter called for an extra couple of buckets.' Verna Kirkness, who grew up in a Cree community in rural Manitoba, remembered her 'mother trying to keep me home because we had to either melt snow or haul water and so she'd want me to help her ... Either I was terribly lazy or I really loved school!'[17] Dave McIntosh, who worked on his uncle's New Brunswick farm, explained that 'carrying water from the well was a sort of test of growing manhood. The object was to carry two pails from well to house or barn [about forty metres] without once putting them down to rest.'[18]

Where the creek was far away, parents or children hitched horses to stoneboats or wagons and went there to fill wooden barrels, milk cans, or drums. On nice days children found this to be an agreeable task; it was certainly more pleasant than weeding the kitchen garden or hilling potatoes. In winter, however, it could be one of the most unpleasant chores a child had to do. 'We went to the creek with a stoneboat, pulled by a horse, with a barrel on it. We [then] chopped a hole in the ice,' recalled one woman. Children then used numb hands to fill buckets and pour near-freezing water into the barrel. Their mittens got wet and froze, and they accidentally splashed water over themselves. The canvas tops and the ropes used to tie them over barrels to prevent splashing became rigid with ice. Any water that slopped over the edge froze on the side of the barrel, on the stoneboat, and on clothes.

When he was a boy on an Alberta ranch, H. 'Dude' Lavington was 'cutting waterholes half a mile or so from the house one day when it was around 30 below. On the last waterhole my axe got away from me ... I reached to make a grab for the disappearing handle and slipped into the waterhole ... Panic struck me. I was sure I would freeze to death before I could get home ... In no time my pants, boots, and socks were frozen solid, and my legs and feet just like encased in splints.' When Lavington made it home, he was surprised 'to find out that I was warm as toast and even sweating from all the effort and panic!'[19]

In her recollections, Bulkley Valley pioneer Nan Bourgon explained that 'everything was brown – soil, house, kids, farmers.'[20] One woman's story nicely emphasizes this point. 'My dad was clearing land,' she recalled, 'and I was supposed to take a message to him ... I could see my dad walking and a black bear was walking with him on its hind legs.' In fact, it was not a bear but another man 'who was so black from clearing land, doing it by hand.' A constant battle with the 'brown' and the 'black' formed a central characteristic of the work of pioneer women and their children. Much of the battle took place inside, in the early years especially, in a house often unevenly floored with planks, or even poles. Fathers and children brought dirt in on their shoes and clothes, with the never-ending supply of wood and kindling for the stoves and, during dry, dusty periods, it blew in through doors and windows. Stove ash added to accumulations. 'On Saturdays,' one woman recalls, 'Mom would have me clean the upstairs ... dust with the dust mop, change the beds, and just generally clean up.'

Washing was the most onerous task connected with keeping things clean. Since hauling water was so difficult, one family built a wash house right on their creek: 'it was cold in winter.' At another home, about a hundred feet from the creek, the large washing was done 'in a large tub on top of a huge block of wood' which sat outside on the back porch. A woman reported that, 'if a neighbour was sick, my mother [would come] home with a big sheet full of wash. We'd light a fire by the creek rather than carrying [the water].' In a third family, one of the boys helped with the water: 'the night before I had to make sure that there was enough water to do the washing.' After the clothes were boiled, 'they were washed on scrub boards' and then wrung out 'with a hand-turned wringer.' Most people 'hung out washing all year round.' In winter they 'brought in frozen articles as needed.' For clothes and other things that needed ironing, mothers and daughters used 'sad' or flat-irons.

Some families were, as one woman put it, 'haphazard about caring for themselves and hygiene.' Such families caused distress to some of their neighbours. As members of the first generation acutely aware of the role of germs ('microbes') in spreading disease, to some mothers 'dirt ... was often synonymous with disease and infection' and they laboured hard to keep it at bay. What one must marvel at is not the shabbiness, and sometimes even dirtiness, of those children and adults who sometimes offended insensitive teachers, public-health nurses, and other outside observers, but that so many children, at the cost of tremendous labour on their part and that of their mothers, went to school and community events relatively clean and tidy, and remained remarkably healthy.

After children completed all their chores, they sometimes had school work to finish. As one woman remembered it, she had homework only 'occasionally'; it was not a 'ritual that you had to do a certain amount when you got home.' A man recalls having to do 'lots of memorizing,' while another did 'no homework; never!' On days when they had none, or completed it quickly, youngsters might read, or be read to, sing, play or listen to a parent play a musical instrument, or play cards or other games. In later years they might gather round a battery radio to listen to such distant stations as KGO, San Francisco, or to 'Mr. Good Evening' (Earle Kelly), who read the news from CKWX in Vancouver. On evenings and weekends, girls also began to learn how to mend, darn, sew, knit, and embroider. One woman, for example, had 'knitted myself a sweater by the time I was twelve.'

Since early rising mandated an early bedtime, their relaxing time was not as long as most youngsters would have liked. Children generally slept in unheated rooms in uninsulated, drafty houses. As one person reported, 'there was frost around the edges of the floor in the house,' and another explained that, in her bedroom, sometimes there was 'snow on the window-sills inside.' In consequence, going to bed in the wintertime involved certain routines. One woman recalled that she wore 'longjohns, pyjamas, her housecoat, a nightcap, and took a hot-water bottle with her.' In another home, the kids 'all moved down [from upstairs] to the living-room beside the heater' when it got really cold. Cold bedrooms and outdoor privies, in turn, led to constipation, the consequent pain, and one of the then popular treatments.[21]

The many chores relating to the wood supply fitted into both daily and seasonal rounds. The cold climate and the need to do everything, including felling the trees, made gathering fuel a much more onerous job than it was for urban youngsters. To pioneer children, their family's need for wood seemed insatiable. As one man put it, 'it seemed like there was no end to getting wood.' People often started out with only a single stove. As families and houses grew larger, they also added to the number of their stoves and heaters. Some homes had 'air tight' heaters which 'took a whole block of wood' and kept the house 'warm all night.' The Bourgon house in Hubert, a few miles southeast of Evelyn, eventually had seven stoves.[22] Since 'green' wood was difficult to ignite, produced a low level of heat and copious amounts of smoke as it burned, and built up heavy deposits in stovepipes and chimneys (which brought on dangerous and frightening chimney fires), most families organized themselves so that they always had a plentiful supply of dry, well-seasoned firewood. Therefore, on the short days in the midst of winter, when the ground was frozen hard and before the sap started to run, they cut enough trees to provide firewood for the whole of the next year. 'On weekends,' reported one man, he and his father 'went to the woodlot. We cut the wood and, with horses and sleighs, would haul it in.'

Next, in the wood area near the house, they cut the logs into stove-length rounds. In some families, fathers and sons placed it on the sawhorse and 'bucked it by hand with a cross-cut saw.' In families in which the father worked away from home, or where there were no boys of an appropriate age, mothers and daughters undertook this task. One woman recalled being 'on one end of a cross-cut saw, with one of my brothers on the other.' Some families cut up their wood on a 'motorized' cross-cut saw, or, more commonly, with an unprotected circular saw mounted on a frame and driven by a gasoline engine. Victor Carl Friesen vividly described this dangerous work: 'My brother, or sometimes my mother, dragged the logs to the saw. At the saw stood my father, who repeatedly pushed each log into the whining blade ... I stood right next to the open blade and grasped the end of the log ... and followed it through its journey into the biting blade until it was severed. Then I threw the piece of wood over my shoulder.'[23] After it was sawed off, each round had to be split, a process most easily done while the wood was still 'green.'

Many families tried to get ahead in their wood splitting over the summer months. They created enormous piles of chopped wood outside, and then stacked it in sheds so they had a good supply on hand for the winter, and especially in case of heavy storms, serious illness, or other emergencies. As one woman explained, the children in her family 'had to spend a half-hour each day stacking up the cut wood in the shed so that it would dry for the winter.' Other families cut their wood over the winter. A man recalled that he and his father each spent an hour a day splitting wood: 'Sometimes on the weekends we might get a little ahead.' One woman recalls that, by the time she was six, she was splitting wood and kindling. Since in even the warmest months families needed to use their stoves for cooking, for preserving, and for heating water, wood and kindling chopping and carrying had to be done over the whole year. 'We packed wood in every day,' reported one man, and a woman recalled that 'one night I went to bed without cutting the kindling. My father rooted me out at midnight to do it.'

Evelyn farms grew hay, oats, wheat, barley, turnips, and potatoes as their principal crops. Some kept sheep as well as the ubiquitous cattle. In addition, mothers planted 'kitchen gardens' in which they grew radishes, lettuce, beets, cabbages, cauliflower, carrots, peas, spinach, beans, rhubarb, parsnips ('I hated parsnips!'), and other vegetables and small fruits. (The climate of the Bulkley Valley was too severe for fruit trees.) Both the major crops and the kitchen garden involved children in a succession of tasks that began early in the spring and came to a halt only in the late fall. Before the ground thawed, families hauled loads of manure from beside the barn and scattered it over the fields.

As soon as the ground thawed and dried out, families prepared it for planting. Although no Evelyn woman told of learning to plough, those who grew up elsewhere did. Mary Henderson, of Unionville, Ontario, reported that she began to learn to plough at the age of nine or ten.[24] Annie Donald, oldest of seven girls and the 'boy' of a family pioneering in Alberta, was, at age eleven, 'taken out of school and became the full-time "hired hand"' who drove 'a team of oxen which in turn pulled the plough and other farm implements.'[25]

In Evelyn, after fathers and older sons completed the ploughing, all the children helped with the further preparation of the soil. As one woman explained, for her 'there was always disking and harrowing ... [and she] used to harness and unharness the [part Percheron] horses by the time I was twelve.' Children also helped get the kitchen garden ready, by digging, raking, and planting the seeds, this last task often done on or near the 24th of May school holiday. One family put in 'a large garden; one acre of potatoes, one half-acre of small vegetables – it seemed like more than that – and one half-acre of turnips.' Another planted 'at least three acres of potatoes,' and a third had 'a large vegetable garden of almost an acre.' After the sheep were shorn in the spring, children helped to wash, card, and spin the wool.

Of all their chores children remember weeding with the most distaste. It was, recalled one man, 'a wearisome sort of thing.' Another remembered that 'we had a vegetable garden. I had to weed and thin the bastards.' 'I'll never forget the long rows of turnips I had to weed,' noted one woman; 'it seemed like there was no end to them.' Some farmers used a horse-drawn cultivator to weed between the rows, but in many families, and especially in the early years, such work was usually done with a hoe. Boys and girls would also 'crawl on hands and knees, pulling weeds out of the garden.' Weeding also seemed never-ending: 'everything that grows is more weeding than gardening,' as one person lamented. During and after rainfall, damp soil clung to boots, building up into large clumps on the soles. These clumps made walking even more difficult and uncomfortable but were hard to dislodge and grew again almost immediately.

Weeding went on over the late spring and summer, which were also the seasons of black flies and mosquitoes. As one woman explained, 'holidays were from school only; that is when parents got the most out of you.' After one woman had her tonsils out, she was absolutely delighted to hear the doctor instruct her father that 'I wasn't to pull weeds. I remember it very clearly. I wasn't to work in dirt!' In addition to the weeding of vegetable gardens and root crops, children also cleared grain fields of such noxious weeds as wild oats and stinkweed. In one family, the father 'made each child responsible for a certain area. Dad checked it at night.' Once a year, families dug new holes for their privies and filled in the old one.

If children remember weeding as their most distasteful chore, they fondly recall gathering wild vegetables and berries as their most-liked spring and summer activity. As one man explained, 'I liked ... picking huckleberries up on the hillsides ... there were kind of endless dreamy days like that, and you had bright, sunny weather.' Another recalled that, 'in the springtime for greens you gathered nettles, pigweed ... and dandelions for salads.' A

Evelyn children weeding turnips in the 1930s.

woman explained that to pick wild strawberries in June 'was a thrill ... We would take a lunch ... we were picking them for Mom to make jam with; that was a serious business.' A man explained that 'children picked wild strawberries, raspberries, low-bush blueberries, and huckleberries. Sometimes we would take two or three hours to walk to a site for picking.' His mother 'put them up in jars; if it was a good year, we often had berries for dinner.' And on the prairies, Ferne Nelson wrote, 'we picked quarts and quarts of summer's bounty, to be spooned from Mama's mason jars when the winter winds blew and summer was only a memory.' [26] While picking berries, children had to keep a wary eye out for bears, especially those with cubs. Children called out to each other regularly or shook 'a tin with stones in it to keep animals away.'

Evelyn residents began harvesting in the summer and continued until late into the fall. Especially in the early days, harvesting was very labour-intensive. Long hours of sunlight made hay ready for cutting by mid to late July. At haying time, reported one woman, 'it was always hot.' While families might scythe hard-to-reach patches – 'I used a scythe a little bit for hay among the trees' -, they customarily employed a horse-drawn mower to cut the hay. With a wary eye on the look-out for rain, families then left their cut hay laying in its swaths or rows to dry.[27] As soon as it was dry, they used either long-handled or horse-drawn rakes to collect it together, and then their hands or pitchforks to put into haycocks (stacks) or piles. From there it was pitched onto horse-drawn hayricks (hay racks) to be carried to sheds, barns, or large outdoor stacks.

Mothers and children helped in all phases of this work. As one woman reported: 'Haying was a ... family job. Dad did the mowing and I [and the other children] stooked and cocked it.' Another woman reported that, at age twelve, she ran both mower and hay rake, and drove the hayricks. Older children pitched hay onto the wagons, while the younger ones rode on the wagons, tramping the hay down. 'At about [age] nine or ten, Dad had me on the hay rig,' reported one man, while a woman recalled that she didn't like 'tramping the loads; ... it was hot, dusty work.' When the rick reached the barn, in one family, an eight-year-old girl drove the horse-drawn 'fork' that lifted the hay off the rick and unloaded it in the hayloft. Adults and older children did the very heavy work of spreading the hay, and children then 'tramped the loft' to level it out.

Grain – oats, wheat, and barley – were harvested later on in the year. Fathers or older children drove the three- or four-horse binders, which cut and bound the grain into bundles or sheaves. The rest of the family would follow behind and stook (sometimes 'shock') the grain, that is, stack the bundles upright, leaning in towards each other. As one person explained, 'we made a field of these [bundles] because, if it rained, it ran off and did not rot the grain.' Only older children took a direct part in the heavy labour of threshing. 'As soon as I was old enough, twelve or thirteen,' reported one woman, 'I joined the team of threshers.' Younger children, as another woman explained, helped 'Mother feed the hungry workers and to carry drinks out to the fields.'

When threshing was done early in the season, two or three teams pulling wagons with racks on them took stooks from the fields directly to the threshing-machine. Two 'field pitchers' pitched sheaves onto the rack while the driver loaded them, heads in, butts out. After the driver had taken a full load to the machine, he or she helped the 'spike pitcher' pitch or toss them onto the belt and into the machine. Twelve-year-olds could load, drive, and help pitch off the stooks.

If the threshing-machine was not expected until late in the season, then families brought their sheaves to a central point and stacked them. Sheaves were pitched from the wagon to the stack builder, who placed them heads in, butts out, to keep them dry. Although throwing up sheaves was too heavy for most girls and younger boys, they could load and drive the wagons. When the threshing-machine arrived, two pitchers on the stack threw the bundles onto the belt. Grain came out of the machine via a spout into sacks or a bin. Again, only older children could help with these tasks and were often kept out of school to do so.

In the Bulkley Valley 'potato picking' and 'turnip picking' were the last major harvesting operations of the year. Children helped with all phases of this work. 'We had a large potato field,' one woman recalls. 'We did the potato picking in the fall. I would come home from school and change. We would load sacks onto the stoneboat and ride it home to the root cellar.' Another woman explained that 'potatoes [were] ... always picked in October ... and it was so cold. I can remember crying at the cold ... picking them.' Floyd Frank, whose family pioneered in the Skeena Valley at about the same time as Evelyn was settled, explained that the potatoes he picked 'were lying on the top of the ground' and were 'picked into half-bushel baskets, thirty pounds capacity, and dumped into gunny sacks that held three to four baskets.'[28] Often children rewarded themselves by turning one of the largest turnips into a Hallowe'en jack-o'-lantern.

Summer and fall brought mothers the added burden of preparing, preserving, and storing as much food as possible for the long months of winter and early spring. In the summer, children helped clear out and clean the root cellar to make it ready for the new crop. Then, over the late summer

Youthful potato pickers in East Kildonan, Manitoba, in the 1920s.

and fall, they placed cabbages, potatoes, turnips, carrots, and other root vegetables directly onto storage racks in the cellar. Together with the wild berries, mothers canned (in glass sealers) such vegetables as cauliflower, peas, and beans.

If chickens, pigs, or cows were slaughtered in summer, then the meat had to be preserved by pickling, smoking, or canning. 'We would,' one man reported, 'kill one pig for ourselves and the rest were sold ... All the meat was canned; jars and jars of canned meat.' His 'mother did all the canning and, since she had no daughter, I helped with whatever was necessary.' A woman recalls 'slaughtering time ... and then the meat was hung ... and then brought into the house, and cut up, and canned.' If the weather was cold enough, some meat was allowed to freeze untreated. As one man reported, 'we would eat a milk cow in the fall if Dad didn't get a moose; ... [we] had to wait until it was cold ... to kill a moose or other animals.' In the summer, a woman reported, First Nations people from their nearby village of Morice-town, 'came with horses and wagons to sell salmon, big beautiful salmon ...

and Mom would can it ... [which was] lots of work ... [since it] had to be cooked on the woodstove, and the house would be hot.' Another woman explained that their 'ham was smoked and cured ... in a little smokehouse ... [which] needs some special kind of bark ... and a salt mixture ("Habicure") you rubbed into it.'

Evelyn pioneers had to integrate their regular rounds into a generation-long process of settling in. Settling in first involved creating basic shelter for families and animals.[29] Families often spent the first summer, and sometimes longer periods, on or near the new site, living in a tent, shed, or abandoned cabin.[30] While her father built their house, one woman explained, he lived in a tent on the site, while the family lived in a vacant cabin 'five miles away through the bush ... We would take a lunch down and watch as he used horses, and a block and tackle to build ... It had to be built before cold came.' The first home was sometimes a small log cabin, chinked with clay or moss, and roofed with poles covered with canvas, sod, shakes, or corrugated iron. At first, these cabins contained but a single room, with sometimes a sleeping loft at one end and perhaps a lean-to on the side. Hard-packed dirt, poles, or rough planks served as the floor. If a family had animals, then it also had to construct a barn before the first winter: the Evelyn woman quoted above explained that 'Dad built the barn before the cold came.'

Those with a little capital as well as their labour to invest in their homes built a permanent home right from the start, or after only a brief stay in a cabin that could then be converted to other uses. Other families, whose time was completely absorbed by the need to clear, or to work elsewhere, lived in their gradually extending initial home for many years. Some families thus spent most of their child-rearing years in the cabin, with only the youngest children spending some of their youth in the second, 'permanent' home. Nan Capewell married Joe Bourgon in June 1915 and moved into a little house with a lean-to kitchen on their partially cleared farm. Only after very considerable family stress – Nan left Joe for a time – and the birth of their first child did they move into their permanent home, in the spring of 1917.[31]

'School holidays! No one asked where you were going for holidays. You knew you were going to do your part to help clear the land during Easter Holidays,' wrote one Evelyn pioneer, one of those whose 'family was starting out from scratch.'[32] For most, 'trying to make a farm' in a heavily wooded area was a long process, and some were still doing it when they died or sold their farms. As with their other work, children, as one man put it, 'began [helping] earlier than I can remember.' They helped to cut down and cut up trees, to pile them on the fire, to pull stumps or gather up the pieces after they were blown with stumping powder. As one woman explained, 'if they blew stumps they ... would blow three at a time ... and you would count so long and wait for the bang ... a boom you would hear for miles and ... feel it too.' She would then 'pick up sticks for hours.' One boy 'got a wagon as a toy but used it to pick roots.' Farther west, near Terrace, Floyd Frank's father had a team of horses 'which we used, along with pulley blocks and cable, to clear out the stumps. My brother Ivan and I, before we were teenagers, were experts at handling cables and blocks.'[33]

Root and rock picking went on for years, with children spending hours and hours collecting them, especially during ploughing season. Lena Capling of Evelyn recalled 'picking rocks from the fields' and putting them into a stoneboat drawn by a 'huge ox.'[34] Cyril Shelford, pioneering farther east, near Ootsa Lake, wrote that both his father's and his uncle's ranches were 'infested with rocks' which he and his brothers had to help clear, despite the fact that they 'did everything possible to avoid picking them.'[35] As one man summarized the experience of clearing and preparing the land, 'each year the fields got a little bigger and each year the boys got a little bigger.' They cleared 'a couple of acres a year' and, by the time of his father's death, had cleared 125 acres.

Even some urban children from middle-class backgrounds could sometimes find themselves in 'pioneering' situations. In 1937, Dr Herman A. McLean established an outpost hospital and evangelical mission in Nootka Sound, on the west coast of Vancouver Island. In their first year there, at eleven and twelve years of age, Don and Max McLean brought the hospital's supplies by rowboat from a mile away, cut all the wood, and carried the enormous amounts of water needed in buckets from a creek. Their eight-year-old sister, Shirley, helped in the hospital itself, serving food to the patients, and doing such other nursing tasks as applying balm to and fomenting muscle injuries. In that year the children were unable to finish their school year because of their workload.[36]

Evelyn School closed in June 1946. Wartime and postwar prosperity enabled British Columbians to look to the future with a sense of hope that they had not had since the end of the 1920s. [37] Rural school consolidation, long advocated but only very partially implemented, became a postwar goal and a province-wide plan, for it was laid out in the Cameron Report.[38] Consequently, in September 1946, Evelyn children travelled by taxi to school in Smithers. They continued to do their allotted share of the daily, weekly, and seasonal routines on farms, most of which still lacked such amenities as running water, electrical power, and tractors. 'We got our first tractor in 1950,' reported one man, and another noted that 'we got our first electricity in '57.' Many families continued to add to the store of cleared land.

The closing of the Evelyn School marked the end of the initial phase in the history of the district. The 'pioneer fringe' had passed beyond postwar Evelyn and the Bulkley Valley as a whole, leaving behind a relatively prosperous agricultural and lumbering region with well-established patterns of seasonal work.[39] If the workload of Evelyn's postwar youngsters remained similar to that of earlier years, for most of them there was little of the sense of desperate ugency that had characterized the lives of their predecessors.

This major event in the history of the community provides an opportunity to make some more general comments. Here, I will discuss why pioneering children worked, and continued to work, as they did; the practical dimensions of education in Evelyn and similar communities; the differing effects of their work on the development of gender identity among girls and boys; and, very briefly, the overall quality of children's lives in a pioneering community.

At this point I must emphasize that my description of pioneering childhoods at Evelyn is a case-study. Evelyn did not exemplify all aspects of pioneering childhoods in Canada during these years. A different landscape, different crops, a harsher or milder climate – each would structure children's tasks in ways that were somewhat unlike those followed in Evelyn. Thus, some Peace River pioneers did not have to clear their land, but all were farther from markets for their products than those in the Bulkley Valley. Despite accounts of childhood illnesses and accidents, the Bulkley Valley seems to have been a reasonably healthy place to bring up children. Its rates of infant and childhood mortality seem to have been lower than those which Cynthia Comacchio Abeele discovered for 'outpost' Ontario at the same time.[40]

None the less, pioneering children anywhere in Canada would have had in common with their Evelyn contemporaries a heavy load of work, and would have taken a major share in what Elizabeth Varley, a pioneer child in the Kitimat area, called 'the rush to get things done.'[41] Descriptions of pioneer life in the Peace River district, for example, contain many Evelyn-like accounts of youthful work, such as that of Stanley (Punch) Landry. 'When I was nine and my brother Waldo ten,' Landry wrote, 'I remember helping thresh oat bundles with Tremblay's machine when it came to our area ... It was operated with 12 horses and, to save power, had a feed table and a straw conveyor ... Waldo and I were band cutters even though we had to stand on boxes to reach the bundles.'[42]

Even as a case-study, this description of Evelyn is incomplete. In contrast to my account of urban neighbourhoods, this chapter is built almost entirely on the recollections of those who went on to live reasonably successful lives. Families who failed usually moved out of the district. We heard a few stories of siblings and neighbours who encountered problems and difficulties in their adult lives, but have no sense as to whether these were in some way rooted in their childhoods or were the product of later events. Except for the casual and very occasional observations of neighbours or teachers, rural and pioneer children with ephemeral or permanent 'problems' do not appear in records in the way in which some of their urban counterparts did. Thus, in 'the winter,' Nan Bourgon wrote, 'I would see some of the children coming to our Hubert school so poorly clothed that it worried me. I always begged shoes and warm clothes from my friends in town for them.'[43]

Through a short vignette from elsewhere, however, we can glimpse two children in homely situations that were not uncommon in pioneering areas. In the Peace River district, Monica Storrs took an interest in 'Gladys, a girl I am rather sorry for. She is about sixteen, and is a "hired girl" at the store, i.e., general slavey to the storekeeper's wife. She has no mother and her father has just gone to prison for distilling moonshine ... The poor girl is terribly shy now, and I think feels a sort of outcast.' Gladys's brother, Hughie, was twelve 'and he is the most delightful little boy in the school; desperately eager, full of fun and completely unselfconscious.' A year later, Storrs wanted Hughie to attend a summer camp. Hughie now lived 'as chore boy with some people who are very kind to him, but, alas, said they were too busy and could not spare him. Poor Hughie said nothing at all through the conversation but stood at the door and stared and stared at us. He was the life and soul of the camp last year. But of course there was nothing for it but to say, "Better luck next year, Hughie," to which cheap comfort he made no reply but only went on staring till we had gone.'[44]

In the previous chapter, I said that urban children worked as hard as they did both because they had to and because they wanted to. If not impossible, then creating a farm out of the 'bush' would have been extremely difficult without the free, and generally freely given, labour of children. Isaiah Bowman's research showed that, on the land, boys and girls were useful at eight and ten years, and by sixteen they could take the place of men and women.[45] In Evelyn, children of both sexes seemed to be more than 'useful' at eight and, depending on their pattern of growth, capable of working as adults when they reached school-leaving age. Farther east, on the Chilako River, twelve-year-old Earl Baity, eager to be grown up, helped to clear land, drove a team skidding logs used to build a school, learned to trap, and for a

time left school to look after his father's camp so the latter could go on long
trapping expeditions. Then, 'the vast emptiness which would crowd in
round me, spinning and almost roaring and filling all the space was too big
for me to cope with.' Although he wanted to 'sneak home ... I couldn't quite
let myself do it. The same lack of maturity which threatened to bring tears
to my eyes, refused to let me disregard a lifetime's discipline and shirk my
responsibilities.'[46]

What also comes through clearly in accounts of Evelyn childhoods is
how proud children were of what they had been able to do, that as girls and
boys they had done 'a man's work.' As one woman put it, 'You did [any job]
if you could possibly do it.' One man was more explicit, explaining that of
any physical work ... as soon as you were able, you did it ... It was partly that
I liked doing it, I liked this responsibility, those chores.' Elizabeth Varley
'was proud, too, to be doing adult work with the adults, and felt very
grown-up,' despite the fact that her mother said she 'would ruin my hands,
make them coarse and rough.'[47] Nevertheless, a few informants conveyed a
sense that fathers aspired to more than they had or could reasonably acquire
through their own and their children's efforts. Such families pushed their
children into more work than they really had time to do, and more than
could be fairly asked for in the circumstances. One man noted that,
although 'he never stayed out of school for farm chores,' certain other Evelyn children were sometimes kept out of school and 'worked like a bugger'
by their fathers.[48]

Implicit in this account of children's work is the sense of the family's central role in the education of Evelyn's youngsters, including helping them to
decide what they would do when they they grew up. Parents encouraged
some, and especially daughters, to use the school to provide an opportunity
so that they need not settle on, or drift into a life in, the local community.
Accordingly, for those Evelyn children who went on to secondary education, and then to trade, semi-professional, and professional training, the
school assumed a major role in their vocational education. Those entering
such practical or semi-practical fields as nursing or the mechanical trades
found their home training also provided them with a substantial base in
practical experience onto which their later theoretical learning could be
built. The student nurse who had helped butcher the family pigs had a head
start in anatomical studies (and the control of squeamishness) over most of
her urban counterparts.

For those Evelyn young people who embarked on careers as farmers, loggers, and the wives of farmers and loggers, their childhood and youth had
provided them with most of the practical knowledge they would need in

their working lives. Both girls and boys could use and repair tools and machinery. Both could care for livestock. Both knew the seasonal routines of planting and harvesting. Both could do most of the domestic chores involved in running a household. Both knew the local vagaries of weather and climate and how to incorporate this knowledge into their seasonal planning. In short, both possessed the full complement of what they needed to know to succeed, even to thrive, in a rural environment.

When the pioneering generation of children came to marry, they could base their family economy on a farm or ranch. Especially after 1939, and in an economic climate of fairly continuous development, wives could manage much of the farm work. Meanwhile, husbands could work away seasonally at land clearing, logging, sawmilling, rough carpentry, labouring on construction sites and on road building, and other related jobs with an almost equal ease. As the seasons and the economic climate changed, such men moved with deceptive ease from one job to another. Sometimes they worked for themselves, sometimes they hired others to help them, and sometimes they worked as part of someone else's small crew. Occasionally they found work in large, fully regulated concerns, although this sort of monotonous employment was not their first choice. Serving their own needs as well as those of a capitalist society, many such families did and do reasonably well, shrewdly customing a good standard of living out of their land, their wide range of abilities, and their mastery of the informal economy.[49] In roughly analagous situations, other families, less skilled or, perhaps, less adept at the ways of the world, lived or live sometimes despairing lives just above or below subsistence.

Whatever their eventual fate, Evelyn and other pioneering and rural youngsters had acquired their substantial fund of practical knowledge and skills in time-honoured ways. They observed their parents and siblings, mimicked their activities or were shown how to do them, or to share in them, and soon grew into full responsibility for them. As Elizabeth Varley put it, 'We were like all primitive people and those in frontier places, learning almost everything by working with our parents.'[50] After describing how she had helped with the birth of a calf – 'I was asked to put my smaller hand in to pull the foot forward and the calf was born instantly' – one woman expressed amazement 'at what six-year-olds can learn.' Andy Russell elaborated: 'We learned by watching, helping, and doing. We found out that there is a skill in about everything ... even using a spade or a pitchfork.'[51] While Ian Mahood was still in elementary school, his forester father 'taught me how to run a compass, estimate the width of a cruise line, tally the volume in a tree and grade it, draw the cruise map and write a report.'[52]

Such practical learning could, of course, be dangerous. H.A. (Bud) Cole recalled, for example, that when he was younger than five, he all but cut one finger off 'while trying to chop kindling.'[53] In this regard we must note that my informants reported remarkably few youthful injuries. They also explained that, while certainly not fool-proof, farm machines of the era were much simpler and less dangerous than their modern counterparts.

If pioneering in Evelyn was a way of life that employed girls and boys almost interchangeably as workers, it was also a way of life that encouraged both sexes to see themselves as growing into sex roles characteristic of the late nineteenth and early twentieth centuries. As one man accurately observed, Evelyn 'was a chauvinistic society.' It was also a paternalistic one. In childhood, Evelyn girls and boys mostly had their mothers and fathers to model appropriate forms of adulthood for them, including the core sense of what it was to be a woman or a man, and one form of the relationship between men and women. If they looked beyond the confines of their own nuclear family, they could see in the lives of their relatives and neighbours only mildly different arrangements of family relationships. If they looked more widely in the community, they could see the different sorts of life possibilities portrayed by such locally visible occupations as storekeeping, teaching, nursing, medicine, preaching, agriculturalist, and some of the railway trades. Ferne Nelson, who grew up on a prairie homestead, vividly described their 'Rawleigh lady' who 'had a husband and a houseful of kids at home ... [who] spent her days bumping over rutted roads, making a living. An early independent business woman.'[54]

None the less, Evelyn children absorbed most of what they learned on these matters from their own families. In them they saw the range of overlapping skills that each parent possessed, the tremendous amount of work that each put into the family enterprise, and what each felt about the experience. In one family, for example, the daughter recalled that 'Dad was happy: he was working towards his dream. Mother not so much ... it was a full day's work just to cope with the family's needs.'[55]

Children also saw the distribution of power in the family. In some, fathers exercised an almost biblical domination over their families.[56] In most others, while each parent exercised it in his or her own sphere of the family's activities, the father exerted a residual but none the less final overall authority. These fathers held the final authority in matters of discipline, and usually administered the still widely prevalent corporal punishment. Within the framework set by the seasons, they made the decisions and allocated the tasks, and whether or not sewing or harvest took precedence over schooling. They decided whether new machinery was more essential to family welfare than new clothes or further schooling. They conducted most of the family's dealings with the outside world, making most of the trips into town. Finally, and beyond the range of a book about childhood, it was against fathers that many of the youngsters, and especially the boys, came in their adolescence to rebel.

Most pioneering boys and girls thus observed male behaviour models who, though they were by no means sole 'breadwinners' of the sort common in urban society, were clearly heads of their families in the broadest sense of that term. For most boys, therefore, there was an easy continuity between their practical education and their developing identities as males of their time and place. As they acquired 'male' skills through their chores, boys also learned to value such supposedly male characteristics as bodily strength, stamina, stoicism in the face of pain, an aggressive sense of self, and the vulgarity that permeates all-male environments. Evelyn boys, for example, absorbed some of this last quality as they told dirty stories to each other or conducted urinating contests behind the school privy. After school consolidation, however, Evelyn boys in the early grades found that their clothes, haircuts, and lack of experience of such village phenomena as running water subjected them to teasing. In high school, however, 'things turned around' and their status in the male hierarchy rose sharply. As one man explained, 'farm kids were stronger, could win at arm wrestling and the like ... Later, we could get jobs, we knew how to work hard, we had the skills and could go to work right away.' After their first day of part-time work away from the farm in the 1930s, 'cutting logs and hauling them out of the bush,' Mary Cook's three school-aged brothers talked 'as if they couldn't wait to get back into the bush next Saturday. They talked about being men, doing men's work and how the other workers treated them just like the rest of the crew.'[57]

On the other hand, Evelyn children saw women who, although they worked at least as hard as men, generally played a distinctly secondary role in the management of the family enterprise. For most girls, who possessed virtually the same range of skills as boys, and some of the other 'male' characteristics as well, there was discontinuity between their practical education and experience and their developing identities as females. The local cultural ethos valued and reinforced paternalistic patterns that called girls to a sense of nurturing and sustaining womanhood. No matter how severe the weather, they wore girls' clothes to school, and usually when they worked outside as well. Their mothers modelled appropriately female roles for them (they always addressed each other as 'Mrs'). Their parents and teachers instructed them in sexually appropriate ways of behaving; peers influ-

Pioneering pupils and their teacher outside a school in the Bulkley Valley.

enced them at school and in the neighbourhood; and books, newspapers, Sunday-school papers, magazines, and other printed material expounded traditional modes of female behaviour.

A few informants told of mothers who regretted where their lives had led them. In these cases, however, the fault was usually seen as a failure to choose a spouse wisely rather than being rooted in the structure of the traditional family situation itself. Capable as they clearly were, none of the Evelyn girls seem to have aspired to be a farmer, rather than a farmer's wife. (However one woman recalled that, 'when war broke out in '39, I thought what I could do would be to run a farm if necessary.') Those who moved off the farm entered such 'women's' occupations as waitressing, nursing, or teaching.

By concentrating, as it does, on the work of children, this chapter may suggest a somewhat bleaker picture of pioneering childhood than was actually the case. Although one of the earliest children in the Evelyn area recalled that 'there was no time for childhood,' most youngsters found release from their work in family and community activities, in school, and in the culture of childhood.[58] Most families read books (some from the circulating library to which they subscribed) and newspapers, taking an interest in public affairs. They made occasional visits to Smithers to shop and to visit. They celebrated birthdays and Christmas. They came together for church services in the school, and then in the community hall that they had banded together to build. The United Church minister from Smithers, for example, 'came to the schoolhouse every other Sunday,' and some children regularly attended services. Families gathered for dances, the school Christmas concert, the school closing activities, and community picnics. Especially with those teachers whom they liked, some children found pleasure in the generally informal and relaxed atmosphere of the Evelyn School. While one man felt 'school was something you had to do, and worse than working by far,' another 'looked forward to going to school because it got you out of the boredom of being at home.'

Evelyn children also shared in the 'culture of childhood,' described more fully in chapter 10. They walked to school together, and played together there before school, at recess, and over the lunch hour. Except at peak times in the seasonal round, they found time to roam the countryside. As they did so, they fished and hunted. They went horse-back riding, sledding, skiing, hiking, and skating. Sometimes they made pocket money through cutting wood for sale, doing the school chores, collecting bottles, trapping, or shooting crows and other creatures on which the province paid a bounty. When she was about ten years old, Elizabeth Varley took complete charge of a flock of chickens, and the next year of one of ducks. With her profits from the sale of the former, she bought her 'most precious possession,' a .22 Winchester rifle.[59] As Evelyn became more established, it also entered into more organized sports. 'When all the chores were done, we played ball; ... once a week there were community ball games.' If work continued to constitute a major element in the lives of Evelyn children, it was no longer as all-pervasive as it had been in the early years.

8

Children in Their Families: Special Occasions

No account of children's experiences within families would be complete without reference to those special, sometimes cherished moments, events, and occasions that still stand out vividly in adult memories. 'Those were,' as one woman put it, 'the best things, the little things.' Many such special memories have a strong emotional dimension, binding children to their parents, grandparents, and other family members. Most grew out of the homely, routine scripts of daily life. 'I used to go to meet my father as he came off shift,' reported a man who grew up in Coleman, Alberta. 'Dad came out of the mine and then showered. I would meet him in the shower room and we would walk home together.' On hot summer nights in the 1930s, remembered a Kerrisdale woman, 'my father would sometimes walk up to the drugstore ... and he'd get a brick of ice cream and a bottle of ginger ale and bring it home and we'd polish it off.' Another woman remembers coming home on 'baking day,' when 'Mom always had a plate of hot buns, butter, and jam ready for us when we got in from school. I can still taste them.' 'Once I went out with Dad,' recalled one man, 'and on the way home we stopped at a restaurant. Dad bought me a glass of milk and a piece of raisin pie. It was the best I have ever eaten. I was never able to recapture the flavour of it.'

One Saturday, when her mother went to town, a young girl decided 'to do a surprise for Mother. I got the scrub brush and mop and water. After a while I had made big puddles on the floor.' In contrast to her mother, who 'would deflate you if you had a problem, even when you felt good about what you were doing,' her father came to help 'without making me feel so bad. He was gentle, but I learned. I never have puddles on the floor when I mop.' Of an evening when his father organized a special outing to a movie, Pierre Berton wrote, 'everything about that evening comes back sharply ...

but more than anything else I remember the pains my father had taken to make me happy and the realization which swept over me like a warm bath, that he really cared.'[1] People warmly recall when their parents got them a pet. One day in Kerrisdale in the 1920s, related one woman, 'we heard a commotion and opened the back door to find a red cocker spaniel eating our fudge. Dad was at the foot of the stairs laughing ... Of course we named the dog "Fudge."'

Some well-remembered events of childhood were sad ones. It was in their families that children made their first meaningful acquaintance with death. When a family member died, children learned to feel the fears and grief that accompany the death of someone close. After her father died away in Britain during the war, followed by the grandfather who lived in the same house, a woman recalled, 'I remember as a child going to school and sometimes I would worry ... not sometimes but a lot, that something would happen to my grandmother. Everybody seemed to be leaving.'[2] And, indeed, some parents, grandparents, and other relatives 'left.' A woman vividly recalled that, when she was almost five and her mother was dying of cancer, her father read to her from the Bible.

The death of grandparents figure in many memories. 'In Grade One my grandmother died,' reported an east-side Vancouver man. 'She was laid out in her living-room for three days ... That was very traditional in those days.' A woman believed that her artistic talent was 'a gift from my grandmother, who taught me to paint when I was four or five, even though she was bedridden.' Soon, 'my grandmother died ... and it was a very traumatic experience because I was so close to her.' Of her grandmother, Helen Porter wrote, 'Nanny lay there, still and white and cold, with a bandage over her sore eyes. It wasn't Nanny, of course, Margie [Porter's sister] and I soon realized that, but if she wasn't in the casket, where was she?'[3] When, in the early 1960s, Derek McNaughton's grandfather died 'on that cold sunny morning, I sat in my mom's car car for a long time. It was not until Mom drove me home from the house, when I gazed at the brown fields of an Ontario countryside, that I felt a warm and steady path of tears on my cheeks.'[4]

Those who grew up before the advent of antibiotics in the 1940s more commonly than later cohorts recalled the death of brothers and sisters. When she was three and a half, one Winnipeg woman remembers, 'my younger sister died of pneumonia. There were lots of flowers in Mother's room, where the little casket was.' In the 1930s, reported another woman, 'my younger sister died at six months of summer complaint.' While Verna Kirkness's family was still in the midst of grieving the very recent death of her stepsister from tuberculosis, 'my sister, who was two years younger than

Both brothers and sisters mourned the death of this child.

me, got a nosebleed and it got to be very bad ... and in those days it was very difficult to get a doctor ... and before long she really got ill ... and she died that night.'[5] When MacDonald Coleman was twelve, his fourteen-year-old brother, Rolly, died of sarcoma of the lymph glands. 'As I came down the stairs his eyes seemed to be fixed on me with some slow-burning fire in them ... As I watched ... the fire burned out and was gone ... the bed where Rolly and I had rump fights now seemed to have become half a mile wide.'[6]

Others of their own generation also died. A man who grew up in the Bulkley Valley recalled the death of two friends. One boy died of spinal meningitis, 'which was quite a shock ... at our age. You didn't think about this.' Later in his childhood, the same man went with another boy, an only child, to watch 'a massive salmon run ... He was on the rocks, and he slipped and fell in and drowned.' In the days before almost universal swimming lessons, such drownings were more common. E.A. Harris's Grade One seatmate, seven-year-old Peter Herman, played truant from the Port Essington school, 'fell off the float into the water, and the current carried him under it ... Peter, like most Port Essington kids at that time, had never learned to swim.'[7]

Children lamented the death of relatives in the Second World War. One woman's brother was 'shot for trying to escape.' Her mother 'took to her bed and died four years later.'[8] A man reported: 'In 1943, my brother was killed ... It was very sad ... My mother and father were never the same after that. None of us were. They never got over it, especially my mother.'[9] Another man explained that his grandmother's brother in England had been 'killed in a bombing raid. I never met him, but with Gran so sad, we kids all grieved a bit too.'

Children were also affected by the death of pets. When Mildred Young Hubbert was ten her mother took her to Scotland for an extended stay with family. As they were about to leave, Mildred was persuaded to leave her dog with the Humane Society 'to look after it until we got back.' Then, 'little by little the awful truth became real. They had killed my dog! ... He loved me totally, and I had handed him over to the executioner. I would never forgive myself, nor Mother, nor Life. I was never quite a child after that. I knew that the very worst life could offer was indeed possible. I learned that a child's heart can break and mine did. Sixty years have not dulled the pain of remembrance.'[10]

Children also suffered injuries or came down themselves with serious illnesses, events that etched themselves deeply into memory. 'I broke my arm when I was about five,' reported one woman, 'and Dad set it himself. He thought it was just a strain. Later, the doctor looked at it, said it had not set properly, and broke it again. It often aches still, especially when there is a change in the weather.' When he was three in 1953, Garth Drabinsky came down with polio: 'I opened my eyes to find myself in a cavernous room lined with small, neat, white beds. I could hardly move. There was no one there I knew, no one to say comfortable words, no one to hold my hand or hug me.'[11]

Many 'special' memories of childhood, however, are happy ones. People fondly recall occasions when families entertained themselves. Although some families 'didn't play [them] on Sundays,' various board and card games contributed to family pleasure. 'We'd play 'til bedtime – cards, crokinole – [but] never for money: Dad would have been horrified;' 'We'd play Crazy 8s ... 'cause remember, like, my brothers and sisters were younger than me ... and it was my dad's way of teaching us to count, too'; 'We played cards, we played checkers, we played Monopoly ... a whole gamut of games'; and 'Grandad sat at one end of a long stool and I straddled the other and we'd

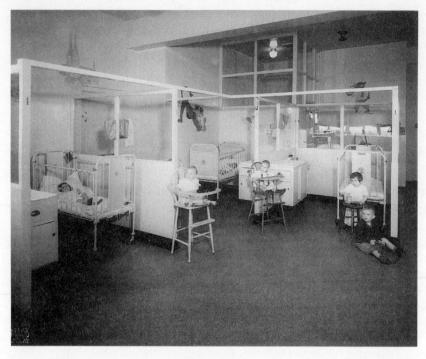

The baby ward in the Vancouver Crippled Children's Hospital in 1943.

play game after game of Snap.' When Dorothy Wardrop and her siblings visited their grandparents, 'Granddad would go around the corner into the pantry to get us a slice of buttered bread. When he came back with the slices, in a serious voice, he would say, "Oh, I accidently dropped these in the sugar bin. Do you mind?"'[12]

Music was central in the life of many families. People variously reported: 'Mother would play the piano and we'd have sing-songs'; 'We'd have family gatherings and singing around the piano'; and, perhaps more rarely, 'We were opera buffs ... We had records on a wind-up gramophone with cylinders ... I can remember listening to Caruso.' Mary Cook's family was 'a singing family. Intermittently we sang in the church choir and at concerts, with our mother accompanying us on the harmonica. We spent hours daily with our voices raised in song ...'[13] Born in Vancouver of Croatian parents, Mary Trocell Veljacic remembered that 'we had our own music, and our own musical instruments, the "tamburitza" ... And we sang a lot ... even we that were born here sang all the old songs.'[14]

Many parents regularly read or told their youngsters bedtime stories. People recalled being read the Thornton W. Burgess stories that appeared in many daily newspapers with, as E.A. Harris recalled, 'illustrations by Harrison Cady, about such animal characters as Peter Rabbit, Reddy Fox, Old Man Coyote, Jimmy Skunk and Sammy Jay.'[15] A woman reported, 'when my dad read Burgess to us, each of the animals had a different voice.' Others remember hearing the novels of Sir Walter Scott or Charles Dickens. Every year, John Charters's mother read *A Christmas Carol* from an illustrated edition, 'and I can still remember the pictures: Scrooge, old, bent and miserable in a snowy Victorian street ...'[16] Tony Smith's father read stories 'at bedtime; stories of adventure and valor, of rising above adversity.' He gave his children 'heroes, martyrs, dragons and trolls. He gave them a love for reading and learning; he gave them survival.'[17]

In some families, a certain amount of game-playing, singing, and being read to gave way to radio listening. In the early 1920s, radios, in the form of crystal sets listened to through earphones, served as a novelty item for children and adults alike. 'We would listen on head sets' and, although 'Dad had a crystal set ... kids rarely listened because we only got stations clearly late at night.' With the addition of amplifiers, radios became more a centre of family rather than an individual entertainment. In the late afternoon, some radio stations carried programs for children: 'I listened to *Just Mary* on the CBC'; 'My best friend, David, and I listened to *Little Orphan Annie* together.' *Little Orphan Annie*, *Dick Tracy*, and other children's programs had 'clubs' that children could join, usually in exchange for cereal boxtops or other proofs of purchase of the sponsor's product. In exchange, children received badges, secret codes, and other inexpensive paraphernalia.

Most radio stations devoted the lunch, supper, and early evening hours to programs directed to family audiences. Parents usually controlled the choice of station. Both rural and urban families listened to *Don Messer*; *The Happy Gang*; *The Carsons*; 'My favourites, *Saturday Night Barn Dance* and *Red River Jamboree*,' and to hockey and baseball games. In many parts of the country, Saturday evening's *Hockey Night in Canada*, with Foster Hewett describing home games of the Toronto Maple Leafs, was a high point of the week. For some families in Atlantic Canada, however, 'their' teams were the Boston Bruins and, especially, the Red Sox.

By the late 1930s, American entertainers and programs had also become very popular. 'I'll never forget Wilf Carter as long as I live,' recalled present-day country singer Gary Fjellgard. 'I used to wonder how he could get from Moose Jaw to Regina to Saskatoon so fast ... we used to pick up all those stations, [but] I didn't know about records.'[18] Others remembered, 'there was Edgar Bergen and Charlie McCarthy to listen to, and later Jack Benny and Fred Allen'; and 'Dad and I loved to listen to Amos and Andy, Jack Benny and Rochester, and *Twenty Questions*.' Billie Housego recalled '*Lux Radio Theatre* on Monday nights, which was a great drama ... The whole family listened. I mean, the dishes weren't done until after the programmes were over.'[19]

The Second World War increased radio listening. Families gathered – often including even very young children – to hear the latest news of the war. They listened to a morning newscast before going to school or work, and then an evening one. In one family, 'we listened to the radio every evening. I can remember being shushed every night at 7 o'clock. The news was taken very seriously in our house.'[20] People particularly remember hearing about the declaration of war and the sinking of the *Athenia* (with Vancouver families and children on board) in 1939, the Battle of Britain, the Dieppe raid, D-Day, and the German and Japanese surrenders. Many Vancouver children have vivid memories of their families listening to the radio all day on Sunday, 7 December 1941, and adults speculating excitedly that 'they'll be here, next!'

After the war, the appearance of radio stations and programs directly focused on children, and especially adolescents, together with children's acquisition of their own radios, sharply reduced 'family' listening. However, as television reception spread across Canada – often first from nearby stations in the United States – many families began to spend time together in front of their single black and white set. They watched the news, *Howdy Doody*, *Highway Patrol*, *George Gobel*, wrestling, and, as the CBC network came to their community, National League hockey in the televised version of *Hockey Night in Canada*. 'Although both Mom and Dad said they were appalled, they sat with us as we watched Elvis on *Ed Sullivan*, explained one man. A woman reported, 'My dad made us watch the opening of the Legislature or Parliament or something soon after we got our TV. Who knows, maybe he got it for that or the elections, or something. Anyway, as my kids now say, "Boring!"'

Families went out together. 'We went to friends' homes to visit and played games'; 'we'd visit some friends in North Vancouver ... or other friends on Capital Hill. We'd take the Hastings Street car and walk miles'; 'my uncle would take us all out in his car'; 'Sunday afternoon Father might say, "Let"s go for a drive in the car," maybe to Stanley Park, the airport, or New Westminster.' 'Sundays, we'd go for walks on the farm ... Dad would teach us to look for different birds, animals, and plants'; 'Father would take me on his back and go for long hikes and walk the trestle and look at the scenery.' Kenneth Boyd and his family 'used to visit with our cousins ... quite often, and get together for Christmas and such holidays. We used to have a great time playing in his hayloft, and I can imagine the work entailed to feed us all. I remember we used to eat in shifts in their home as they had six kids and we were seven ...'[21] Although youngsters did most of their movie-going at Saturday matinées – discussed later, in chapter 10 – it was still 'a big treat to go to the picture show with Mom and Dad.' It was also 'real special to go to a restaurant ... for dinner for fifty cents. Once Mother was really excited at having sardines there'; 'We'd ... meet my father downtown on Wednesday nights and go to dinner, then go to the Pantages Theatre. There would be vaudeville and a show.'

For Evelyn and other rural youngsters, the trip to 'town' was a particularly memorable family event. Until after the Second World War, these trips tended to be rare ones. One Evelyn family took the children to 'town' (Smithers) about three times a year: 'We got twenty-five cents and made it last.' After the war, trips became weekly affairs, with shops staying open into the evening to cater to their rural customers. While their parents shopped, or mothers shopped as fathers visited the pub, children roamed up and down the streets. The trip often ended with a treat, such as a snack in a coffee shop or a movie. 'Every Saturday' after the Second World War, an Evelyn family 'went by car to the movie in Smithers.' Very rarely, rural families made longer excursions to larger centres. A man who grew up on a farm vividly recalled his only childhood visit to Vancouver, seventy miles away: 'We went in the farm truck to Chilliwack and took the interurban to town. We shopped at a department store, and then went to a show with live entertainment between the features. We stayed overnight with some of Mom's relatives. On Sunday, we went to Stanley Park. My brother and I talked about the trip for years afterward.'

Summer, with its trips to the beach, picnics, and, for some, travel and visits to far-away relatives, provided people with rich stores of warmly recalled family events. In Vancouver, parents took their children to Trout Lake or they 'spent marvellous wonderful days at Kits[ilano] beach.' 'Mom, she would take us down to Locarno, or Jericho ... You know, we'd get on the bus ... And those were nice times 'cause it was a picnic.' At the beach, they would swim, make rafts, fish, build driftwood fires, beachcomb, and skip rocks. 'In those days,' wrote Hugh Palmer, 'one of the supreme pleasures for a child who had stayed too long in the freezing water was to ... buy five cents' worth of French fries, and drown them in vinegar; ... the bizarre sensation of eating food that scalded the roof of my mouth even as I shivered from the cold was something close to ecstacy.'[22] In Evelyn, mothers took children 'out to Lake Kathryn to swim,' in Toronto to the 'Islands,' and in Halifax by ferry 'to where the Memorial Tower now stands. It was a big trip and we took the picnic basket for the day. It was great to line up for the ferry, our anticipation was so great for that trip.'

Sunday school, community, or organizational picnics marked a high point in summer. 'We have pictures of picnics where my father has his bathing suit on and all our friends have theirs ... and here Mother is in a long-sleeved [swimming] dress with stockings'; and, on Bowen Island, 'we'd go in the father-and-son three-legged races'; and, 'Mother liked picnics – especially the races – and she'd come in first.' For Jacqueline Gresko, in New Westminster, 'a highlight of our summer time weekdays was ... the civic workers' picnic. There we played in a hollow tree, ran the races, ate hard icecream that had rested on that mysterious dry ice, raced over to see all of the zoo, went swimming, drank pop, had hotdog-eating contests, went to the swings, discovered we caught blisters from sand in our runners, and had tummy aches.'[23] For a Cedar Cottage family in the 1940s, 'our Sunday school's picnic at Belcarra Park was really great. We took the little ferry, and then played all sorts of games. We ended up with a family baseball game.'

In Evelyn, whole families gathered for dances at the community hall; one woman remembers 'sleeping on top of coats as my parents were dancing.' Others who grew up in Evelyn described the school Christmas concert, the school closing activities, and, especially, community picnics as social high points of the year: 'every family in the community went.' In the words of one man, 'Boy, it was fun!' to go to the annual picnic at Trout Creek and, when 'Dad played ball and I was amazed to see him [at age thirty-two] hit a ball and running; I'd never seen him run!' One woman recalled, 'We had races; sack races, running races, three-legged races; ... we made ice cream [to which] everyone shared in contributing cream, eggs, ice.' These neighbours then finished the day with a pot-luck supper.

A family visit to the local exhibition and fair marked the end of summer. These ranged in size from small, local events up to Toronto's Canadian National Exhibition. Whether the fair was small or big, children looked forward to each with growing excitement. After a 'wonderful day' at the August fair in Viking, Alberta, in the 1920s, Ferne Nelson and her siblings 'would look forward to next year and another school fair.'[24] Grant Buday has written that fairs should be seen 'from the perspective of a nine-year-old. As a child, the Pacific National Exhibition [in Vancouver] ranks with the cardinal events of the year: Halloween, Christmas, Easter, your birthday. At nine, the fair is magic. It means rides, music, faces, freaks, the hot sweet scent of candy apples, seagulls swarming spilled popcorn, three-day

Youngsters at the fair in Boissevain, Manitoba, in 1938.

tattoos and having your fortune told by a mouse.'[25] Youngsters felt they had taken a major step towards maturity when they were permitted to tour the midway and, eventually, go to the fair itself on their own.

It was not until after the Second World War that many families, even middle-class ones, went away for summer vacations.[26] Before this time, if working-class fathers had vacations, they, like many middle-class fathers, generally could not afford to take their families away. Thus, although a Halifax lower-middle-class father 'took annual vacations in the summer, we didn't go anywhere. We didn't have a car or the money.' However, in the Cedar Cottage family of a hospital orderly, 'Mother was resourceful and would find us a cottage to rent for a week or two. I remember lots of rain.' Maureen Forrester's grandfather, who lived with her family, had a lifetime railway pass. 'Because I never fussed or cried, he would take me along on his trips to visit relatives in far-off Ontario. In those days, when people in our circle couldn't afford to travel, the next province seemed worlds away from Montreal.'[27] Throughout the Depression, social agencies such as the Hebrew Maternity Aid Society of Toronto and the Alexandra Fresh Air Association of Vancouver ran 'Fresh Air' camps for 'tired mothers and needy children.' The latter's camp was at Crescent Beach, an hour's train ride from the city.[28] Of it, a Cedar Cottage informant recalled, 'My mother, my younger sister, and I had a very pleasant if somewhat chaotic time.'

Before and during the Second World War, those families who did go away visited relatives or rented a cabin or cottage at a nearby vacation spot. Ebbitt Cutler's mother took her from Montreal to a village in the Laurentians that seemed 'very remote' because of 'the dusty four-hour train trip during which I slithered restlessly about on the rattan seats while mother gave me oranges to peel, pointed out the engine pulling us each time the train went around a turn, and warned me to "sit small" when the conductor passed to collect tickets.' Her father joined the family on the weekend.[29] An Evelyn woman remarked that 'it was lovely when I went to stay with relatives [in nearby Smithers] for a week in the summer.' A Kerrisdale woman 'had an aunt and uncle who lived at Sidney on Vancouver Island. My brother would stay with them for a longer time, [but] the rest of us would stay a couple of weeks. One of my cousins had a boat and would take us sailing.' A Kerrisdale woman from what was not usually a very happy family 'remembers that we always went on an annual holiday. One year we rented a cabin at Eagle Harbour and another ... at Cultus Lake. These were always fun times when the whole family could be together.' On vacations, said one Cedar Cottage man, 'we went down to White Rock, my aunt and uncle had a place there. We would go for a month, my mother, myself, and my younger sister. My older sister and Dad would come down on weekends on the train.'

After the war, a higher standard of living, a wider ownership of automobiles and better roads to drive them on, and a sharp rise in the number of paid vacations combined to make travelling vacations more a part of a family's annual routine. In the 1950s a 'tightly knit' Kerrisdale family 'went to Kelowna a couple of times, [and] camping in the Cariboo ... I remember eating lots of fried tomatoes on our camping trips.' On one summer's camping trip to Vancouver Island's Oyster River, Susan Mayse 'would hang in the current for hours at a time, holding my place by grasping a projecting cottonwood root, watching the dappled clouds float high above and the first falling leaves float on the river's reflected sky ...[30] After spending most family vacations in cabins on Bowen Island, one Kerrisdale woman especially remembers 'one time my parents saved up and we went to Disneyland. We drove. That was sure a one-time event!' Those who drove into the United States still recall keeping 'an eye out for "Burma Shave" signs and reading them aloud: "The barefoot boy with cheeks of tan ..." and that's all that they can remember!'

Vancouver children watch a department store's toy parade in 1929.

In his Burnaby home in the 1930s, Alistair Ross wrote, 'Christmas was always a family affair for me.'[31] Indeed for most children, Christmas was both a 'special family day' and the most important single, long-awaited day of the year; 'whole centuries intervened between one Christmas and the next.'[32] Christmas was also a time characterized by small and large elements of family ritual. Before Christmas, parents took their children to visit Santa Claus, to tour Toyland in a department store, and to look at the specially decorated store windows. In Vancouver, the locally owned Spencer's store had many youngsters' favourite window display, together with a train in Toyland. In small towns, merchants combined to set up a local Santa's house. In the home of Eve Rockett and her older sister, a lamp 'was always placed on the windowsill in our home in Oshawa, Ont., at Christmas with the three wise men painted on the shade. Warmed by the light bulb, the wise men kept turning and turning, and we felt glowy and safe.'[33]

Christmas trees figure in many memories. In one working-class Halifax family in the 1920s, 'Mother kept Christmas very special ... We would clean the fireplace out for Santa to come down. On Christmas morning the Christmas tree would be there. There would be candles on the tree.' In Otto Tucker's Newfoundland home, the presents, 'hardly ever wrapped, were placed upon the branches so that on Christmas morning the tree looked like a figure with numerous outstretched arms holding yaffles and yaffles of gifts.'[34] In 1944, when he was six, Leonard Wilson went with three siblings to cut down their tree: 'We crested a small hill and there it was. The sun hung over the top like a giant halo. The snow on its branches glittered like silver specks. Then Isabel started singing the Christmas carol her class had learned for the concert. Her words rang clearly in the cold air. Tears welled in my eyes.'[35]

For some families, Christmas routines included religious activities. 'My fondest memories of the Cumberland Chinatown Mission,' wrote Philip Low of the 1910s and 1920s, 'were the annual preparations which the Sunday school children had to make for the Christmas tree and the mission hall; the rehearsals, which they had to go through for the play on "the birth of Christ"; and the arrangements for the Christmas party.'[36] Even the youngest children in one Roman Catholic family were taken to midnight Mass. Afterwards, 'we had a cookie (the same kind that we left out on a plate for Santa), hung up our stockings, and went to bed.' Children in an Anglican family in Cedar Cottage 'longed to be old enough to attend the midnight service at St. Margaret's.' In Saskatchewan in the 1920s, a Lutheran family went to church on Christmas Eve, 'and then to our grandparents' home ... where the children had a treat of candy and nuts. We opened presents on Christmas morning' and then went back to the grandparents for a noontime Christmas dinner.

In some families the season was split in two. In Bill Maciejko's Ukrainian Canadian family, 'the 25th was when the hockey equipment and toys and games and the sleds and etc. came, but when I look back at it, what I remember more is the family's spiritual and social connections for the 6th and 7th rather than the commercial Christmas.'[37] In Aubrey Tizzard's Newfoundland outport, 'Christmas holidays would begin at noon on December 24th, to end on January 6th (Old Christmas Day) ... The first mummers would appear on Christmas Eve, and on Old Christmas Night everyone that had an inclination at all to dress up was out that night because it was the last night to go mummering until next December 24th.'[38]

Presents are at the centre of many memories of Christmas. Until after the Second World War, most presents were practical ones. As one Cedar Cottage man explained, 'Christmas wasn't a big giving time. You used to hang up your stocking and Mother would fill it with candy and nuts. She would

knit a pair of woollen socks as a gift.' Another man from the same neighbourhood noted, 'We would have stockings and Mother would fill them up.
I believed in Santa Claus for a long time.' In another family, 'every year we
would get back from Christmas Eve dinner with our relatives and the ham-
pers [from the local United Church] would be sitting on the steps full of
candies, clothes, and toys.' Sam Roddan, one of the seven children of a Vancouver United Church minister, wrote that 'the Christmas presents I
remember best ... were the mitts, socks, and sweaters knitted by my Granny
... Everything was always several sizes too big to allow for growth and
expansion ... All gifts had to be carefully spread around ... One Christmas I
got the checkers and my brother the board.'[39] One woman remembers that
one year her non-practical 'present under the tree was a cup and saucer. I
was disappointed.' None the less, another woman spoke for many when she
reported that 'Christmas was always a great occasion in our family, even
though we were hard up. Mother made things. We always had one toy or
something special.' Gary Saunders was 'bursting with pride' when Santa left
a 'scrawly note saying "Your red sleigh will come on the steamer next week.
Love, Santa."'[40]

Even before postwar affluence, however, some children received imprac-
tical, sometimes expensive presents. Robert Thomas Allen and his brother
'never got what were known as sensible gifts ... We got what we wanted.
Snowshoes, shoe packs, tins of Dubbin to keep out the Arctic ice, toy farms
that gave you the feeling of being able to bring under control the sprawling
stuff of the adult world ... mechanical toys ... big sets of building blocks,
erector sets.'[41] Marjory Narroway's 'wealthy and indulgent grandfather ...
asked me for a list of all the things I really wanted and, to my surprise and
delight, Father Christmas brought them all, even ... the splendid rocking
horse on which I spent many delightful hours.'[42]

Some toys and other presents, such as Narroway's rocking horse, games
such as snakes-and-ladders, checkers, Chinese checkers, 'old maid' cards,
and ludo, were given to both boys and girls. Others, including dolls, doll
carriages, and clockwork and then electric trains, were meant for one sex or
the other. Some presents, exemplified by one girl's 'darning egg painted like
a doll' or one boy's 'small but usable – and very sharp – hatchet,' reinforced
other lessons in gender identity.

Presents also tightened family ties with other places. 'We always had a
parcel from Denmark,' recalled one man, 'sometimes with clothes in it that
were not necessarily good for Canada. Once I got plus fours, but my
mother adapted them.' In another family a 'highlight of Christmas was a
parcel' that came from Scotland, one containing a precious 'brown mohair

sweater.' English relatives sent their Canadian nephews '*Chums* annuals, that we read and reread over the years to come. My own nephew eventually devoured them as well.'

Christmas dinner figures prominently in many memories. In Maria Campbell's family, 'Christmas dinner was the highlight of the day. It consisted of meat balls rolled in flour, stewed moose meat, all covered with moose fat, mashed potatoes, gravy, baked squash and pemmican made of dried meat ground to a powder and mixed with raisins, smashed chokecherries, and sugar. After that we filled ourselves with the pudding and cakes until we could hardly move.'[43] After trying to make the meal of the farm animals special – 'extra wheat for the chickens, choice scraps for dogs and cats, a carrot for each horse and cow' – the Christmas dinner in Robert Collins's home 'was a triumph of the farm.' They had 'roast chicken, mounds of creamy mashed potatoes, carrots, peas, turnips, bread, butter, pie, cake, cookies. Only the Japanese oranges, cheddar cheese, walnuts and filberts were store-bought treats – but *such* treats.'[44]

Christmas meals often tied children to customs brought from 'the old country.' 'We had,' recalled one Evelyn man, 'a Swedish dinner; lutfiske, pork roast, some chicken, rice for dessert, and Swedish baking with carraway seeds that at first I thought were mice droppings.' In another home, where 'my grandmother was English so we had to do things properly,' they had 'beefsteak pudding that was better than turkey, vegetables, and plum pudding,' while 'a gramophone with a horn played Christmas carols.'

Christmas also stood out for those children whose families did not or could not celebrate it. In 1933 or 1934, an east-side Vancouver father 'lost his business' and, his son reported, 'that Christmas was non-existent, except for a gift from my grandparents in Ontario.' Fredelle Bruser Maynard movingly described the sense of separateness brought on by being a Jewish child in a strongly Christian town on the prairie during the 1930s.[45] Richard Wagamese wrote that, in 1960, when he was five and in a foster home with his two older brothers and his sister, they scraped together enough money to buy him 'a tiny red truck with a blue cab and one wheel missing ... It was the only present the four of us shared that year.' Otherwise, 'with about six other kids, Christmas was a tree and a meal shared at one long table apart from the foster family who ate in another room.' In the following spring, Wagamese was separated from his brothers and sister, not to see them again for almost twenty years.[46]

Religious observances formed the heart of other family occasions. Easter was widely observed. As Helen Sigurdson explained, her family, who lived near Starbuck, Manitoba, 'began preparing for Easter at the beginning of

Lent ... On Ash Wednesday, everyone went to church and ... the priest made a cross on our forehead with ashes.' Her family followed strict dietary rules during Lent 'and there were no weddings or parties ... Good Friday saw us in church at three o'clock in the afternoon to pray the Stations of the Cross.' The preparations culminated on Easter Sunday, 'a joyous celebration with choruses of Halleluiah! Christ has risen!'[47]

Like Christmas, Easter had its secular side. Custom decreed that Easter Sunday was the day for the wearing of new clothes, or even whole new outfits. Those with only a nominal connection to a church would dress in their new best and promenade to church. 'During the '30s and the war, we might just have one new thing – a pair of gloves, a hat, or a scarf for Easter,' reported a woman of Cedar Cottage, 'but after the war we kids and Mummy as well usually had a completely new outfit. Even Daddy would buy a new tie for his annual visit to church. If it was a nice day we would then walk in Stanley Park.'

Other traditions also had their special, memorable occasions. Sing Lim wrote that one of his 'favourite festivals was Ch'ing Ming, or annual remembrance day, when offerings to the dead were made.' At Vancouver's Mountain View Cemetery, food, wine, cigarettes, and paper 'money' and paper 'clothes' were all laid out, and the money and clothes burned. After the dead had been honoured, the group adjourned to a meeting hall for a feast. 'By the end of the day we were exhausted but happy. I liked to think of our dead relatives having "a big meal," "money" to spend and new "clothing to wear."'[48]

Many Jewish families observed the sabbath and High Holidays, such as Rosh Hashanah and Yom Kippur. Rita Goldberg reported, 'my mother would always prepare the chicken soup and the chicken, and we knew this was the sabbath and everything would be – the tablecloth and the candles, she would light the candles for the sabbath and there would be wine.'[49] Reuben Slonim sang in the choir of the Winnipeg Jewish Orphanage, which practised Saturday evenings. 'How we sweated in the summer months rehearsing for the fall holidays.' On those days in the synagogue at the Home, 'we sang everything and gave no quarter to the congregation, made up of adults from the community.'[50]

Occasionally children stored certain regular or unique public events among their special memories. In Toronto, one boy went regularly to the Eaton's Santa Claus parade, and 'one year Dad pulled me to it on a sled, and then we went to Aunt Edna's house for hot dogs and drinks.' For Lawrence Freiman, Armistice Day in 1918, when he was nine, 'meant being awakened at 5:00 in the morning, bundled into the car decorated with lots of Union

Jacks, and given a big wash tub to bang.'[51] In the 1930s, his mother woke up one Toronto boy at a very early hour. 'It was the Coronation [of George VI] with the sombre voices of the officials and commentators. Mother was quite nuts about the royal family.' People of elementary school age have stronger memories of VE rather than VJ day, partly because most of those in the Canadian services served in the European war, and partly because, as a man exclaimed, 'we got the day off school!'

Families (and schools) made much of royal tours. In 1939, after one family watched 'King George and Queen Elizabeth drive by from the roof of a commercial building' in Kerrisdale, their uncle 'drove us all over town ... to different spots to see them again.'[52] They also visited their unmarried aunt 'and with her help we would put scrapbooks together of all the royal visits across Canada.' Smithers had 'a big celebration' to mark the royal visit there, and an Evelyn woman's cousin 'picked up all the kids in a truck and we went to town. It was a very special occasion, and we got a big ice-cream cone.' In the 1950s, one Kerrisdale family 'drove somewhere to see Princess Margaret. She went by in a car with a light on inside. She was wearing a white gown and a tiara.'

As this and other chapters reveal, most emotionally charged memories are embedded in the innumerable routine scripts and rituals of childhood. One expects people to recall characteristic events related to much-loved (or much-hated or much-feared) parents, siblings, peers, or teachers. We have seen, however, that most people also store away certain personal recollections that stand outside regular routines. Often they are of events so superficially insignificant ('the little things') that even those other than their subjects who took part in them probably neither noted them at the time nor could later recall them. This chapter has dealt with the special memories that occurred within the family. The next two chapters include others associated with school and with the culture of childhood.

There is another sort of personal, sometimes unique memory – those neither involving others nor illuminating particular scripts – that rarely appear in this book. A woman told me of the 'fairy lights' of her childhood: 'They circled round and round the room as I waited to fall asleep. Their magic remained even after Mom told me that they were only reflections from the headlights of passing cars. Even now – this is foolish – I sometimes, often, feel the warmth and comfort, you know, of my childhood bed, knowing Mom and Dad, they're downstairs – when I see the fairy lights going round our room now.'

A man who grew up in Cedar Cottage told of one morning when he got up to deliver the morning *News-Herald*. 'There was something different about the morning and it took me a moment or two to notice that it was much quieter than usual. We lived right at Kingsway and Victoria, and even in the early morning we heard cars and streetcars as they came up the rise, and especially those that screeched as they turned up Victoria.' After he lighted the kitchen stove for his mother, dressed, and went out, he found that a heavy snow had fallen overnight. No traffic was moving. 'The clouds were moving off and the moon shone on the snow. I was the first out and broke path all the way to where I picked up my papers. They never came, and finally I slowly walked home through the fresh snow. I think I can still retrace every step of that walk in my mind.' Other people also recounted memories that had made an indelible impression on them.

Both sorts of intensely personal memories are at the very edge of or outside the scope of this book, concerned, as it is, with the recurrent. What is within its scope, and should be noted, if not discussed in any detail, is the fact that children store away memories of such unique and idiosyncratic events, and value, even cherish, them over the whole of their lives. Since people 'can still retrace every step' of them, they are as much a part of childhood as those dimensions discussed in this book.

9

Children in 'Formalist' Schools

Of the three central elements in adult memories of childhood – family, friends, and school – those of school display the greatest amount of consistency from one person to the next. Whether as children they loved, hated, or were indifferent to school, they described in interviews and memoirs a structure and set of classroom scripts that, over the whole of these years, were characterized by a remarkable degree of similarity from school to school, from place to place, and from public to separate and parochial systems. That structure, in turn, was a product of a mode of thinking about schooling that its critics came to refer to as 'formalism.' Advocates of this theory believed that education consisted of training such 'faculties' of the mind as memory and reasoning because such training generalized itself. Studying algebra and formal grammar, for example, trained reasoning ability. Acquiring competence in these subjects also enabled one to apply reasoning to actual situations throughout life.

While formalist pedagogy assumed a much more elaborate form in large urban schools than it did in small rural ones, it characterized the latter as much as it did the former.[1] Although I refer to rural schools in what follows, I lay out formalist schooling as it elaborated itself in an urban elementary school that I have assembled out of the memories of those who attended such schools in Vancouver and other parts of Canada.[2] There I follow the pupils through their day, their week, and their school year, describing how their teachers taught and what they learned. Next, I explain how the school ensured its 'peace, order, and good government.' Finally, I show how schooling extended, reinforced, or countered notions of self-identity begun in family and extended in congregation and culture of childhood.

Most children starting school were initiated into its ways long before they arrived for their first day. Parents, brothers and sisters, playmates, and older children helped to craft in the preschool child expectations of a traditional sort of schooling. The characteristics of the teachers, the rituals of discipline, and the content of the curriculum were part of the lore of childhood. On a bright summer day, a brother, a sister, or an older playmate had taken the prospective beginner to the schoolyard. Together they had climbed the fire escape to peer into the shadowed classrooms; the neophyte heard exaggerated tales of 'rubber nose,' or 'weasel mouth,' or 'Pussy Foot,' or 'Dynamite Dunsie,' or 'the strap,' or 'Mr Robb,' who cast so all-pervasive an aura over the school of which he was the principal that in the minds of some pupils he and his school almost merged together as one being.

Some children were afraid to start school, and often remained frightened by it throughout the whole of their school careers. They knew about events which gave a grim touch of reality to apocryphal lore – of the boy from down the lane who was strapped for throwing a spitball, of a girl who had a rash brought on by fear of physical-education classes, of another child's stomach cramps before each weekly spelling test, of a sister's outburst of tears when a page of her exercise book had been ripped out by her teacher. They expected such things to happen to them, too. Those whose families moved occasionally or frequently had to go through the ritual of 'starting to school' a number of times.

Most beginners were only partly taken in by ritual tales of 'horrors' ahead. They recalled the carefree departures of friends and neighbours to school as recently as the previous June, and themselves set off in the same way; typically, most children were 'very excited about school.' Although some people have few memories of the early years of their schooling, few have forgotten the excitement of the very first day: 'I could smell how clean my clothes were that day.' Most departed for their first day with their mothers or an older sibling. ('The first day arrived and my mother escorted me to school that morning'; 'My mother took me up there and that was all there was to it.') As she went with her sister to her first day in Bonavista, Newfoundland, Jessie Mifflen repeated 'the first page of the Primer over and over ... for no respectable child ever started school without having learned all the letters of the alphabet and without knowing the first page of the Primer by heart.'[3]

Other first-day memories are equally vivid but less pleasant. On his first day in a rural school in Ontario, Roy Bonisteel and the other Grade Ones were strapped, the teacher explaining, 'This is to get you started out on the right foot.'[4] 'I remember wetting my pants on the first day of school,' noted one woman. 'I was very upset and went back home ... After lunch my mother took me back and my teacher was very kind to me and let me carry around the waste-basket to help her.' Some children insisted that their mothers accompany them for the first few days and, very occasionally, the first few weeks. Some, even among those who were really keen to go to school, cried when their mothers left them on the first day.

However they came and whatever their expectations of how the school would be ordered, most beginners shared one very clear idea of what they would do in school. They were going to learn to read. Even after a half-century or more, many can recall stories, such as 'Chicken Little,' and even phrases and sentences such as '"A" says "ah" like in apple'; 'pretty pink ice cream from a pretty pink glass'; '"Cut, cut, cut," said the King'; 'I am a boy. My name is Jerry'; and 'See Spot run,' which were among the first that they decoded.[5] Older children also had a clear idea of the purpose of schooling. Susan Eng, born in Toronto in the early 1950s, said, 'School was fascinating for me ... I knew precisely what I was there for. I was to learn and I did what I was told and I got very good marks.'[6]

Despite problems posed by periods of rapid growth, many Canadian cities provided substantial buildings to house their pupils.[7] In Cedar Cottage and Kerrisdale, Lord Selkirk and Kerrisdale schools stood out as the most impressive buildings in their neighbourhoods. The front of each presented its best side to the community; the buildings were set back behind low fences which protected lawns and shrubs. At about 8:00 o'clock each morning, the janitor or a monitor raised the flag in front of the school. Schools had a boys' entrance and a girls' entrance, generally at ground level. Behind the school lay the main playing field. Since intensive use made grass impossible, this part of the playground was usually covered with packed earth, gravel, or even cinders, which meant that those who fell on the playing field often tore their skin or pitted their knees. Those who attended Kerrisdale fondly recall the small clump of trees in one corner of the school ground.

Most children arrived at school well before the bell. As they did so, they joined in the complex culture of childhood, described in chapter 10. There they also met the first symbol of the school's authority. The 'duty' teacher circulated from field to field, sometimes carrying the brass bell by its clapper. If she taught one of the primary grades, she might have a small chain of girls attached to each hand. Unless they were one of those privileged youngsters – generally girls – who had minor housekeeping or administrative tasks to perform before school, pupils were not admitted to the corridors or classrooms before the bell.

There was a ritual to entering school. At about five to nine, those schools equipped with bell towers or electric bells sounded a warning ring. In other schools a senior pupil or a teacher circulated through the corridors and on the grounds, ringing the brass hand bell. At the bell, monitors collected the meagre ration of sports equipment.(In the late 1920s, South Park School in Victoria provided its boys 'one softball and bat, one basketball, one rugby ball, and one soccer ball.')[8] Children moved rapidly to the inside or outside assembly point for their classes. There they lined up in pairs – girls in front, boys behind, younger children holding hands with their partners. Since the front was a much-coveted position, girls who wanted it reserved it by placing coats, lunch bags, or other possessions there, or even lined up well ahead of the bell to ensure their prime positions. One girl would 'race to school so I could be the first in line to enter.' At the bell, boys raced up and tussled either for first position behind the girls or for the very last position in the lines. The principal, vice-principal, or the duty teacher appeared and stared – or roared – the children into silence. He or she then signalled the classes one by one to march into the school.

Once inside, classes passed more or less silently along the corridors, some of which had a traffic line painted down the middle. Teachers stood vigilantly by the doors of their rooms. After the children entered their rooms, they placed their coats and lunches in the right place – some classes had dark, high-ceilinged cloakrooms which were often the scene of semi-silent scuffling, shin-hacking, and the like – and then moved to their desks. Those with problems in hearing or seeing – more did then than now – sat at the very front of the room. In the 1920s, some teachers still arranged their pupils according to their academic rank in the class, a practice that had generally disappeared by the 1950s.

Children entered classrooms that were dark and gloomy by today's standards. On the left-hand side of the room were windows that could be opened and closed. In most schools, freshly washed black slate chalkboards – on which white chalk was used – covered two, or even three, of the other sides of the room. In the new schools of the 1950s, the brighter fluorescent lights were installed, and yellow chalk was employed on green chalkboards. The floors were oiled wood or, later, tan-coloured 'battleship' linoleum. The former gave off the characteristic odour of raw linseed oil.

Much of the board space was already full. The morning's seat work covered much of it, sometimes concealed by a rolled-down map of the world, British Empire in red, or of a Canada surrounded by Neilson's chocolate bars. On a side panel, the teacher or some favoured pupils had gently tapped chalk brushes on onionskin stencils to etch out a ghostly scene appropriate to the season – autumn leaves, or Santa Claus, or valentines – and filled it in with coloured chalk. Another space displayed the list of classroom monitors whose tasks included cleaning blackboards and chalk brushes (*never* on the wall of the school), operating the pencil sharpener, filling ink-wells from copper containers or glass bottles with delicate glass stems, watering plants, and so on. Beneath the monitors' names came the 'detention' list, which, first thing in the morning, held only the names of those who had collected more of these punishments than they had yet been able to serve. Other lists showed those receiving milk, those who had bought war savings stamps, and other unofficial records. On one panel, a timetable dictated the regular pattern of the events of the day and of the week.

Portaits hung above the front boards. Over the years public schools displayed King George V and Queen Mary, and then George VI and Queen Elizabeth, and then Queen Elizabeth II. From 1927 onward in Vancouver, children also gazed at a lifeless copy of Robert Harris's *Fathers of Confederation*, that the Canadian Club had presented to schools in celebration of the fiftieth anniversary of Confederation. In 1940 it was joined by a coloured picture of the Union Jack, beneath which appeared the words:

> 'One Life   One Fleet
> One Flag   One Throne
> Tennyson'[9]

For children whose classrooms had one, as did that of E.A. Harris, 'the clock was the main focus of attention at the front. The pendulum swung back and forth behind its little glass door, and the minute hand slowly, sometimes ever so slowly, edged its way around the dial's circumference in a series of sixty spasmodic jerks.'[10] Above other boards hung such scenes of British prowess as the capture of Quebec, the Battle of Trafalgar, and the signing of the Magna Carta, and model alphabets, health posters, or murals created by the pupils.

Roman Catholic schools had a different display. A crucifix occupied the centre position above the front blackboard. In place of the monarch there was a picture of Pope Benedict XV, Pius XI, or Pius XII. Instead of political or military scenes, pictures showed events in the lives of Jesus or one of the saints. Otherwise, the classrooms contained the maps, the plants, the displays of children's work, and the piles of text and exercise books that characterized other schools.

Pupil desks, by the 1920s commonly individual rather than double ones (although the latter persisted in some places right through the 1950s), were generally screwed onto wooden runners. A metal ink-well or glass ink bottle sat in a hole that had been bored into the top right-hand corner of the

A class taught by a member of the Sisters of Charity in the 1940s.

slightly sloping desk. A pencil trough crossed the top of it. Beneath lay a shelf for storing pencil boxes, crayons, textbooks, and exercise ('copy') books. On the days when the windows could not be opened, the characteristic classroom odour was particularly strong: on the one hand, Plasticine, sour paste, pencil shavings, orange peels in the waste-baskets, chalk dust, oiled floors, and dustbane; on the other, stale bodies and sweaty feet, occasionally enriched by 'sneakers' or 'fluffs.' Characteristic sounds complemented these smells: steam radiators clanked, 'blakeyed' toes and heels clattered down the aisles, chalk screeched on the blackboard, and bells divided the day into its segments.

Teachers began the day by calling the roll and marking the class register, a process repeated in the afternoon. In public schools in British Columbia in the 1920s and 1930s, some teachers followed roll call with a scriptural reading or biblical story, and then a prayer. From 1944 onward, British Columbia public-school teachers read, without introduction or comment, a prescribed selection from the King James version of the Bible. After the reading, the teacher said, 'Class stand,' paused for quiet, and the children recited 'The Lord's Prayer' in unison.[11] In Catholic schools children took part in more elaborate morning devotions, and went once a week as a class to Mass.

Other routines followed the religious exercises. Teachers conducted a daily health inspection; they looked for nits, clean hands, clean nails, clean faces, combed hair, and possession of a handkerchief. Once a week they collected the milk money and, during the war, quarters for war savings stamps. They gave iodine tablets to whose who had paid a dime for a year's supply.[12] Pupils who aspired to be nurses, one recalled, 'would count out the tablets with a tongue depressor onto a tray and then carry them around the room, pushing out each kid's with the depressor.' Monitors gave out new pen nibs to those who needed them, from which children had to suck the thin coating of wax before they would hold ink. As these routines came to an end, the children took out their texts and exercise books for the first lesson. Many called the latter 'scribblers,' a practice that annoyed some teachers because it suggested slovenly work.

Whether pupils attended school cheerfully or apprehensively or in a state of fear, curriculum, teaching methods, and the pattern of school discipline combined to press them into the formal mode of learning. Its system was based on teachers talking and pupils listening, a system that discouraged independent thought, a system that provided little opportunity to be creative, a system that blamed rather than praised, a system that made no direct or purposed effort to build a sense of self-worth. Even those who enjoyed it then now recall a system that put its rigour into the rote learning of times tables, of spelling words, of the 'Lady of the Lake,' of the capes and bays of Canada, of 'the twelve adverbial modifiers (of place, of reason, of time ...),' and of the Kings and Queens. 'I can still name and date every monarch from Elizabeth the First to George the Sixth,' boasted one man. Such rigour began early. While talking to a social worker about the problems her son was having in the first grade, 'Donald's' mother described 'with what tension he arrived home, took a piece of paper from his pocket to show her the words he got wrong that morning, begging her to help him. He was also worried about getting stars.'[13]

Teachers in both rural and urban schools taught groups of children rather than individual youngsters. Of the former, Frances Fleming recalled, 'Every morning work for each class was set out on the blackboards. Miss Warburton would start with the beginners and work her way across the room, teaching, marking, assigning.'[14] In urban schools, the very size of classes made other forms of teaching and learning virtually impossible. In classes that, in Vancouver, for example, averaged for most of these years about forty pupils, teachers could not get to know much about their charges as individuals. Classes of this size forced them to teach to the whole class, to let the good look after themselves, and to let the weakest fall by the wayside.

Their responsibility for so many children also forced many teachers to take a stance in their classrooms that emphasized children's weakness and propensity to err, to capitalize on their vulnerability, and to keep an extremely wary look out for bad behaviour. They tested their pupils' memories and evaluated their work habits; they commented freely on these and other characteristics of their pupils. In the jargon of a later era, they unashamedly ran 'teacher-centred' classrooms. 'I didn't think a thought in the whole of school,' recalls one person with an excellent school record; 'I just regurgitated.'

Small-group teaching found its most extensive articulation in the teaching of reading. In the 1920s, a few teachers still taught reading as it was done in the nineteenth century: in one cryptic recollection, 'Well, you had to learn your ABCs to know what it is about. Then you found out that the words were not what they meant.' Most primary teachers, however, divided their pupils into reading groups roughly based on ability. In the 1920s, these groups were usually labelled by letter or number: thus, groups 'A,' 'B,' and 'C,' or '1,' '2,' or '3.' Later, it became fashionable to name groups in ways that concealed ability designations: thus, 'Bluebirds,' 'Robins,' 'Tony's,' or 'Pauline's' groups. Such euphemisms did not fool the children; they soon grasped the reality behind them.

Whatever they were called, primary reading groups went, in turn, to the front of the room, where they sat on little chairs or on the floor in a semicircle in front of their teacher. After the teacher conducted a 'phonics' drill, she introduced and drilled the new words. Then, in what was often the highlight of the day, the children each read a short segment of the day's story; 'I enjoyed it when it was my turn to read,' recalled one; another explained that the dull repetition didn't matter at all because 'learning to read was such a fabulous thing.' One man recalled 'sitting in front of a giant-sized book and the teacher using a pointer for each word of Dick and Jane.' After the Second World War, new readers with detailed guidebooks brought ability grouping and related practices to reading in the upper grades as well.

While one reading group worked with the teacher, the others did seat work at their desks. (One page of an unlined scribbler, completed in 1933, shows, in its owner's printing, 'the cat sits on the rug'; 'the rug is by the fire'; 'the fire is warm'; followed by a coloured drawing of a cat, a fire, and a rug.) Some classes had library corners or 'interest centres' or sand tables to which the children who had finished their seat work could go. Others had a dress-up box or a store where children quietly practised using money made from cardboard circles or milk-bottle tops. Intermediate-grade teachers encouraged those who had finished their work to move onto other tasks or to read library books.

Although the tone varied from room to room, the methods of teaching the whole class were remarkably consistent from teacher to teacher and subject to subject. Teachers began each lesson by reviewing what they had taught in the previous one. In arithmetic, teachers conducted individual or group drills of the number facts, or the times tables: 'Daily we had arithmetic first; always drill, drill, drill, flash cards, flash cards'; 'What a proud thing it was' to come first in an arithmetic race. Children also chanted drills of spelling words, or times tables, or number facts, or capitals of the provinces.

When teachers decided that the class was ready for the next segment of the topic, they instructed the pupils to put down pens, pencils, and rulers; to place their hands on their desks or behind their backs; and to 'sit up straight and face the front.' With all pupils' eyes on the blackboard, teachers then demonstrated, sometimes through question-and-answer, the letters for handwriting, the syllables in and the pronunciation of the new spelling words, or took the pupils a further step in the language, arithmetic, or grammar sequence. Then, some pupils moved eagerly and more moved reluctantly to work examples on the blackboard. The rest of the class was instructed to watch for mistakes. Teachers moved along the board, releasing those who had the correct answer or taking those in error through the question again. A man remembered a girl sent to work at the board 'almost as a punishment'; the 'teacher wouldn't let her sit down and she peed her pants. It was quite devastating.'

In reading, history, geography, and science lessons, pupils often read sequentially from textbooks. Teachers broke into the sequence to read themselves, to 'thrust a question at wandering minds,' or to explicate some point in the text. Some teachers followed a regular and predictable pattern, up one row and down the next. Others, to keep pupils alert, 'called out our names at random and we would respond immediately.' In Franklin Horner School in Long Branch, Ontario, in the early 1930s, 'Miss Healey ruled Third Book with an iron hand ... When one child was reading, the rest of us were required to follow word for word against the terrible moment that Miss Healey would point her finger and demand to know what the next word was. It was the strap if we were lost.'[15]

In some classes, children were allowed to volunteer to read. Those who read well read long bits, and those who read badly short ones. 'I could read with "expression",' reported one woman, 'but sometimes would say the wrong word, and would be embarrassed.' Some teachers passed over really

Pupils in the Nanaimo Indian School practise their handwriting in 1942.

poor readers altogether, or had them read later while the class did seat work. Most pupils found these sessions boring. Those who read well had long since read ahead and mastered the content. Those who did not worried about getting through their own portion.

Terrified by the thought of public performance on their part, some children never volunteered an answer to a question, and avoided any other oral participation as much as they could. 'In grade school,' wrote Lynn Fiddes, 'I lived in terror – not imagined terror, but real, physical, terror – that someone would try to talk to me, or, worse, that a teacher would call on me. Neither happened very often. Like most shy children, I became adept at being invisible.'[16] Kathryn Furlong recalled herself as 'sitting quietly at the back of the class, very studiously not bringing attention to myself ... I found it safer to withdraw. I had learned how to melt into the class. It was too scary to stand out.'[17]

Teachers occasionally varied their routine in science classes by performing experiments for their pupils. In a format that was 'progressive' in form rather than content, they laid out on the board what they were doing step by step, tackling a 'problem' through a precisely prescribed sequence that led from a 'plan' through 'apparatus and materials,' 'method,' 'observations,' to a 'conclusion,' the last sometimes written out even before the experiment was begun.[18] 'We put some rocks in a glass container, poured some liquid over it, and it bubbled and stank,' reported one man, while a woman recalled that 'a match went out when you put it into carbon dioxide.' Similar practical demonstrations characterized the introduction of something new in manual arts, manual training, and home economics.

Teachers closed the oral part of lessons by explaining and initiating the seat work which was to follow. Admonished to 'keep between the lines,' pupils wrote a couple of rows of 'ovals,' and other practice elements in handwriting. In the rooms of teachers who were writing 'purists,' pupils had to use H.B. MacLean's 'whole arm' or 'muscular movement' method of handwriting.[19] Pupils wrote a sentence to illustrate each of the spelling words or 'syllabicated' the list. In primary classes children went to 'number work' tables on which they manipulated such objects as blocks, pop or milk-bottle caps, or, later, Cuisinaire rods. They worked arithmetic questions that employed the new skill, or wrote out and 'diagrammed' sentences in ways that showed understanding of the newest wrinkle in usage or parsing form. They wrote out dictated drills in arithmetic and spelling. They wrote friendly letters, business letters, and thank-you notes. They answered questions, *always* answered in sentences ('that were never to start with "Because", or "And", or "But"'), that tested their comprehension of what they had read in their texts. They wrote short essays. One Grade Eight work sheet from the time instructed: 'Study pages 94, 95, 96, 97, 98, and the first paragraph on page 99 and write ... a full account of Edward the III's reign ...'

In the upper grades, much seat work consisted of copying notes from the blackboard. Sometimes notes were so copious – 'reams and reams' of them, covering board after board after board – that pupils groaned inwardly and sometimes outwardly at the sight of them, and even the recollection of them can still create a sinking feeling in some stomachs. One teacher 'covered the blackboard with notes and that's how we learned English.' Teachers often left blank spaces in the notes that pupils were to fill in by referring to the textbook.

Until schools permitted fountain pens and, later, ball-point ones, many found note-taking a difficult task. Straight pens with steel nibs that had to be dipped frequently in the ink-well and often blotted challenged everyone; they were particularly hard on those whose motor coordination was not very good, or whose teachers insisted on 'muscular movement.' 'I had terrible coordination,' remembered one man, 'and wrote very poorly. When we did MacLean's I was even worse. There was ink from hell to breakfast.'

Some teachers harassed the left-handed. 'My sister was dragged to the back of the room by her hair and dunked in cold water,' said one man. The teacher said, 'Maybe that will teach you to write with your right hand.' (It didn't.) When, in 1928, Hubert Smith entered South Park School in Grade Six, he was given special permission to remain left-handed. The principal, however, lamented, 'I'll be the only principal in all of Victoria to have one of these in my school.'[20] By the 1930s, British Columbia forbade teachers from making the left-handed changeover, but some teachers continued to do so right through the 1950s. For pseudo-theological reasons, many teachers in Catholic and other denominational schools forced right-handedness on all pupils, often employing corporal punishment as they did so.[21]

Pupils freed themselves from the bonds of these routines as best as they could. Some learned to talk to neighbours in such a way that they were rarely seen or heard, or to throw balls or wads of paper when the teacher was not looking. Some, as one person boasted, 'mastered the skill of copying ... without ever needing to comprehend' and were thus able 'to dream of outdoor matters while rarely missing a word.' Others travelled to the lavatory or pencil sharpener as frequently as they felt they could get away with the practice. This latter activity was especially popular in classrooms where the sharpener was on the bookcase under a window; then one 'could have a look out of the window.' Many doubted that the period or the day or the week would ever come to an end. 'Wednesday was usually the lowest point in the week,' wrote Hugh Palmer. 'By Thursday noon, however, I was ready to believe again that Saturday would really come.'[22]

Pupils welcomed any small change in routine. They enjoyed health classes, in which they copied diagrams, and geography ones, in which they sketched or traced maps, recording on them the names of mountains, rivers, and cities, and then colouring the product. Occasionally pupils did history or geography 'projects' on such topics as 'British Columbia,' or 'totem poles,' or the 'Loyalists,' or 'Our New Allies, the Russians.' Some recall making models, such as a fort in history class, using Plasticine and card paper, or crafting 'a salt and flour map of Australia, and painting it.' Most recall that they made butter in Grade One or Two: 'We each took a turn shaking.' One woman remembered her teacher's poetry lessons: 'To this day, when I see a full moon on a windy night I still hear her reading "the moon was a ghostly galleon tossed upon cloudy seas."'

While the pupils worked, some teachers moved about the room, correcting questions, checking on the neatness of the work, and adding to explanations. They awarded gold, blue, and red stars or coloured stickers to those whose work reached a high standard. Other teachers increased the store of notes on the blackboard, erasing and adding new material to one panel after the other – sometimes more quickly than some pupils could copy – in what in many rooms became an endless sequence. Still others sat at or on their desks, or watched the children from a favourite position by a window. All regularly surveyed the class to ensure that heads were down, that no whispered conversations took place, and that no notes were passed. They acknowledged hands that were raised, answered questions, or permitted pupils to go to the pencil sharpener or the lavatory, one child at a time.

As the period drew to a close, teachers summarized the main points that they had tried to make in the lesson. They reminded the pupils of what was to be finished before the next period, they assigned even more material for homework, or they dispatched monitors to collect exercise books for marking. Over the course of the day, teachers collected many piles of scribblers.

Music, art, industrial arts, home economics, and physical education had welcome or unwelcome characteristics that made them different from the other subjects. First, children generally found classes in these subjects somewhat livelier than the others. Second, they often brought their competence to the classroom rather than learning it there. Finally, their competence, or lack of it, often made the children look upon them as either high or low points in the weekly routine.

Aside from a small amount of what was called 'music appreciation' – that is, listening to a classical piece played by teacher or pupils, or on a phonograph record or school radio broadcast – most school music consisted of singing. Some teachers taught rudimentary music reading. William Macklon recalled, 'our teachers drilled away at us until some of us ... could recite "Every good boy does fine" and "f-a-c-e" and stick 'em on the lines in more or less the right places.'[23] Classes began with vocal exercises using the tonic sol–fah scale. Pupils then sang such 'ridiculous songs' as 'Heart of Oak' and 'Early One Morning' from Sir Ernest MacMillan's inaccurately titled *A Canadian Song Book*.[24] Some teachers could make this bill-of-fare enjoyable: 'We had a good music program, with lots of British songs,' one person recalled, and another remembered that her music teacher made it 'so enjoyable we really wanted to sing for him.' Other pupils enjoyed the variety provided by school music broadcasts.[25] Some youngsters, especially self-styled 'crows,' did not enjoy music very much but really disliked it only when they were asked to sing alone. A woman noted, 'I couldn't carry a tune, and I felt so ... I was determined to do it, but I was no good.'

In many schools teachers sorted out the best singers to prepare for the annual music festival, in Vancouver sponsored by the Kiwanis Club. Those selected to take part remember the festival as one of the 'really great' days in the school year; we 'got at a minimum a complete day off.' Melinda McCracken, who grew up in Winnipeg, recalled that, on festival day there, children 'would come to school squeaky clean, their hair shining, the runs in the girls' black stockings sewn up, the sleeves of their white shirts rolled down and buttoned, their ties neatly tied and their tunics pressed. The boys' hair was stuck down with water; they wore white shirts with ties.'[26] A Halifax man whose class sang in festivals boasted: 'We won the trophy three times in a row, so we kept it!'

In physical education, teachers concentrated on those who already could perform well. They paid less attention to basic skills than they did in reading and arithmetic. If the facilities were available and their parents had provided the 'strip,' pupils changed into white shirts, blue shorts for boys, tunics and bloomers for girls, and running shoes. If the class was conducted on a hardwood floor in a gymnasium or school auditorium, the school would insist on rubber-soled shoes as the minimum acceptable strip. There the class would line up in rows or teams and the teacher would take them through such exercises as 'toe touching' and 'astride jumping.'

After these 'physical jerks,' as the children called them, the teacher would conduct activities that practised skills related to whatever sport was emphasized at the moment. In softball season, for example, pupils tossed balls back and forth, and practised batting and bunting, and teachers batted out 'grounders' to be retrieved. The period then culminated in the playing of one or more games of softball. In some classes, teams would be picked to last over the season; in others, the best players were picked as captains each day and, as captains selected their teams, children received a finely honed demonstration of exactly how their peers evaluated their competence. Those who were picked towards the end still recall the sense of inadequacy, or even self-contempt, this system engendered. Sometimes, however, even the incompetent were lucky. One less-than-athletic student still has a 'vivid recollection of when I was on third base and just reached out and caught the ball; what a fabulous feeling it was, just to catch a ball!'

Since the subject had neither text nor festival to ensure consistency, art programs differed more than most subjects from teacher to teacher and from school to school. Recollections of art in the primary grades focus on craft activities involving making such things as woven place-mats, bookmarks, and pen wipers out of burlap. Intermediate-grade pupils also sewed burlap, and measured, folded, and pasted cardboard, and sometimes made things out of soft wood. They also sketched still lifes, copied drawings illustrating perspective ('why a thing at the upper part of the page should *have* to be smaller than that at the bottom *always* mystified me'), made designs that 'always involved a ruler,' and did a variety of paintings.

Until the 1950s, tasks in art tended to be specific; there was 'no freelancing at all,' and 'there was no freedom to draw what you wanted, so everyone [was] compared to each other.' In painting many recall a misordered sequence that began with watercolours – in their 'little Reeves tins' – in the early grades, and permitted only the most senior and capable to work with the easier-to-use poster paints. Some had art teachers who made the subject really exciting for the pupils; we did 'all kinds of sketching, watercolours, poster paints; we put up big displays at one end of the school ground on sports day for our parents to see the work.'

Most former pupils recall their home-economics and manual-training classes with pleasure. While children may not always have enjoyed these subjects, only really nasty teachers could make them actively dislike them. Those who had some practical bent often looked on them as the high point of the week and remain grateful for what they were taught. One man explained, 'I figured out how many hours in the week and would count down to the time to go to carpentry.' Of one teacher, a woman remembered, 'She was fussy, and taught me to be fussy.' Girls who had already learned some cooking or sewing at home sometimes became impatient at the slow pace of their classes, but they enjoyed the annual tea or 'parade of fashion' at which they showed off their skills to their mothers. In industrial arts, one man remembered, 'you got to make the occasional simple object that had a use ... So we did pencil boxes, simple stands for Mom's flower pots, some sort of wall bracket, etc. I remember spending five or six months alone remaking the lid to my pencil box until I managed one that fit snugly. Meanwhile more adept pupils finished small end tables in time for Mother's Day.'

Beginning in the mid-1920s, some elementary schools made traditional classroom practices more efficient by 'platooning.'[27] In such 'departmentalized' schools, pupils moved from room to room, some of which had special equipment, to visit specialist teachers, many of whom had some extra training leading to a provincial 'specialist' certificate. Platooning also had its special set of routines. On the bell or, in those rooms in which the teacher regularly said, 'The bell is for me, not for you,' on his or her signal, the pupils would gather up their materials. The children then lined up in pairs to move from room to room. Although forbidden to talk in the corridors, pupils looked upon moves as pleasant breaks in the day. However, those moving to the rooms of the vicious fretted at what was ahead, and those leaving them were sometimes giddy with relief at having survived another day in their presence.

Friday brought variation in school routines. Pupils did the final draft of the week's writing exercise in their copy books or 'compendiums.' Teachers conducted the weekly tests. In language, pupils wrote out as exactly as they could – correctly spelled, punctuated, and capitalized, 'with one mark off for each mistake from a total of ten' – the texts of such poems as 'Silver,' or 'Sea-Fever' that they had memorized.[28] Some teachers then 'read out the results of these weekly and other tests so all would know who came first and last.' On those occasions, one Toronto woman remembered, 'I hated the good spellers!' In the 1920s, test results could still lead to a shuffling of classroom seating based on how each pupil ranked. As a man from that era proudly recalled, 'I had missed several days of schooling and when I came back I was right at the bottom ... So, anyways, this word came up and it came right down the line until it got to me and I answered correctly so I went to the top of the class!' Tests might be followed by spelling bees or games such as arithmetic baseball. Pupils in Catholic schools went to confession.

Friday afternoon brought a relaxation in the rigidity of the week's work. Teachers read stories or perhaps a chapter from *The Wind in the Willows*, or a novel by Sir Walter Scott or Charles Dickens, or a heroic account of the life of a saint – sessions recalled with special warmth. In an increasing number of schools, at least up to the 1950s, pupil officers conducted the weekly meeting of the Junior Red Cross, during which Maurice Hodgson (and likely many others) accepted as necessary 'the need to care for others; not others like family or town or even country, but that truly nebulous "other" that encompasses the world.'[29] In other schools, older pupils dispersed to a range of 'clubs' for the last period of the day. 'I enjoyed especially Grades Five and Six, perhaps because the principal and myself organized a successful stamp club,' noted one man. 'We had a lot of clubs,' reported one woman: 'stamp, science, chess, tennis, badminton, cooking, service, library; everyone had to belong to some organization, to learn to work with others.'

Many schools marked the end of the week with a school assembly. After the pupils had filed, class by class, to their appropriate places, the principal or music teacher led the school in 'O Canada.' Two or three classes then presented items that they had prepared; a song that they would later sing in the music festival, a play taken from a reader, or some acrobatics learned in physical education. Sometimes assembly programs drew attention to talented individuals who would perform a dance, or recite an item learned in elocution lessons, or sing or play a classical piece: 'The Foley kid played his violin a few times every year. He was really good.' Classes that had had the best turn-out of parents at the previous Home and School or Parent–Teacher Association meeting received a banner. Those whose writing came up to standard were presented MacLean's writing certificates. ('Getting a MacLean's ... certificate was a big deal!') During the Second World War, the principal or a visitor would honour the classes which had bought the most war saving stamps, or collected the most metal or paper for the regular salvage drives. In some schools the pupils would all join together to sing a hymn, a patriotic song ('The Maple Leaf Forever!'; 'There'll Always Be an England'), a Christmas carol, or a round such as 'Row, row, row ....'

In nearly every school the penultimate item on the program was the principal's message: he – or, in a very few public schools, she – usually addressed some problem of school or community governance.[30] The principal explained that some pupils were 'hanging around' too long after school, or that there was too much talking in the halls, or that there was too much fighting to and from school, or that the police were about to crack down on those who rode their bicycles on the sidewalk or who had not renewed their bicycle licences. Finally, the children all stood to sing 'God Save the King' or 'God Save the Queen,' and then marched back to their classrooms.

Some events broke irregularly or infrequently into class and school routines. Pupils enjoyed those occasions when the teacher wandered, or was drawn from the subject under discussion. 'The room hushed' because pupils did not want to break the thread. Some teachers recounted personal adventures or told war stories. ('He sure had an exciting time during the First War, or at least he told us he did!'; 'He flew a Spitfire!') Others talked about their families; one told 'about all the people in her family who had TB, and how terrible it was.'

During outbreaks of such infectious diseases as measles, chicken pox, mumps, and scarlet fever, or during the seasonal visit of lice, the school nurse would inspect each of the pupils. Sometimes the teacher, or principal, or nurse would warn children about men hanging around the school grounds, admonishing them to go directly home after school and not talk to any strangers on the way. At other times individual children would be called out of class to visit the nurse, the school doctor, or the school dentist, or to attend a toxoid or vaccination clinic. Those who did well in school enjoyed receiving report cards and comparing them with friends before they took them home. Those who did badly met the occasion with bravado or tried to keep their results to themselves.

Among irregular interruptions, pupils particularly welcomed fire-drills:

'Who knows, the school might really have been burning down!' They also enjoyed not only the events themselves, but also preparing for the music festival, for maypole dancing on May Day, for sports day, for a tea or fashion show in home economics, for a production of a play or operetta, and especially for the Christmas concert.[31] Those who attended one Vancouver elementary school in the 1930s remember the delight they took in their production of *The Mikado*. Valentine's Day sometimes brought a class party, but also the misery of those who received few if any valentines. ('She said, "My mom made me bring one for everyone, that's why you got that card."')

Occasionally, events outside of the school impinged on what went on in it. Influenza closed schools right across the country for some weeks in 1918, and a fuel shortage did so in Vancouver in 1943. Severe winter weather sometimes closed schools for a day or two. One interviewee recalls forming up to see the Prince of Wales in 1919, and giving him a cheer when he gave them the day off. Another remembers being urged to listen to the coronation of George VI on the radio, and making in class a little crown to wear while doing so. More remember how their school marked the Royal visit of 1939 or the visit of Princess Elizabeth and Prince Philip not long after their marriage. Some made scrapbooks of these events in their classes or learned to sing 'Land of Hope and Glory.' All classes went out to watch at the place assigned to their school, with great excitement, 'as they whisked by' on their drives about the city.

During the Second World War, its major events were frequently discussed, or even more directly impinged on the classroom.[32] The war felt very real and very close to those who had relatives in the services, or who lived in such seaports as Montreal, Halifax, Sydney, St John's, and, later, Prince Rupert and Vancouver. Sometimes teachers would explain that a classmate was away because a relative had been killed. In all parts of the country, pupils bought war savings stamps and knitted for the Red Cross. As one Powell River woman reported, 'My dad made knitting needles for the whole Grade Three class and we knitted squares.' In some schools that early casualty among the elements of the 'new' education, the school garden, reappeared for a time as the 'Victory garden.' 'We planted things that grew quickly'; pupils were supposed to persuade their parents to plant such gardens at home. Some school gardens had short-term and long-term effects: 'I persuaded my parents to plant potatoes in our yard; ... to this day my hobby is vegetable gardening.'

On a more frightening note, pupils practised what they would do in an air raid; in one school they went to the school basement, in another they filed out into the playground, where 'the principal blew a whistle and we would all fall down.' In another the principal gave a vivid description of just how bombers would destroy Vancouver in air raids. In a fourth the janitor added to the fear occasioned by a Japanese submarine shelling the lighthouse at Estevan Point, in June 1942, by telling the children it was 'the beginning of the end.' In St John's, Helen Fogwill Porter reported, 'We had regular air-raid drill on Thursday mornings in school and we had to bring tinned food to have it stored away in case we ever had to stay there.'[33] In the 1950s, children learned about 'fallout' and practised how to shelter from atomic blasts under their desks.

The ways in which pupils and teachers behaved towards each other were what bound them and the curriculum together to make a school. Thus recollections of what was taught, how it was taught, and who taught it led naturally into an elaboration of what is implicit therein about how elementary schools controlled their pupils, and how the pupils responded to that control. First, an overall observation. Discussions of what was 'fair' and what was 'unfair,' usually initiated by informants themselves, often burn through with an intensity that belies the fact that the events discussed took place, not the day before, but sometimes four or more decades earlier. Here one must note that children seem to have been predisposed to accept the consequences of just about any code of conduct so long as the school administered it fairly. One teacher 'was very annoyed and took four of us into the cloakroom, where she used the ruler on our knuckles. It was grossly unfair: she had watched a note go through the four people before she intervened.' Another, by whom the pupils felt 'cheated' and 'betrayed,' marked a set of tests without noting anything on the papers, returned them to the children to mark their own, asked the youngsters to call out their marks, and then excoriated those who had yielded to the temptation to pad.

One man, who believes that corporal punishment is a 'beneficial' device and that schools would be better places if strapping were restored, 'to this very day feels wrongly punished' on two out of the three occasions he was strapped. As a six-year-old child who emigrated to Canada in 1955, Mary di Michele had some 'unpleasant encounters' before she became fluent in English. One day, 'a nun dressed formally in black cloth and veil saw me standing quietly and waiting. For some reason ... the very sight of me sent her into a rage ... She dragged me into her class of senior students and strapped me soundly in front of the girls ... I discovered later that I had been standing in the wrong spot; the entrance to the school had been declared off-limits for the students ...'[34] Mass punishments were always considered unjust. Eric Adams recalled 'one episode when two entire classes of boys, totalling about 80 children, some of whom had persisted in whispering during an assembly period, were lined up on the spot and "slugged" once on each hand, I was one of them. I hadn't been whispering.'[35]

People's recollections of teachers divide them into four rough categories. They give their highest rating to those teachers who emphasized fundamentals, who drilled frequently and tested often, who concentrated on having their pupils learn those things that both community and educational tradition told them were the 'core' curriculum. These teachers knew their business and they taught this curriculum thoroughly and systematically. 'Good' teachers also taught this curriculum in a particular way. They had dominant personalities. They conveyed a sense that what they did, and what they wanted their pupils to do, was of immense importance. They ran 'no nonsense' classrooms in which routines were all-pervasive, and cast in a code that itemized many 'thou shalt nots.' Some pupils also knew that these were good teachers because 'you *knew* you'd learned a thing. The evidence was there because you could *repeat* the learning accurately – even years later.'

Good teachers often fare better in memory than they did at the time. In Powell River, one man reported, pupils 'always shuddered when ... we got Miss Cedar. She was an old spinster ... but I thought she was the greatest thing. When you got out of her room, you knew you had spent a year of learning. No nonsense.' Many former pupils reported that Anna B. Dunsmuir, who taught at Lord Selkirk School in Cedar Cottage from 1921 to 1950, was such a teacher. Colleen Wright Manness, for example, reported of her that 'we all thought the world of her and were terrified of her. When we pleased her we felt like a million dollars. If we went back to the school, she was the one we went back to see. We loved her. We didn't know it then, though.'[36]

Good teachers were also fair teachers. They dispensed their rebukes and punishments rarely, in an even-handed way, and in strict accordance with the rules. It was appropriate, it was fair, for these teachers to give special attention to the best pupils – to those who learned the rote packages, obeyed the rules meticulously, and did everything neatly – so long as these children did not receive blatant favouritism. Pupils also believed it was 'fair' for teachers to ride herd on those who did not do their homework, or who were often unruly, and sometimes even on those who were not very bright, so long as the teachers did so without malice and so long as the breach in the rules was evident to all.

There is some objective evidence that such teachers had, strong, positive, and lifelong effects on their pupils. One well-documented example was Iole Appugliese, who taught Grade One for thirty-four years in Montreal's

Royal Arthur School, a Protestant school serving a working-class district. Pupils recalled that she gave them a 'profound impression of the importance of schooling, and how one should stick to it'; that 'she gave extra hours to the children who were slow learners'; a former colleague explained: 'How did she teach? With a lot of love!' Although Grade One pupils in this school were randomly assigned to teachers, a far higher proportion of Miss Appugliese's former pupils eventually achieved higher adult status than did those of the school's other two Grade One teachers: of Miss Appugliese's, 64 per cent did so, of Miss 'B's,' 31 per cent, and of Miss 'C's,' only 10 per cent.[37]

A larger group of teachers were 'nice.' Such teachers are remembered less sharply, less vividly than the others; recollections of them tend to be enveloped in a pleasant haze. One was 'always warm and friendly'; another was a 'lovely person, an excellent teacher'; a third was 'a very quiet man; we kids thought he was really nice'; a fourth was 'a very kind man, the first one who really challenged us; he made you think about things.' When Geiri Johnson started school in 1927 near Hnausa, Manitoba, 'it was a shock to both myself and the teacher that I knew only two English words – yes and no – ... My teacher was Icelandic, and a very kind, understanding lady who ... kept me in while all the other kids played outside. She taught me the basics so I could learn school work.'[38] In Elphinstone Elementary School on British Columbia's Sechelt Peninsula, in 1940, 'Miss [Florence] Evans gave vitamin pills to a student who lived in a make-shift home where the meals were neither regular nor nutritious. She taught back exercises to a boy with round shoulders. She encouraged me with my written compositions.'[39]

Such people apparently taught well and easily, they mothered or fathered their charges without all the elaborate apparatus that characterized the classroom of the 'best' teachers. They did, however, use a pedagogy almost identical to that of their more overbearing colleagues. Of a Powell River teacher, one former pupil explained, '[He] was a good all-round teacher. You couldn't beat him. We could have fun, but you blinkin' well had to work ... If we started horsing around there would be a strap come down.' Although few people remember them in this way, I suspect that they were probably as effective in carrying out the bread-and-butter tasks of teaching as were their more famous and martinet-like colleagues. (One person who had both kinds, however, argues that what the 'nice' teacher taught didn't seem to have the same mental precision or self-evident value and worthiness as the product of the 'good' teacher's efforts.)

If the above are memory's satisfactory elementary teachers, two other sorts also stand out. One was made up of teachers and principals who were mean, nasty, sarcastic, cruel, or even vicious. One woman recalled a teacher who called her, alternatively, 'Dummy' and 'Fatty'; another remembered a teacher who remarked, when he mispronounced a word in the reader or made some other mistake, 'What else can you expect from bohunks?'; and another who described her classmate as a 'filthy little pig' because she ate garlic. One teacher 'plunked a kid in the waste-basket ... She said he smelt like garbage.' There was also the teacher who 'smiled when you stumbled, and then waited for the moment to pin the truth on you,' another who announced that she was 'sick and tired of calling out "foreign" names,' and a third who mocked those who stuttered until they cried. One of Cessie McLaren's teachers was 'a churlish brute of a woman whose method for maintaining order was simple and effective – fear. Her humorless, disapproving demeanor bespoke the possiblity of unimaginable horrors inflicted with pointers, yardsticks or the inevitable "strap" ... a length of leather that everyone knew lay coiled in her lower left-hand desk drawer.'[40]

In the Depression, while most teachers were discreet, some drew attention to those on relief and in receipt of shoes, clothes, or school supplies. 'Our school books were given to us because we were on relief,' reported one man. 'It was very embarrassing getting up in front of the class to get those books.' When 'Arlene' came to school without supplies, her teacher declared, 'Oh, I know your family, they are all the same.' This and other belittling remarks led to deep resentment on Arlene's part; she naïvely explained that the teacher 'doesn't know my family. She has never met my mother and father.'[41] On the really dark side, there were, as well, the principal who fondled girls and the school physician who sexually assaulted some of the boys. Such teachers usually employed a pedagogy that was not very different from that used by other teachers. They differed from their colleagues mostly in that, instead of being respected or liked by their pupils, they were feared and hated. Only in retrospect did these people achieve a dubious sort of merit; some former pupils gradually came to look upon the fact that they had 'survived' these teachers as evidence that they had in their classes taken a major step towards adulthood.

Finally, pupils looked on a few teachers with contempt. These unfortunates displayed their ineffectiveness or their incompetence in a variety of ways. They could not explain things clearly. The oral parts of their lessons rambled and their notes were incoherent. They could not keep order; they sometimes broke down and wept. Some tried to bribe the children to behave with candy, or even money. While most disappeared in a year or less, a few persisted to become almost legendary objects to be scorned by class after class of pupils. Whether they stayed or left, they received no compassion or mercy from either pupils or parents.

Those who went to Catholic schools divided their teachers (usually sisters of a teaching order) into the same four groups. 'We were terrified of the nuns,' wrote Michael Enright, 'as we had been taught to be terrified of religion. With their severely cut black robes, the starched wimples and leather belts with the rosaries hanging down, they were God's Amazons who would brook no deviation from their established orthodoxy. We ate fish or macaroni on Fridays because we would burn in hell forever if we ate meat.'[42] On the other hand, one man said, 'This one sister was like a second mother to us; even the bad kids really loved her.' Of the nuns in his east-side Vancouver parochial school in the early 1940s, Ray Culos reported, 'some of them were quite strict, and corporal punishment was a means of getting at you ... But they *did* help a group of young kids who might not have had the direction or the religious instruction that in all likelihood saved them [from] problems as they grew up.'[43]

Two main themes characterize overall school discipline in this era. The first and dominant mode was that imposed by the school. It displayed itself in a continuum that at one end had the presence, the personality, the aura of the teachers and the principal, and, at the other, the strap and expulsion. School staffs held back the latent barbarism they perceived in the children with an increasingly severe range of sanctions that began with displeasure and ended with corporal punishment. Teachers joined parents, police, mag-istrates, and most other adults in justifying this range of measures by appealing to a very long-standing tradition; to the proverbial 'Spare the rod and spoil the child.' In Catholic schools, tradition held that discipline helped produce 'perfect human beings according to the example and teach-ing of Christ.' Thus bad behaviour was a sin as well as a crime.

The second mode saw some schools introducing a range of 'progressive' practices through which the children were to learn 'democratic self-control.' Through a system of monitors, older and abler pupils joined teachers and principals in the task of teaching and maintaining appropriate standards, especially among the younger children. Democratic self-control, however, was tightly circumscribed by traditional disciplinary means, which were brought in these years to a peak of effective performance.

The presence of a seasoned teacher was clearly the first line of defence against barbarism. Teachers had presence; pupils, and their parents expected them to possess it. Teachers with this quality said, 'Do this,' and the children did it. All but ineffectual teachers exerted their personalities with more or less intensity on their pupils, and expected, and received, a reasonably automatic compliance with their directions. Even those who created a loving atmosphere in their classrooms did so in this broader con-text. The woman who now recalls that 'I knew who the teacher was and did as I was told,' speaks for her classmates as well as herself. Presence came with experience, but neophytes set out, self-consciously, to acquire it. Eighteen- and nineteen-year-olds stare at us from the Normal school annuals of these years with an intensity that makes them look older, more severe, and altogether more formidable than the much older beginning teachers of later years.[44]

Teachers used an armoury of sanctions to back up their demands that pupils meet certain standards of behaviour and work habits. They gave children 'the ray.' They gave them the cutting edge of their tongues; they spoke sharply; they made nasty, and sometimes sarcastic, remarks; they spoke more and more softly, coldly, ominously; they shouted, and even raged against their charges. ('She really lambasted us; she had a short fuse'; 'I recall his scarlet face and his ferocious temper.') Many maintained full control solely through verbal means. Others made children sit or stand in a corner; they kept children in at recess, at lunch hour, and after school. One person recalls being kept in after school, asking to leave the room, being refused, and then wetting his pants: 'I stayed away for three days.' Teachers made pupils sit up straight, motionless, with hands behind their backs, for periods of time up to half an hour. They forced chewers to put their gum on the ends of their noses or behind their ears. As punishment, they gave extra work of an excruciatingly boring and valueless sort, such as eight- or nine-digit long-division questions and their proofs, the writing of lines – some wrote such things as 'I will not chew gum,' or 'Silence is golden,' five hundred to a thousand times - the copying of pages out of textbooks or dictionaries, and the memorization of poems.

Teachers assigned offenders to those classroom and school chores not popular with 'monitors' such as picking up paper and other garbage in the school and on its grounds. In Burnaby in the late 1950s, Allan Safarik, instead of an expected strapping, 'was to pick up garbage on the school ground every day after school for one week. I was thrilled ... I worked like a fiend ... Every now and then I would glance over my shoulder and see [the principal's] grey muzzle looking from an upstairs window.'[45] Teachers sent offenders to school detention halls, where the duty teacher or vice-principal imposed sanctions, often with great severity of tone. Some teachers and schools kept elaborate systems of 'demerit' records, through which offending pupils progressed through an increasingly severe range of sanctions. Other schools and teachers employed the opposite of this system by giving out merit points for good behaviour, and providing minor rewards – such as being dismissed first – to those pupils or rows of pupils which collected the most points.

Teachers and principals kept corporal punishment as their ultimate sanction short of expulsion. 'I got the strap ten times in one year,' remembered one man. 'I was very inattentive ... and she tried to make me pay attention.' 'I wasn't a good student,' reported another: 'I remember being strapped three times in one day.' Classroom teachers often employed less formal – and, in most provinces, unlawful – sorts of physical punishment. Former pupils recall teachers who spanked them on the bottom, or slapped them on the hands or about the shoulders and, occasionally, on the face. Other teachers pinched the upper arm or the earlobe, or hit victims on the top of the head with tightened knuckles. Still others used pointers, rulers, chalk brushes, gym shoes, or other things to hit children on their bottoms, hands, knuckles, shoulders, elbows – especially on the 'funnybone' – and, less often, on their heads. A somewhat fondly remembered Grade One teacher, who that year enrolled forty-six pupils, 'stepped on their toes as she hit them with a ruler.' A few, carried by temper almost beyond control, sometimes dragged children from their desks to shake them, to bang them against walls, or even to manhandle them out of the classroom.

Unlike the cold, ritualized formality that characterized corporal punishment by a principal, classroom teachers sometimes struck out in a high pitch of unleashed emotion. A few teachers tried to be light-hearted, even affectionate, in their physical punishment. On these occasions the ritualized rules of the 'game,' especially as it was played between boys and male teachers, and in such all-boy classes as those in physical education or industrial arts, required that the victim accept, however reluctantly, that his physical punishment was part of a game. In the same jocular way, some teachers threw chalk, chalk brushes, and even textbooks at their charges.

For really serious violations of class or school codes, children were sent to, or summoned by, the school principal. Pupils found these interviews with the principal to be extremely stressful occasions; some were tongue-tied into silence. Being strapped was not an inevitable product of a trip to the 'office,' but it happened often enough for youngsters to be extremely wary of visiting there. 'Getting THE STRAP was to us the same as going to the gallows,' wrote Pete Loudon of his school in Anyox, British Columbia. 'You didn't just get THE STRAP, you were sentenced to it.'[46]

Once a principal decided to strap a pupil, he followed a routine – transformed into a formal and unvarying ritual in many schools – laid down by the Department of Education.[47] He summoned the required witness, explained the crime and punishment to the latter, positioned the subject carefully, administered the strokes and counted them out in a firm voice, and then recorded the event in a special book. Some principals removed their jackets and hung them up on a coat hanger. Others emphasized the formality of the occasion by buttoning their jackets. If there was more than one victim, those waiting their turn either watched or listened from just outside the door. The worst thing was when friends were there, 'because then you couldn't cry.' One man, recalling his first four on each hand, said, 'I couldn't understand the pain, it was so intense.' Another 'died a thousand deaths but refused to show it [by crying] ... afterwards I held my hands between my legs trying to get the fire out of them.' Robert Thomas Allen, on the other hand, claimed that the strap 'didn't really hurt ... and when you got back to class among friends, you were able to hold your hands against the cast-iron sides of your desk, putting on a great act of cooling the unbearable heat and grinning in a worldly way at the girls.'[48]

Since principals used corporal punishment as much to deter as to punish, they often permitted the sounds to carry their warning through the school; the appearance back in the classroom of a red-eyed and red-handed victim quickly reinforced the message. A few principals even prolonged the misery by administering punishment over more than one session, or by announcing it and then postponing its administration to noon hour or after school, or even to another day.[49] Although girls sometimes received corporal punishment of the informal classroom sort, they rarely took part in the ritual in the office.

Expulsion constituted the school's most serious sanction for bad behaviour. None of my informants was ever expelled or, if any was, did not admit to it. Unless the transgression was really heinous, schools did not expel pupils on a first offence; they reserved this punishment for a series of serious offences, and especially those that posed a threat to the very order of the classroom or school. In January 1951, twelve-year-old 'Peter' threw a waste-basket at a teacher who 'was a little abrupt' with him. 'Later that week he was rude in class, the teacher kept him in after school, and Peter threatened the teacher with a baseball bat.' Peter was then expelled.[50] Another 'Peter' was twice expelled from elementary schools for 'severe behaviour problems,' including theft. In adolescence this lad embarked on a career of automobile theft and breaking and entering and, before he was eighteen, received a three-year sentence to the penitentiary.[51]

If parents and teachers often justified stern discipline and corporal punishment by appealing to proverbial wisdom, their approach was also deeply rooted in fear. On the one hand, they feared that, without severe sanctions, family, classroom, school, and society would quickly descend into disorder, and even barbarism; on the other hand, they feared for the future of the unchastened. Many still believed that the 'old Adam' was very close to the surface in boys, and especially those in early adolescence. In eight-grade elementary schools, some teachers in the upper grades seem to have seen a barely suppressed violence in some of the boys; in responding to it savagely, they perhaps transformed their own fears into realities. In turn, these violent episodes communicated such beliefs and fears to the younger pupils and gave them notions of a sort of behaviour that one day they might well perform.

The school's informal communication system passed down and exaggerated stories of epic disciplinary events in the upper grades. These tales seem to have kept certain youngsters in a state of anticipatory tension over much of their school days, 'feeling ... that the certainty of it occurring to you was not only high, but preordained.' Many now recall the paradox in this system; it terrified the good children who only very occasionally got caught up in its machinery, but gave those who were often punished and who 'could take it' a heroic status among their peers. One boy, for example, was one of those 'who was strapped two or three times a year.' One day he kicked a football at a school window; 'it took him three kicks to get it through the window. He just stayed there until the teacher came and took him away' for the usual punishment.

By the 1920s nearly all school-aged children in English Canada spent at least a few years in school. Despite the general belief that they all would benefit from the experience, a few may actually have been worse off than their counterparts in earlier times. In the era before attendance laws were vigorously enforced, fractious boys – and, occasionally, girls – who fell behind because of large classes, poor teaching, irregular or poor attendance, or with little or no disposition or perhaps ability to learn, dropped out of school and found a place in the community. Now their parents, or economic conditions, or truant officers forced them to stay in school. Some may have benefited from the extended experience; others, no better or more appropriately taught, or more able to profit from formal learning than their predecessors, were oppressed by it. Of his brother, Fraser Miles wrote: 'So maybe he was a bit slow in school, but nobody is likely to learn any better sitting in class all day terrified he would beaten at the end of it. The strappings sure didn't help Lloydyboy learn any more ...'[52]

Others found their outlet in being 'tough.' They moved along the very edge of forbidden practices and behaviours, they dominated the cloakroom and the boys' playground, they used bad language just at the edge of earshot of the teacher, they fought each other, and they carried 'rollings' or cigarettes in their pockets, which they smoked just out of sight of the school. They quit school as soon as they were old enough to do so, or when they received the school's ultimate sanction and were expelled.

What has come to be called the school's 'hidden' curriculum has been an implicit part of what appears above. Learning to survive was perhaps its most important element. Pupils had first of all to learn how to deal with their fears: their fear of the other children in their own class; their fear of the bigger children who might harass them to and from school, or on the playground; their special fear of 'tough' boys and girls; their fear of teachers and the principal; their fear of the strap. Others feared that they would not measure up to family expectations for them. Most children obviously learned to manage, or at least to live with, their fears.

The foundation for children's sense of themselves as persons, of who they were and who they would be, was laid in their families. When they went to school, they found both the overt and hidden curriculum taught them still more about themselves. The merit of belonging to certain ethnic groups was reinforced. Those of British background found that their history and culture formed the basis of much of what they learned. During and after both world wars, those of 'enemy' origin experienced both the cultural hostility that permeated formal and informal classroom discourse and the personal hostility of some teachers and many classmates. In Gertrude Story's trenchant words, 'What I call the Holy British Imperial Empire Saskatchewan School System did a heck of a lot more for the British Empire ... than it ever did for Saskatchewanians. We learned to be loyal British Empire subjects, proud as punch that the sun never set on the British Empire ... [but] you did not (indeed, you dared not) play Norwegian singing games in the schoolyard (and under pain of death, German ones).'[53]

Many children found that, so far as the school was concerned, a culture they had been taught to cherish by family and congregation did not exist. Mary di Michele 'suffered from an acute sense of otherness because my home language and culture were not reflected at all in my education, nor in my reading, nor in the American dramas of film and television I liked to watch.'[54] Children were also the butt of the racial and ethnic sterotypes and slurs that were part of popular culture. Norm Alexander, descendant of a pioneering black family in British Columbia, was cast as 'Little Black Sambo' in a school play in Victoria in the 1930s.[55] Gloria Steinberg Harris recalled, 'We were never, ever allowed to forget that we were foreign. I was born in this country, but I was "foreign."'[56] School subsumed other cultures into larger conglomerations; Ukrainians, Georgians, and others from that Empire found themselves labelled Russians, German-speaking Mennonites from Russia and even the Dutch and Dutch-speaking Belgians became Germans, all Eastern Europeans were 'bohunks,' and so on. The Second World War euphemism for refugees, 'Displaced Persons,' was employed pejoratively in its abbreviated form, 'DPs.' Teachers Anglicized pupils names or even gave them new ones: 'I can"t pronounce all that, so I"ll call you Mary.'

Schools also affected religious identities. Public schools were clearly Christian schools, and generally presented a non-denominational form of liberal Protestantism.[57] Those interviewed who attended them offered few direct comments about the religious dimension of schooling. Some mentioned hearing Bible stories and readings and saying the Lord's Prayer as part of their accounts of classroom routines. If parents so requested, children could be excused from taking part in religious exercises. Usually, these pupils waited in the hallways until this part of the opening activities was over. Such children had an intense dislike of drawing attention to themselves in this way, an attitude reinforced when teachers made derogatory comments. In Toronto in the 1950s, for example, 'one teacher accused us [Jews] of being Communists because we wouldn't say the Lord's Prayer.' Others who were not Christian often found the prejudice against them expressed in ethnic – Sikhs labelled 'ragheads' or 'dirty Hindus,' for example – rather than religious terms.

Parochial and separate schools created an environment suffused with Catholic doctrine and practice. Unlike their public counterparts, wrote Harry J. Boyle, 'Catholics had holidays on holy days ... But in return they had an admixture of catechism every day and a Friday afternoon grilling on matters of faith by the parish priest.'[58] 'We learned the catechism by heart,' wrote Patrick O'Flaherty, 'and it is still all there somewhere in my deepest memory, triggered now by some chance word or phrase, as when I heard someone recently say the word "chrism."'[59]

Schools also played a major role in developing gender identity.[60] This process began, of course, long before youngsters entered school, but in the new setting identity was presented in a more structured and systematic way. And, if gendered expectations grew out of an adult agenda, they none the less received strong support from the youngsters themselves.[61]

Schools presented a gendered physical message; there, boys and girls inhabited sharply differentiated spaces. Some schools, and especially parochial and other Roman Catholic ones, enrolled only boys or girls, as did most private schools.[62] As the next chapter will show, playgrounds and play patterns of large schools were sharply segregated by deeply rooted custom, often reinforced by administrative fiat. Although play on the grounds of small rural schools was often more coeducational than on large urban ones, each also had a boys' and a girls' area, often on the way to or near the widely separated privies. Many schools had separate entrances for girls and

The end of a race in the 'Little Olympics' elementary-school track meet in New Westminster in June 1959.

boys. Once inside, children went to girls' classes or boys' classes, or to the boys' side or the girls' of cloakrooms and classrooms.

Schools insisted that pupils, and especially girls, dress appropriately. As one woman explained (among many who emphasized the point), 'If we wore slacks in cold weather, we had to put them under our dresses or skirts, and take them off in class.' Inside as well, children saw that women nurtured and men administered. If the former provided adult role models for girls, the latter did not always do so for boys. Some men, for example, recalled their male teachers in elementary school as 'wimps,' and a couple referred to their principals as 'men among boys, but boys among men.'

Classroom discourse and behaviour reinforced the messages of the setting. On the one hand, teachers seem to have demanded, and usually received, more docile conduct from girls than they did from boys. 'We had a very fine teacher,' reported one man, 'and he would have stayed; but he wouldn't use the strap on a girl, and the girls simply took advantage of him;

and ... he resigned.' On the other, the culture of childhood itself structured much of the different ways that boys and girls came to behave. Most beginners of both sexes probably came to school disposed to conduct themselves in a way designed to please teachers. However, as they got to know other children; as they formed same-sex friendships, groups, and gangs; as they integrated themselves into the playground pecking order, the sexes came to have different norms as to how they should behave towards each other and how to conduct themselves in the classrooms. Responding to both sorts of expectations, girls tended to work more conscientiously, to complete tasks more expeditiously and neatly. They did the major share of classroom housekeeping. Their work became the classroom model; their answers were more likely to conform to teacher expectations. Since neither parents or teachers questioned these differences, both boys and girls came to see them as being rooted in the natural order of things.

Curricula and texts strengthened gendered messages, prescribing both childhood and adult roles. In the 1957 version of the British Columbia primary curriculum, the 'desired outcomes' for the first grade included:

An understanding of the dependence of the family upon father.
An appreciation of the various kinds of work fathers do.
An appreciation of mother's contribution to our welfare, comfort, and happiness.[63]

Primary readers became more gender-specific over these years. In the first-grade reader prescribed in British Columbia from 1923 to 1934, nursery rhymes, poems, and a miscellaneous collection of stories made up most of the content. When 'Mother Goose' had a tea party, she asked, 'Is the table set, Boy Blue? Please get the bread, Miss Muffett. Please bring the cake, Jack Horner.'[64] In 1935, this reader was replaced with one dealing with a single cast of characters, six-year-old twins Jerry and Jane, their sibling Baby, their parents, and their pets. In the late 1940s, this family in turn gave way to that of Dick and Jane. Both series focused on middle-class family life of a traditional sort. As well, the teachers' guides and optional workbooks for the latter series structured class discussion along traditional gender lines.[65]

In fact, in all the subjects in the elementary grades, children studied content that looked on the world from a male perspective and emphasized traditional patterns of work and play. In geography, they learned that, in all sorts of societies all over the world, men worked and mothers nurtured. In the late 1940s, J.M. Dent brought out a new, 'postwar' series of readers for the intermediate grades that was used for nearly two decades in the schools of British Columbia, Alberta, and Ontario. In the one prescribed for Grade Five, thirty-eight stories had a clearly identified protagonist. In 29, the protagonist was a male human, in eight, a male animal, and in one a teenaged girl.[66] Further, notions that one sex or the other was 'better' at, or 'needed,' particular fields of study, often learned outside of school, were confirmed in the upper elementary grades. Language and literature became 'girls'' subjects, and mathematics and science 'boys'.' 'When I came home from school all excited about a science class, Mom would say, "What does a girl need to know about that for?,"' declared one woman who came herself to accept the opinion.

Children's experience of schooling is obviously more than its parts. It is important to reiterate that most of those whom we interviewed reported that, overall, they enjoyed their schooling. In the words of one, 'I sure enjoyed my days at school, even if I wasn't good at it,' and another stated, 'The years in grade school were the best in my life.' Fredelle Bruser Maynard wrote: 'In many respects my early education was narrow, repressive, unimaginative,' but the 'curious truth, though, is that I *liked* school and acquired there a love of learning.'[67] For those from large families, school provided a setting in which their individual characteristics could be recognized and developed. As the sixth in a family of eight children, Max Braithwaite found that, in school, 'I soon discovered that I was pretty quick to learn, and this gave me status. I was in a new pecking order now, not one governed by age or sex or rotundity, but by ability.'[68] For those from both rural and urban families, in which children had lots of hard work to do, school provided a some relief from their labours. For those frightened, harassed, or even persecuted by other children, the classroom provided some sanctuary. For those from extremely poor, crowded, abusive, or disrupted families, school provided a warm, ordered, and structured environment. As Percy Janes's protaganist explained, he was 'glad' to start school, 'for here I began to feel that I had at least some small measure of control over the things that happened to me, in a violent and bewildering world. By close attention and diligence I could influence and therefore predict my rulers' behaviour toward me ...'[69]

Other children were less fortunate. Someone who did well enough to complete high school reported that visiting his elementary school at a recent reunion gave 'a bad feeling even now ... I have bad memories of that place.' Another, hearing about my research through a radio interview, telephoned to insist I talk to him: 'I know things you have to know.' When we met, and after he had savagely criticized his own schooling, he asked what sort of alternatives to the public system I could suggest for his own child.

In the context of this overall assessment, I want to make two final comments about schooling in this era. First, it is clear that the whole community – pupils, teachers, parents, employers – believed that the 'learning out of a book' sort of schooling described in this chapter was the way it ought to be. In particular, parents of all social classes shared in this common viewpoint as to the nature and value of elementary schooling. They knew what children should learn, they knew how teachers should teach it, and they knew how principals and teachers should maintain order. They were sceptical of anything new. ('Why learn to cook on those [electric] stoves if you'll never afford one, anyway?'; 'We didn't have any of that colouring nonsense when I went to school – we learned proper drawing.') Indeed, because parents and employers lacked the daily empirical testing of their expectations against the real world of the classroom, they often held the most rigid of formalistic expectations of what school should be like.

That working-class parents apparently held the same views on elementary education as did their middle-class counterparts may seem somewhat surprising. As other chapters show, the lives of children outside of school clearly displayed differences based on class. Recollections of school are surprisingly similar, however, whatever the neighbourhood or class background of the children. Schooling sorted children within rather than between schools.[70] Thus, all schools encouraged the 'bright,' and told those who were not as able as their peers that they were not going to climb very far up the educational ladder.

None the less, formal schooling met, in a rough and ready way, somewhat different class needs. At the political level, organized labour supported free public education, and, in Vancouver at least, working-class people ran for, and were elected to, school boards.[71] At the personal level, in a city composed of people born elsewhere, or the children of those born elsewhere, parents took seriously their role as educational strategists for their children.

My second closing comment is to note how far classroom practice was from educational theory. The 'new' education – by the 1930s often called 'progressive' education – embodied notions of learning by doing, and of building child-centred curricula out of the interests of children. In the context of these ideas, most provinces gradually introduced a series of what were really administrative reforms. They standardized curricula and time allotments for each subject, adopted the notion of the junior high-school, eliminated high school entrance examinations, tightened standards for admission to Normal schools, and promoted school consolidations. In British Columbia in the 1930s, for example, the province undertook a major revision of the curriculum. By 1937, the Department of Education had produced a new course of study that was more than 1,600 pages long. In the words of one of its chief architects, H.B. King, the philosophy characterizing this new curriculum 'may be briefly expressed as the promotion of individual growth and social adjustment through purposeful activity.'[72] None the less, if my informants are to be believed, then all of the changes that took place in education outside of the classroom had very little effect on what went on behind its doors. For children, their schooling was still epitomized in the time-honoured response of their teachers: 'Yes, neatness counts!'[73]

10

Children in the Culture of Childhood

Imagine the playground of a Vancouver school as it was on a dry October morning sometime between the 1920s and the 1960s.[1] In the few minutes before the bell rang for the first time, it became a noisy, and overwhelmingly physical, scene that could be heard for a couple of blocks in all directions.[2] Most boys in the upper grades had assembled on the boys' field. Some raced after the soccer ball, trying, as they said, to get a 'kick in.' Sometimes a group of the older boys tried to keep the ball to themselves, passing it within a tight circle. A single mistake put it back into play for all. Other boys lounged in clumps. If the ball came arcing down their way, these clumps dissolved as the boys raced for the ball. The lucky victor booted it as hard as he could across the field, and another clump dissolved after it.

On the girls' playground, many youngsters bounced lacrosse balls, and one could hear, among other chants, 'One, two, three, alery-o.' Others skipped, some on their own with short ropes, more in groups. In the latter arrangement, two girls twirled a longer rope, while the rest lined up to take turns skipping over it. While younger girls employed relatively simple routines and rhymes, older, and more adept, girls followed elaborate sequences, some of which involved two, or even more, girls skipping at the same time. Those who faltered went to the end of the line. On smaller playgrounds younger children played with balls, or played tag and other chasing games.

Many children stood in pairs, some girls holding hands, or in small groups talking to each other. Other pairs or small groups promenaded the schoolyard so that they would be seen and would know what was going on everywhere. Except for the boldest of the Grade Sevens and Eights, these pairs and small groups were composed of children of one sex only; rule or custom separated girls and boys on most school grounds. Some groups talked loudly, argued, laughed, and the boys particularly, but also some of the girls, hit, pushed, and shoved each other playfully, and sometimes not so playfully, and wrestled in 'play' fights. Others talked quietly, exchanging gossip and telling jokes. ('Did you hear "The Great Gildersleeve" last night?'; 'Old Bell is wearing a new sweater today'; 'Why did the little moron ...?') At the edge of the playground, a few children stood alone looking on.

Teachers who surveyed the scene saw a boisterous, noisy world, but also one that they were sure they controlled. The bell symbolized their authority, and the response it brought from the children demonstrated its strength. Passers-by, parents, and neighbours who heard the clamour from afar, looked upon this lively gathering as one through which children had moved easily from the control of their families into the control of the school.

On the other hand, to the children on the playground the scene displayed, as it would again during recess, just before the afternoon bell, and right after school, the culture of childhood in one of its most rigid and complete forms. 'Recess lasts only fifteen minutes,' recalled Sylvia Fraser, 'yet whole playground societies, based on a tennis ball or a skipping rope, rise and fall.'[3] Divided, as it was, along gender, age, ethnic, and other lines, this culture controlled who played in which games and who did not play at all. It gathered together the smaller groups, and it pushed to the side of the playground those who observed the world from there.[4]

The culture of childhood was not confined to the school playground. To a quite remarkable degree, it structured the lives of children throughout their waking hours and may have affected their dreams as well. It exerted its influence within the homes of the most strong-minded of parents. It controlled some behaviour in the classrooms of even the most tyrannical of teachers. Outside of home and school, it affected relationships between the young, even when they were immediately under the eyes or ears of adults with authority over them. As they moved away from adult-structured arenas, children also moved more deeply into a world in which they had to come to terms with a culture passed on directly from one generation of children to the next.

As they had already learned in their families, they discovered that the power of some over others also governed their relations with their peers; they found the third locus of power in their lives. 'When we start school,' wrote Charles Dougan, 'the lessons we are taught in the classroom pale in comparison to the lessons learned when we are immersed in the school yard society ... One better be quick to understand that "might is right."'[5] In these instances, however, children learned that power could be relative as well as

The girls' field of a Toronto school (Pape Avenue Public School) in a working-class neighbourhood in April 1960.

absolute; that as they were subject to those older, bigger, stronger, or more confident than themselves, so they could dominate those younger, smaller, weaker, or less confident than themselves.

In this chapter, I first explain what I mean by 'the culture of childhood.' Next, I describe the key role that siblings, friends, peers, and the neighbourhood as a whole played in that culture. Finally, I discuss the workings of the culture – the constraints surrounding it, how children found their place in it, some of the things they did within the culture, and how they felt about it. Although this is not a history of children's games and pastimes, the complexity of the culture, with its multitude of venues, requires some description of the actual activities of youngsters. The culture of childhood played as large a role in the lives of rural youngsters as it did in those of their urban counterparts. Since the urban form of it was more elaborate (although no more important) than the rural, I lay it out in urban terms. My account of the scripts of the culture itself, however, draws on both rural and urban examples.

What do I mean by the 'culture of childhood'?[6] Most of the institutions

in which children spent their lives – family, congregation, voluntary association, school, truant home, industrial school, and so on – had as their principal goal the socializing of the young into the whole cluster of ways of living
that characterized the larger cultures of which they were a part. At the same
time, however, children had to learn to be children, to become members of
both the almost timeless world of childhood and their own brief generation
within it.[7] At its simplest level, this meant learning to *do* certain things.
Learning to skip, for example, involved mastering a complex system of
rhymes and physical activities. But learning to skip also involved learning to
behave in appropriate ways with other girls. In learning how to behave
towards each other, children absorbed the knowledge, customs, expectations, beliefs, norms, values, and social roles that governed relationships
between them. They also absorbed the multitude of unwritten rules that
regulated social behaviour. 'For months,' wrote Elizabeth Brewster, 'the
two Corcoran girls, Eileen and Blanche, used to beat me up on the way
home from school ... I didn't tell any of the grownups, teachers or parents. I
knew that tattling was the greatest of all sins.'[8]

Sometimes this social learning harmonized with what adults also wanted
of their children. Most parents, for example, approved of their children
learning the sharing, the give-and-take that characterized real friendship.
Sometimes learning which children valued highly appeared irrelevant to the
goals of adults; parents and teachers attached no particular merit to youngsters mastering the words of a skipping song, or the rules of 'conkers.'
Sometimes this childish learning ran contrary to what adults expected of
children; adults tried to prevent children from teasing or tormenting the
weak, the afflicted, or the merely different in their midst. In consequence,
many points of great tension between adults and children had their roots in
the competing requirements of childhood and adult cultures.

One can visualize the geography of the culture of childhood as a personal
landscape made up of concentric circles, with the child's family at the centre
and the whole community encompassed by the outer ring. Children entered
the culture of childhood when they first established a relationship with
another child or group of children. Most infants made their first connections with siblings, with cousins, or with the children of friends or neighbours met while parents took part in adult activities to which their children
accompanied them. As children moved outside of their households, they
met the boys and girls who lived nearby. As they grew older, and extended
the range of their travels, children began to associate more extensively with
their peer group; those who were relatively close in age to one another and
who came together because of schooling, for neighbourhood play, or for

activities sponsored by a congregation. In the next outward ring, and much more important than the psychological and sociological literature makes clear, was the whole youthful population of the neighbourhood; at one end, those just emerging from infancy, and, at the other, adolescents just on the verge of adulthood.

Children entered the culture of childhood as they interacted with their sisters, brothers, and other close relatives. Since relationships among siblings were discussed in an earlier chapter, all that needs to be noted here is the connection between these relationships and those that prevailed among children generally. Thus, as children got older, they found that the norms of the childhood culture increasingly prevailed within the family as well. Brothers and sisters who told tales on each other learned that such behaviour was wrong. ('My brother called for Father; it was unfair.') Possibly these norms were less effectively enforced between siblings than they were in the wider community – things had a way of slipping out at home – but they were surprisingly strong, and especially so when they involved one sibling's knowing about another's visiting a forbidden place or engaging in a forbidden practice. A younger child might be aware of an older sister's habit of shoplifting, or a brother's cigarette smoking, know that both were wrong, both were against family rules, and yet not report either.

Since, until well into the 1950s, Vancouver possessed few nursery schools or kindergartens, most children there entered the world of other children as it existed immediately around their own homes, in extended family, and in congregational activities.[9] 'All my friends,' said a Winnipeg man, 'were from the immediate vicinity.' A Vancouver man 'had twenty-four first cousins on Dad's side. We had huge family gatherings.' A Vancouver woman noted, 'I saw a lot of [a friend] because his parents were involved in our church.' Young children played inside their own homes, in the hallways outside their apartments, or on the covered, shared porches of Vancouver's characteristic wooden tenements. They played in their own yards, in other yards, on the sidewalk or the street in front of or the back alley behind their homes and those a few doors away in either direction. A Vancouver boy 'was sent out to play in the back alley. It was my main area of play as a smaller child.' Some ventured to nearby vacant lots.

Play in these local settings was generally simple. A Montreal brother and sister 'made forts out of chairs on our verandah.' The more fortunate or well-to-do rode tricycles, or pulled wagons, or laid out roadways for small cars in sandboxes or on patches of dirt. Many children played with home-made or self-made toys: washed-out tin cans, blocks of wood, old pots or pans, pieces of metal, and so on. They played in puddles. They used rocks or sticks to lay out floor plans for homes, and in these settings practised parental or other roles with each other, or with dolls. ('We played house a lot.') Sometimes they picked flowers for their playhouse or mother; 'good' flowers from their own or neighbourhood gardens, or dandelions, daisies, or brown-eyed Susans that they would put into a glass jar or tin can.

In this early neighbourhood play, children began to acquire some of the secret knowledge of childhood. They learned the truth about Santa Claus and the Easter Bunny, which they wisely did not tell their parents that they had learned. They began to pick up the separate language of childhood, to understand that certain things could be said only with one's own sex, and never in front of adults, to master a more complex set of 'we's' and 'they's' than those of the family, and to comprehend the basic rules of the child's culture. They identified those children on whose behaviour they modelled their own, and those whom they disliked. As adults, people remember both those whom they liked and those whom they disliked, but have little recollection as to why they felt the way they did. Clearly, both friends and enemies came from those who lived close by. If we can be guided by the psychological literature, then these feelings were less a consequence of personality than they were of behaviour; aggressive children, who pushed their way into the play of others, were generally disliked by other children.[10]

As they got older, and particularly after they started school, children began to sort special friends out of the larger group of their peers. To most children, the role of 'chum' or 'friend,' and especially 'best friend,' was the most important relationship they had with other children.[11] Two friends who, however temporarily, had woven their lives together – talking, playing, walking, laughing, giggling, arguing, fighting, holding hands in school lines, attending the Saturday matinée, window shopping, buying penny candy together – formed the smallest component of the culture of childhood. A woman reported, 'I always had a good friend,' and a man explained of himself and another: 'We were friends for sixteen years.' According to the Gage *Dictionary of Canadian English*, the most common meaning of the term 'friend' is a 'person who knows and likes another.' Children grew into and within their friendships in this sense of the term; the older they were the more they expected from a friendship. Young children became friends because they lived close to each other and shared activities. As one woman said, she and her friend 'were together all the time. She lived just down the street.' Older children became or remained friends because, as well as activities, they came to share values, and the same attitudes towards the way in which their world worked. Best friends were usually, although not always, of the same sex.[12]

Three friends who live on the Musqueam Reserve in Vancouver stop to chat in 1958.

In the intermediate and senior elementary grades, children may have added to their friendships a certain intimacy, a degree of sharing, and a level of feeling that, in its most complete form, might be, as Harry Stack Sullivan argued, 'something very like full-blown psychiatrically defined love.'[13] As one man put it, 'best friends are fantastic because you share so much with them that you can't share with anyone else, even your parents.' A woman noted, 'My girlfriend and I were like blood sisters, and we had a secret code and we used to write backward or had our own language.' Some research in social psychology suggests that girls may enter into this level of friendship more often than boys.[14] Whether between girls or boys, such close relationships outside the family could go some way towards alleviating the misery brought on by unhappy home life. Unfortunately, those whose circumstances made them most in need of such a close relationship were also those who had the most difficulty forming them.

Friends spent as much time together as possible. If they could, they walked to school together, and played together at recess and noon hour. Although friendship was reciprocal, occasionally one-half of a pair would apparently invest more in a particular friendship than the other, with consequent tension, heartache, and jealousy. One woman explained, 'I placed heavier emphasis on friendship than did those who were my friends,' and a second noted of herself and another girl, 'I was a second-string friend and she kept up with the first string.'

The *Gage Dictionary* also defines 'friend' as 'a person who favours and supports.' This definition omits the 'likes' of the first, but accurately describes some childhood friendships that had characteristics of an alliance. Certain children came together, for example, through a forced propinquity; they were both new to the neighbourhood, they were rejected by others, they shared a disability or the fact that both were disabled, or they were the only peers that lived in a certain area. Most such children tried to make more satisfactory friendships, and the fortunate ones did so. A woman recalled, after moving, 'It was hard to start school, but I made friends easily.'

Most children also forged increasingly tight memberships for themselves in the peer group. One man, however, recalled, 'I had two or three close personal friends, whereas the rest of the neighbourhood would go out in a gang, of eight or ten.' A child's peer group was made up of those youngsters of roughly the same status and stage of development with whom he or she talked, played, argued, fought, or otherwise interacted on a reasonably regular basis.[15] One woman said, 'We had a gang if you want to call it that ... we would hang out under the lamp on the corner. We didn't do any harm; mostly we just talked.' A man declared, 'We had friends that did things together but no hoodlum gangs.' As did friends, the peer group helped youngsters develop a sense of belonging, and provided a common view as to how its members should dress, think, and behave towards one another and other children. Generally, a hierarchy developed within a peer group, with a few children at the core providing leadership, and a fluctuating group following along.[16] Youthful leaders proposed what the rest should do, and to a considerable degree controlled and sanctioned the behaviour of the group.

For young children, the peer group of the neighbourhood might be very different from that of the classroom or school ground. As children got older, and extended their boundaries, peer groups began to blend together. As children got older, as well, the peer group became a stronger and stronger influence on them or, perhaps more accurately, they acquired enough sense of autonomy and even physical independence that they were able to adopt at least some peer norms or practices even when these conflicted with those of parents or teachers. For this reason both parents and teachers tended to distrust the peer group.

Most children also interacted with the other young people of their neighbourhood. Indeed, for rural youngsters the whole community of the young formed a sort of peer group. If youthful culture in urban areas could no longer be characterized by the 'promiscuity of ages' that Joseph Kett ascribed to it in the preindustrial world, intermixture had not declined to the extent that research based on age-graded classroom groupings has suggested.[17] At the broadest level, children merely knew who the other children were in their neighbourhood ('I knew the names of all our neighbours'; 'I've a lot of good memories of the neighbourhood kids. They were a very friendly group. The boys and girls were all pretty good people'; 'Kerrisdale was a small town; I knew everybody.') From neighbourhood young people, children picked out those whom they admired from a distance, or even emulated them in clothing or behaviour. They also sorted out those whom they avoided – the cruel, the vicious, the bullies, those likely to tease or torment them. Generally, they kept away from the handicapped. Sometimes they avoided those of other religious denominations, ethnic groups, or races.

In the neighbourhood, children sometimes discovered their first loves. A Cedar Cottage man came to 'adore' a classmate during the first or second grade. 'I often looked across the room at her.' Even after he became a teenager and began to date other girls, he 'retained a certain fondness for her. I finally told her about my "crush" at our high-school class's twenty-fifth reunion. She was really surprised.' Dorothy Livesay wrote, 'in those years between nine and twelve, I experienced the "ideal" love ... It was a kind of obsession. Any day that passed without my seeing him was a day weighed down. My fantasies about him were intense. Yet if he had come near, or spoken, or touched my arm, I would have been speechless with embarrassment.'[18]

Parents and guardians controlled the extent to which children participated in the lives of other children. At one extreme, certain parents kept their children away from other youngsters for most or all of the time. Some parents decided on this course as a matter of principle: they feared the physical effects or the social consequences of relationships with other children. Other parents took this route out of necessity: they needed their children for domestic activities and chores. Some parents organized their children into studies of various kinds – singing, dancing, elocution, a second language, piano or other musical instrument – so that lessons and practices took up much or most non-school time. Parents sent their children to visit grandparents or other relatives; to attend meetings of children's groups such as the Junior Catholic Youth Organization, Brownies, Cubs; and to Sunday school or catechism classes.

Parents confined their youngsters to particular places, such as the home block or the local street or neighbourhood park. As one person reported for others, 'I was not allowed to play outside our yard, and inside it only with certain other children.' For a Vancouver woman, 'the northern boundary was the cemetery at Fraser and 41st Avenue ... the church at Fraser and 47th would be about the southern boundary.'[19] Parents put such places as the city dump, the newspaper 'shack,' certain areas of 'bush,' 'the flats,' the lake, log booms, the Fraser River dikes, the swamp, the bogs, and railway or interurban rights-of-way out of bounds. As we saw in chapter 3, they discouraged, and sometimes even forbade, their children to associate with certain other children. Most parents took a strong stand against such practices as smoking (in part because of their fear of fire); using slingshots or air rifles; using bad language; engaging in talk, discovery, and experimentation regarding sex; vandalism; turning in false fire alarms; and indulging in shoplifting or other forms of petty theft. Finally, parents set time limits on their children's play, a practice governed partly by the season and partly by family requirements as to meals, chores, music practice, and the like.

Certain parents rarely set or enforced boundaries. They let – or pushed – their children out of the home at an early age and left them to fend more or less for themselves. Again, parents took this step for a variety of reasons. Some lone parents went out to work and could not afford much or any child-minding. Other parents, emotionally disturbed, abused, abandoned, alcoholic, or otherwise cast down by their lives, seemed to have lost the capacity, or perhaps the energy, to care. Some parents, and especially those with large families, encouraged their children to assume responsibility for themselves from a very early age onward. Such children chose themselves what to do with the time that they did not have to commit to school or such family activities as chores or meals. A few parents so lost control over their youngsters that the latter ignored wishes or demands that went contrary to their own. Such 'free spirits' were envied by their more restricted peers.

As parents set spatial, temporal, and behavioural boundaries, however, so children tested them. Even the most timid and most rigidly controlled youngsters at some time or another ventured to forbidden places and attempted forbidden practices. Children were most likely to test their boundaries when there was conflict between family and youthful norms and values. Nearly every child, for example, experimented with smoking. 'We would,' declared one man, 'pick up cigarette butts and end up getting sick smoking them.' Both Kerrisdale and Cedar Cottage had merchants who would sell children single cigarettes. Probably fewer children attempted shoplifting than smoking, but soft drinks, penny candies, fruit, and make-up presented strong temptations, and undoubtedly justified the watchful eye that shopkeepers kept on this merchandise.[20] The confectioner, who 'had the patience of Job as we picked out our penny candies,' also possessed a shrewd sense of what would happen should he turn his back. Children sometimes felt guilty when discussion or play with friends or peers became overtly sexual. None the less, the play began with preschool children trading 'peeks' and continued right through elementary school. 'Two girls,' reported one man, 'tried to take me home to be the "doctor."'

For most youngsters, school became the most important theatre for the enactment of their culture. For nine or ten months of the year, going to school, being at school, and returning from school absorbed much of their waking hours. Schools sorted children into age and class divisions, within which they divided themselves into more intimate groups. In the school-yard, declared one man, 'you had your own group of kids you played with at school in your class, and that was it. You didn't get in with this other group that was a year older [or] ... with the group that was a year younger.'

Although parents and teachers viewed the children's trips to and from school each day as a means to an end, many children looked upon them as separate, special elements of the day. In the opinion of one woman: 'Half the fun of school was the walk to and fro, having a friend, going home for lunch, and admiring the flowers in people's gardens.' As youngsters left their own home and yard or apartment block, they also moved towards the edge of the circle of family authority. They knew that the school's efforts to

control the territory between home and school were mostly directed at regulating conduct, and especially conduct that could put children into danger,
or bring the school itself into disrepute.[21] Those who felt particularly
hemmed in by the constraints of family and school took special delight in
these periods of freedom, and stretched them out as much as they could.
For some this was not very far. One woman who could not leave until just in
time for school, who came home for lunch and again right after school,
reported that she 'always had a good time' on the playground, 'with lots of
friends,' that 'her playground was recess.'

Parental concerns, school regulations, personal habits, and one's own
attitudes towards, and place in, a group governed how children made this
trip. If time was pressing, or the playground activity of particular interest to
the children, they walked, sometimes roller-skated, or, in the upper grades,
cycled fairly quickly to school. 'I rode my V-handled bike to school; they
were a big thing then,' said a man, and a woman reported, 'We were always
there by 8:30.' On cold days those inadequately clothed or from unheated
homes left early and moved quickly to get to a place that was warm. Some
children did the trip to school on the run. Some ran because parents kept
them at chores or music lessons until just before the bell. From the first
grade onward, 'in the morning,' said one woman, 'I stayed home and practised the piano until the last minute before the first bell.' Others rose late: 'I
leaped from the breakfast table when the first bell rang,' reported someone
who lived near the school, and 'I arrived just as soon as the second stopped
ringing.' Some arrived exactly on time because they feared other children.
Out of 'sheer fear of those kids' who persecuted one boy, he 'hid in a ditch
by the school until the school bell rang.' Fear of in-school consequences,
however, made most children resolve not to be late for school.

For other children, the trip followed a leisurely pattern. Many children
began to gather with their own group while on their way to school. A
Kerrisdale woman 'would leave about twenty to nine and jaunty off to
school. I would meet my friends at the corner or they would come and yell
for me.' In the era before telephones became universal, both boys and girls
practised this mode of, literally, calling on their friends. They stood in the
lane behind the house or on the sidewalk in front, calling out the name of
the friend inside. 'We'd just yell and yell from the road until the person
came out,' explained one woman. As they gathered together, children followed a regular route along certain streets, down back lanes, and through
vacant lots and bits of 'bush.' Certain dogs could be provoked into fits of
furious barking. Children examined the changing characteristics of creek
beds and ditches. After a rain, they stomped in puddles, built dams and

Some Winnipeg children on their way to school in 1925.

bridges, or tried to catch tadpoles. They broke ice wherever they found it. In the spring, they looked for salmonberries, and in the fall they picked overhanging apples in the back lanes. In marbles season, they played 'chase.' They admired houses and gardens and observed changes in the neighbourhood.

Some children carefully selected their routes to avoid such things that frightened them as unpleasant neighbours, fierce dogs, and quarantine signs. They avoided routes on which one might meet children whom they feared or disliked. During the Second World War, certain Halifax young-sters whose homes were inside a restricted area had the extra excitement of passing through a military check-point on their way to school. Some of these children delighted in finding illegal short-cuts in which they went 'across the tracks and into town illegally.'

Most children arrived at school in time to join the kaleidoscopic but highly structured activities described in the opening paragraphs of this chapter. The seasons, the weather, and the pecking order governed what and where they played. In large schools, each level – primary (Grades One to Three), intermediate (Grades Four to Six), and senior (Grades Seven and Eight) – had a core group who dominated the activity that the season dictated. This group also controlled the best bit of the playground that custom assigned to children in that grade or level. Those not in the most exclusive group played the same game close by. A small group of youngsters played, or watched, from the edge, some of whom 'spent a lot of time observing ... and talking about people.' If there was a 'special' class of some sort in the school, its pupils were generally ignored by the 'regular' pupils. 'They didn't talk clearly or walk right; they didn't socialize with us,' said one person, and another declared 'one boy with CP talked funny and other kids didn't want to talk with him.'

Although most Vancouver schools possessed separate basement play areas for boys and for girls, most children preferred to be outdoors unless the rain was teeming down. On such days, children had no choice; word came from the principal that all children would play inside. With concrete floors, walls, and sometimes ceilings, on rainy days these generally unventilated basements were extremely noisy, 'hard on the bones,' and usually odorous places to be: 'They smelled like wool in the rain; a real stink.'

Pupils played traditional games, most of which involved at least some physical contact.[22] Some were common to both girls and boys. Younger children played hide and seek. Children of all ages built snow and other houses and 'forts.' Both boys and girls employed traditional chants and starting rhymes: 'Liar, liar, your pants are on fire!'; 'Cry baby'; 'You're getting warm'; 'Sticks and stones ...'; 'On your marks ...!'; and so on. Both girls and boys played with milk-bottle tops, using their 'stickers' to increase their supply. Both boys and girls promenaded the school ground to see what was going on, or to spot a particular member of the opposite sex. Both boys and girls stood in pairs or small groups talking, sharing the secret knowledge of childhood, telling jokes, and sometimes 'dirty' stories. (X: 'Do you want to hear a dirty story?' Y: 'Yes.' X: 'A white horse fell into a mud puddle.') Both boys and girls talked about sex when, as Margaret Atwood's 'Elaine' aptly put it, 'a long whisper runs among us, from child to child, gathering horror.'[23] Both boys and girls played poison tag, tag ball, dodge ball, andy-andy-eye-over, the fox and the geese, pom-pom pull-away, follow-the-leader, and 'single basket.' On wet days in the separate basements, both boys and girls played a version of tag sometimes called 'British bulldog.' Both boys and girls played, separately if there were enough of each sex, otherwise together, a transformed softball game called 'scrub.' One woman 'loved baseball and enjoyed it best if boys and girls played it together.' On those school grounds where the practice was not forbidden, they had snow-ball fights.

Girls also had their own games. They skipped in a variety of games – 'Dutch,' 'Double Dutch,' and so on – of increasing physical and verbal complexity. In Burnaby in the 1920s, Frances Fleming learned:

> House for rent, apply within,
> People moving out for drinking gin.
> Drinking gin is a very bad sin,
> As you move out, then I move in![24]

Girls bounced balls – 'there were lots of games with lacrosse balls' – on the sidewalk, or against the wall of the school. They played with jacks and balls together. One woman 'loved jacks,' and another still has 'callouses on my fingers from playing jacks on concrete.' They played hopscotch 'with favourite things sewn together.' They played house and 'Initials,' which 'involved knowing the initials of Hollywood stars.'

Football and baseball were 'the' games of boys. ('Soccer was our game!') In the fall, they played 'conkers' with horse chestnuts 'to see who was the king of the chestnut bashers.' In the spring, they played with marbles or 'alleys' (called 'steelies,' 'dibs,' 'glassies,' 'cat's eyes,' and 'cobs'), carried in a draw-string bag – 'preferably the purple one that came from Seagram's Crown Royal whisky' – in such games as 'round pot,' 'square pot,' 'odd or even,' 'poison,' 'stink,' or with marble boards. 'I was very good at [marbles],' claimed one man. 'I had a small 3-pound lard pail full of them that I had won.'[25] They chased and shot at each other with finger-guns, while making appropriate noises in their throats. In the school basement, they played a game called, variously, 'ship ahoy,' 'ships and sailors coming in,' or 'piling on.'[26] They played handball, murder ball, 'two finger whacking,' tag ball, and 'pie.'

Although most of the school-related activities of children were sharply gendered, they also had an undercurrent of sexual awareness. As most youngsters walked to school and played with members of their own sex, they were acutely aware of nearby members of the other. By the intermediate grades, certain girls would begin to take routes to school or around the grounds that paralleled those of some of the boys, or vice versa. Only the boldest girls or boys at this stage would actually walk or play with a single friend of the opposite sex, and they were teased when they did so. Some games had a deliberate sexual dimension. On some school grounds, for example, older girls played variations of 'kiss,' during which 'we would chase some of the boys to grab and kiss them. They pretended it was awful, but came close enough to get caught sometimes.' Both boys and girls deliberately invaded each other's space. Girls chanted or sang such slightly risqué rhymes as 'Chinese (pull up eyes), Japanese (pull down eyes), look at these! (turn around and flip up skirt to show underpants to boys).'

Indeed, as this rhyme exemplifies, much play unselfconsciously involved racist sentiments. The version of 'eeny, meany ...', of the time, the chants shouted at passing vegetable trucks driven by Chinese or loads of wood driven by Sikhs, and caustic references to ungenerous givers embedded racial slurs and slanders. As William Macklon shrewdly observed, 'We'd never heard of racism. We just practiced it ... Of course it was just ignorant ... But it was destructive, for it must have clung to us like a tick burrowing into a soft and neglected place and making poison, so that we never felt perfectly comfortable with people of other races no matter what kindness and what courtesy and good will they may have shown us or what allowances they have made for our shortcomings.'[27] Not all Canadian children were racist. Caroline Wong arrived in Prince Rupert from China in 1953. At school, she made friends quickly and, by Valentine's Day, 'was the most popular girl in the class; I received a valentine from everyone. Summer that year I was invited to several birthday parties ...'[28]

Although the commercial world then intruded far less into childhood than it does now, each year saw the arrival at the school grounds of the salesmen/demonstrators of Yo-Yos, Bolos, or other patented toys.[29] There they demonstrated the vast array of tricks that one could do with one of these mechanisms. In the spring in Vancouver, many of the older boys practised hardball pitching in order to enter the *Vancouver Sun*'s Ace Pitching Club contest.[30] In the 1950s, Hula Hoops arrived on Canadian school grounds. A toy that initially appealed to both sexes, it eventually became almost solely a possession of girls, probably because they were more adept at using it than boys. 'I could,' one woman claimed, 'keep one hoop going around my waist, another around my wrist, and a third around my ankle, all at the same time!'

Although the ringing of the school bell dissolved all the elaborate arrangements of the playground, they quickly re-formed at recess, lunch hour, and after school. A few children tried to remain in the classroom or, contrary to school regulations, 'came home at recess because I hated school.' More came out 'the back door and onto the field; all of us kids roaring around, chasing the soccer ball.' Children who enjoyed the activities of playground and basement also tried to spend as much of their noon hour there as possible. One child 'ran home for lunch ... and ran back; I wanted to be at school with the action'; for, as one woman explained, 'The order you got back to school was the order you got up to bat.' However, another's mother 'always said, "You'll come for lunch because teachers need a rest." I was not allowed to go back early.'

The trip home after school was the reverse of that to school in the morning. Many children had to hurry home to be under the eye of a parent, to babysit or undertake other family chores, or to attend to lessons of various kinds, or to practise. 'I went home to music; all my after-school time was taken up by music' reported one girl, and another noted that she practised for two hours every day after school. Others could make a more leisurely progression, replicating a more relaxed version of the morning's activities. Those who could afford to bought penny candies, and sometimes shared broken cookies from Dad's or Bader's, or day-old, or 'sinker' doughnuts.

Playground relationships and mores spilled over into the classroom. In contrast to their lively manifestation outside, however, inside they had to be conducted with considerable subtlety. Perhaps more often in memory than in fact (it was, after all, both a difficult and a strapping offence), girls had their braids dipped in ink-wells. Bigger boys stepped on the feet of smaller ones and pricked others with compass or pencil points. On Valentine's Day, popular children and unpopular children had their status confirmed by the number of cards they received. Those whom the children taunted, bullied, or picked on continued to be treated in this way. Pupil monitors gave them the oldest textbooks, or 'accidentally' knocked things off their desks as they went by. One person recalls how, as a pupil monitor, he ground away as much of their pencils as possible. Until the 1950s, this 'game' was more serious than it now sounds. Even middle-class parents provided school supplies charily, and expected them to last an appropriate amount of time.

Victimized children were extremely reluctant to inform on those plaguing them. Except under the most severe interrogation, the code that forbade tattling held sway in the classroom as strongly as it did on the playground and in the wider community. In the third Grade, a man reported, 'Charlie got beaten up for telling that Billy had stolen his crayons.' Perhaps to retaliate, certain children developed careers as informers but suffered the penalty of being despised and ostracized by their peers, and not really liked by the teachers with whom they tried to ingratiate themselves. Other unpopular children drew attention to themselves by their behaviour, as did the boy who reported that 'Teacher says I'm the silliest boy in school, and I am, too.'[31]

Even greater diversity than that of the school ground characterized the culture of childhood in the neighbourhood. Most children played with other children as much and as often as they could. They played after school

('I came home from school and put on my play clothes'), in the evening when the days lengthened, on the weekend, and over the summer vacation. As they did so on the school ground, children projected a kaleidoscopic image of changing groupings, movement, and sound that only partly concealed the fairly rigid structure that actually governed their relationships. The neighbourhood provided more scope for parents and children to differ over boundaries of place, time, and friendship. In it, as well, most children found a wider opportunity to explore forbidden places, to spend time with forbidden people, and to partake of forbidden pastimes.

Childhood culture included a solitary core, often centred in a private space. Since few children had their own rooms, they searched for privacy elsewhere. In Alice Kimoff's Vancouver home in the 1930s, there 'was a tiny landing with a small window, and it was here that I would bring a book or some homework. It was my secret hideaway.'[32] Others repaired to the 'forts' or other secluded spaces they shared with their friends. There, children day-dreamed about and wished for changes in their lives. As a 'child of the Great Depression,' Gerald Paul 'attributed to the wishbone the auspicious power of wish-fulfilment. I wished for pants without patches, protection from polio, and pocket money for pop and peanuts.'[33] 'I dreamed of our family becoming a happy one, like, you know, well, those I met in books,' one woman reported. In their solitary time, children also cared for pets, read, played musical instruments, and built models. They played with blocks, cut-out books, dolls, doll-houses, model soldiers, model airplanes, and trains, or sorted through their collections of movie magazines, comic books, pop-bottle caps, streetcar transfers, cigarette and bubble-gum cards, or other 'collectibles.'

On their own, children practised certain skills, sometimes for their own merit, but more often to enhance their status among their peers. Both sexes tried to walk on railway tracks; to ride their bicycles 'with no hands'; to spit through their teeth; to whistle, both with and without the help of fingers; to pump, sitting or standing, a swing up really high: 'I wanted to be able to reach the tree with my feet.' Girls practised ball bouncing, skipping, and Hula-Hooping. Katherine Dedyna explained that, in skipping, girls 'strove for personal bests on the pavement – mine was 1104 uninterrupted jumps, an impressive number even to my 11-year-old self.'[34] Boys practised marbles, whittling, throwing baseballs, and using Yo-Yos. Some boys practised muscle-building exercises, such as those of Charles Atlas that they found advertised in comic books. While only a minority of children persisted to the point of complete mastery, few were like the boy who, 'if I couldn't do it properly first time, I didn't practise to get it right!'

Neighbourhood play lacked the rigid constraints of that on the urban school ground. In this regard it resembled the play arrangements of rural schools. Without the press of time and a large crowd of children, neighbourhood play was less frantic, less intense than that of the schoolyard.[35] It was also less spatially confined. Children played in their yards, on the street and sidewalks, in vacant lots, and on playgrounds. On one Kerrisdale block, 'the end lot ... was on two levels, with two of the original stumps from the days the place was first logged. All the neighbourhood children spent a great deal of time playing there.' Although older children played with younger ones, they exacted a price. 'I usually directed the whole operation,' explained one woman, 'as I did when I played school with my brothers. I was always the teacher and they were my pupils.' Although their clothing sometimes constrained girls' play, children none the less shared in activities that on the schoolyard were felt to be the exclusive property of one sex. A man recalled, for example, that he spent a lot of time playing with his next-oldest sister, including jacks and hopscotch.

Friends and peers repaired to their private spaces. A room in a house, on or under the porch, in the garage, in a corner of the basement, or other small places served as the locales of friendship. In good weather, locations outside the house – a fort, a 'cave,' a tree-house, the space beneath advertising billboards, a shelter in the bush, an ice-house – permitted children to gather in private. ('I spent a lot of time building forts'; 'We spent a lot of time playing in the woods.')[36] There they would sit and read together, or play 'Snap,' checkers, Monopoly, or other games, or talk about parents, siblings, friends, teachers, the movies and other aspects of popular culture, their wishes, hopes for the future, and so on. As one woman reported, 'We spent long periods of time lying and talking,' and one man and his friends 'spent a lot of warm summer days reading books or comics on sun-porches.' In the 1950s, they listened to records of popular songs, including, in the words of one woman, 'Elvis Presley records played over and over, nearly driving my parents mad.'

In their private places children exchanged rumours. They claimed that Lost Lagoon (in Stanley Park), Trout Lake (in Cedar Cottage), Mt Tolmie pond (in Victoria), Deer Lake (in Burnaby), Grenadier Pond (in Toronto's High Park), and other bodies of water across the country were bottomless, 'and many drowning victims had been lost forever in [their] inky depths.' Many became convinced 'that one out of a thousand Cracker Jack boxes would contain a genuine diamond ring,' or that Player's cigarettes would award a prize for an enormous but generally unspecified number of its sailor trademark torn off cigarette packages.[37] Older children taught

Children playing on a Montreal street in June 1942.

younger ones the superstitions of childhood; when to cross their fingers, that to 'walk on a crack would break your mother's back,' that to cut your hand between finger and thumb brought on lockjaw, and countless other ones.

Play and discourse in private spaces was often gendered. At a very early age, girls began to play 'house.' They also played with dolls, each of which had a name and a set of personal characteristics. They wheeled their dolls around in buggies and wagons. They dressed up their pet cats and dogs. More so than boys, girls collected and compared the autographs of friends and teachers. ('True friends are like diamonds, precious and rare / False ones like autumn leaves, found everywhere.')[38] Girls observed, discussed, and rehearsed such dimensions of adulthood as the nature of beauty in women, good grooming, fashionable clothing, and how to deal with men. They planned their weddings, furnished their homes, and selected names for their children. In these discussions they used dolls, and especially figures that could be variously clothed cut out of Eaton's catalogues or from comic papers or special cut-out books. For girls born in the late 1950s and early

1960s, the arrival of Barbie dolls on the market gave them a three-dimensional version of the adult cut-out that soon became enormously popular.[39]

Boys talked about sport, girls, making money and spending it, especially on the cars they would eventually buy. In the bush, boys more than girls experimented with smoking, conducted exploratory sexual play, and discussed and explored bodily functions in such activities as spitting, wind-breaking, and urinating contests. As one man recalled, 'We would try to mark the wall for height. My legs were shorter than the other boys,' so I never won.' On these occasions, and when they swam in the nude, most boys felt, as Farley Mowat has put it, 'the primordial fear which haunts most men — even when they are little boys — that their organ is smaller than it ought to be.'[40]

Children's talk sometimes turned to 'where babies came from,' and other aspects of human sexuality. Patricia Graham recalled 'an unforgettable moment of revelation. I was in grade school and it was the time when girls were growing breasts ... No slight swelling, no change in posture, no new brassiere escaped our notice.'[41] As noted in chapter 3, for some children friends provided all their sex education (or miseducation). Such discussion sometimes added to the sexual myths taught by parents. For some years, for example, boys in British Columbia marvelled about the supposed phallic characteristics of a locally famous rapist and murderer.[42]

Boys' neighbourhood games tended to be more active than those of girls. They played 'cowboys and Indians' (or Canadians versus the 'Nazis' or 'Japs'), 'peggy' (in Halifax called 'tiddlies'), or they would get 'boxes [cartons] and open both ends of them, crawl in, and walk on hands and knees like a tank.' Boys employed the stalks of ferns as spears: 'You'd pull it up and it's got a long stem with a straight root on it; no branches. It made a dandy spear.' They made scooters, for which 'you needed a half a roller-skate on each end [of a two-by-four] and an apple box on top.'

Some activities were seasonal. In spring, children picked pussy willows and collected birds' eggs. In spring and summer, 'scrub' and other versions of baseball were particularly popular. Summer baseball, reported Kerry Banks, 'wasn't recess baseball, where an alarm bell cut short every rally ... but summer holidays baseball: the games began and ended according to whim and Tuesday became Wednesday, then Thursday and on around again with only different scores to mark the days.'[43] For many children, as for Eric Stofer, 'summer days seemed endless. No school forever. Each morning brought new adventures.'[44] In the summer, they 'burnt bugs with a magnifying glass,' followed the ice-wagons to collect chippings, chewed warm tar from the street, and blew grass stems between thumb and forefinger to see who could make the most noise. Those who lived near the sea, a river, or a stream regularly went swimming, and fished for trout, salmon, cod, and crabs. 'We used to love to fish,' said a Powell River man. 'We'd fish from the beach to the creek and fry them up!'

Fall and winter also brought their characteristic activities. In the fall, youngsters played in the leaves and collected chestnuts. They made bonfires, around which, reported Gary Saunders, 'shadows swooped like huge black birds, our voices were lost in the seething roar, our eyes were mesmerized by coruscations of violet and crimson and gold.'[45] Then they roasted beans over or potatoes under the coals. When it snowed, they made snowmen and snow forts, and threw snowballs. They rode their sleds or sleighs (the term varied from family to family and district to district) sometimes 'roped together, one behind the other, in a formation called a "hitch-bob,"' reported E.A. Harris. 'The first rider lay down on his belly to do the steering, and the others flopped on to the sleighs behind.'[46] In the winter, they also skated, for brief occasional periods on the west coast, for months at a time in other parts of Canada. On the prairies, Robert Thompson reported, 'when we played road hockey we wrapped magazines around our legs as shinguards, and used frozen horse manure, known as "roadapples," for pucks.'[47]

For many youngsters, Hallowe'en stood out as a particularly important day. They carved jack-o'-lanterns out of turnips or pumpkins. As it got dark, they garbed themselves in a variety of home-made costumes – ghosts, witches, pirates, and, during the war, the uniforms of service men and women were popular choices – and headed into the neighbourhood to 'trick or treat.' Small children went with parents or older siblings; it was 'a great year' when one was at last old enough to go with friends to collect apples or a small handful of candies wrapped in orange-coloured paper. In Vancouver in the late 1950s and early 1960s, Gerry Sheanh and his brothers 'would make three or four forays out into the night, returning home to dump our bags for Mom and Dad to sort.'[48] More boys than girls invested in fireworks, including 'long strings of tiny firecrackers which exploded with the noise of machineguns; "salutes"; cannon-crackers and bombs ...; sparklers; Catherine's wheels; snakes .... All could be lit from long stick-like fuses with a pungent incense-like odour ....'[49] Men's recollections abound with stories of soaped windows, disappearing gates, turned-over privies, and the like. As I noted in chapter 1, many such sagas, generally related about the adolescent years, must be greeted with considerable scepticism.

Sometimes children's play involved harassing adults. Although these activities reached a peak at Hallowe'en, some went on all through the year. Men who gave the rough side of their tongue to children who crossed their yards or played too close to their houses found, as the neighbourhood 'meanie,' that their woodpiles were knocked over. Older women, living alone, and sometimes described as 'witches,' were taunted from a distance. Children played the 'purse game,' 'or rapped on doors or rang doorbells, and then ran away.[50] Of the Quebec village in which she spent her summers, Ebbitt Cutler wrote, 'each afternoon terminated with the kind of ritual play that distinguishes children from adults ... we flung chunks of charcoal high up the sloping tin roofs [of an abandoned factory], listening as long as we dared to their bumpy trip back down, then ran to hide in the nearby wood' before the watchman appeared 'and shouted threateningly at us.'[51]

In neighbourhood play there were certain times when the rules were – by common but tacit consent – relaxed. In the growing darkness of warm summer evenings, older children would revert to earlier patterns and play with younger ones, girls and boys would play together, and all would avoid loud debates over the rules, and other confrontations between themselves that might prompt parents to intervene and declare the day's activities at an end. To Lorraine Brander, who moved to Vancouver's east end when she was nine, kick-the-can 'was most fun after it was dark, hiding around the woodsheds and backyards and along the alleys when you were supposed to be getting ready for bed.'[52] For others such evenings sometimes included 'a post-supper stroll to Twigg Island Dairy, where one could buy many varieties of ice cream, especially tutti-fruiti, at five cents a scoop.'

Older children ventured out of their neighbourhoods with friends and peers. As described in chapter 8, for young children, their trips to Stanley Park, to the beach, to skate at the old Forum or at newer postwar rinks, to Santa Claus, to picnic at Bowen Island, or to the Pacific National Exhibition were usually family expeditions. One sign of growing maturity was being allowed out, unaccompanied, on Hallowe'en. Another was when parents permitted children to go to these places with friends and without adults. 'Every year,' explained one person, 'we went to the PNE, even if we didn't have any money. We would go just to walk around.' 'When I got older,' explained a woman, 'I could come ... with my sisters and brother and spend just about the whole summer down at Kits pool, and that was just marvellous.' They also cycled long distances on Saturday, Sunday, or on summer outings. 'We went to Spanish Banks, to Little Mountain, even Birch Bay and White Rock,' said one person, and another said, 'My brothers and I would come home from gaffing salmon in Seymour Creek. We had two bikes between the three of us.' A man reported, self-righteously, 'when we were at the beach my friend would steal money, watches, and other things from the clothes bundles of people in swimming. I never did that!'

While some children read to escape loneliness or illness, for others the practice had a social dimension.[53] Children read the same books as their friends, and went together to the public library to borrow books. People described the pleasures they found in reading and sharing Nancy Drew, the Bobbsey Twins, the Henty books, the Elsie Dinsmore books, the Anne books, the *Boy's* and *Girl's Own Annual, Chums*, and even the *Books of Knowledge*. 'We read and re-read *Huckleberry Finn*,' noted one man, 'and planned to raft down the Fraser.' In Grade Six, another man and his best friend 'set out to read every Tom Swift book,' and, at ten years of age, Marion Engel and her friend decided 'to read "serious" books part of the time.'[54] A westside Vancouver woman reported that 'a group of us formed what we called the "Bookworm Club." We went to each other's homes and we read books out loud, and the mothers would make hot chocolate.'

A woman recalled, 'I had a set of the Books of Knowledge ... I loved them; they were the only books we had. I can't recall reading anything else,' and a man remembered trying, generally unsuccessfully, 'to make all those model things they showed you how to do.' Girls had a special fondness for books about horses. For Margaret Gunning, and probably many others, for 'the crème de la crème of horse lore ... absolutely nothing in the realm of kids' literature could top Anna Sewell's *Black Beauty*.'[55] Mordecai Richler has argued that, for his generation, 'there was nothing quite like comic books.'[56] While many of my informants mentioned comic books and 'Big Little Books' – 'We traded comics; it was a big activity'; 'I really liked Mary Jane and Sniffles' – none confessed to a real fascination with them.

Newspapers reached out to children. They ran daily and weekly comic strips – then commonly called 'the funnies' – which attracted a wide readership among adults as well as children. ('I only read the comics and the sports pages.') They often ran a regular 'children's corner' which included a club which children could join. The *Vancouver Province*, for example, conducted its Tillicum Club (Chinook jargon for 'friend'; Motto: 'We're all friends together'; Greeting: 'Kla-how-ya'), which provided a membership badge and listed each child in the newspaper on his or her birthday. By 1935, it claimed to have 65,000 members.[57] Lloyd Person described how, one summer, the 'kids' supplement in the Saturday edition of the *Morning Leader* became the highlight of my week; it was really and truly the only bright spot during the six unending weeks of Bible School.'[58] Weekly newspapers also gave considerable attention to children. At eleven or twelve, Geiri

Johnson himself subscribed to the *Free Press Weekly* in order to read its page for children and to solicit pen-pals. He ended up with many, 'mostly girls' from all across the country. 'Some of us kept in touch for many years.' When, in the late 1930s, Johnson started riding the freight trains, one of the reasons was to call on pen-pals.[59] Such denominational weeklies and monthlies as the United Church's *Canadian Girl* and *Canadian Boy* were also widely read.

Although they enjoyed both the 'funnies' and radio programs, Canadian children of these years clearly valued motion pictures above all other forms of popular culture.[60] The stories themselves, and the movie stars, captured a central place in the imagination of some children. 'I was fascinated by the movies,' reported one man for nearly all of his contemporaries. 'I recall the opening of the Park Theatre, Anna Neagle and her husband, Arthur Hornblower, were there in person.' While children clearly enjoyed the features and the serials ('The serial I recall was "Jack Mandy and the Indians Are Coming"' and 'My favourite was this Jungle Queen one'), they also enjoyed movie-going, and especially Saturday matinées, as a social experience.

The 'good day was Saturday,' recalled one person, because of the matinée. On Saturday afternoon two friends 'each got ten cents; we went to the Fraser Theatre for five cents and bought five cents' worth of candy to take to the movie'; another reported that, 'at my mother's discretion, I could be given a dime to go to the show'; and a third, whose family was on relief in the Depression, said, 'I don't know where Mom found the money, but she always scraped together [enough] for us to go every week.' Some theatres added 'movie' or 'birthday' clubs to their Saturday fare. When the latter provided a piece of birthday cake to each child having a birthday that week, one boy 'put a different name in all of the time and they never caught him.'

If over these years the fare changed – silent films accompanied by piano music gave way to the 'talkies,' colour replaced black and white in the major films, and the technology of cartoons improved greatly – the children's response to the Saturday matinée did not. In an atmosphere of what one described as 'disorganized bedlam,' 'they stamped their feet, went on an endless procession to the bathroom,' hissed scenes they didn't like, 'threw stuff over the edge of the balcony and at each other,' and otherwise 'did all the things you couldn't do at school.' Movies sometimes frightened their youthful audiences, and might even bring on nightmares. However, most children learned to know what to expect, looking forward, as one explained, to 'the safe but delicious terror' brought on by certain movies. Sometimes they employed such mechanisms as closing, or partly closing, their eyes, covering their ears, or putting their heads down during the parts they both did and did not want to watch. Occasionally, events from the wider world displayed in news reels penetrated children's consciousness. Thus scenes of Nazi concentration and death camps, and of released prisoners of war who had been captured by the Japanese, affected some youngsters in 1945.[61]

Girls and boys looked at films in different ways, and movies thus added another dimension to emerging gender identities. Boys identified themselves with the leading male characters, especially when they were involved in vigorous activities: fighting, shooting, riding horses, and so on. When the male lead turned to romance, boys jeered. In their fantasies, boys saw themselves in the hero's role as he dealt with the villain. A Halifax man declared that, after 'action' movies, 'I deliberately walked on the "tough" side of Barrington Street, hoping a sailor would try to jump me, and I would beat him up.' Girls identified with female leads in a more romantic way. They enjoyed the tender moments between romantic leads, and studied the garb worn by attractive women. They disliked the noise made by boys during 'love' scenes and tried to hush them. In their fantasies, girls saw themselves in a romantic relationship with the male lead. Since movies were then both less violent and less sexually explicit than later became the case, these day-dreams led neither to an understanding of the grim realities of death nor, in male–female relationships, beyond dreams of hand-holding, gentle kissing, and so on. Children then could still retain a child's view of the world.

The social value of the motion picture continued into the next week. One man explained, 'You were nothing in school if you didn't know what happened in the serial the Saturday before,' and a woman noted, we 'would get together and retell the movie with much arguing over the sequence of events.' In the case of a particularly good movie, a number of women reported, they 'would spend the whole week reconstructing it with an effort to get the dialogue correct and facial expressions described accurately.' As Marion Engel put it, 'Janie practised her Deanna Durban imitations' as she and her sister rode in the back seat of the family car in the early 1940s.[62]

Not all children went to the Saturday matinée. Some stayed away through choice; they found the noise, and the press of so many children confined in a small space, uncomfortable, or even frightening. As noted in earlier chapters, some families took up all of their youngsters' non-school time with family chores. Other families objected to movies on religious, moral, or safety grounds, and forbade their children to attend them.[63] 'I was embarrassed to say I didn't go to the movies,' explained one woman, and another reported, 'I cried when I saw *Bambi* so I was not allowed to ... see another movie that might be sad.' Some children were unable to scrape up the necessary admission and so attended only irregularly. Many older children worked on Saturdays. As they got older some of these children ignored or defied the parental ban. Whether they attended or not, however, most children made it their business to have at least a rough idea of what was going on in the world of the feature film, the cartoons, and the weekly serials.   ·

Although their families sometimes marked a rare trip to Smithers or some other town by taking their children to a film, Evelyn children did not really enter into the world of the cinema until after the Second World War. Sometimes in the 1930s, films were shown in the Evelyn Community Hall, and, during the war, the whole community turned out for the regular presentations of the travelling programs of the National Film Board. Only with school consolidation in 1946, however, were Evelyn children able to participate in the whole of the youthful discourse that grew out of regular attendance at the movies. On the other hand, children who lived right in Smithers and other towns shared this part of childhood culture with their urban counterparts: 'The big thing in Powell River was going to the show, the Patricia Theatre on Saturday nights.'

Together with their relationships with their parents and with the school, children believed that their place in the culture of childhood was one of the most important elements of their lives. 'I was more afraid of kids ... than of adults,' reported one person. The culture governed how children experienced their childhoods, how they felt about themselves and their families, and how they came to see their place in the world. As they moved from one neighbourhood to another, they left one cultural edifice behind to enter into another, just as complex, in the new environment. 'My mother was a mover,' exclaimed one man. 'I had to make new friends each time. I hated it,' and a woman reported, 'Life was hard [at her new school] until I made a special friend.' Although some hoped that moving might raise their status and others feared it might lower it, most who moved seemed to end up in a place similar to the one they had left behind. Children remained in the youthful culture until they were almost adults. Indeed, for some, the effects and memories of their place in that culture would affect their relationships with certain people over the whole of their lives.

Children, of course, varied greatly in the intensity of their introspection regarding their status in the youthful culture. Some children entered the culture of childhood mostly for positive reasons, because they found great pleasure there. One recalls the 'feeling of warmth. It was more like a family.' Some entered it for negative reasons, because it kept them away from chores, from child-minding, or from unpleasant parents. Some children moved into it, and through it, in an almost automatic way, absorbing its norms, obeying its codes, and generally participating unselfconsciously in it. They immensely enjoyed their time with other youngsters. More moved through the culture with a certain caution, especially when they decided to extend their personal boundaries, or when they moved from one neighbourhood to another. Some retreated from it into private worlds of their imaginations. Some children were excluded: 'There was a whiney kid across the street. She'd call and call and we wouldn't go out. We didn't want to play with her. She'd keep yelling.' A few children saw the territory as being almost analogous to a war zone that held innumerable threats and dangers they had to circumvent as best they could. In the poignant words of one such person: 'My strongest memory is of running to and from school; to school in the morning, home at lunch time, to school at the last minute in the afternoon; running home after school ... Recalling school, I'm overwhelmed again by a childhood sense of inadequacy.'

How did children establish positions for themselves in the complex structures of schoolyard and neighbourhood? As were relationships in families, those among children manifested the effect that power plays in close relationships.[64] Children acquired their place, their position with others having power over them, and they, in turn, having power over others through the interaction of such personal qualities as their physical attributes, their psychological characteristics, their possessions, and the way in which they took part in the process of creating and sharing group behaviours and group values. Group standards applied to such matters as speech, clothing, and, especially, the way in which children behaved towards each other.

First, children evaluated themselves and other children according to physical attributes. They compared themselves as to age, size, and physical maturity in relation to their age; their strength; their physical dexterity; the shape of their bodies; their facial features; the sound of their voices; whether they stank because they did not bathe often; and their possession of birthmarks, harelips, buck-teeth, or other disfigurements. As adults, both men and women still have vivid recollections of their personal characteristics: 'There was an awning over the drugstore window,' explained a Cedar Cottage woman. 'When you were little, you couldn't reach it. You kept jumping up, hoping to touch the awning. As the years went by ... one day you realized you could jump up and reach the awning.' Men variously explained: 'Smaller kids had to show that they were tougher'; 'They tended to think of me as more mature because I was bigger'; and 'I was small but fast, a good fighter, and good at other sports.' Women explained: '... because I excelled in sports, I think that's why I was accepted'; and 'From Grade Four onward I was the "baby" to everyone, and written off in a number of ways. It didn't bother me.'

Next, children measured themselves and other children on the basis of their temperament, their courage, their intelligence, and the sense of the freedom of choice that they projected. As a result of some school successes, one boy 'saw myself in a different light, and saw myself as seen differently by the other kids.' Children were acutely conscious of each other's sense of self, especially as they revealed this quality in their attitudes to, and their behaviour towards, their peers, and the weak and the strong in their midst. How, for example, did they respond to teasing or bullying? How did they treat parents, teachers, and other adults with authority over them? They noted how newcomers behaved: did they avoid any social contact; did they initiate themselves gradually and cooperatively into the group; were they willing to assume appropriate roles, did they try to threaten, insult, or fight their way into it?

Children placed enormous importance on how their own and their family's possessions compared with those of friends, peers, and neighbourhood acquaintances. Lawrence Freiman was proud of his family car, 'a big limousine.'[65] For some girls, 'it was socially important to have the best hopscotch tassels, the neatest hopscotch squares.' Children felt their status was threatened by a family or home that did not conform, sometimes in even minor ways, to the supposed norms of the neighbourhood: by the habits of parents or by the absence of one of them; by their lack of the customary quantity and quality of clothes, toys, and other personal possessions; by the size of their bedrooms, if they had one, and whether or not they had to share it, or even a bed, with siblings; and so on. One boy recalls that he was 'never one to take kids to my house' because his mother worked and he was 'embarrassed that his was not a normal situation.' Another 'became embarrassed because his father was a janitor.' A third 'never took people home because there might be a fight on.'

Children could do little to change their personal characteristics or family possessions. Short children could not make themselves taller ('I was still short!'), and those with hand-me-down clothing could not buy a new wardrobe at the Army and Navy, Woodward's, Spencer's, or 'the Hudson Bay.' However, as they talked, played, argued, and fought together, all could join in creating and sharing the cluster of behaviours and values that governed their relationships with each other. Friends and peers influenced one another's behaviours through a combination of modelling, discussing, and reinforcing. Older children, and those with the most prestige, set group standards and, through their behaviour, demonstrated them to the rest. Sometimes ethnic, class, or behavioural differences led to the emergence of more than one group or gang in a neighbourhood. Then the core members of each would model the standards which other members or aspiring members followed as they tried to find their place in the group, and to behave appropriately and play correctly. All had to learn, for example, to avoid behaviour that might draw the attention or the intervention of parents, teachers, or other adults. As one woman put it: 'The code of conduct for children was mostly not to sneak on each other.' While group membership was relatively open at the bottom, only the right combination of qualities – in an as yet incompletely understood process – made one a leader.

Children most clearly demonstrated the dynamics of their relationships when they differed with each other. While the community of children was perhaps more stable than the almost constant noise and movement suggested, four sorts of activities led to arguments, and sometimes to minor or major incidents of violence. In a general context in which youngsters believed that games should be played properly and the code of conduct followed meticulously, children of roughly equal status debated exactly what the rule or code was and how it should be interpreted in individual circumstances. From a children's perspective, the code possessed the characteristics traditionally ascribed to natural law. Through this discourse the older children taught the rules to the younger, and established their application to particular situations in the way in which adults applied case law. Children settled these sorts of differences relatively quickly. After a certain amount of shouting and arguing – 'Do you want a knuckle sandwich?' – either they came to a consensus or the minority noisily withdrew from the game or discussion which immediately resumed.

Bullying, vicious, and seriously disturbed children posed more serious challenges to playground and neighbourhood harmony. Even though they rarely followed through on their most severe threats, such children were a source of disquiet, fear, and sometimes even dread on the part of smaller or more peaceable youngsters. Women reported, 'I was attacked without provocation by aggressive kids,' and 'One large family acted strange. They killed a batch of kittens by putting them in a hole with a boulder over them.' Men variously stated: 'I stayed as far as possible from those capable of dismembering animals. I didn't hang around with kids like that'; 'The tough kids would use their boots to hack at ankles, to kick in the rear, and to hack shins'; '[he] wore loggers' boots with hobnails to play soccer and he shinhacked'; 'he gave me wrist-burns'; and 'he spat "goobers" at us.' These subjects felt particularly vulnerable when their tormentors were also able to stimulate other children to join in their taunts or physical threats, or even assaults.

Some differences between children arose from conficts over status.

While the particular status arrangements of a schoolyard or neighbourhood remained stable over long periods of time, a number of events could disturb it. Probably most important were changes in physical or other characteristics that occurred as children moved through the various stages of their development. When one combines these with the grade structure in school, and the crowded nature of schoolyards, then the evidence suggests three points of increased tension among children. Even though beginners came lowest in the school's status hierarchy, they had to work out an initial status relationship among themselves. Similarly, when children moved into either the intermediate or the senior grades, some, and especially those whose relative size or self-concept changed, made an effort to alter their positions in the group. Pupils moving in and pupils moving out could raise tension, especially if those moving vacated or expected to assume a high-status position.

At a very early age, children began to learn how they differed from each other on racial, ethnic, or religious grounds. As a Cedar Cottage man explained, 'after a while everybody knew if you were Catholic or Protestant.' A woman of the same neighbourhood reported, 'As we were one of the few Catholic families in the area, I felt isolated when I returned from [parochial] school. This limited my opportunities for making friends.' In each neighbourhood and on each school ground, a tacit truce generally characterized the relationships between self-classified different groups of children. Sometimes, children of different groups played together. Sometimes children of a particular group came to 'own' a part of the playground or neighbourhood, and the rest generally respected or tolerated their possession of it. Nevertheless, children could and did draw attention to these differences, and most often did so in a negative way. As we have seen, most children, employed fairly regularly the racial, ethnic, and other slurs they picked up from their parents and from their own culture. As a woman explained, 'we used to make jeering remarks like "cat-likers" and stuff like that.' Sometimes, even, children physically attacked those whom they disdained. 'We'd pass Catholic kids and fight them,' noted one man. In his part of Toronto, Michael Enright reported: 'Some kid on our side would be beaten up on his way home from parochial school by some kids from Rose Avenue or Winchester Public School. The day of retribution took the form of a brief stone fight between the two sides. On one occasion I was trapped behind enemy lines and had my head bloodied.'[66]

Children settled most of their differences verbally. In their arguments they employed such weapons as scorn and merciless teasing. They probed for failures in skill, school mastery, and other weaknesses ('You failed!');

mocked those who had physical defects ('Four-eyes'; 'gimpy'); taunted those who differed in some way from the norm ('Buckle shoes'; 'You are a "bloody Englishman"'; 'Dirty DP'); and tried to bring those who wept easily to tears. ('A couple of kids were school martyrs. Pupils could do what they liked with them ... Teachers had contempt for them as well.') If not close friends, then those of relatively equal status often developed severe rivalries, and were particularly harsh on each other. Those who were younger, smaller, or of inferior status found themselves vulnerable to the whole range of childish sanctions. Older and bigger youngsters employed peremptory instruction with younger and smaller peers, and sometimes reinforced their demands with threats. At times, all children found themselves bullied by older, bigger, or stronger children, and, in turn, most indulged in some bullying of those younger, smaller, weaker, or merely different from themselves.

Some such occasions left permanent imprints. 'This evil little boy,' remembered one woman, 'then threw the worm and it landed in my hair. It was horrible, disgusting. I ran home so fast that day it seemed that I must have broken some world records. My mom had to wash my hair several times before she could quiet me down and convince me that all remnants of that worm were gone.' Rick Parkinson recalls a neighbourhood boy 'tied to a pole in the backyard of a neighbour's house. His mouth is open in a scream as he hurls expletives at us, his tormentors. We are all dancing around spitting at him until he drips.'[67]

Sometimes, disputes moved beyond verbal exchanges into what was called a 'mad' fight. Since most children tried to avoid them, these battles were rare events. As Robert Thomas Allen remembered, 'school fights didn't happen often, their value preserved, like the Victoria Cross, by rarity ...'[68] A man recalled 'I had a hard time in fighting. I was easily intimidated and ran home and felt embarrassed about it.' In his recollections of growing up in Vancouver in the 1920s and 1930s, Ted Ashlee argued that fighting 'was undoubtedly a natural reaction to iron discipline: whether the teacher was in the right or not, we did exactly as we were told or were severely punished.'[69]

In any case, a certain ritual characterized youthful fighting. As a fight began, children shouted, 'Fight, fight,' and a crowd quickly gathered. Fights generally comprised a combination of boxing and wrestling. Thus fighting youngsters most commonly punched at or pushed or shoved each other, or attempted to twist their opponent's arms or to trip them. ('I got him in a scissor grip.') Although children generally considered kicking, hair pulling, biting, or using weapons such as sticks unfair practices, outraged opponents would occasionally indulge in them. One man succinctly summarized:

'There were certain rules upon which we were beaten up, or beat each other up: (a) You didn't hit when someone was down; (b) You didn't kick, ever.' Spectators would sometimes intervene when rules were blatantly broken. Fights ended when the victor held the vanquished flat on the ground, when the latter said 'uncle,' when parents or others intervened to break it up, or when a teacher arrived to take the opponents to the 'office.' In the words of a Powell River boy: 'Well, this time up in the school ground, Evan and I got into a fight. The teacher warned us if there was any fighting there we would get the strap, you see. So the teacher comes out; ... yes, we got a licking all right!'

Girls fought less often than boys. Although they tussled with and hit back and forth with siblings and neighbourhood children, they rarely battled on the school ground. Only one woman told me of such a fight. 'My mother didn't like it,' she reported, 'but I used to wrestle all the time with my brother, who was only a year older than me. At school there was this girl who was always making nasty remarks, see, about me: my hair, my clothes, my schoolwork. One day she said something really nasty about my mom, so I grabbed her, put my foot behind her leg, and flipped her over. I sat on her and she tried to bite me, so I hit her on the nose and it started to bleed a bit. When she saw the blood, well then, she started to scream. One of the teachers pulled me off her. What a fuss. You'd have thought, you know, I started the war or something. The teacher yelled at me and then the principal yelled at me. I guess I was lucky I didn't get the strap. I look on that day as one of my best in public school!'

Children were generally not aware of how closely their culture resembled that of the adults from which they thought they were escaping. When they finally 'grew up' and had greater control over their own lives, they found they were able to continue to use, and to refine, the social skills that they had learned among the other youngsters of their neighbourhood or schoolyard. If it was no longer important to be able to skip, or to break another's conker, it was still important to employ the social devices that accompanied these pastimes. In the company of their peers they had learned uses of power that also worked in a wider world. They had learned skills of understanding others, of getting along with them, of accommodating oneself to their wishes and desires as one also tried to fulfil one's own.

The adult world, however, was not an exact mirror image of that of children. If adult emotions remained much the same as they were in childhood, their expression often had to be reined in, or expressed in more subtle ways. As they grew older, youngsters were able to find friends and acquaintances from much wider geographical circles. They could also escape the lack of privacy, even what was often the tyranny, of a community characterized by an all-enfolding propinquity. For those who wished desperately to grow up so they could escape family and community, adulthood sometimes provided, at least for a time, joys that their childhood had denied. Others, of course, found as little happiness as 'grown-ups' as they had as children. And, only when they were long past youth and entering into middle age did people begin to believe that their childhoods had been the best years of their lives, to begin to look back on a schoolyard fight as one of life's great days.

11

Conclusion:
Continuity and Change in
the Lives of Children

In the Preface I described how this book followed on from *Children in English-Canadian Society*. As I came to the end of it, I began to reflect on what I had learned from writing both volumes, and also from my research on the period since the 1950s. In consequence, I decided to extend this final chapter both backward and forward in time from the rest of the book's contents. In this conclusion, I comment on the present condition of English-Canadian children in the light of continuities and changes in childhood over the years from the concluding decades of the nineteenth century to the concluding ones of the twentieth.

If this book has one overarching theme, it is that growing up was and is a very complex process that does not lend itself to easy generalizing. Not surprisingly, then, I conclude that the evidence over a century or more suggests no simple formulation of either improvement or decline in the state of being a child. Further, I argue that some intended and unintended developments have wrought many important, and mostly practical, positive changes in the lives of the young, and also that some intentional, even 'progressive,' transformations did not in fact improve the lives of the children at whom they were directed, and sometimes even made them worse. Finally, I argue the emotional dimensions of childhood have remained virtually unchanged.

There is a bittersweet quality to recollections of childhood. As one of those I interviewed put it, childhood 'was the best time in my life but I didn't realize it.' Since they are adults, most of those interviewed saw their own childhoods from both perspectives. Many looked back on their childhood as a time of considerable happiness and joy. People variously reported: 'I had a very pleasant childhood. We were not as afflicted by the Depression as most families'; 'I had an enjoyable childhood, an active one, without many fears'; 'I have nice memories of a great childhood'; 'The days weren't long enough because we had so much fun'; and 'Everyone seemed happy in those days.'

As earlier chapters showed, however, others did not recall theirs as happy childhoods. They reported: 'My life was not happy, generally, either at home or at school'; 'I was very unhappy at home'; or 'The happiest day of my life was the one I ran away for good.' When the woman whose farmer father worked his children very hard indeed reported that he had told her that 'we were among the luckiest ... We never have to worry,' there was more than just a touch of irony in her voice.

But these are judgments in retrospect. When they were children, those interviewed took the circumstances of their lives as givens: 'We didn't know any different,' as one explained. Or, as they saw other ways of life, they also concluded that their own circumstances were immutable. In their power-lessness, like children everywhere, English-Canadian children of these and all other years had to take life as it came. If nearly all had some moments of love, of delight, of physical and mental exuberance, of great joy, they also had periods of acute boredom, of weariness, of fear, of anger, of hatred, of hunger, and of despair. Only from the perspective of adulthood could they compare their own experience with that of people who grew up in different families, or in different environments, or at different times; only as adults could they come to more or less objective judgments or summative evalua-tions of their childhoods.

How, then, do people now evaluate their own childhoods, how do they compare them with those of previous and future generations? The topic came up during many interviews. It is frequently raised by students, friends, colleagues, and others with whom I find myself discussing my research. People's opinions on the topic – often firmly held and vigorously expressed – are to some degree influenced by where they are in their own life course. Not surprisingly, for many the times of their own childhoods were the *best* times to have been a child in Canada. This view was expressed even by those whose own childhoods were desperately unhappy ones; it is hard to think of living outside of one's own time. The elderly tend not only to put a rosy glow over their own childhoods, but also sometimes to put an even rosier one on those of their parents and grandparents. For them, the expres-sion 'the good old days' conveys no irony.

Others focus on the future. The middle-aged, of the middle class, with children of their own, are generally committed to the notion of 'progress' that permeates our society. Despite temporary set-backs, their children will, or should, have the 'better life' that flows from a combination of their good parenting and of 'progress.' Middle-aged working-class parents are hopeful if less optimistic, less certain that 'progress' will characterize the lives of their children. Although many young adults are now deeply concerned about their own future, most of those of both classes with small children are committed to crafting a better future for them. (We are generally environmentalists when talking about our own youngsters!)

Not altogether consistently but not surprisingly, some in each group also employ another perspective to comment on childhood. Yes, by and large, their childhoods were better in many, mostly material and physical, ways than those of their parents. On the other hand, they wonder if the long period of relative prosperity may be over; if their children's and grandchildren's future may not be as assured as was theirs. Further, some see the young evidencing Canada's supposed social, moral, and intellectual decline.

This generally negative assessment of the present situation finds widespread support. Much of a century or more of rhetoric surrounding childhood and public services for children has cast what currently prevails as being in a critical or nearly critical condition in need of considerable reformation. Thus to many, the children of today (whenever the 'day') are 'spoiled rotten.' From that time in the nineteenth century when schooling became primarily a state responsibility, right up to the present, the supposed failure of schools to teach the 'basics' has been a perennial theme of popular discourse. The 'lax' treatment of youthful offenders has been an issue for at least the same length of time. Public investigations, such as those conducted by royal commissions, and professional and academic research directed at social situations, are also, at least implicitly, conducted within an alarmist framework. One is not therefore surprised to find that such investigations tend to confirm popular suppositions regarding the 'decline' of the family, of the quality of education, and of other dimensions of childhood. This stance contrasts with that of many front-line workers in the professions that help children, who often see themselves, in the face of difficult circumstances, doing a better, more professional, job than their predecessors.

In the 1960s, and in a climate of increasing social concern, if not yet one of crisis, Canadians held the first and second Canadian Conference on Children, and the first Canadian Conference on the Family, and established the Vanier Institute of the Family. The research for this volume was partially funded by the Social Sciences and Humanities Reseach Council of Canada out of its 'strategic grants' program in the area of the family and the socialization of children. This program, initiated in the late 1970s, grew out of the council's belief that, while the 'quality of relationships within the family has a profound effect on the quality of our daily living,' there were 'indications that in recent years the stability of the family has deteriorated considerably with the increased incidence of divorce, adolescent pregnancies and family violence.'[1] By the 1990s, sociologist John F. Conway argued that the 'crisis of the family in Canada is of monumental proportions, and it touches us all.'[2]

In response to popular opinion and conventional wisdom, one can, of course, apply certain objective measures to childhood over time.[3] Public health, bacteriology, and medicare have improved enormously both the life chances and long-term physical well-being of infants and children. Cholera infantum, diphtheria, poliomyelitis, tuberculosis, measles, mumps, scarlet fever, and other illnesses rarely exact their traditional toll of youthful lives or of lifelong affliction. That often-used index of a nation's social health, the rate of infant mortality, has in Canada declined from well over 100 per thousand live births at the turn of the century to fewer than 8, one of the lowest in the world.[4] At a more mundane level, children suffer far fewer of the earaches, toothaches, and other causes of pain that made many childhoods miserable.

Smaller families and a higher standard of living have substantially increased the amount of family resources, both physical and emotional, that can be devoted to each child. Thus most Canadian children today live in warmer, more comfortable homes (and, much more often than their predecessors, they have their own beds, and even their own bedrooms), they have money to spend as they like, and are better fed and better clothed than youngsters of any earlier generation. Communities make extensive provision for their recreation and entertainment. And, despite arguments to the contrary, smaller classes and better-educated teachers ensure that most children are better, and certainly more humanely, schooled.[5] Indeed, in the era since the Second World War we have perhaps gone some way towards 'sacralizing' childhood, to employ American historian Viviana Zelizer's vivid term for the process. By this she means that as, the economic value of children to their families declined, their emotional value increased.[6]

On the other hand, improvements in the condition of children are not distributed evenly across Canadian society. The greatest have been made in child health, the least in child and family welfare. These unevenly distributed outcomes are a direct reflection of the amount of resources we have invested in each area. Even in the area of child health, while infant mortality has declined, this decline has not been the same for all groups. In the 1980s, for example, the infant mortality rate of the 'most poor' in British Columbia was twice that of the 'least poor,' and that of the aboriginal population four times that of the most favoured group.[7] Within the public system, the rewards of schooling still vary according to the class, sex, and ethnic group to which children belong.[8] Further, upper-middle-class parents can give their youngsters the added edge that comes from attending élitist private schools (now publicly supported in British Columbia) established to attract their patronage.[9]

As the stories told below vividly illustrate, poor children continue to live different lives from those who are not. Many of them are still ill housed, ill clothed, and often hungry. Indeed, the Canadian Institute of Child Health argues that the proportion of children living in poverty has been increasing in the last couple of decades.[10] The Vancouver children interviewed by Sheila Baxter for her book *A Child Is Not a Toy* (the title in the words of an eleven-year-old girl), for example, tell the almost timeless story of what children feel about living in poverty.[11] In describing a sketch he made of a kitchen, twelve-year-old Chris told Baxter that it showed 'when my mom didn't have money and we couldn't afford to buy food ... There was hardly any clothes to wear ... I felt so sad and embarrassed when I went to school. I was afraid that kids would make fun of me. My mom was full of stress, she would sometimes cry at night thinking about the rent ... At night I would cry as well because I would be hungry ...'[12]

Juanita and Billy, two 'healthy-looking and well-adjusted' First Nations youngsters, were living in Vancouver in 1994. They got good grades in school. They and their single-parenting mother, Freida, lived on welfare for two years while she completed a manpower training program and then found a job. While on welfare, the family were 'binners' who searched back-lane garbage bins and dumpsters for pop bottles and cans. They used the money to buy food. They also searched the dumpsters behind discount and second-hand stores. As Frieda reported, 'That's where we got our kids' clothes ... If you find something that will fit a neighbour's child, you take that, too.' Of the experience, eight-year old Billy remarked, 'I don't feel bad about it, because we needed the money.' Ten-year-old Juanita added: 'I'd rather eat than starve, even if I have to do that [binning]. The welfare cheque isn't enough for three people to survive.' Now their mother has an adequate income, the family doesn't go binning any more. As Juanita explains, 'I leave it for the kids who really need it.'[13]

Other aspects of childhood also remain much as they were. Most children grow up in families in which some form of the modern patriarchal order is the norm.[14] Throughout their childhood girls and boys continue to absorb traditional notions of gender identity and gender roles. None the less, some of the ideology of domesticity has changed over time. Although most children grow up believing that family responsibilities will be the first charge on a woman's life, they also learn that this responsibility can be combined with part- or full-time work outside the home. Recently, and generally not until late adolescence or early adulthood, some women and fewer men are questioning what until then they accepted as a 'given' of social life; appropriate gender relationships are still a matter of relearning rather than initial learning.

Many children still live in emotionally cold, even abusive families. Even if families employ psychological rather than physical means of control, the former can be applied as with as much severity as the latter. If the incidence of the physical and sexual abuse of children has not increased, it also seems not to have declined.[15] In *Children in English-Canadian Society*, I argued that the supposed increase in juvenile crime at the end of the nineteenth century was mostly a product of middle-class members of society establishing new standards of public order for themselves, and then imposing these standards on everyone. In the same way, we have now, and certainly not before time, come to circumscribe much more tightly certain kinds of physical and sexual behaviours and to label them as abusive. However, as many children in the past found no family or other haven in their lives, so, too, many children today find none. It is also clear that many of those as yet unborn will also find no haven in theirs. We seem more able to punish transgressors than to intervene in, and prevent, cycles of abuse that persist in some families from generation to generation.

Many children in need of foster and or other sorts of care live lives similar to those of their predecessors. Welfare and other agencies that try to help such youngsters find the structures and relationships that characterize a good child-rearing environment continue to lack the resources to do so; case loads are large, neglected children often more difficult than others to rear, and foster parents minimally trained and rewarded. A few youngsters who leave or are taken from their families find satisfactory placements, but many do not. They move from foster home to foster home, from foster home to group home, from foster and group homes to courts and custodial institutions. Others take to the streets. There they are as vulnerable as were the nineteenth-century 'waifs and strays' who attracted the attention of the child-savers of that time. Now, as then, few children in need of care find themselves in the sort of happy foster family that Anne Shirley found in turn-of-the-century Prince Edward Island.

Consider but one recent example. Richard Wolfe was born in 1974. When he was four years old, his father deserted his mother and her three boys. Her task of child-rearing was exacerbated by the fact that they lived on welfare, and that she had a drinking problem. Wolfe was first arrested, for breaking and entering, when he was eight. By the time he was ten, he was living on the streets and had been arrested more than twenty times before he was twelve. After each arrest, the *Winnipeg Free Press* reported, 'Wolfe was simply escorted back to his mother by police officers ... [who] could do nothing because the Young Offenders Act precludes anyone from under 12 from being arrested.' In the years since he turned twelve, and was subject to jailing, Wolfe had, by 1994, been out of institutions, mostly the Manitoba Youth Centre, for a total of only nine months, seven of which were after one of his eight escapes from the centre.[16]

Throughout history, an unchanging characteristic of being a child is a sense of powerlessness. As earlier chapters showed, even those who were lovingly cared for occasionally felt imprisoned, bound in by conditions over which they had no control, subject to the arbitrary authority of parents, teachers, and other adults often unwilling to explain or even to listen. Indeed, an all-enfolding love can sometimes form a prison. Children felt powerless in such minor matters as how they could employ their spare time to such major ones as being separated from their family and being placed in care. Such freedom that they did have was in the gift of adults, and could be withdrawn as easily as it was granted.

Most feelings of youthful powerlessness and the fears it often engendered were rooted in family and community circumstances. Our century, however, has been one of war, and rumours of war, and these also impinged on many children. Those with relatives in the armed services helplessly feared and sometimes grieved. The German Pacific fleet frightened many in British Columbia early in the Great War, and Pearl Harbor and the shelling of Estevan did so in the Second. From the 1950s onward, the Cold War was never far from the minds of young people. 'In Junior high school during the early 80s,' wrote Airdrie Hislop, 'my English teacher gave us the bleak task of writing about what we would do in the 15 minutes preceding the arrival of a barrage of Soviet nuclear warheads. I sat in front of my Keytab notebook for what seemed like hours – I was paralysed with fear.'[17]

Today, children absorb visions of apocalyptic collapse from the population explosion, from the destruction of the environment, from random violence, and from parental and congregational expectations of an imminent 'rapture.' In 1996, an eight-year-old Vancouver girl asked, 'Can a man come into my class and kill us?'[18] We have found new stories to replace those of ghosts, goblins, witches, and bogeymen that used to terrorize the young.

If some changes over a century or more clearly fit onto a 'positive' list or a 'negative' list, other data require more complex interpretation. The stability of families over the child-rearing years of the life cycle is one example of complexity. Death from disease, during childbirth, from farm, woods, and industrial accidents made nineteenth-century family life far less stable than popular memory would have it. In more recent years, after decreasing for thirty or more years, the proportion of lone-parenting, mostly mother-led, families in Canada has returned to that prevailing in the Depression.[19] Some children of these families have lost the benefits of being raised by both a mother and a father. Others have escaped from harmful situations endured by predecessors in the era when some unhappy parents came or stayed together for 'the sake of the children,' or because the mother and children had nowhere else to go. This latter situation was common until recently, and certainly still persists.

A similar complexity surrounds the fact that in many families both parents work away from the home. After nearly a century during which the notion of the 'family wage,' earned by a male breadwinner, prevailed in theory if not in practice, a family economy roughly analagous to that of earlier eras has again become the norm. If in some, especially middle-class families, it is a matter of choice for both parents to work outside the home, in many working-class ones it is clearly a matter of economic necessity. While the former are usually able to make good alternative arrangements for their children, the latter often lack the means to do so, and the state has made only a grudging and minimal effort to assist them.[20] And, whatever the form of family in which they live, children themselves have no say in the making of it, or of its social and economic circumstances.

Perhaps even more complex is the matter of the moral education of children. According to the traditional formula and practice – the latter very much a product of the nineteenth century – children began to acquire what were called 'virtues' in the home. Good behaviour was seen to be rooted in religious beliefs. Parents instructed children in behaviours and beliefs that were often an inextricable mix of morality, on the one hand, and politeness, and even gentility, on the other. Other family requirements, such as individual or family prayers, learning the commandments or other codes of belief and practice, and asking the forgiveness of parents or siblings for transgressions, were more explicitly religious and moral.

Both congregation and school extended and systematized what parents had initiated. All denominations gave religious and moral instruction to youngsters, most beginning it at a very young age. In the early years of school, what was right and wrong continued to mix moral and genteel behaviours. Separate and parochial schools systematically inculcated the moral code and set of beliefs of a very conservative Catholicism. Jewish,

Mennonite, and the private schools of other denominations made similar provisions for their pupils. Public schools were generally conducted in the context of a non-denominational Protestantism. There, while the difference between right and wrong were taught, and appropriate behaviours enforced, religious and moral instruction displayed more variety than that in parochial schools.

Although the range of religious belief and practice in Canada has greatly expanded, many children still receive in their families and religious institutions instruction in religiously based moral and behavioural codes. Those who attend public schools are still expected to behave in accordance with traditional strictures in favour of honesty, kindness, politeness, and generosity, and against lying, stealing, cheating, tattling, and so on. Far less often, however, are schoolchildren taught a religious basis for their behaviour. Secondary-school classes, especially those in the humanities, often focus on what are called 'value' questions, usually with at least an implicit commitment to a search for shared, although not necessarily religiously based values.[21] The surveys conducted by Reginald Bibby and Donald Posterski show that adolecents who received formal religious training are more likely to affirm such values as honesty, forgiveness, and generosity than those who do not. Bibby and Postersky also point out, however, that affirmation does not necessarily translate into practice.[22]

Whether these changes in moral education and in the beliefs of young people are evidence of a social decline is not nearly as clear, however, as some of the rhetoric surrounding the topic may suggest.[23] On the one hand, the history of social behaviour clearly shows that traditional moral inculcation may have been superficially understood and observed, and only sometimes transformed into practice. How effective, for example, were such common-practice exercises or punishments as writing such lines as 'It is never too late to do good' or 'Honesty is the best policy,' sometimes hundreds of times? On the other, in times when social convention does not demand even superficial commitment to traditional beliefs, or even to social civility, those who do subscribe to them are perhaps more likely to put them into practice. Is ours really a less civil, less virtuous, society now than it was in the nineteeth century, during the construction boom at the turn of the century, in the Depression, in the years of juvenile unrest at the end of the Second World War, in the turbulent late 1960s and 1970s? Are our present concerns merely the latest manifestation of the usual wariness that age customarily displays towards the manners and morals of youth? Our uncertainty in these matters argues that the subject is one needing both more thought and more investigation.

For most young people, the end of childhood no longer means entering the world of work and relative independence, but that of adolescence and its culture. As well as the expansion of life choices it provides, the gradual lengthening of the number of years children spend in school has given some youngsters longer periods of time to be physically away from such tight bonds as those imposed by abusive, tyrannical, or emotionally overpossessive parents. (The current fad for home schooling – turning the family into a form of 'total' institution – gives rise to the concerns that attach to all such arrangements.) Children raised or fostered for the work they could do benefited from a tightening of school-attendance regulations. On the other hand, those of thirteen or fourteen who, as they entered into full-time work in earlier eras might have become fairly independent, now find themselves dependent through, and even beyond, adolescence, or as runaways in the culture of the street. Thus a longer period of dependency may have benefited many, but not all, young people.

When one moves away from these more or less objective criteria to more subjective ones, the question as to whether the lives of children have improved, declined, or remained unchanged becomes even more difficult to resolve. In the mid-1980s, about one-quarter of Grade Four children responding to a survey reported that 'most of the time' they couldn't sleep worrying about things, or had trouble making decisions; 40 per cent did not have confidence in themselves; and half of them felt they did not make friends easily or did not feel good about the way they looked.[24] Surely these sorts of anxieties were felt by many in each cohort of children over the century, but perhaps media and other aspects of contemporary culture have exacerbated them.

None the less, when one tries to compare the totality of one childhood with others at different times, one faces an insuperable task. I quoted novelist Gabrielle Roy at the end of the first chapter, and what she wrote bears repeating here. 'Is it possible,' she asked, 'to record in a book the spellbinding powers of childhood, which can put the whole world inside the tiniest locket of happiness?'[25] At whatever period they lived, some children found innumerable 'lockets of happiness' in their lives. And, at whatever period they lived, others found few. Whether they did so depended, of course, on how they were treated at home, at school, and by their peers, and perhaps on their temperament.

Of these variables, the home was and remains the most important. As previous chapters made clear, family conditions provided the foundation of most happy and unhappy childhoods. Some children in unhappy family circumstances, however, received solace through their association with their friends and peers. If the content of the discourse of the culture of childhood has changed over time – some traditional activities such as skipping and marbles have faded in importance – it remains second only to the family in crafting the emotional dimensions of growing up. School could also provide a refuge. As one person explained, 'Some kids really liked school because it was the only place they had an out from wonky homes.' Other children did not do well in school, and did not make close friends or fit in well with their peers; for them, the community mirrored the emptiness, the rejection, and sometimes the abuse that characterized their lives at home. There are still many such children.

Children saw, and see, their own situation mostly as it relates to that of others in their local cohort. Although the children of welfare families are today more colourfully dressed than even their middle-class counterparts of a generation or so ago, it does not mean that they feel any less about the inadequacy of their clothing, say, than did the child of the 1930s who went to school in runners but without socks. In April 1989, fourteen-year-old Steven told the Surrey, BC, Child Poverty Forum, 'I cannot afford all the designer clothes that are worn by my fellow classmates. We shop at Value Village and those clothes are used and sometimes stained and ripped, and that makes me feel like dirt.'[26]

I will conclude by reemphasizing another truism: that we can live our own lives only in our own times. None the less, it seems clear that happiness or unhappiness in childhood is only very lightly connected to the era in which it is lived. This book shows both happy and unhappy childhoods. They were not unique to the years described: the years before the Great War and the years after television also had, and have, many examples of both. To emphasize the point, let me conclude with two vignettes.

Writing of a moment in his life in the 1970s, when the whole panoply of the welfare state was in place, Richard Cardinal noted that, although

I was not considered an outcast this year ... I was halfway through the school year when a Social Worker came to our home and I was to be moved and asked me how soon I would be ready ... and I answered, one week. I should have answered never. When I would move alone, Charlie and Linda [his brother and sister] would stay.

I had four hours before I would leave my family and friends behind and since Linda and Charlie were at school, I went into the bedroom and dug out my old harmonica and ... sat on the fence and began to play real slow and sad like the occasion, but before halfway through the song my lower lip began to quiver and I know I was going to cry and I was glad so I didn't even try to stop myself.[27]

Cardinal had been taken into care as a toddler and, when he committed suicide at age seventeen in 1984, he was living in his twenty-eighth placement or institution.

In 1897–8, thirteen-year-old Christina Young kept a diary. This document, written long before modern developments began to affect the children of rural families, surely displays a girl as happy (and sometimes as sad) as any girl was before, during, or after that year. On 4 October 1897, Christina wrote: 'This has been a good, good day, and I expect when we are old ladies, and our bodies have grown too feeble to move around much on the earth ... and we wander back in our spirits to these days when we were thirteen and will find among them beautiful days, and we'll live it all over again.'[28]

Children in English-Canadian Society described the origins and early development of the child-centred agenda of earlier reformers. While we may now think some elements of their program naïve, surely their goal was not: 'to ensure for every child a fair chance to attain self-reliant and self-respecting citizenship.'[29] All children still need to live in circumstances that enable them to grow and flourish in self-reliance and self-respect. For them to do so may not solve all our social problems, but might sharply reduce those rooted in childhood circumstances.[30]

If we do take up the challenge of crafting a better life for all children, we can learn from a century or more of experience. Substantial investments in child health have brought substantial social rewards. Mediocre investments in child and family welfare have brought mostly superficial changes in the treatment of the most vulnerable of the next generation. At the beginning of this century, Swedish social activist Ellen Key made a widely read appeal that the twentieth century should be 'the century of the child.'[31] The 1959 United Nations Declaration of the Rights of the Child said each youngster had the right to 'grow up ... in an atmosphere of affection and of moral and material security.' In 1989, Canada voted for the Convention on the Rights of the Child that both reaffirmed the principles laid out in 1959 and articulated them in greater detail.[32] The following year, Canada, as one of the many countries represented at the World Summit for Children, committed itself to a far-reaching declaration and a plan of action.[33] Canadians are obliged, for example, 'to protect the child from all forms of physical and mental violence, injury or abuse, neglect or negligent treatment, maltreatment or exploitation, including sexual abuse, while in the care of parent(s), legal guardian(s) or any other person who has care of the child.'[34] Even if we failed to meet these goals in this century, should we not continue to try to reach them in the twenty-first? And, what are our responsibilities to the rest of the world's children?

Notes

Preface

1 *Children in English-Canadian Society: Framing the Twentieth-Century Consensus* (Toronto, 1976).
2 I use 'Great War' rather than 'First World War,' because that was the way people referred to it for much of the time covered in this book.
3 Neil Sutherland, 'Social Policy, "Deviant" Children and the Public Health Apparatus in British Columbia Between the Wars,' *Journal of Educational Thought* 14 (August 1980), 80–91.
4 Jean Dunbar, 'School Nursing in a Mining Town,' *British Columbia Public Health Nurses' Bulletin* 1 (April 1926), 17.
5 For what has already been written about the history of childhood in Canada, see Neil Sutherland and Jean Barman, 'Out of the Shadows: Retrieving the History of Urban Education and Urban Childhood in Canada,' in *The City and Education in Four Nations*, ed. R. Goodenow and W.E. Marsden, 87–108 (Cambridge, 1992); Neil Sutherland, Jean Barman, and Linda L. Hale, eds., *History of Canadian Childhood and Youth: A Bibliography* (Westport, CT, 1993); and Patricia T. Rooke and Rudy Schnell, 'Canada,' in *Children in Historical and Comparative Perspective*, ed. Joseph M. Hawes and N. Ray Hiner, 179–215 (New York, 1990).
6 Originally I intended to include a chapter on children's experiences of voluntary organizations. Although mentioned briefly in many recollections, they took a far less central place than I had expected. They are, however, in need of a separate, focused investigation.
7 See also Jane Ursel, *Private Lives, Public Policy: 100 Years of State Intervention in the Family* (Toronto, 1992).
8 Paul Rutherford, *When Television Was Young: Primetime Canada, 1952–1967* (Toronto, 1990), 49–50.

268 Notes to pages vii–5

9 Ibid., 478; see also Edwin D. Parker, *The Impact of U.S. Media on Canadian Children* (n. p. 1961).
10 See Howard Chudacoff, *How Old Are You? Age Consciousness in American Culture* (Princeton, 1989).
11 While Jane Synge correctly notes that, for working-class adolescents, 'there was no stage before marriage at which they experienced a formal rite of passage,' these events shared some of the characteristics of a formal rite: 'The Transition from School to Work: Growing Up Working Class in Early 20th Century Hamilton, Ontario,' in *Childhood and Adolescence in Canada*, ed. K. Ishwaran, 249–69 (Toronto, 1979).
12 'Twelve stands out in my mind as a definite turning point. It was like a bridge between childhood and the grown-up world, and though I sometimes find it difficult to remember what it was like to be eight or fourteen or twenty-two, I have no trouble ... to recall vividly what it was like to be twelve': Helen Porter, *Below the Bridge: Memories of the South Side of St. John's* (n. p., 1979), 86.

1: Listening to the Winds of Childhood

1 Gabrielle Roy, *The Fragile Lights of Earth: Articles and Memoirs, 1942–1970*, trans. Alan Brown (Toronto, 1982), 147.
2 David Lowenthal, 'The Timeless Past: Some Anglo-American Historical Preconceptions,' in *Memory and American History*, ed. David Thelan (Bloomington and Indianapolis, 1990), 149.
3 I have explored psychological research on memory through Elizabeth Loftus, *Memory* (Reading, MA, 1980); David C. Rubin, ed., *Autobiographical Memory* (Cambridge, 1986); Ulric Neisser and Eugene Winograd, eds., *Remembering Reconsidered: Ecological and Traditional Approaches to the Study of Memory* (Cambridge, 1988); and Edmund Blair Bolles, *Remembering and Forgetting: An Inquiry into the Nature of Memory* (New York, 1988). The field is currently an extremely active one, and the literature appears to be growing exponentially.
4 Until recently, the most influential work was Paul Thompson, *The Voice of the Past: Oral History* (Oxford, 1978). The essays and notes in Thelan, ed., *Memory and American History*, are an excellent introduction to current historical approaches to the topic.
5 Eric Stofer, *Growing Up in Victoria* (Victoria, BC, 1994), 7.
6 Katherine Nelson, 'The Ontogeny of Memory for Real Events,' in Neisser and Winograd, eds., *Remembering Reconsidered*, 268.
7 See Paul Thompson, 'Introduction,' in *Our Common Heritage: The Transformation of Europe*, ed. Paul Thompson with Natasha Burchart (London, 1982), esp.

15–16; for the psychological perspective see Loftus, *Memory*, chs. 6 and 7, and Bollus, *Remembering and Forgetting, passim.*

8 Leslie Thomas, *In My Wildest Dreams* (London, 1984), 11.

9 Craig R. Barclay, 'Schematization of Autobiographical Memory,' in Rubin ed., *Autobiographical Memory*, ch. 6.

10 See Isabelle Bertaux-Wiame, 'The Life History Approach to the Study of Internal Migration,' in Thompson with Burchart, *Our Common Heritage*, 195; and Susan Friedman, 'Women's Autobiographical Selves, Theory and Practice,' in *The Private Self: Theory and Practice of Women's Autobiographical Writings*, ed. Shari Benstock (London, 1988), esp. 40–2.

11 See, for example, William Kurelek, *Someone with Me: An Autobiography* (Toronto, 1980), and Charlotte Vale Allen, *Daddy's Girl: A Very Personal Memoir* (Toronto, 1980).

12 Jean Peneff, 'Myth in Life Stories,' in *The Myths We Live By*, ed. Raphael Samuel and Paul Thompson (London, 1990), 45.

13 Barclay, 'Schematization.'

14 Thompson, *Voice of the Past*, 113.

15 Robert Roberts, *The Classic Slum: Salford Life in the First Quarter of the Century* (Harmondsworth, 1973), 25.

16 Lawrence W. Barsalou, 'The Content and Organization of Autobiographical Memories,' in Neisser and Winograd, eds., *Remembering Reconsidered*, 236.

17 Thompson, *Voice of the Past*, 119.

18 Alessandro Portelli, 'The Peculiarities of Oral History,' *History Workshop* 12 (Autumn 1981), 96–107; Bruce Curtis, 'Gender in the Regime of Statistical Knowledge/Power,' unpublished paper presented to the joint ANZHES/CHEA Conference, Melbourne, December 1993.

19 See, for example, Sylvia Fraser, *My Father's House: A Memoir of Incest and Healing* (Toronto, 1987), and Women's Research Centre, *Recollecting Our Lives: Women's Experience of Childhood Sexual Abuse* (Vancouver, 1989).

20 See Thompson, *Voice of the Past*, 96, and his 'Introduction' in *Our Common Heritage*, 9–20.

21 For an analysis of the major historiographic problems facing the historian of childhood, see Jean Barman, '"Oh, No! It Would Not Be Proper to Discuss That with You": Reflections on Gender and the Experience of Childhood,' *Curriculum Inquiry* 24 (Spring 1994), 53–67. Also of interest is Michael H. Frisch, 'The Memory of History,' *Radical History Review* 25 (1981), 9–23, as are the many items cited in Barman's notes.

22 *Greek Historical Thought from Homer to the Age of Heraclius*, introd. and trans. by Arnold J. Toynbee (New York, 1952), 40–1.

23 Craig R. Barclay, 'Schematization of Autobiographical Memory,' in Rubin, ed., *Autobiographical Memory*, ch. 6; Ulrich Neisser, 'What Is Ordinary Memory the Memory Of?,' in Neisser and Winograd, eds., *Remembering Reconsidered*, ch. 14.

24 Roger C. Schank and Robert R. Abelson, *Scripts, Plans, Goals and Understanding: An Inquiry into Human Knowledge Structures* (Hillsdale, NJ, 1977), 17–19.

25 Katherine Nelson, Robyn Fivush, Judith Hudson, and Joan Lucariello, 'Scripts and the Development of Memory,' in *Trends in Memory Development Research*, ed. Michelene T.H. Chi, Contributions to Human Development series (Basel, 1983), 9: 108–15. History based on the analysis of shared scripts may help bridge the gap between 'people's' history and 'social science' history: see Louise A. Tilly, 'People's History and Social Science History,' *International Journal of Oral History* 6 (February 1985), 5–18; Paul Thompson, Luisa Passerini, Isabelle Bertaux-Wiame, and Alessandro Portelli, 'Between Social Scientists: Responses to Louise A. Tilly,' ibid., 19–46.

26 Mildred Young Hubbert, *Since the Day I Was Born* (Thornbury, ON, 1991), ii, 103; Jim Caplette, *Haywire* (Madeira Park, BC, 1993), 103.

27 Joy Kogawa, *Obasan* (Toronto, 1981), 2.

28 Toronto *Globe and Mail*, 21 December 1984, 14.

29 Northrop Frye, *The Great Code: The Bible and Literature* (Toronto, 1982), 50–1. Our interviews revealed little sense of what girls and boys felt was taking place in their bodies at such moments of change as they moved into adolescence. How children imaged or image their bodies is a fascinating topic but one that is beyond the scope of this book. See Barbara Duden, *The Woman Beneath the Skin: A Doctor's Patients in Eighteenth-Century Germany*, trans. by Thomas Dunlap (Cambridge, 1991), and Patricia Vertinsky, 'The Social Construction of the Gendered Body: Exercise and the Exercise of Power,' *The International Journal of the History of Sport* 11 (August 1994), 147–71.

30 Marcia K. Johnson and Mary Ann Foley, 'Differentiating Fact from Fantasy: The Reliability of Children's Memory,' *Journal of Social Issues* 40/2 (1984), 33–50.

31 David Ireland, *A Woman of the Future* (Harmondsworth, 1979), 117. Sensitive researchers can, of course, work with children in a way that permits them to see much of the social world through the eyes of children; see, for example, Bronwyn Davies, *Life in the Classroom and Playground* (London, 1982).

32 Alice Munro, 'Privilege,' in *Who Do You Think You Are?* (Toronto, 1979), 25.

33 On this point, see James West Davidson and Mark Hamilton Lytle, *After the Fact: The Art of Historical Detection* (New York, 1982), especially ch. 7, 'The View from the Bottom Rail: Oral History and the Freedmen's Point of View,' 169–204.

34 David Vincent, *Bread, Knowledge and Freedom: A Study of Nineteenth-Century Working-Class Autobiography* (London, 1981); see also Edvard Bull, 'Industrial Boy Labour in Norway,' in Thompson with Burchart, *Our Common Heritage*, 231–2.

35 Vincent analysed 142 mostly male autobiographies. Thompson drew on the recollections of 500 men and women: Vincent, *Bread, Knowledge and Freedom*, 3; Paul Thompson, *The Edwardians* (London, 1975), 7.

36 Glen Elder, 'History and the Life Course,' in *Biography and Society: The Life History Approach in the Social Sciences*, ed. Daniel Bertaux, 77–115 (Beverly Hills, 1981).

37 John Updike, 'The Importance of Fiction,' *Esquire*, August 1985, 62.

38 The research assistant was the late Elizabeth Lees, then a doctoral student in history at Simon Fraser University. Her untimely death was a great loss to the profession.

39 Thompson, *The Edwardians*, 7.

40 A series of visits to a Vancouver Grade Two classroom in the early 1980s emphasized the merits of consulting overlapping memories. There, the teacher followed the common practice of having the children begin the day by writing in their journals. When one girl let me read her journal, I was impressed by the quality of her thinking and writing. How fortunate, I thought, for some future historian who comes across this documentary evidence of the quality of education at this time. Another visit, however, demonstrated how that quality was achieved. Towards the end of each day, the teacher asked her pupils for interesting bits of news. When the children arrived next morning, they found 'their' journal entry for the day – the same one for the whole class – all ready to be copied into their exercise books!

41 See, for example, Robert McIntosh, 'The Boys in the Nova Scotian Coal Mines: 1873–1923,' *Acadiensis* 16 (Spring 1987), 35–50.

42 For a discussion of 'respectability' in another community, see Suzanne Morton, *Ideal Surroundings: Domestic Life in a Working-Class Suburb in the 1920s* (Toronto, 1995), ch. 2.

43 Loftus, *Memory*, 134–7.

44 If I had decided to identify those I interviewed by name, then the ethics of research on human subjects required that I obtain their permission for each quotation as it would appear in the text. This is not an unreasonable requirement when one is building life histories, or using long, self-identifying quotations. Since my goal was to re-create the common scripts of childhood, and to illuminate each with short quotations drawn from a number of lives, the task posed by getting individual permissions for thousands of quotations was both insuperable and unnecessary.

45 For a convenient introduction to this work, see University of British Columbia, School of Social Work, *Social Work Research at the University of British Columbia, 1947–1956* (Vancouver n.d.). A sentence in one of these theses reveals the theoretical stance of most: 'The worker who is trained in psycho-analytic con-

cepts can recognize in such a casual contact and conversation important and significant information ...': Mary Thomson, 'The Social Worker in the School: An Experimental Study of the Liaison and Service Functions of the Social Worker in a Vancouver Elementary School,' unpublished MSW thesis, University of British Columbia, 1948, 73. See also Joy Parr, 'Case Records as Sources for Social History,' *Archivaria* 1/4 (1977), 122–36.

46 Mordecai Richler, 'The Great Comic Book Heroes,' in *Hunting Tigers under Glass: Essays and Reports* (London, 1971), 78–9.

47 Roy Daniells, 'Plymouth Brother,' *Canadian Literature* 90 (Autumn 1981), 25–37.

48 Elizabeth Anderson Varley, *Kitimat My Valley* (Terrace, BC, 1981), 72.

49 The methodology for the first large-scale project in which I took part and in which interviews comprised a major component is described in Eleanor Duckworth, 'Assessing the Canada Studies Foundation, Phase 1: An Approach to a National Evaluation,' *Canadian Journal of Education* 2/1 (1977), 27–34.

50 On the merits of unstructured interviews, see also Dagfinn Slettan, 'Farm Wives, Farm Hands and the Changing Rural Community in Trongelag, Norway,' in Thompson with Burchart, *Our Common Heritage*, 153.

51 Loftus, *Memory*, 16–17.

52 Betty Bell, *The Fair Land, Saanich* (Victoria, BC, 1982), 126. Those who grew up on the prairie often recall the smell of the wolf willow.

53 For a sceptical view of the notion that memory can be stimulated by either hypnosis or drugs, see Loftus, *Memory*, 54–62.

54 Max Braithwaite, *Never Sleep Three in a Bed* (Toronto, 1969), 55–6; Roy Bonisteel, *There Was a Time* ... (Toronto, 1991), 201–3; Lloyd H. Person, *No Foot in Heaven* (Saskatoon, 1978), 47; Lew Duddridge, *The Best 70 Years of My Life: It's All Downhill from Here* (Victoria, BC, 1988), 10–11.

55 On this point, see the eminent autobiographer Ved Mehta, *Vedi* (New York, 1982), i.

56 Howard S. Becker, *Sociological Work: Method and Substance* (New Brunswick, NJ, 1970), 39–62. For a recent, critical comment on contemporary fieldwork, see Y. Michal Bodemann, 'Review Essay/Note de lecture,' *Canadian Journal of Sociology* 9 (1984), 85–95.

57 For an example of what such a researcher can actually accomplish, see Diana Kelly-Byrne, *A Child's Play Life: An Ethnographic Study* (New York, 1989).

58 Roy, *Fragile Lights of Earth*, 149.

2: Children in Their Families: Contexts and Settings

1 Betty Bell, *The Fair Land, Saanich* (Victoria, BC, 1982), 30.

2 Quoted in Emilie L. Montgomery, '"The War Was a Very Vivid Part of my

Life": The Second World War and the Lives of British Columbian Children,' in *Children, Teachers and Schools in the History of British Columbia*, ed. Jean Barman, Neil Sutherland, and J. Donald Wilson (Calgary, 1995), 173.

3 Shizuye Takashima, *A Child in a Prison Camp* (Montreal, 1971); Montgomery, '"The War"'; Norah Lewis, '"Isn't This a Terrible War?" Children's Attitudes to Two World Wars as Demonstrated through Their Letters,' *Historical Studies in Education* 7 (Fall 1995), 193–215.

4 For a fine examination of the effects of the Depression on children in Montreal, see Wendy Johnston, 'Keeping Children in School: The Response of the Montreal Catholic School Commission to the Depression of the 1930s,' Canadian Historical Association, *Historical Papers*, 1985, 193–217.

5 However, when the children of the 1950s reached adolescence they could see no evidence that justified their parents' cautious use of family resources – they didn't remember the Depression or the war – and therefore rejected such a stance for themselves. They spent rather than saved their allowances and outside earnings, and later in life became really enthusiastic consumers.

6 Elizabeth Gordon, 'Reminiscences of Ridgeway,' *Bank of British Columbia Pioneer News*, June/July 1987, 14.

7 Mildred Young Hubbert, *Since the Day I Was Born* (Thornbury, ON, 1991), 51.

8 Robert Collins, *Butter Down the Well: Reflections of a Canadian Childhood* (Saskatoon, 1980), 74.

9 Mary Cook, *One for Sorrow, Two for Joy* (Ottawa, 1984), 73.

10 Ellen Davignon, *The Cinnamon Mine: Memories of an Alaska Highway Childhood* (Whitehorse, 1988), 61.

11 Hugh Palmer, *Circumnavigating Father* (Surrey, BC, 1990), 67.

12 Robert Thomas Allen, *My Childhood and Yours: Happy Memories of Growing Up* (Toronto, 1977), 91.

13 *Vancouver Sun*, 1 February 1992, D4–D5.

14 Lloyd H. Person, *No Foot in Heaven* (Saskatoon, 1978), 194.

15 Roy Bonisteel, *There Was a Time ...* (Toronto, 1991), 113, 141.

16 John V. Friesen, *Never Never Give Up! An Autobiography* (Cloverdale, BC, 1986), 52.

17 Suzanne Morton, *Ideal Surroundings: Domestic Life in a Working-Class Suburb in the 1920s* (Toronto, 1995), and John R. Seeley, R. Alexander Sim, and E.W. Loosley, *Crestwood Heights: A Study of the Culture of Suburban Life* (Toronto, 1956), describe Canadian neighbourhoods made up almost entirely by people of a single class.

18 For the historical development of Vancouver's neighbourhoods, see Bruce Macdonald, *Vancouver: A Visual History* (Vancouver, 1992). For the suburbs themselves see Donna McCriride, 'Opportunity and the Workingman: A Study

of Land Accessibility and the Growth of Blue Collar Suburbs in Early Vancouver,' unpublished MA thesis, University of British Columbia, 1981: and the informal accounts in Reuben Hamilton, *Mount Pleasant Early Days* (Vancouver, 1957); Chuck Davis, *The Vancouver Book* (North Vancouver, 1976); Seymour Levitan and Carol Miller, eds., *Lucky to Live in Cedar Cottage: Memories of Lord Selkirk Elementary School and Cedar Cottage Neighbourhood, 1911–1963* (Vancouver, 1986); *The Days Before Yesterday in Cedar Cottage* (Vancouver, 1968); *The Kerrisdale Story* (Vancouver, n.d.); Michael Valpy, 'Going Home,' Toronto *Globe and Mail*, 24 December 1993, A1, A6.

19 Levitan and Miller, eds., *Lucky to Live in Cedar Cottage*, 8.

20 For the social and economic nature of Vancouver neighbourhoods, see Jean Barman, 'Neighbourhood and Community in Interwar Vancouver: Residential Differentiation and Civic Voting Behaviour,' *BC Studies* 69–70 (Spring/Summer 1986), 97–141. In this paper Barman uses the term 'working people' rather than 'working class' because she found the former had become a self-definition by the 1930s. I have employed 'working class' because invariably those I interviewed described themselves in that way: see the discussion below, in chapter 3. None the less, Ethel Wilson, who had a fine ear for local speech, had two of the protagonists in 'Tuesday and Wednesday,' originally published in 1952, identify themselves as 'working people' or as a 'plain working man': *The Equations of Love* (Toronto, 1990), 17 and 45. I employ 'middle class' in the sense that Paul Axelrod describes it in *Making a Middle Class: Student Life in English Canada during the Thirties* (Montreal and Kingston, 1990), 168–77. Axelrod separates a wealthy, élite upper class out from the middle class that he deals with in his book. Among accounts of the childhood of the wealthy in Canada are Palmer, *Circumnavigating Father*; Elizabeth Aikins Ney, as told to Adele Rose Wickett, 'A Girlhood in Government House,' *The Beaver* 70 (April/May 1990), 14–21; Lawrence Freiman, *Don't Fall Off the Rocking Horse: An Autobiography* (Toronto, 1978); and Joan Michener Rohr with Terrence Heath, *Memories of a Governor General's Daughter* (Toronto, 1990).

21 In his 1951–2 survey of 200 Kerrisdale boys, Allan Hare compared the occupations of the fathers of his sample with the 1951 census. The Census Tract he employed was not identical to Hare's Kerrisdale, but it did overlap considerably. Both sets of data show that just over 20 per cent of the fathers were in labouring occupations, while about 75 per cent were in financial, business, and professional occupations: 'Kerrisdale Youth,' unpublished MA thesis, University of British Columbia, 1954, 33.

22 Isaiah Bowman, *The Pioneer Fringe*, American Geographical Society, Special Publication no. 13, ed. G.N. Wrigley (New York, 1931); and Cole Harris, 'Reflections on the Surface of the Pond: A Review Article,' *BC Studies* 49 (Spring 1981), 91.

The sequence of modern settlement is mapped in 'British Columbia Settlement 1911–1930' and 'British Columbia Settlement 1931–1954,' in *British Columbia Atlas of Resources* (n.p., 1956), 31–2. The political, economic, and social context of agricultural settlement after the Great War is described in Morris Zaslow, *The Northward Expansion of Canada, 1914–1967*, The Canadian Centenary Series, vol. 17 (Toronto, 1988), especially ch. 2. See also David Demeritt, 'Visions of Agriculture in British Columbia,' *BC Studies* 108 (Winter 1995–6), 29–59.

23 Some Evelyn pioneers told their stories in *Bulkley Valley Stories, Collected from Old Timers Who Remember* (n.p., n.d.) especially 139–47, 153–6, and 167–8; see also Olive Storey, 'The Early Days of Evelyn,' *The Smithers Interior News*, 23 April 1980, A5.

24 [Della Herman, ed.,] *Bulkley Valley School Days* (n.p., n.d.), 56–62, gives both dates. The school first appears in provincial records in June 1923, where it is noted that Miss E.S. Miller enrolled sixteen pupils in the Evelyn School, which had been open for 173 1/2 days over the 1922–3 school year: British Columbia, Department of Education, *Report*, 1923, F86–7. Recollections and other local records show that Miss Miller was preceded by James Muir, Laura Hunter, and Kathryn Wilson. Among the most interesting of local records is an untitled, profusely illustrated mimeographed pamphlet of some twenty pages, put together for the Evelyn School reunion in 1985, which lists all of Evelyn School's pupils and teachers.

25 Nan Bourgon, *Rubber Boots for Dancing and Other Memories of Pioneer Life in Bulkley Valley*, ed. by Marjorie Rosberg (Smithers, BC, 1979), 118.

26 For an excellent account of Vancouver housing over these years, see Jill Wade, *Houses for All: The Struggle for Social Housing in Vancouver, 1919–1950* (Vancouver, 1994). Donald G. Wetherell and Irene R.A. Kmet, *Homes in Alberta: Building, Trends, and Design, 1870–1967* (Edmonton, 1991), provides an outstanding overview of many aspects of a complex topic. See also Harold F. Greenway, *Housing in Canada: A Study on the Census of 1931*, Census Monograph no. 8 (Ottawa, 1941), 411–578; John G. Bacher and J. David Hulchanski, 'Keeping Warm and Dry: The Policy Response to the Struggle for Shelter amongst Canada's Homeless, 1900–1960,' *Urban History Review/Revue d'histoire urbaine* 16 (October 1987), 147–163; Ross Paterson, 'The Development of an Interwar Suburb: Kingsway Park, Etobicoke,' *Urban History Review* 13 (February 1985), 225–35; John R. Miron, *Housing in Postwar Canada: Demographic Change, Household Formation, and Housing Demand* (Kingston and Montreal, 1988); Mary Beeler Galloway, 'User Adaptations of Wartime Housing,' unpublished MED thesis, University of Calgary, 1978. Photographs and floor plans for some Vancouver houses over these years are displayed in *Western Homes and Living* (January 1958), *passim*.

27 See Wade, *Houses for All*, ch. 1. Rolf Knight provides a good description of a boathouse in *Along the No. 20 Line: Reminiscences of the Vancouver Waterfront* (Vancouver, 1980), 75.

28 Dorothy Sutherland, 'A Visit to Vancouver,' *Vancouver Historical Society Newsletter*, March 1975, n.p.

29 Freiman, *Don't Fall Off the Rocking Horse*, 17–18.

30 A survey of houses for sale on one spring day in 1926 showed that a Kerrisdale home could be bought for prices that ranged from $3,700 to $5,600, with a down payment as low as $100. On the same day, an east-side house could be bought for as little as $1,100, with many others offered at less than $2,000. On a similar day in 1933, west-side homes were listed from below $3,000, while houses on the east side could be had for as little as $495 for 'a nice 4-room cottage and two lots close to Kingsway and School': *Vancouver Province*, 16 May 1926, 27–8; ibid., 14 May 1933, 19–20; see also Wade, *Houses for All*, ch. 2.

31 Wade, *Houses for All*, table 2, 43. See also Canada, Dominion Bureau of Statistics, *Census, 1931* (Ottawa, 1941), vol. 12, 557–8.

32 Canada, Dominion Bureau of Statistics, *Vancouver Housing Atlas* (Ottawa, 1944), 2. See also Catherine Jill Wade, 'Wartime Housing Limited, 1941–1947: Canadian Housing Policy at the Crossroads,' unpublished MA thesis, University of British Columbia, 1984, 28–30.

33 Albert Rose, 'Rental Problems of 1000 Canadian Families,' *Canadian Welfare*, 25 (1 March 1950), 40.

34 Galloway, 'User Adaptations,' 3. She shows this process in action as it took place in the Renfrew Heights district of east-side Vancouver (28–30).

35 Miron, *Housing in Postwar Canada*, 264–7; Susan Balcom describes her family's move, over three generations, to larger and larger houses: 'House Building as a Hobby?' *Vancouver Sun*, 28 April 1987, G1.

36 Bacher and Hulchanski, 'Keeping Warm and Dry,' 159–60; Wade, *Houses for All*, ch. 5.

37 Max Braithwaite, *Never Sleep Three in a Bed* (Toronto, 1969), 115.

38 *Vancouver Sun*, 20 February 1990, A1, A11; the building of Burkeville by Wartime Housing Limited is described in Wade, *Houses for All*, ch. 5.

39 A 1931 census monograph concluded that 'lodgers prefer rooms of good quality as measured by the rent paid for the houses in which they lodge; they avoid overcrowded households; they avoid children only in so far as the children monopolize the available accommodation and they are more common in families whose earnings are above average than in families with low earnings, since the former families can provide the most suitable accommodation. The keeping of lodgers, therefore, can seldom be resorted to as an amelioration for poverty': Canada, Dominion Bureau of Statistics, 'The Canadian Family,' by A.J. Pelletier, F.D.

Thompson, and A. Rochan, *Seventh Census of Canada, 1931: Monographs*, vol. 12 (Ottawa, 1942), 6. The proportion of households taking in lodgers began to decline after the Second World War, from 9.6 per cent in 1951 to 7.6 per cent in 1961: Canada, Dominion Bureau of Statistics, *Canada Year Book, 1965*, 185.

40 Allen, *My Childhood and Yours*, 100. Allen's father worked as a jewellery repair-man for Eaton's. The family's boarders obviously helped meet the mortgage payments on their house.

41 *Vancouver Sun*, 11 March 1985, A5.

42 Gillian Crees, 'The Politics of Dependence: Women, Work and Unemployment in the Vancouver Labour Movement before World War II,' in *Class, Gender, and Region: Essays in Canadian Sociological History*, ed. Gregory S. Kealey, 121–42 (St John's, 1988); Margaret Conrad, '"Sundays Always Make Me Think of Home": Time and Place in Canadian Women's History,' in *Not Just Pin Money*, ed. Barbara K. Latham and Roberta J. Pazdro, 1–16 (Victoria, 1984); Louise A. Tilley and Joan Scott, *Women, Work, and Family* (New York, 1978), 228–9.

43 In the last week of October 1949, for example, only 22 per cent of wage-earners in British Columbia worked fewer than 40 hours, while 63 per cent worked from 40 to 44 hours, and 15 per cent worked more than 44 hours. For Canada as a whole, the comparable figures were 18 per cent, 35 per cent, and 47 per cent: Canada, Dominion Bureau of Statistics, *Canada Year Book, 1952–53*, 706.

44 Canada, Statistics Canada, 1981 Census, *Canada's Lone Parent Families* (Ottawa, 1984), table 1. The census of 1966 showed a continuation of that decline, but the proportion began to rise again in 1971. By 1981, 11.3 per cent of Canadian families were lone-parent ones. Preliminary reports from the 1991 census showed 13 per cent of all families were lone-parent ones: *Vancouver Sun*, 8 July 1992, A1, A20.

45 Jack Munro and Jane O'Hara, *Union Jack: Labour Leader Jack Munro* (Vancouver, 1988), 20.

46 'For many loggers who worked in coastal camps, Vancouver remained their main place of residence and, when they quit, were discharged, or laid off, they returned to the city': Gordon Hak, 'The Socialist and Labourist Impulse in Small-Town British Columbia: Port Alberni and Prince George, 1911–33,' *Canadian Historical Review* 70 (December 1989), 524. None the less some men who worked away from home in the resource industries were able to take their families with them. In the late 1920s or early 1930s, M. Wylie Blanchet visited a small logging camp at the entrance to Kingcome Inlet 'built on a series of huge log-rafts ... There were comfortable homes for the married men; bunkhouses for the bachelors ... Also a school': *The Curve of Time* (Sidney, BC, 1989 [1961]), 84; such 'floating schools' are described in Joan Adams and Becky Thomas, *Floating Schools and Frozen Inkwells: The One Room Schools of British Columbia* (Madeira Park, BC, 1985). In 'The Bomb that Mooed,' Howard White describes the

almost idyllic years he and his two sisters spent at their father's gyppo logging show on Nelson Island between 1950 and 1954: *Writing in the Rain* (Madeira Park, BC, 1990), 31–51. The lives of Newfoundland loggers who left their families to spend many months working in the woods is described in Dufferin Sutherland, '"The Men Went to Work by the Stars and Returned by Them": The Experience of Work in the Newfoundland Woods during the 1930s,' *Newfoundland Studies* 7 (Fall 1991), 143–72.

47 Some such houses are preserved at the Port Edward Cannery Museum at Port Edward, near Prince Rupert. Others are shown in photographs in Gladys Young Blyth, *Salmon Canneries: British Columbia's North Coast* (Lantzville, BC, 1991), 56, 58, 127, and 158.

48 Rudy Wiebe, 'Father Where Are You?' *West*, December 1989, 53–4. J.K. Bell, who grew up in Halifax in the 1910s, also had a father who 'used to drift around': Sue Calhoun, ed., *Ole Boy: Memoirs of a Canadian Labour Leader* (Halifax, 1992), ch. 1.

49 Fraser Miles, *Slow Boat on Rum Row* (Madeira Park, BC, 1992), 9–13.

50 Sean Rossiter, 'Perrault of the Senate,' *Vancouver*, July 1981, 56.

51 Munro and O'Hara, *Union Jack*, 20.

52 Daphne Marlatt and Carole Itter, ed., *Opening Doors: Vancouver's East End* (Victoria, BC, 1979), 101.

53 In the earliest stages of the Second World War, while the army preferred to recruit men without dependants, it did pay dependants' allowances, to a maximum of three, and refused to enlist those with four or more dependants. As the need for men increased, the regulations were gradually relaxed, so that, by 1943, all ranks could 'draw dependents' allowance for up to six dependent children, and a dependent father or mother in addition': C.P. Stacey, *Six Years of War: The Army in Canada, Britain and the Pacific*, vol. 1: *Official History of the Canadian Army in the Second World War* (Ottawa, 1955), 52–3.

54 Robert MacNeil, *Wordstruck: A Memoir* (New York, 1989), 11.

55 'Childhoods Revisited Series: Prairie Girlhoods,' Canadian Childhood History Project, University of British Columbia, 23 February 1989.

56 Rohr with Heath, *Memories of a Governor General's Daughter*, 6.

57 Iris Allan, *Mother and Her Family: Memories of a Railway Town* (Cobalt, ON, 1977), 74.

58 Howard White and Jim Spilsbury, *Spilsbury's Coast: Pioneer Years in the Wet West* (Madeira Park, BC, 1987), 31.

3: Children in Their Families: Relationships and Identities

1 'The History of the Family and the Complexity of Social Change,' *American Historical Review* 96 (February 1991), 120.

2 For an outstanding recollection – perhaps somewhat romanticized – of a warm and loving upbringing, see Fredelle Bruser Maynard, *Raisins and Almonds* (Toronto, 1973); for a clear-eyed but extremely bitter account of an unhappy family, see the autobiographical novel by Percy Janes, *House of Hate* (Toronto, 1970).

3 *Vancouver Sun*, 4 May 1992, A1.

4 Christopher Lasch, *Haven in a Heartless World: The Family Besieged* (New York, 1977).

5 Sometimes described as 'social patriarchy' in contrast to the 'familial patriarchy' of preindustrial Canada: Jane Ursel, *Private Lives, Public Policy: 100 Years of State Intervention in the Family* (Toronto, 1992), part 1.

6 Ignatia Lanigan Grams, *Never Borrow Trouble* (Aldergrove, BC, 1995), 36.

7 Scriptural references cited in support of this formulation included Exodus 20: 12, 21: 15; Ephesians 5: 21–33, 6: 1–4; and Colossians 3: 18–21. The first passage is the fifth commandment, 'Honour your father and your mother ...'

8 Melinda McCracken, *Memories Are Made of This* (Toronto, 1975), 16.

9 Although family-allowance legislation was introduced in 1944, and the first family allowances were paid in 1945, no interviewee mentioned whether this new social service had any effect on family life. The fact that the cheques were made out to the mother may have changed the power relationships in certain families, but, if that did in fact occur, no one mentioned it in any of the interviews, nor does it appear in any of the autobiographical material I consulted.

10 Robert MacNeil, *Wordstruck: A Memoir* (New York, 1989), 174.

11 Allan Cecil Hare, 'Kerrisdale Youth,' unpublished MA thesis, University of British Columbia, 1954.

12 Leslie Warde Laidlaw, 'Premature Withdrawal from Treatment in a Child Guidance Clinic: Exploratory Study of the Factors which Underlie Clients' Decision to Withdraw from Social Work Treatment at the Provincial Child Guidance Clinic, North Burnaby, British Columbia,' unpublished MSW thesis, University of British Columbia, 1957, 26.

13 Fredelle Bruser Maynard, *The Tree of Life* (Markham, ON, 1988), xiv.

14 Hugh Garner, *One Damn Thing After Another!* (Toronto, 1973), 17–19.

15 Fathers also occasionally helped out when children were ill: see, for example, Scott Young, *Neil and Me* (Toronto, 1984), 30–6.

16 Helen Sigurdson, *I Wanted You to Know* (Winnipeg, 1994), 16.

17 Roy Bonisteel, *There Was a Time ...* (Toronto, 1991), 162–3.

18 MacDonald Coleman, *Once Upon a Childhood* (Red Deer, AB, 1978), 57; a fine evocation of the sense of powerlessness felt by a ten-year-old boy in relation to a basically loving but remote father is found in Hubert Evans's autobiographical novel *O Time In Your Flight* (Madeira Park, BC, 1979).

19 *Vancouver Sun*, 15 June 1985, A6. See also Rick Ooston *Finding Family* (Vancouver, 1994), esp. ch. 1.

20 Arthur Mayse, *My Father, My Friend*, ed. Susan Mayse (Madeira Park, BC, 1993), 53.

21 Horace Goudie, *Trails to Remember* (St John's, 1991), 2, 8.

22 Stuart Keate, *Paper Boy* (Toronto, 1980), 4–5.

23 Toronto *Globe and Mail*, 8 November 1986, D5.

24 R. Margaret Cork, *The Forgotten Children: A Study of Children with Alcoholic Parents* (Toronto, 1969), 140. See also the five case-studies reported in Toronto *Globe and Mail*, 8 November 1986, D5.

25 Joyce Fairchild Rolston, 'Clinical Treatment of Adolescents with Behaviour Disorders: An Evaluative Survey of Patients Admitted to Crease Clinic (British Columbia), 1956–1958,' unpublished MSW thesis, University of British Columbia, 1959, 34–5. For an account of how alcohol transformed what had been a warm daughter–father relationship, see Bronwyn Drainie, *Living the Part: John Drainie and the Dilemma of Canadian Stardom* (Toronto, 1988), 207–13, 304–5.

26 Cork, *Forgotten Children*, 59.

27 *Vancouver Sun*, 4 February 1992, A11.

28 In an unusually frank autobiography, Kenneth C. Boyd comments candidly on each of his six siblings. The whole family, for example, gave his brother Cecil the role of the 'bad apple,' and then both deplored and celebrated his transgressions: *When the Ship Comes In!!!* (Duncan, BC, 1993), *passim*.

29 Olive O'Brien, *Running with the Wind* (Fernwood, PEI, 1977), 81.

30 Lew Duddridge, *The Best 70 Years of My Life: It's All Downhill from Here* (Victoria, BC, 1988), 10, 22–4.

31 Charles A. Dougan, *My Daughter's Request: Spotlight on the Yesterday of Country Folk* (Duncan, BC, 1991), 8.

32 'Gender' is now commonly defined as the social organization of sexual difference. For contemporary discourse on the topic, see Jane Gaskell, *Gender Matters: From School to Work* (Toronto, 1992), esp. ch. 4.

33 On the centrality of practice in the formation and retention of gender identity, see Stephen Richer, *Boys and Girls Apart: Children's Play in Canada and Poland* (Ottawa, 1990), 123.

34 Iris Allan, *Mother and Her Family* (Cobalt, ON, 1977), 4.

35 Pierre Berton, *Starting Out: 1920–1947* (Toronto, 1987), 43.

36 Evelyn Huang with Lawrence Jeffery, *Chinese Canadians: Voices from a Community* (Vancouver, 1992), 35.

37 Women's Research Centre, *Recollecting Our Lives: Women's Experience of Childhood Sexual Abuse* (Vancouver, 1989), 50.

38 See Patricia Vertinsky, 'The Social Construction of the Gendered Body: Exer-

cise and the Exercise of Power,' *The International Journal of the History of Sport* 11 (August 1994), 147–71.

39 Hugh Palmer, *Circumnavigating Father* (Surrey, BC, 1990), 42–3.

40 Continuity and change in the lives of women between the end of the Great War and the 1960s are explored in Veronica Strong-Boag, *The New Day Recalled: Lives of Girls and Women in English Canada, 1919–1939* (Markham, ON, 1988), and Veronica Strong-Boag, 'Home Dreams: Women and the Suburban Experiment in Canada, 1945–60,' *Canadian Historical Review*, 72 (December 1991), 471–504.

41 'Childhoods Revisited Series: Prairie Girlhoods,' Canadian Childhood History Project, University of British Columbia, 23 February 1989.

42 *Vancouver Sun*, 4 May 1992, A1.

43 Jean McKay, *Gone to Grass* (Toronto, 1983), 15.

44 *Vancouver Sun*, 15 June 1992, A3.

45 Ellen Davignon, *The Cinnamon Mine: Memoirs of an Alaska Highway Childhood* (Whitehorse, 1988), 58.

46 One of the 'Oriental' families then living north of Broadway was that of businessman Lee Bick, whose four Vancouver-born sons graduated from the University of British Columbia and two of whom became businessmen, and the other two a lawyer and a physics professor: Huang with Jeffery, *Chinese Canadians*, 20–9, 50–7.

47 Charles Ritchie, *My Grandfather's House: Scenes of Childhood and Youth* (Toronto, 1987), 1.

48 Thomas Greenfield and Peter Ribbins, eds., *Greenfield on Educational Administration: Towards a Humane Science* (London, 1993), 232. Greenfield spent much of his childhood in east Vancouver.

49 Harold Winch sat as CCF member for Vancouver East from 1933 to 1953. He later became member of Parliament for the same area. Arthur Turner sat for the dual-member provincial riding from 1941 to 1966.

50 Maureen Forrester with Marci McDonald, *Out of Character: A Memoir* (Toronto, 1986), 39.

51 Daphne Marlatt and Carole Itter, eds., *Opening Doors: Vancouver's East End* (Victoria, BC, 1979), 68.

52 'Childhoods Revisited Series: First Nations Childhood,' Canadian Childhood History Project, University of British Columbia, 18 October 1989.

53 Marlatt and Itter, eds., *Opening Doors*, 64.

54 Gertrude Story, *The Last House on Main Street* (Saskatoon, 1994), 175.

55 'Childhoods Revisited Series: Growing Up Mennonite in Western Canada,' Canadian Childhood History Project, University of British Columbia, 12 January 1989.

56 See Phillip Buckner, 'Whatever Happened to the British Empire?' *Journal of the Canadian Historical Association*, new ser., 4 (1993), esp. 31–2.

57 Denise Chong, *The Concubine's Children* (Toronto, 1994), xii.
58 Sing Lim, *West Coast Chinese Boy* (Montreal, 1979), 26.
59 R.F. Sparkes, *The Winds Softly Sigh* (n. p. [St John's], 1981), 91.
60 *Vancouver Sun*, 23 October 1987, A10. See also Jimmy Pattison with Paul Gresco, *Jimmy: An Autobiography* (Toronto, 1987), esp. chs. 1 and 2.
61 Isabelle (Doyle) Daley, 'The Geography of Home,' *The Island* 30 (Fall/Winter 1991), 25.
62 Millicent Blake Loder, *Daughter of Labrador* (St John's, 1989), 14.
63 Sparkes, *Winds Softly Sigh*, 109.
64 Grams, *Never Borrow Trouble*, 56.
65 In F.G. Paci, *The Father* (n. p. [Ottawa], 1984), 23–9, the author gives a detailed description of a first communion, together with a child's reflections on the event. In the late 1930s and 1940s, many Vancouver children attended the special interdenominational children's 'missions' conducted by Lionel A. Hunt and his wife: Lionel A. Hunt, *Mass Child Evangelism* (Chicago, 1951), 7, 29, 34, 36, and 142.
66 Morley Torgov, *A Good Place to Come From* (Toronto, 1974), 13.
67 Harry J. Boyle, *Memories of a Catholic Boyhood* (Toronto, 1973), 42.
68 *Vancouver Sun*, 7 May 1994, A3.
69 Roy Daniells, 'Plymouth Brother,' *Canadian Literature* 90 (Autumn, 1981), 28.
70 Eugene Vaters, *Reminiscence* (St John's, 1983), 11–12.
71 John Norris, *Wo Lee Stories: Memories of a Childhood in Nelson, B.C.* (Nelson, 1986), 44–6.
72 Lloyd H. Person, *No Foot in Heaven* (Saskatoon, 1978), 211–12. Person's two-volume memoir, realistic but generally light in tone, portrays various religious denominations in a harsh light. See also his *Growing Up in Minby* (Saskatoon, 1974).

4: Children in Their Families: Using and Abusing Parental Powers

1 Robert MacNeil, *Wordstruck: A Memoir* (New York, 1989), 179.
2 For the relationship between working-class Vancouverites and their schools, see Jean Barman, '"Knowledge Is Essential for Universal Progress But Fatal to Class Privilege": Working People and the Schools in Vancouver during the 1920s,' *Labour/Le Travail* 22 (Fall 1988), 9–66. See also Craig Heron, 'The High School and the Household Economy in Working-Class Hamilton, 1890–1940,' *Historical Studies in Education/Revue d'histoire de l'education* 7 (Fall 1995), 217–59.
3 Mitchell Sharp, *Which Reminds Me ... A Memoir* (Toronto, 1994), 4.
4 Charles A. Dougan, *My Daughter's Request: Spotlight on the Yesterday of Country Folk* (Duncan, BC, 1991), 46.

5 Rolf Knight, *Along the No. 20 Line: Reminiscences of the Vancouver Waterfront* (Vancouver, 1980), 48.

6 Tommy Hunter with Liane Heller, *My Story* (Toronto, 1985), 97.

7 By 1958, the Dominion Bureau of Statistics estimated that just over half of British Columbia pupils completed Grade Twelve: see British Columbia, *Report of the Royal Commission on Education* (Victoria, BC, 1960), 43–9. By 1988, 'Ministry of Education statistics showed that approximately 60% of students who enter Grade 9 graduate from Grade 12': British Columbia, *A Legacy for Learners: The Report of the Royal Commission on Education, 1988* (Victoria, BC, 1988), 104.

8 See also the 'retention' table in British Columbia, Department of Education, *One Hundred Years: Education in British Columbia* (Victoria, BC, 1972), 82.

9 Charles E. Phillips, *The Development of Education in Canada* (Toronto, 1957), 289.

10 Ina Small and Ernie Mutimer, *Ina of Grand Manan: A Stranger from Away* (Halifax, 1989), 73, 81.

11 Alvin L. Flood of the Canadian Imperial Bank of Commerce was born in 1935 and joined the bank in 1951. Matthew Barrett of the Bank of Montreal was born in 1944 and joined the bank in 1962: *Who's Who in Canada* (Toronto, 1993), 284, 41–2.

12 Norman Lidster, *No Time for Why* (Vancouver, 1972), 2.

13 Norah L. Lewis has used children's letters to newspapers to great effect in '"Isn't This a Terrible War?": The Attitudes of Children to Two World Wars,' *Historical Studies in Education* 7 (Fall 1995), 193–215, and in *'I Want to Join Your Club': Letters from Rural Children, 1900–1920* (Waterloo, ON, 1996).

14 MacNeil, *Wordstruck*, 3.

15 *Vancouver Sun*, 24 January 1985, D6.

16 Gene Lees, *Oscar Peterson: The Will to Swing* (Toronto, 1988), 23.

17 Robert Thomas Allen, *My Childhood and Yours: Happy Memories of Growing Up* (Toronto, 1977), 48.

18 Morley Torgov, *A Good Place to Come From* (Toronto, 1976), 43.

19 Joan Michener Rohr with Terrence Heath, *Memories of a Governor General's Daughter* (Toronto, 1990), 22.

20 Richard Austin, *Lynn Seymour: An Authorized Biography* (London, 1980), 15.

21 George Dorman, *Up in the Morning, Out on the Job: The George Dorman Story*, vol. 1 (Nanaimo, BC, 1994), 18.

22 Margaret Visser, *The Rituals of Dinner: The Origins, Evolution, Eccentricities, and Meaning of Table Manners* (New York, 1991), 15–27, describes how mostly middle-class youngsters learned table manners over the centuries.

23 Rohr with Heath, *Memories of a Governor General's Daughter*, 14.

24 Knight, *Along the No. 20 Line*, 70.

25 Lloyd H. Person, *Growing Up in Minby* (Saskatoon, 1974), 4.

26 *Vancouver Sun*, 1 April 1982, A5.

27 Provincial Archives of Ontario, RG 10, Box 475-F-1-B, Squires to Knox, 28 August 1923.

28 Kenneth Edward Bell, 'The Recognition and Treatment of Emotionally Disturbed Children in Grades One to Four of a Public School System: A Sample Survey of the Children from Twelve Burnaby Schools Reported by Their Teachers on Maladjusted Children, with Further Study of the Children from Three Schools and the Help Presently Given Such Children to Overcome Their Emotional Disturbance,' unpublished MSW thesis, University of British Columbia, 1951, 58–61.

29 The current state of academic discourse on the disciplining of children is discussed in Rhonda D. Lenton, 'Techniques of Child Discipline and Abuse by Parents,' *Canadian Review of Sociology and Anthropology* 27 (May 1990), 157–85.

30 Norah L. Lewis, 'Creating the Little Machine: Child Rearing in British Columbia, 1919–1939,' *BC Studies* 56 (Winter 1982–3), 38.

31 W.E. Blatz, *The Management of Young Children* (New York, 1930), 38, quoted in Norah Lillian Lewis, 'Advising the Parents: Child Rearing in British Columbia During the Inter-War Years,' unpublished EdD thesis, University of British Columbia, 1980, 108. See also Jocelyn Matyer Raymond, *The Nursery World of Dr. Blatz* (Toronto, 1991).

32 S.R. Laycock, 'Innoculating for Character,' *The Bulletin of the Saskatchewan Teachers' Federation, 1945*, unpaginated, quoted in Mary Chernesky, 'A Touch of Laycock,' unpublished MA thesis, University of Saskatchewan, 1978, 183. In addition to the references cited above, see Veronica Strong-Boag, 'Intruders in the Nursery: Childcare Professionals Reshape the Years One to Five,' in *Childhood and Family in Canadian History*, ed. Joy Parr, 160–78 (Toronto, 1992). For changing fashions in advice literature in the United States see Julia Wrigley, 'Do Young Children Need Intellectual Stimulation? Experts' Advice to Parents, 1900–1985,' *History of Education Quarterly* 29 (Spring 1989), 41–75.

33 Even the quintessentially middle-class families of 'Crestwood Heights' employed corporal punishment: John R. Seeley, R. Alexander Sim, and E.W. Loosley, *Crestwood Heights: A Study of the Culture of Suburban Life* (Toronto, 1956), 193–203.

34 The nature of such jobs is described by Craig Heron, whose steelworkers 'stand in for a wide range of workers in the new mass-production industries – auto workers, chemical workers, pulp and paper workers, packinghouse workers, and many others in industries using sophisticated machinery in immense factories ...': *Working in Steel: The Early Years in Canada, 1883–1935* (Toronto, 1988), 10.

35 Raymond Gareth Atkinson, Mary Nora Clark, Marjorie-Guy Wickeet, and Gary Steeves Wright, 'The Battered Child Syndrome: Medical, Legal and Social

Work Machinery for Dealing With the Battered Child Syndrome,' unpublished MSW thesis, University of British Columbia, 1965, 26.

36 Roy Bonisteel, *There Was a Time ...* (Toronto, 1991), 83.

37 *Victoria Times-Colonist*, 8 August 1995, 2.

38 Ellen Davignon, *The Cinnamon Mine: Memories of an Alaska Highway Childhood* (Whitehorse, 1988), 52.

39 See, for example, J.D.A. Widdowson, 'The Function of Threats in Newfoundland Folklore,' in *Explorations in Canadian Folklore*, ed. Edith Fowke and Carole H. Carpenter, 277–88 (Toronto, 1985).

40 Dr. Maara Haas, 'On the Street Where I Live,' Historical and Scientific Society of Manitoba, *Transactions*, ser. 3, 31 (1974–5), 22.

41 Adults often cited scriptural authority for the use of corporal punishment, especially Proverbs 13: 24: 'A father who spares the rod hates his son, but one who loves him keeps him in order.' For a critical evaluation of the role of scripture in the disciplining of children, see Philip Greven, *Spare the Child: The Religious Roots of Punishment and the Psychological Impact of Physical Abuse* (New York, 1992), especially 'Religious Rationales,' 46–96.

42 E.H. Cayford, *Barefoot Days* (Saskatoon, 1974), 116–17.

43 Fraser Miles, *Slow Boat on Rum Row* (Madeira Park, BC, 1992), 10.

44 Pat Capponi, *Upstairs in the Crazy House: The Life of a Psychiatric Survivor* (Toronto, 1992), 5, 37.

45 See Jean Barman, *Growing Up British in British Columbia: Boys in Private School* (Vancouver, 1984).

46 Wilma Mary Gibson, 'The Social Worker in Adoption Practice: An Exploratory Study of 28 Adopted Children Who Were Referred Privately to the Vancouver Child Guidance Clinic, 1953–55,' unpublished MSW thesis, University of British Columbia, 1955, 86–7.

47 John S. Mozzanini, 'An Evaluation of the Facilities and Services of the Vancouver B.C. Juvenile Detention Home,' unpublished MSW thesis, University of British Columbia, 1950, 46–7.

48 Edwin Francis Watson, 'What Happens to Children in Later Adolescence? A Study and Evaluation of the Adjustment of Thirty-One Wards of the Superintendent of Child Welfare for the Province of British Columbia, Who Have Been in Foster Care, and Who Reached Eighteen Years of Age during the Year January 1, 1954–December 31, 1954,' unpublished MSW thesis, University of British Columbia, 1955, 60.

49 Audrey Mary Coppock, 'Children in Group Homes: A Survey of Wards of the Children's Aid Society Living in These Units, Vancouver, 1954,' unpublished MSW thesis, University of British Columbia, 1955, 88.

50 It seems reasonable to conclude that some of those who declined to be inter-

viewed about their childhood on the grounds that talking about it conjured up unpleasant memories that they wished to avoid discussing, or even recalling, were victims of sexual and other abuse. In one example, when I followed up my initial letter of approach to her by telephone, a woman wept as she declined to be interviewed. In another, a man who did agree to an interview broke into tears more than once as he described being abused.

51 *Vancouver Sun*, 11 June 1992, 21.

52 Some studies have tried to estimate the incidence of child abuse, or to compute trends. In a 1989 study, staff at the Children's Hospital of Eastern Ontario in Ottawa reported that there was a 'striking similarity in the reported prevalence rates [for childhood sexual abuse] comparing the 1940s with the 80s.' They concluded that such abuse 'is not increasing but, in a new social climate, more children and their families are coming forward,': W. Feldman, E. Feldman, J. Goodman, P. McGrath, R. Pless, L. Corsini, and S. Bennett, 'Is Childhood Sexual Abuse (C.S.A.) Really Increasing in Prevalence? An Analysis of the Evidence,' Canadian Paediatric Society, *Abstract*, January 1989; see also Toronto *Globe and Mail*, 28 June 1989, A5. In 1983, the Badgeley Committee – Canada, Committee on Sexual Offences Against Children and Youths, *Sexual Offences Against Children: Report of the Committee on Sexual Offences Against Children*, 2 vols. (Ottawa, 1984), discussed below – had the Canadian Gallup poll conduct a national survey employing questionnaires answered anonymously and privately. On the basis of this survey, the committee concluded that 'at some time during their lives, about one in two females and one in three males have been the victims of unwanted sexual acts. About four in five of these ... happened ... when they were children or youths' (175). Although this and other findings of the committee came under sharp criticism for combining trivial with extremely serious examples of abuse, the survey and other personal accounts it collected clearly showed that many people in the years covered by this study concealed, or were forced to conceal, what happened to them.

53 Donald Garth Homer, 'A Survey of Wards Not in Foster Homes: A Study of the Group Who Severed Contact with the Agency (Children's Aid Society, Vancouver),' unpublished MSW thesis, University of British Columbia, 1956, 61–72.

54 Helen M. Finlayson, 'Play Therapy Techniques: An Examination of a Children's Aid Society Experimental Project for Disturbed Children, 1948 to 1951,' unpublished MSW thesis, University of British Columbia, 1951, 61. Although brother–sister incest is apparently more common than that perpetrated by fathers, this was the only example of the former uncovered in my research. See Julia Krane, 'Explanations of Child Sexual Abuse: A Review and Critique from a Feminist Perspective,' *Canadian Review of Social Policy/Revue canadienne de politique sociale* 25 (May 1990), 13.

55 *Vancouver Sun*, 28 April 1989, B6.

56 *Sexual Offences Against Children*, 159–60. For critical evaluation of the Badgeley Report, see J. Lowman, M.A. Jackson, T. S. Palys, and S. Gavigan, eds., *Regulating Sex: An Anthology of Commentaries on the Findings and Recommendations of the Badgeley and Fraser Reports* (Burnaby, BC, 1986), and Gary Kinsman and Deborah Brock, 'Patriarchal Relations Ignored: A Critique of the Badgeley Report on Sexual Offences Against Children and Youth,' *Canadian Criminology Forum/Forum canadien de criminologie* 8 (Fall 1986), 15–29.

57 Badgeley Committee, *Sexual Offences Against Children*, 162. Various sorts of sexual abuse are recounted and analysed in Women's Research Centre, *Recollecting Our Lives: Women's Experience of Childhood Sexual Abuse* (Vancouver, 1989), especially ch. 2.

58 Gordon Bates, 'A Survey of the Incidence of Venereal Disease in Toronto in 1937,' *Canadian Public Health Journal* 28 (December 1937), 581. I am indebted to Christabelle Sethna for pointing this situation out to me.

59 See Women's Research Centre, *Recollecting Our Lives*, ch. 4.

60 John Norris, *Wo Lee Stories: Memories of a Childhood in Nelson, B.C.* (Nelson, 1986), 36–7.

61 Ibid., 56–62.

62 The Canadian Social Hygiene Council advocated that 'sex education should be given by parents rather than by teachers': Laura E. Jamieson, *Sex Education in the Child Welfare Programme, A Paper Read Before the Conference on Child Welfare in ... 1927* (Victoria, BC, 1928), 3; see also Christabelle Sethna, 'The Facts of Life: The Sex Instruction of Ontario Public School Children, 1900–1950,' unpublished PhD dissertation, University of Toronto, 1995.

63 The phrase is that of one of the women interviewed for Women's Research Centre, *Recollecting Our Lives*, 57.

64 Millicent Blake Loder, *Daughter of Labrador* (St John's, 1989), 26.

65 Such materials are described in Michael Bliss, '"Pure Books on Avoided Subjects": Pre-Freudian Sexual Ideas in Canada,' Canadian Historical Association, *Historical Papers*, 1970, 88–108.

66 Hugh Garner, *One Damn Thing After Another!* (Toronto, 1973), 18.

67 Fredelle Bruser Maynard, *Raisins and Almonds* (Toronto, 1973); Fredelle Bruser Maynard, *The Tree of Life* (Markham, ON, 1988).

5: Children in a Wider Environment of Care

1 See, for example, Victor Malarek, *Hey Malarek!: The True Story of a Street Kid Who Made it* (Toronto, 1984), and Dereck O'Brien, *Suffer Little Children: An Autobiography of a Foster Child* (St John's, 1991). O'Brien lived in foster homes

and in the Mount Cashel Orphanage. On the latter, see Newfoundland, *Royal Commission of Inquiry into the Response of the Newfoundland Criminal Justice System to Complaints* [the Hughes Commission] (St John's, 1991). In contrast to Malarek and O'Brien, Reuben Slonim described the Jewish Orphanage in Winnipeg in which he spent part of his childhood in the 1920s as 'a congenial place.' Its staff 'were often more severe in their discipline than they needed to be, but this severity was balanced by their dedication and the affection of volunteers ...': *Grand to Be an Orphan* (Toronto, 1983), 11, 13.

2 Diane Purvey examined, from the family perspective, an agency designed to be a 'short-term strategy used by parents to keep their families together in the long-term': 'Alexandra Orphanage and Families in Crisis in Vancouver, 1892–1938,' *Dimensions of Childhood: Essays on the History of Children and Youth in Canada*, ed. Russell Smandych, Gordon Dodds, and Alvin Esau, 107–33 (Winnipeg, 1991). A recent book describes a grim example of 'baby farming': Betty L. Cahill, *Butterbox Babies* (Toronto, 1992). See Patricia T. Rooke and R.L. Schnell, *Discarding the Asylum: From Child Rescue to the Welfare State in English Canada, 1800–1950* (Lanham, MD, 1983), and Andrew Jones and Leonard Rutman, *In the Children's Aid: J.J. Kelso and Child Welfare in Ontario* (Toronto, 1981), for the origins of such institutions.

3 H. 'Dude' Lavington, *The Nine Lives of a Cowboy* (Victoria, BC, 1982), 12.

4 On step-parents, see Natasha Burchardt, 'Stepchildren's Memories: Myth, Understanding, and Forgiveness,' in *The Myths We Live By*, ed. Raphael Samuel and Paul Thompson, 239–51 (London, 1990).

5 Marjory Helen Munro, 'A General Survey and Evaluation of an Institution for the Observation and Treatment of Problem Children,' unpublished MA thesis, University of British Columbia, 1946, 82.

6 Patrick James Fogarty, 'Relation of Children's Disorders to Limiting Parental Influences: An Essay in Classification and Analysis, Concerning a Certain Group of Children Who Were Referred Privately to the Vancouver Child Guidance Clinic between 1948 [and] 1951,' unpublished MSW thesis, University of British Columbia, 1952, 58–9.

7 Helen M. Finlayson, 'Play Therapy Techniques: An Examination of a Children's Aid Society Experimental Project for Disturbed Children, 1948 to 1951,' unpublished MSW thesis, University of British Columbia, 1951, 129–35.

8 As a result of her interviews with sixty adults who were adopted between the 1930s and 1960s, Karen March concluded that 'a strong image of adoption as a social stigma' was an important trigger in their decision as adults to search for their birth mothers. Other triggers included the medical and social need for more complete genealogies: *The Stranger Who Bore Me: Adoptee–Birth Mother Relationships* (Toronto, 1995), 39.

9 Dorothy Jean Morrow, 'I Met My Birth Mother When I Was 50,' *Chatelaine*, February 1985, 52, 93–4. March concluded that 'contact with the birth mother increased the adoptees' appreciation for their adoptive backgrounds ...': *The Stranger Who Bore Me*, 134.

10 Toronto *Globe and Mail*, 16 November 1985, D1.

11 'Childhoods Revisited Series: Ukrainian Childhoods,' Canadian Childhood History Project, University of British Columbia, 22 November 1989.

12 Mary Cook, *One for Sorrow Two for Joy* (Ottawa, 1984), 33–4.

13 An American historian of welfare writes that research there shows that 'recent generations have undoubtedly seen a decline in the interdependence among members of the functionally-extended kinship system ...': Clarke A. Chambers, 'Towards a Redefinition of Welfare History,' *Journal of American History* 73 (September 1986), 425. So far as I know, no one has investigated the situation as it exists in Canada. I must say, however, that I am very sceptical of this conclusion.

14 Mildred Young Hubbert, *Since the Day I Was Born* (Thornbury, ON, 1991), 69.

15 Silver Donald Cameron, 'The Great White Father – and Other Tales of Informal Adoption,' *Homemaker's Magazine*, December 1987, 12–24.

16 Pete Loudon, 'Pride of the West: A Canadian Family Battles the Great Depression, 1935,' *The Beaver* 70 (April/May 1970), 29.

17 Mary Twigg Wynn Woodward, 'Juvenile Delinquency among Indian Girls: An Examination of the Causes and Treatment of a Sample Group and the Resulting Social Implications,' unpublished MSW thesis, University of British Columbia, 1949, 31.

18 Ferne Nelson, *Barefoot on the Prairie: Memories of Life on a Prairie Homestead* (Saskatoon, 1989), 51.

19 Robert H. Thompson, *Penny Candy, Bobskates and Frozen Road Apples: Growing Up in the Thirties and Forties* (Victoria, BC, 1990), 5.

20 *Victoria Colonist*, 3 June 1925, quoted in *Victoria Times-Colonist*, 11 June 1993, A 3.

21 *Vancouver Sun*, 13 June 1992, A6.

22 Stompin' Tom Connors, *Before the Fame* (Toronto, 1995).

23 *Victoria Times-Colonist*, 20 August 1995, M1.

24 One of the five, daughter Anna Stuber, told their story in the *New Westminster Royal City Record*, 7 June 1992, 8–9. I am indebted to Jacqueline Gresko for drawing my attention to this account.

25 Erna Vaitmaa, 'A Study of C.A.S. Wards Not in Foster Homes: Being a Study of Eighteen Cases of Children in Correctional Institutions as of October 31, 1954,' unpublished MSW thesis, University of British Columbia, 1955, 31.

26 Edwin Francis Watson, 'What Happens to Children in Later Adolescence? A Study and Evaluation of the Adjustment of Thirty-One Wards of the Super-

intendent of Child Welfare for the Province of British Columbia, Who Have
Been in Foster Care, and Who Reached Eighteen Years of Age during the Year
January 1, 1954–December 31, 1954,' unpublished MSW thesis, University
of British Columbia, 1955, 51.

27 Vivian Mauretta Ellis, 'Multiple Placement of Foster Children: A Preliminary
Study of Causes and Effects, Based on a Sample of Fifty Foster Children in Vancouver,' unpublished MSW thesis, University of British Columbia, 1949, 67–8.

28 Donald Garth Homer, 'A Survey of Wards Not in Foster Homes: A Study of the
Group Who Severed Contact with the Agency (Children's Aid Society, Vancouver),' unpublished MSW thesis, University of British Columbia, 1956, 46.

29 Henry Moncrieff McLaren, 'Adjustment of the Adolescent in Rural Foster
Homes: A Pioneer Study of the Problems in Giving Service to Adolescent Boys
and Girls, and the Difficulty This Age Group Has in Adjustment to Foster
Homes in Rural Communities,' unpublished MSW thesis, University of British
Columbia, 1954, 71–2.

30 Maggie MacDonald with Allan Gould, *The Violent Years of Maggie MacDonald:
An autobiography* (Scarborough, ON, 1987), 12.

31 Elizabeth Ursula Townsend Tuckey, 'Family Influence in Child Protection Cases
at the Point of Apprehension and in Later Foster Care: An Exploratory Study of
a Group of Wards (of the Children's Aid Society, Vancouver) in Foster Care
More Than Two Years (1958),' unpublished MSW thesis, University of British
Columbia, 1958, 51–3.

32 Watson, 'What Happens,' 36, 57–8.

33 Ibid., 55.

34 Ellis, 'Multiple Placement,' 103–5.

35 Rosemary Lansdowne, 'The Concept of Non-Adoptability: A Study of the Concept of Non-Adoptability on Case Work Services to the Unmarried Mother, and
an Examination of the Validity of This Concept,' an unpublished MSW thesis,
University of British Columbia, 1949, 19–22. These attitudes were not confined
to the Vancouver CAS. In her annual report in 1944, British Columbia's superintendent of child welfare wrote: 'If we can prevent a child who has not a good
background from being placed in a [adoptive] home, the matter is simple. Our
legislation provides other and adequate ways of caring for the dependent child':
British Columbia, Superintendent of Child Welfare, *Report*, 1944, 3.

36 Rose Blinder, 'Treatment for Emotionally Disturbed Wards of the Children's Aid
Society,' unpublished MSW thesis, University of British Columbia, 1954, 77–8.

37 Magda Elizabeth de Rimanoczy, 'Some Aspects of Adoption Probation: An Illus-
trative Study of a Sample of Wards of the Vancouver Children's Aid Society
Placed on a Boarding Basis with a View to Adoption,' unpublished MSW thesis,
University of British Columbia, 1956, 29–31, 42–3, 56–7, 71–2.

38 A sample of fifty white children between seven and twelve years old (born
   between 1936 and 1941) who had been in the care of the Vancouver Children's
   Aid Society or the Vancouver Catholic Children's Aid Society for two or more
   years, showed that 22 per cent had over that time been in one foster home, 20
   per cent had been in two, 24 per cent had been in three or four, and 34 per cent
   had been in from five to ten foster homes: Ellis, 'Multiple Placement,' 15. Thus,
   by the time she was fifteen in 1954, 'Evelyn,' who came into care when she was
   six, had been in and out of the Receiving Home, was under the care of her
   twelfth social worker, and was in her seventeenth foster home: Audrey Mary
   Coppock, 'Children in Group Homes: A Survey of Wards of the Children's Aid
   Society Living in these Units, Vancouver, 1954,' unpublished MSW thesis, University of British Columbia, 1955, 50–83. Between the time he came into care at
   nine and his being sent to jail at twenty, 'Dick' went through thirty-two placements, including nine in correctional institutions: Vaitmaa, 'Study of C.A.S.
   Wards,' 34.
39 Kenneth Edward Bell, 'The Recognition and Treatment of Emotionally Disturbed Children in Grades One to Four of a Public School System: A Sample
   Survey of the Children from Twelve Burnaby Schools Reported by Their Teachers on Maladjusted Children, with Further Study of the Children from Three
   Schools and the Help Presently Given Such Children to Overcome Their Emotional Disturbance,' unpublished MSW thesis, University of British Columbia,
   1951, 75.
40 *Vancouver Sun*, 16 March 1991, B5. Ronda Eyben, born in 1969 and also adopted
   as an infant, described the mother she hopes to meet as 'the black hole in my
   mind': *Vancouver Sun*, 9 September 1992, A3. See March, *Stranger Who Bore Me*,
   ch. 3.
41 Ellis, 'Multiple Placement,' 35, 62–5.
42 McLaren, 'Adjustment,' 80–3.
43 The nightmare nature of many children's experience of fostering is surely one of
   the saddest but most persistent dimensions of the history of childhood in Canada
   and elsewhere. In his *The Canadian Home Boy* (London, 1913), S.A. Francis tells
   of his experience in late nineteenth-century Ontario. In Phyllis Harrison, *The
   Home Children* (Winnipeg, 1979), former Barnardo, Quarrier, and other children
   from Britain described their experiences in Canadian foster homes. Joy Parr,
   Labouring Children: British Immigrant Apprentices to Canada, 1869–1924 (Montreal, 1980), provides the indispensable analysis of the recruitment, placement,
   and treatment of these children. *In Nobody's Children: The Foster Care Crisis in
   Canada* (Toronto, 1990), Martyn Kendrick vividly describes the situation as it
   exists towards the end of the twentieth century.
44 Bell, 'Recognition and Treatment of Emotionally Disturbed Children,' 60.

45 Donald Joseph Lugtig, 'The Psychological Factors which May Intensify the Adolescent Foster Child's Concern about His Unknown Parents: An Exploratory Study of Seven Adolescent Wards of the Vancouver Children's Aid Society,' unpublished MSW thesis, University of British Columbia, 1956, 68.
46 Jack M. Cobbin, 'Emotionally Disturbed Teen-Age Boys in a Group Living Residence: An Examination of Children's Aid Society Wards, with Special Reference to Movement Shown after a Period in a Group-Living Institution,' unpublished MSW thesis, University of British Columbia, 1955, 46.
47 Coppock, 'Children in Group Homes,' 56, 80.
48 Lugtig, 'Adolescent Foster Child,' 78–9.
49 Katherine Rider, 'Interviews with Former Wards,' typescript Children's Aid Society of Vancouver, 1974, 2–5.
50 As part of his preparation of a suit against the provincial government, Hale collected 700 pages of material on his childhood through the provincial Freedom of Information Act. The Crown denied liability in the case. None the less, the quality of care Hale received, as evidenced by his recollections and supported by data from the documents, fell far below the standards set by modern child welfare legislation: *Vancouver Sun*, 24 March 1994, B1, B6.
51 *Vancouver Sun*, 30 April 1991, B7. Ooston later wrote about his search for his mother, sister, and other family members in *Finding Family* (Vancouver, 1994). Other such reunions are occasionally described in newspaper articles. See, for example, the story of Steve Kinsman, *Vancouver Sun*, 21 December 1991 B1; the complex story of the four children of Mary Wilson, ibid., 30 October 1992, B1 and 2 November 1992, B9; and the story of Beverly Allen, ibid., 6 July 1994, B1.

6: The Paid and Unpaid Work of Urban Children

1 In 'Orphans, Idiots, Lunatics, and Historians: Recent Approaches to the History of Child Welfare in Canada,' *Histoire sociale/Social History* 18 (May 1985), 133–45, John Bullen noted much of the Canadian and international literature on this topic. Other studies have described boys' work in mining and other industries. For mining, see Ian McKay, 'The Realm of Uncertainty: The Experience of Work in the Cumberland Coal Mines, 1873–1927,' *Acadiensis* 16 (Autumn 1986), 3–57; Lynn Bowen, *Boss Whistle: The Coal Miners of Vancouver Island Remember* (Lantzville, BC, 1982); Robert McIntosh, 'Canada's Boy Miners,' *The Beaver* 67 (December 1987/January 1988), 34–8; his 'The Boys in the Nova Scotian Coal Mines: 1873–1923,' *Acadiensis* 16 (Spring 1987), 35–50; and his 'Patterns of Child Labour: Victorian Labour Markets for Colliery Boys in Nova Scotia and British Columbia,' an unpublished paper presented to the Seventh Atlantic Studies Conference, Edinburgh, May 1988. For a firsthand account, see Dan J.

MacDonald, as told to Ed Payne, 'Into the Mines – as a Child,' *Atlantic Advocate* 57 (August 1967), 21–3. In two fine papers, Jessie Chisholm discusses child labour and youthful strikes – '"Hang Her Down": Strikes in St. John's, 1890–1914,' an unpublished paper presented to the Seventh Atlantic Canada Studies Conference, Edinburgh, May 1988, and 'Organizing on the Waterfront: The Longshoremen's Protective Union (LSPU) St. John's, Newfoundland, 1900–1914,' *Labour/Le Travail* 26 (Fall 1990), 51–5. For current accounts of the nature of children's work around the world, see Elias Mendelievich, *Children at Work* (Geneva, 1979), and Roger Sawyer, *Children Enslaved* (London, 1988).

2 Lorna F. Hurl, 'Restricting Child Factory Labour in Late Nineteenth-Century Ontario,' *Labour/Le Travail* 21 (Spring 1988), 87–121.

3 John Bullen, 'Hidden Workers: Child Labour and the Family Economy in Late Nineteenth-Century Urban Ontario,' *Labour/Le Travail* 18 (Fall 1986), 163–87. The work of children in a family setting is also described in Joy Parr, *Labouring Children: British Immigrant Apprentices to Canada, 1869–1924* (Montreal, 1980), and Jane Synge, 'The Transition from School to Work: Growing Up Working Class in Early 20th Century Hamilton, Ontario,' in *Childhood and Adolescence in Canada*, ed. K. Ishwaran, 249–69 (Toronto, 1979).

4 John Bullen, 'Children of the Industrial Age: Children, Work and Welfare in Late Nineteenth-Century Ontario,' unpublished PhD dissertation, University of Ottawa, 1989, ch. 7.

5 Neil Sutherland, *Children in English-Canadian Society: Framing the Twentieth-Century Consensus* (Toronto, 1976), 164–6. Dan Robert Hawthorne, 'Patterns of 20th Century Attendance: A Systematic Study of Victoria Public Schools, 1910 and 1921,' unpublished MA thesis, University of Victoria, 1984, surveys the complexities embedded in school-attendance data as they played themselves out in a single community.

6 Even today, and especially in rural and in immigrant communities, children are an important element in family economies. In February 1987, a Vancouver family initiated a lawsuit in the death of their fourteen-year-old daughter in a school-ground accident. The parents claimed that she 'did most of the cleaning, cooking and household duties in the family home and just before her death had planned and coordinated the purchase of a grocery store operated by the family': *Vancouver Sun*, 4 February 1987, A3.

7 British Columbia, *Statutes*, 1921, cap 56.

8 Canada, Department of Labour, *The Employment of Children and Young Persons in Canada* (Ottawa, 1930), 36, 6.

9 For an account of how gender determined the ways in which people worked in an earlier era, see Bettina Bradbury, *Working Families: Age, Gender, and Daily Survival in Industrializing Montreal* (Toronto, 1993), esp. ch. 4.

10 Although girls played some part in each of the five categories into which Veronica Strong-Boag has divided women's work in the home, my own somewhat different arrangement reflects the way in which children perceived what they did: Veronica Strong-Boag, 'Keeping House in God's Country: Canadian Women at Work in the Home,' in *On the Job: Confronting the Labour Process in Canada*, ed. Craig Heron and Robert Storey (Kingston and Montreal, 1986), 126–7.

11 Jack M. Cobbin, 'Emotionally Disturbed Teen-Age Boys in a Group Living Residence: An Examination of Children's Aid Society Wards, with Special Reference to Movement Shown after a Period in a Group-Living Institution,' unpublished MSW thesis, University of British Columbia, 1955, 27.

12 Maria Campbell, *Halfbreed* (Toronto, 1973), ch. 9.

13 Provincial Archives of Manitoba, RG4, Box 57, Children's Aid Society of Dauphin, *Minutes*, 7 December 1939. At its meeting of 29 May 1940, the society decided to ask another older daughter to undertake a similar arrangement.

14 As Veronica Strong-Boag remarks, 'no wonder most Canadian women appeared to hate wash day with a passion few other chores evoked ...': *The New Day Recalled: Lives of Girls and Women, 1919–1939* (Markham, ON, 1988), 135.

15 In 1938, a survey of 1,135 self-supporting Canadian families of 'British origin,' with husband and wife present and with one or more children, showed that fewer than 3 per cent had 'regular domestic help.' Of those with the highest incomes, only 6.5 per cent of homeowners and 13.3 per cent of tenants had regular help: 'Urban Wage-Earner Family Housing 1938,' Canada, *Census, 1931*, vol. 12, ch. 10.

16 Italian-Canadian mothers also indulged their sons. Even now, according to Lia Pichini, 'cursed are the households without any female children, for the mothers would never dare ask their sons to lift a finger to help them. For them, this would not seem right': 'Two Generations in Conflict: Sex Role Expectations among Italian-Canadian Women,' *Canadian Woman Studies/Les Cahiers de la Femme* 8/2 (1981), 22.

17 Edwin Francis Watson, 'What Happens to Children in Later Adolescence? A Study and Evaluation of the Adjustment of Thirty-One Wards of the Superintendent of Child Welfare for the Province of British Columbia, Who Have Been in Foster Care, and Who Reached Eighteen Years of Age During the Year January 1, 1954–December 31, 1954,' unpublished MSW thesis, University of British Columbia, 1955, 51.

18 Joan W. Scott, 'Gender: A Useful Category of Historical Analysis,' *American Historical Review* 91 (December 1986), 1053–75; 'Editorial: Culture and Gender: The Separate Worlds of Men and Women,' *History Workshop Journal* 15 (Spring 1983), 1–3; Strong-Boag, *The New Day Recalled*, ch. 1.

19 In June 1940, for example, one could buy the 'new Hi-Ideal sawdust burner,

completely installed with new patent features ...' for $20, while automatic coal stokers, installed, sold for between $150 and $250: *Vancouver Province*, 5 June 1940, 15.

20 By 1961, of Vancouver's 118,500 occupied dwellings, 106,000 were heated by furnaces, 10,500 by space heaters, and the other 2,000 in some other way. In the same year, 10,000 of the dwellings were heated with coke or coal, 3,500 by wood, 64,000 by 'liquid fuel' (fuel oil mostly), 36,500 by piped-in natural gas, and the remaining 4,500 by some other means, such as sawdust or electricity: Canada, *Census 1961: Housing*, vol. 2.2, tables 47, 52.

21 For an account of how families of an earlier generation supplemented their wage income, see Bradbury, *Working Families*.

22 According to the *Oxford English Dictionary* the word *scrounge* appeared in the years immediately after the Great War. It seems likely that it was invented by the troops in that conflict, and then passed into civilian use.

23 Daphne Marlatt and Carole Itter, eds., *Opening Doors: Vancouver's East End* (Victoria, BC, 1979), 106–7.

24 Sheila Baxter, *No Way to Live: Poor Women Speak Out* (Vancouver, 1988), 215–16.

25 In 1944, there were six Curry's Grocery stores in east-side Vancouver: Vancouver, *City Directory, 1944*, 596.

26 *Vancouver Province*, 21 January 1920, 16; ibid., 26 June 1930, 21.

27 Malcolm Harper, 'Newsboy Looks Back in Wonder,' *Victoria Times-Colonist*, 13 October 1991, M2.

28 *Vancouver Sun*, 3 January 1985, A3.

29 Mary Thompson, 'The Social Worker in the School: An Experimental Study of the Liaison and Service Functions of the Social Worker in a Vancouver Elementary School,' unpublished MSW thesis, University of British Columbia, 1948, 111.

30 See the discussion at the Vancouver Trades and Labour Congress meeting of 21 August 1928 of the unfair treatment of delivery boys on the newspapers 'whereby they have to stand the loss of money owing from subscribers moving away.' University of British Columbia Special Collections, Vancouver Trades and Labour Council, 'Minute Book,' 20 July 1926–2 October 1928.

31 *Grant MacEwan's Journals*, ed. Max Foran (Edmonton, 1996), 14.

32 British Columbia, Department of Labour, *Report, 1927*, L64.

33 Ibid., *1928*, J53; ibid., *1929*, L52; ibid., *1930*, E54.

34 Sing Lim, *West Coast Chinese Boy* (Montreal, 1979), 35.

35 Rolf Knight, *Along the No. 20 Line: Reminiscences of the Vancouver Waterfront* (Vancouver, 1980), 37.

36 *Vancouver Province*, 18 June 1930, 15; ibid., 29 June 1940, 18.

37 Ibid., 26 June 1930, 21.

38 University of British Columbia Special Collections, False Creek Oral History Collection of the Vancouver Historical Society, Jacqueline Hooper, interviewed 8 April 1985.

39 Charles A. Dougan, *My Daughter's Request: Spotlight on the Yesterday of Country Folk* (Duncan, BC, 1991), 28.

40 For a survey of child labour as it was seen in Canada in the early 1920s, see Helen Gregory MacGill, 'The Child in Industry,' *Labour Gazette*, October 1925, 983–91. See also Department of Labour, *Employment of Children*, 41.

41 *Vancouver Sun*, 14 January 1985, B2.

42 Two advertisements in the 'Wanted' columns of the *Province*, 18 June 1930, 15, for example, called for 'Boy about 14' and 'Light housework by young girl, 14, in good home.'

43 Canada, *Census, 1921*, v. 4, xlviii; ibid., *1931*, v. 6, table 41.

44 Gainfully occupied fourteen-year-olds in the Canadian workforce declined steadily from 20,745 in 1921 to 13,716 in 1931, to 12,394 in 1941, to 10,179 in 1951: M.C. Urquhart and K.A.H. Buckley, eds., *Historical Statistics of Canada* (Toronto, 1965), ser. C37.

45 Vancouver School Board, *Report, 1930*, 32–3.

46 *Vancouver Sun* 2 January 1991, B4.

47 In 1921, 114 British Columbia boys and girls under age fifteen reported themselves 'in trade': Department of Labour, *Employment of Children*, 66–7. See also Vancouver School Board, *Report, 1919*, 77; ibid., *1923*, 94.

48 British Columbia, Department of Labour, *Report, 1920*, P541; ibid., *1932*, G51.

49 Canada, *Census, 1931*, v. 6, table 41.

50 University of British Columbia Special Collections, False Creek Oral History Collection of the Vancouver Historical Society, Walter E. Dubberley, interviewed 9 February 1985.

51 In May 1923, the South Vancouver School Board permitted a boy who had 'no chance of passing the Entrance Examination,' and who would be fifteen in September, to leave school. In September of the same year, however, it insisted that at least five fourteen-year-olds continue with the new school year: City of Vancouver Archives, South Vancouver School Board, *Minutes*, 16 May 1923; 18 September 1923; 26 September 1923. I am indebted to Jean Barman for showing me these records.

52 Caption, photograph of Phyllis McMillan, North Pacific Cannery Village and Fishing Museum, Port Edward, BC. The whole process is described in Alicja Muszynski, 'Race and Gender: Structural Determinants in the Formation of British Columbia's Salmon Cannery Labour Forces,' in *Class, Gender, and Region: Essays in Canadian Historical Sociology*, ed. Gregory S. Kealey, 103–20 (St John's, 1988).

53 John E. Robbins, *Youth Figured Out: A Statistical Study of Canadian Youth* (Ottawa, n.d.), 15.

54 Carmela Patrias, 'Passages from the Life ... An Italian Woman in Welland, Ontario,' *Canadian Woman Studies/Les Cahiers de la Femme* 8/2 (1981), 70. In Percy Janes's 'semi-autobiographical' novel *House of Hate*, set in 'Milltown' (Corner Brook), Newfoundland, 'Flinsky' was 'plucked out of school' in her thirteenth year, becoming 'the household drudge, working seven days and five or six nights a week without pay and with never a word of praise or appreciation to lighten her burdens': New Canadian Library N124 (Toronto, 1976), 60–1.

55 Baxter, *No Way to Live*, 85.

56 *Vancouver Province*, 2 June 1930, 13.

57 Ibid., 10 June 1930, 14; ibid., 18 June 1930, 15.

58 Ibid., 9, 17, 25 September; 3, 11, 19 October 1935.

59 Theresa Kaufman, 'Child Mothers: Social Circumstances and Treatment Problems of Unmarried Mothers of School Age,' unpublished MSW thesis, University of British Columbia, 1962, 97.

60 Audrey Mary Coppock, 'Children in Group Homes: A Survey of Wards of the Children's Aid Society Living in These Units, Vancouver, 1954,' unpublished MSW thesis, University of British Columbia, 1955, 78.

61 Child-welfare workers expressed concern about the long-term consequence of sending 'children out to work, neither physically, emotionally nor mentally equipped to be permanent wage earners': Nora Lea, 'The Protection of Our Children,' *Canadian Welfare* 17/7 (January 1942), 49; see also Nora Lee, 'Child Labour and the War,' ibid., 17/8 (February 1942), 17–21.

62 Canada, Department of National Health and Welfare, *Report, 1946*, 79–80. In 1959–60, the department suspended allowances for fewer than 7,000 of the 6,220,000 children receiving them: ibid., *1959–60*, 3.

63 Canada, *Census, 1951*, vol. 4, table 3.

64 Helen Des Roches, 'Early School Leavers,' *Canadian Welfare* 38 (15 September 1962), 217–18.

65 Thompson, 'The Social Worker in the School,' 52.

66 Ibid., 57.

67 Ibid., 67.

68 Ibid.

69 Marlatt and Itter, eds., *Opening Doors*, 96.

70 David Weale, *Them Times* (Charlottetown, 1992), 79.

71 See Bullen, 'Hidden Workers'; Synge, 'The Transition from School to Work'; and Sutherland, *Children in English-Canadian Society*, part I.

72 Canada, Department of Health, *How to Take Care of the Father and the Family*, by Helen MacMurchy (Ottawa, 1925), 9.

73 Thompson, 'The Social Worker in the School,' 72.

74 Coppock, 'Children in Group Homes,' 101. Despite this decision the boy soon returned to the Industrial School.

75 John Calam, 'Discovering B.C. Education: A Personal Retrospect,' unpublished Phi Delta Kappa Address, University of British Columbia, 19 March 1980.

76 See Synge, 'The Transition from School to Work.'

77 Cobbin, 'Treatment of Emotionally Disturbed Teen-Age Boys,' 37.

78 In his pioneering study on the history of the family, Friedrich Engels noted that, in the family 'man ... the earner, the breadwinner of the family ... is the bourgeois, the wife represents the proletariat.' A more accurate description would state that 'the woman and the children' formed the proletariat in the family, or, in modern terminology, that a patriarchal structure subordinated them both: Frederick Engels, *The Origin of the Family, Private Property, and the State* (New York, 1972 [originally published 1884]), 81–2. Economists investigating notions that envisage people as the embodiment of human capital have considered children in this context. In a formulation that they believe applies mostly in poor countries, such economists see children as 'in a very important sense the poor man's capital.' On the other hand, parental investment in children in 'rich' countries is 'in many ways akin to the investment in home-grown trees for their beauty and fruit': Theodore W. Schultz, 'The Value of Children: An Economic Perspective,' *Journal of Political Economy* 81 (1973), 53.

79 John V. Friesen, *Never Never Give Up! An Autobiography* (Cloverdale, BC, 1986), 60.

80 Homer Stevens and Rolf Knight, *Homer Stevens: A Life in Fishing* (Madeira Park, BC, 1992), 30.

81 The number of children ever-born to ever-married women declined from 4.2 to 3.1 between 1941 and 1961: Ellen Gee, 'Fertility and Marriage Patterns in Canada, 1851–1971,' unpublished PhD dissertation, University of British Columbia, 1978, 240–2.

82 Synge, 'The Transition from School to Work,' 250.

83 Bryan D. Palmer, *Working-Class Experience: The Rise and Reconstitution of Canadian Labour, 1800–1980* (Toronto, 1983), 196. Glen H. Elder's description of the work of children of 'deprived families' in Oakland, California, in the 1930s suggests that they, too, remained in a distinctive culture: *Children of the Great Depression* (Chicago, 1974), 64–82.

7: The Working Lives of the Children of Modern Pioneers

1 For a charming but unsentimental account of pioneering in the 1970s, written from a child's point of view, see Ann Blades, *Mary of Mile 18* (Montreal, 1971).

2 For the dynamics of rural society in the nineteenth century, see Chad Gaffield

and Gerald Bouchard, 'Literacy, Schooling, and Family Reproduction in Rural Ontario and Quebec,' *Historical Studies in Education/Revue d'histoire de l'education* 2 (Fall 1989), 214–16. Late nineteenth-century pioneering childhoods are vividly described in Imbert Orchard, ed., *Growing Up in the Valley: Pioneer Childhood in the Lower Fraser Valley*, Sound Heritage Series no. 40 (Victoria, BC, 1983).

3 Robert Collins, *Butter Down the Well: Reflections of a Canadian Childhood* (Saskatoon, 1980), 171.

4 See Monica Storrs, *God's Galloping Girl* (Vancouver, 1979); Neil Sutherland, 'Social Policy, "Deviant" Children, and the Public Health Apparatus in British Columbia between the Wars,' *Journal of Educational Thought* 14 (August 1980), 80–91; and John Calam, ed., *Alex Lord's British Columbia: Recollections of a Rural School Inspector, 1915–1936* (Vancouver, 1991).

5 Isaiah Bowman, *The Pioneer Fringe* (New York, 1931), 69.

6 Norah Lewis, 'Reducing Maternal Mortality in British Columbia: An Educational Process,' in *Not Just Pin Money*, ed. B.K. Latham and R.J. Pazdro, 337–55 (Victoria, BC, 1984); Veronica Strong-Boag and Kathryn McPherson, 'The Confinement of Women: Childbirth and Hospitalization in Vancouver, 1919–1939,' *BC Studies* 69–70 (Spring/Summer 1986), 142–74. See also Cynthia Comacchio Abeele, '"The Mothers of the Land Must Suffer": Child and Maternal Welfare in Rural and Outpost Ontario, 1918–1940,' *Ontario History* 80 (September 1988), 183–205, and Cynthia Comacchio, *Nations Are Built of Babies: Saving Ontario's Mothers and Children, 1900–1940* (Montreal, 1993). For a vividly written account of birthing from the point of view of a mother living in conditions at least as harsh as those in the Bulkley Valley, see Elizabeth Goudie, *Woman of Labrador* (Toronto, 1973), *passim.*

7 Lewis, 'Reducing Maternal Mortality.'

8 'Mrs. Jim Owens Reminisces,' *Bulkley Valley Stories, Collected from Old Timers Who Remember* (n.p., n.d.), 145–6.

9 While the Evelyn School displayed some of the difficulties discussed in J. Donald Wilson and Paul J. Stortz, '"May the Lord Have Mercy on You": The Rural School Problem in British Columbia in the 1920s,' *BC Studies* 79 (Autumn 1988), 24–58, it was never an example of 'a pedagogical charnel house' of the sort noted in John H. Thompson with Allen Seager, *Canada, 1922–1939: Decades of Discord* (Toronto, 1985), 156; see also Paul James Stortz, 'The Rural School Problem in British Columbia in the 1920s,' unpublished MA thesis, University of British Columbia, 1988, especially part II: 'The Schools in the British Columbia North Central Interior: Terrace to Vanderhoof.'

10 Ian E. Davey, 'The Rhythm of Work and the Rhythm of School,' in *Egerton Ryerson and His Times*, ed. by Neil McDonald and Alf Chaiton, 221–53 (Toronto, 1978).

11 Although the calendar limits of the school year were laid out in British Columbia as early as 1882–3, rural school districts only gradually fell in line with provincial requirements. School-attendance records suggest that nearly all districts had come to comply by the 1920s: British Columbia, Department of Education, Report, 1882–3, 99; ibid., 1920–1, 76–99.

12 British Columbia, Department of Education, *Report*, 1921–2 to 1944–5, *passim*.

13 Gertrude Story, *The Last House on Main Street* (Saskatoon, 1994), 129.

14 Elizabeth Davis of Tottenham, Ontario, outlined the process as she did it as a child in Allan Anderson, ed., *Remembering the Farm: Memories of Farming, Ranching, and Rural Life in Canada, Past and Present* (Toronto, 1977), 111–12.

15 Ferne Nelson, *Barefoot on the Prairie: Memories of Life on a Prairie Homestead* (Saskatoon, 1989), 14.

16 Elizabeth Anderson Varley, *Kitimat My Valley* (Terrace, BC, 1981), 111.

17 'Childhoods Revisited Series: First Nations Childhood,' Canadian Childhood History Project, University of British Columbia, 18 October 1989.

18 Dave McIntosh, *The Seasons of My Youth* (Toronto, 1984), 52.

19 H. 'Dude' Lavington, *The Nine Lives of a Cowboy* (Victoria, BC, 1982), 22.

20 Nan Bourgon, *Rubber Boots for Dancing and Other Memories of Pioneer Life in Bulkley Valley*, ed. by Marjorie Rosberg (Smithers, BC, 1979), 9.

21 See Norah L. Lewis, 'Goose Grease and Turpentine: Mother Treats the Family's Illnesses,' *Prairie Forum* 15 (Spring 1990), 67–84.

22 Bourgon, *Rubber Boots*, 113.

23 Victor Carl Friesen, 'Sawing the Winter's Fuel,' *Bank of British Columbia's Pioneer News*, August/September 1988, 10. See also Anna Friesen and Victor Carl Friesen, *The Mulberry Tree* (n.p., 1985), for a fine account of pioneering in Saskatchewan.

24 Anderson, *Remembering the Farm*, 58–9.

25 'Resident of the Month – Mrs. Annie Donald,' Evergreen House, [Lions Gate Hospital, North Vancouver, BC], *Residents' Newsbulletin* (September 1988), 2.

26 Nelson, *Barefoot on the Prairie*, 66–7.

27 Settlers brought their agricultural terminology with them. Since my informants came from different backgrounds, I employ the first I heard (of English origin) and include the others within brackets.

28 Floyd Frank, *My Valley's Yesteryears* (Victoria, BC, 1991), 77; see also 'Picking Potatoes,' David Weale, *Them Times* (Charlottetown, 1992), 29–31.

29 The urban centre tried to exert its influence even on the design of 'outpost' houses. See, for example, Canada, Department of Health, *Beginning a Home in Canada*, and *How to Build the Canadian House*, nos. 7 and 8 in the 'Little Blue Books Home Series' written by Helen McMurchy, chief of the Division of Child Welfare.

30 In parts of the province where the climate was milder, a few families employed

tents as reasonably permanent homes. When he was a boy, reported Jim Spilsbury, he 'spent twelve years of my life living in tents,' first on Savary Island, and then at Whonnock in the Fraser Valley: Howard White and Jim Spilsbury, *Spilsbury's Coast: Pioneer Years in the Wet West* (Madeira Park, BC, 1987), 17.

31 Bourgon, *Rubber Boots*, 49–68.

32 Beryl Jones, 'The MacMillans Settle at Evelyn,' *Bulkley Valley Stories*, 155.

33 Frank, *My Valley's Yesteryears*, 44.

34 Mrs Jim Capling, as told to Marjorie Rosberg, 'A Long Time Ago,' *Bulkley Valley Stories*, 140.

35 Arthur Shelford and Cyril Shelford, *We Pioneered* (Victoria, BC, 1988), 10.

36 Louise Johnson, *Not Without Hope: The Story of Dr. H.A. McLean and the Esperanza General Hospital* (Matsqui, BC, 1992), 35–7.

37 Margaret A. Ormsby, *British Columbia: A History* (Vancouver, 1958), 'Epilogue'; Jean Barman, *The West Beyond the West: A History of British Columbia* (Toronto, 1991), ch. 12.

38 Maxwell A. Cameron, *Report of the Royal Commission of Inquiry into Educational Finance* (Victoria, BC, 1945). See also F. Henry Johnson, *A History of Public Education in British Columbia* (Vancouver, 1964), ch. 9.

39 Post-1945 economic development of the Bulkley Valley is described in British Columbia, Department of Lands and Forests, *The Prince Rupert–Smithers Bulletin Area: Bulletin Area No. 8* (Victoria, BC, 1959).

40 Abeele, 'The Mothers of the Land Must Suffer.'

41 Varley, *Kitimat*, 47.

42 Lillian York, ed., *Lure of the South Peace: Tales of the Early Pioneers to 1945* (n.p., 1981), 180.

43 Bourgon, *Rubber Boots*, 97.

44 Storrs, *God's Galloping Girl*, 93, 95, 215.

45 Bowman, *The Pioneer Fringe*, 5.

46 Earl S. Baity, *I Remember Chilako* (Prince George, BC, 1978), 72–3.

47 Varley, *Kitimat*, 75.

48 Martha Ostenso's *Wild Geese* (Toronto, 1961), first published in 1925, gives us a clear view of the role of children in families where the father's desire for land goes beyond the more customary need to use it to provide for his family and for his old age. As I understand the Evelyn experience, no father there resorted to the brutalized tyranny Ostenso's lightly fictional Caleb Gare exerted over his wife and children.

49 In turn they are part of what H. Craig Davis and Thomas A. Hutton call the 'ROP' (Rest of Province) economy in British Columbia, which they separate out from the 'metropolitan' one: 'The Two Economies of British Columbia,' *BC Studies* 82 (Summer 1989), 3–15.

50 Varley, *Kitimat*, 71.
51 Andy Russell, *Memoirs of a Mountain Man* (Toronto, 1984), 18.
52 Ian Mahood and Ken Drushka, *Three Men and a Forester* (Madeira Park, BC, 1990), 32–3.
53 Marilyn Wheeler, *The Robson Valley Story* (n.p., 1979), 199.
54 Nelson, *Barefoot on the Prairie*, 27–9.
55 Capling, 'A Long Time Ago,' 141.
56 Such patriarchal control of family-based production was not confined to farming. In the Labrador inshore fishery, 'men totally dominated ownership of the means of production more completely than any other staple-based activity,' and the location did not permit local markets, or farming activities that women elsewhere employed: Sean Cadigan, 'Battle Harbour in Transition: Merchants, Fishermen, and the State in the Struggle for Relief in a Labrador Community during the 1930s,' *Labour/Le Travail* 26 (Fall 1990), 125–50.
57 Mary Cook, *One for Sorrow, Two for Joy* (Ottawa, 1984), 121–3.
58 Capling, 'A Long Time Ago,' 141.
59 Varley, *Kitimat*, 175–7.

8: Children in Their Families: Special Occasions

1 Pierre Berton, *Starting Out, 1920–1947* (Toronto, 1987), 40–1.
2 Poet Elizabeth Bishop, who spent part of her childhood with her maternal grandparents in Great Village, Nova Scotia, wrote of the time when she was about six that her 'father was dead and my mother away in a sanitorium ... I used to ask Grandmother, when I said goodbye, to promise me not to die before I came home': *Elizabeth Bishop: The Collected Prose*, ed., with an introduction, by Robert Giroux (New York, 1984), 6.
3 Helen Porter, *Below the Bridge: Memories of the South Side of St. John's* (n. p., 1979), 106.
4 *Vancouver Sun*, 19 August 1995, D7.
5 'Childhoods Revisited Series: First Nations Childhood,' Canadian Childhood History Project, University of British Columbia, 18 October 1989.
6 MacDonald Coleman, *Once Upon a Childhood* (Red Deer, AB, 1978), 90–1.
7 E.A. Harris, *Spokeshute: Skeena River Memory* (Victoria, BC, 1990), 116.
8 Quoted in Emilie L. Montgomery, '"The War Was a Very Vivid Part of my Life": The Second World War and the Lives of British Columbian Children,' in *Children, Teachers and Schools in the History of British Columbia*, ed. Jean Barman, Neil Sutherland, and J. Donald Wilson (Calgary, 1995), 173.
9 Ibid.

10 Mildred Young Hubbert, *Since the Day I Was Born* (Thornbury, ON, 1991), 134.
11 Garth Drabinsky with Marq de Villiers, *Closer to the Sun: An Autobiography* (Toronto, 1995), 13.
12 *Vancouver Sun*, 17 July 1995, A3.
13 Mary Cook, *One for Sorrow, Two for Joy* (Ottawa, 1984), 24.
14 Daphne Marlatt and Carole Itter, eds., *Opening Doors: Vancouver's East End* (Victoria, BC, 1979), 69.
15 Harris, *Spokeshute*, 180.
16 John A. Charters, *Over My Shoulder: Reflections & Recollections of a Newspaper Columnist* (Robson, BC, 1988), 175.
17 *Vancouver Sun*, 17 June 1995, A3.
18 Ibid., 5 January 1986, F4.
19 'Childhoods Revisited Series: Prairie Girlhoods,' Canadian Childhood History Project, University of British Columbia, 23 February 1989.
20 Montgomery, '"The War Was a Very Vivid Part of my Life,"' 163.
21 Kenneth C. Boyd, *When the Ship Comes In!!!* (Duncan, BC, 1993), 61–2.
22 Hugh Palmer, *Circumnavigating Father* (Surrey, BC, 1990), 62.
23 Jacqueline Gresko, 'The View from the Centre of the Earth,' *Vancouver Historical Society Newsletter* 14 (November, 1974), n.p.
24 Ferne Nelson, *Barefoot on the Prairie: Memories of Life on a Prairie Homestead* (Saskatoon, 1989), 70.
25 *Vancouver Sun*, 20 August 1994, D10–11; ibid., 3 September 1994, D20. Although Buday mentions birthdays, they did not figure much in our interviews or in other recollections.
26 By the early 1950s, Quebec, Ontario, Manitoba, Saskatchewan, Alberta, and British Columbia had legislation providing for annual holidays with pay for all except farm workers. Except in Manitoba and Saskatchewan, domestic servants were also excluded from this benefit: Canada, Dominion Bureau of Statistics, *Canada Year Book, 1952–53*, 689.
27 Maureen Forrester with Marci McDonald, *Out of Character: A Memoir* (Toronto, 1986), 19.
28 See, for example, *Vancouver Province*, 27 May 1931, 15. The work of the Hebrew Maternity Aid Society is described in its report of 5 May 1936 in Toronto Board of Education Archives, R22, Box 5.
29 Ebbitt Cutler, *I Once Knew an Indian Woman* (Montreal, 1967), 3.
30 Susan Mayes, 'Afterword: One More River,' Arthur Mayse, *My Father, My Friend*, ed. by Susan Mayse (Madeira Park, BC, 1993), 148.
31 *Gulf Islands Driftwood*, 19 December 1990, C1, C3.
32 Charters, *Over My Shoulder*, 172.

33 Eve Rockett, 'Christmas Eve,' *Chatelaine*, December 1986, 49, 136–8.
34 Otto Tucker, 'Events Surrounding the Christmas Line,' *Newfoundland Quarterly* 88 (Winter 1992–3), 5.
35 *Vancouver Sun*, 18 December 1995, C7.
36 Philip C.P. Low, *Memories of Cumberland Chinatown* (Vancouver, 1993), 17.
37 'Childhoods Revisited Series: Ukrainian Childhoods,' Canadian Childhood History Project, University of British Columbia, 22 November 1989.
38 Aubrey M. Tizzard, *On Sloping Ground: Reminiscences of Outport Life in Notre Dame Bay, Newfoundland*, ed. J.D.A. Widdowson (St John's, 1984), 101.
39 *Vancouver Sun*, 23 December 1982, A5.
40 Gary L. Saunders, *September Christmas* (St John's, 1992), 46.
41 Robert Thomas Allen, *My Childhood and Yours: Happy Memories of Growing Up* (Toronto, 1977), 57.
42 *Bank of British Columbia Pioneer News*, December 1986/January 1987, 4.
43 Maria Campbell, *Halfbreed* (Toronto, 1973), 50.
44 Robert Collins, *Butter Down the Well: Reflections of a Canadian Childhood* (Saskatoon, 1980), 100.
45 Fredelle Bruser Maynard, *Raisins and Almonds* (Markham, ON, 1973), 27–37.
46 *Vancouver Sun*, 23 December 1991, A10.
47 Helen Sigurdson, *I Wanted You to Know* (Winnipeg, 1994), 37–8.
48 Sing Lim, *West Coast Chinese Boy* (Montreal, 1979), 52.
49 Daphne Marlatt and Carole Itter, eds., *Opening Doors: Vancouver's East End* (Victoria, BC, 1979), 113.
50 Reuben Slonim, *Grand to Be an Orphan* (Toronto, 1983), 79–80.
51 Lawrence Freiman, *Don't Fall Off the Rocking Horse: An Autobiography* (Toronto, 1978), 31.
52 The excitement of the 1939 royal visit for a boy on a prairie farm is described in Collin's 'The Day the King Came to Moose Jaw,' in *Butter Down the Well*, 119–25.

9: Children in 'Formalist' Schools

1 For affectionate accounts of rural schooling, see Joan Adams and Becky Thomas, *Floating Schools and Frozen Inkwells: The One-Room Schools of British Columbia* (n. p., 1985); and John C. Charyk, *The Little White Schoolhouse* (Saskatoon, 1968); *Pulse of the Community* (Saskatoon, 1970); and *Those Bittersweet Schooldays* (Saskatoon, 1977).
2 For a contemporary perspective on elementary schooling in the 1950s, see Joseph Katz, ed., *Elementary Schooling in Canada* (Toronto, 1961).
3 Jessie Mifflen, *A Collection of Memories* (St John's, 1989), 1.

4 Roy Bonisteel, *There Was a Time* ... (Toronto, 1991), 193.

5 'Chicken Little,' appeared in *The Canadian Readers: Book One: A Primer and First Reader* (Toronto, 1922), 74–80. I have not been able to find out from which books the first two sentences came, but the person who recollected the third is obviously recalling an early story in the reader by Henrietta Roy, Elsie Roy, P.H. Sheffield, and Grace Bollert, *Highroads to Reading: Jerry and Jane: The Primer* (Toronto, 1932). 'Spot' was a pet in the famous American 'Dick and Jane' series, introduced in Canada after the Second World War. The first 'pre-primer' in the series was William S. Gray, Dorothy Baruch, and Elizabeth Montgomery, *We Look and See* (Toronto, n.d.).

6 Evelyn Huang with Lawrence Jeffery, *Chinese Canadians: Voices from a Community* (Vancouver, 1992), 93.

7 School architecture in Canada is surveyed and illustrated in a series of Parks Canada research bulletins. Although they deal only with years up to 1930, because so few schools were built during the Depression and the war, these publications in fact show school design as it was, except for the new buildings of the 1950s. See, for example, Ivan J. Saunders, 'A Survey of British Columbia School Architecture to 1930,' *Research Bulletin* no. 225, Parks Canada, November 1984.

8 Victoria *Times-Colonist*, 22 May 1994, M4.

9 The wording is taken from a copy now in the possession of Jean Barman. See also Vancouver School Board, *Report, 1940,* 55. Mildred Young Hubbert recalled that the same words appeared in a reader she used in Ontario in the early 1930s: *Since the Day I Was Born* (Thornbury, ON, 1991), 79.

10 E.A. Harris, *Spokeshute: Skeena River Memory* (Victoria, BC, 1990), 115.

11 See British Columbia, Department of Education, *Report*, 1943–4, B30; British Columbia, *Statutes*, 1944, c. 45.

12 In 1930, 3.9 per cent of Vancouver pupils had goiter. By 1936, this had declined to 1.1 per cent: Vancouver School Board, *Report, 1937*, 31–2.

13 Mary Thomson, 'The Social Worker in the School: An Experimental Study of the Liaison and Service Functions of the Social Worker in a Vancouver Elementary School,' unpublished MSW thesis, University of British Columbia, 1948, 49.

14 *Vancouver Sun*, 29 August 1981, A5.

15 Hubbert, *Since the Day I Was Born*, 88.

16 *Vancouver Sun*, 14 March 1995, A3.

17 Ibid., 12 January 1994, A3.

18 See George H. Limpus and John W.B. Shore, *Elementary General Science* (Toronto, 1935), 11–12.

19 H.B. MacLean, *The MacLean Method of Writing: Teachers' Complete Manual: A Complete Course of Instruction in the Technique and Pedagogy of the MacLean Method*

of *Writing for Teachers of Elementary Schools, Junior and Senior High Schools, Commercial Schools, and Normal Schools* (Vancouver, 1921). The note at the foot of the title page of the thirty-first edition says that it is authorized for use in British Columbia, Quebec, Nova Scotia, Prince Edward Island, New Brunswick, and Newfoundland.

20 Victoria *Times-Colonist*, 22 May 1994, M4.

21 Stanley Coren, *The Left-Hander Syndrome: The Causes and Consequences of Left-Handedness* (New York, 1992), ch. 1.

22 Hugh Palmer, *Circumnavigating Father* (Surrey, BC, 1990), 64.

23 William C. Macklon, *The Fledgling Years* (Saskatoon, 1990), 32.

24 Sir Ernest MacMillan, ed., *A Canadian Song Book* (Toronto, 1937). The first edition of this text appeared in 1928.

25 The nature of school music and other broadcasts are described in Laurie Elizabeth Ion, 'Over the Airwaves: School Broadcasts in British Columbia, 1960–1982,' unpublished MA thesis, University of British Columbia, 1992. Ion reports that teachers used music broadcasts more frequently than those on other subjects.

26 Melinda McCracken, *Memories Are Made of This* (Toronto, 1975), 54.

27 Lord Tennyson School pioneered platooning in Vancouver in 1924. By 1938, all elementary schools in the city employed some form of specialist teaching: Vancouver School Board, *Report, 1925*, 11–12; ibid., 1937–8, 64–5. The American origins of platooning are described in Raymond E. Callahan, *Education and the Cult of Efficiency: A Study of the Social Forces That Have Shaped the Administration of the Public Schools* (Chicago, 1962), 128–36.

28 Both poems, the first by Walter de la Mare, the second by John Masefield, appeared in E.G. Daniels, T.R. Hall, and H.H. MacKenzie, *Dominion Language Series*, Book 2 (Toronto, 1932), 68 and 179.

29 *Vancouver Sun*, 26 August 1995, A3. A 'demonstration' Junior Red Cross meeting conducted by a class at Tecumseh School in Vancouver in May 1936 is described in 'Practical Citizenship,' *B.C. Teacher*, June 1936, 17–19. See also Nancy M. Sheehan, 'The Junior Red Cross Movement in Saskatchewan, 1919–1929: Rural Improvement through the Schools,' in *Building Beyond the Homestead: Rural History on the Prairies*, ed. David C. Jones and Ian MacPherson, 66–86 (Calgary, 1985).

30 In the 1920s, one woman in Vancouver, one woman in Point Grey, and nine women in South Vancouver held school principalships for one or more years. By the school year 1930–1, and after the three districts had amalgamated, only one woman – a former South Vancouver principal – still held the role. After Miss E.M. Dickieson retired in 1934, all forty-nine Vancouver elementary schools had male principals: British Columbia, Department of Education, *Report, 1935–36*,

H165–82. The next female principal was appointed in 1969. In Catholic schools, however, a sister often served as principal.

31 Christmas concerts are fondly recalled in John C. Charyk, *The Biggest Day of the Year: The Old-Time School Christmas Concert* (Saskatoon, 1985).

32 See Charles M. Johnson, 'The Children's War: The Mobilization of Ontario Youth During the Second World War,' in *Patterns of the Past: Interpreting Ontario's History*, ed. Roger Hall, William Westfall, and Laurel S. MacDowell, 356–79 (Toronto, 1988); Emilie Montgomery, '"The War Was a Very Vivid Part of My Life": The Second World War and the Lives of British Columbian Children,' in *Children, Teachers and Schools in the History of British Columbia*, ed. Jean Barman, Neil Sutherland, and J. Donald Wilson, 161–74 (Calgary, 1995); Patricia Roy '"Due to Their Keenness": The Education of Japanese Canadian Children in the British Columbia Interior Housing Settlements during World War Two,' in ibid., 375–92; Norah Lewis, '"Isn't This a Terrible War?": Children's Attitudes to Two World Wars,' *Historical Studies in Education* 7/2 (Fall 1995), 193–215.

33 *Books in Canada*, 22. The minutes of a staff meeting held at Vancouver's Charles Dickens School on 5 October 1942 note: 'Re Air Raids – (1st) If there is time – Send class home. (2nd) If there is only a little time, send pupils to the basement. (3rd) If there is no time, pupils and teachers under their desks. N.B. If you hear any anti-air craft fire, there is no time to go home.'

34 Mary di Michele, 'Writers from Invisible Cities,' *Canadian Woman Studies/ Cahiers de la femme* 8 (Summer 1987), 37.

35 Toronto *Globe and Mail*, 13 September 1986, D7.

36 Seymour Levitan and Carol Miller, eds., *Lucky to Live in Cedar Cottage: Memories of Lord Selkirk Elementary School and Cedar Cottage Neighbourhood, 1911–1963* (Vancouver, 1986), 46.

37 Robert Collins, 'Miss Apple Daisy,' *Reader's Digest* (Canadian edition), September 1976, 144. A research study on the effects of Miss Appugliese's teaching, involving both a study of school records and interviews with former pupils then in their thirties, is reported in Eigel Pedersen, Thérèse Annette Faucher, with William W. Eaton, 'A New Perspective on the Effects of First-Grade Teachers on Children's Subsequent Adult Status,' *Harvard Educational Review*, 48 (February 1978), 1–31.

38 Geiri Johnson, *My Compass Points North* (Arnes, MN 1994), 4.

39 Mary Razzell, 'Tribute to a Teacher,' Bank of British Columbia's *Pioneer News*, April/May 1988, 15.

40 Toronto *Globe and Mail*, 31 August 1985, A 6.

41 Mary Thomson, 'The Social Worker in the School: An Experimental Study of the Liaison and Service Functions of the Social Worker in a Vancouver Elementary School,' unpublished MSW thesis, University of British Columbia, 1948, 105.

42 Michael Enright, 'Notes of a Native Son,' *Quest*, March 1984, 24.
43 Daphne Marlatt and Carole Itter, eds., *Opening Doors: Vancouver's East End* (Victoria, BC, 1979), 164.
44 John Calam drew my attention to what old annuals and class photographs tell us about the determined maturity of beginning teachers of earlier eras. Perhaps this characteristic reinforced the view of many pupils that all their teachers, as one man put it, 'were as old as the hills.' One woman, recalling a teacher of the 1930s who 'wore her hair in a bun and had dark clothes,' was really surprised, thirty years later, to read that this teacher had just retired.
45 *Vancouver Sun*, 1 February 1992, D5.
46 Pete Loudon, *The Town That Got Lost: A Story of Anyox, British Columbia* (Sidney, BC, 1973), 41.
47 Corporal punishment was rooted in the Canadian Criminal Code. Statutes, precedents, and reported cases for this era are discussed in Peter Frank Bargen, *The Legal Status of the Canadian Public School Pupil* (Toronto, 1961), 125–33; see also *Manual of the School Law and School Regulations of the Province of British Columbia* (Victoria, BC, 1944), 127–8. For a more contemporary summary, with a focus especially on Ontario, see Jeffrey Wilson and Mary Tomlinson, *Children and the Law*, 2d ed. (Toronto, 1986).
48 Robert Thomas Allen, *Your Childhood and Mine: Happy Memories of Growing Up* (Toronto, 1977), 37.
49 Mordecai Richler reported that postponement to after school, or even the next day, was also the practice at the Montreal school he attended: *Saturday Night*, March 1969, 49–50.
50 Jack Macdonald Cobbin, 'Treatment of Emotionally Disturbed Teen-Age Boys in (a Group Living) Residence: An Examination of Children's Aid Society Wards, with Special Reference to Movement Shown after a Period in a Group-Living Institution,' unpublished MSW thesis, University of British Columbia, 1955, 36.
51 Mildred May Wright, 'Social and Family Backgrounds as an Aspect of Recidivism among Juvenile Delinquents: A Compilation and Review for a Group of Juvenile Delinquents Who Failed to Respond to Programmes Provided for Their Rehabilitation,' unpublished MSW thesis, University of British Columbia, 1957, 42–50.
52 Fraser Miles, *Slow Boat on Rum Row* (Madeira Park, BC, 1992), 21.
53 Gertrude Story, *The Last House on Main Street* (Saskatoon, 1994), 168.
54 di Michele, 'Writers from Invisible Cities,' 37.
55 *Vancouver Sun*, 23 February 1994, B8.
56 Marlatt and Itter, eds., *Opening Doors*, 130.
57 Harro Van Brummelen, 'Shifting Perspectives: Early British Columbia Textbooks from 1872 to 1925,' *BC Studies* 60 (Winter 1983–4), 8.

58 Harry J. Boyle, *Memories of a Catholic Boyhood* (Don Mills, ON 1974), 10.
59 Patrick O'Flaherty, 'Caught in the Nets: Growing Up Irish Catholic in New-foundland,' *The Canadian Forum*, March 1986, 9.
60 For an account of the gendered nature of current American schooling, see Barrie Thorne, *Gender Play: Girls and Boys in School* (New Brunswick, NJ, 1993).
61 Rosanna Tite, 'Sex-Role Learning and the Woman Teacher: A Feminist Per-spective,' *Feminist Perspective Feministes* 7 (July 1986), shows how deeply rooted traditional notions are among contemporary children.
62 See Jean Barman, *Growing Up British in British Columbia: Boys in Private School* (Vancouver, 1984).
63 British Columbia, Department of Education, *Program for the Primary Grades* (Victoria, BC, 1957), 143.
64 *The Canadian Readers: Book One: A Primer and First Reader* (Toronto, 1933), 27.
65 This discussion is in part based on Lynne A. Saddington, 'Family Life in Grade One British Columbia Primers, 1900–1985,' MEd Major Paper, University of British Columbia, 1985.
66 Donalda Dickie, Belle Ricker, Clara Tyner, and T.W. Woodhead, *Gay Adventurers* (Toronto, 1947).
67 Fredelle Bruser Maynard, *Raisins and Almonds* (Markham, ON, 1973), 127.
68 Max Braithwaite, *Never Sleep Three in a Bed* (Toronto, 1969), 37.
69 Percy Janes, *House of Hate* (Toronto, 1970), 140.
70 This statement is supported both by my interviews and by an examination of such data as class size and teacher qualification for selected schools from differ-ent neighbourhoods in the city.
71 Jean Barman, '"Knowledge Is Essential for Universal Progress But Fatal to Class Privilege": Working People and the Schools in Vancouver During the 1920s,' *Labour/Le Travail* 22 (Fall 1988), 9–66.
72 British Columbia, Department of Education, *Report, 1939–40*, B32.
73 For an analysis of the dichotomy between theory and practice in Canadian edu-cation at the time, see George S. Tomkins, *A Common Countenance: Stability and Change in the Canadian Curriculum* (Toronto, 1986).

10: Children in the Culture of Childhood

1 Barry Glassner, 'Kid Society,' *Urban Education* 11 (1976–7), 5–21, describes school-ground culture in the United States. Much of Barrie Thorne, *Gender Play: Girls and Boys in School* (New Brunswick, NJ, 1993), also deals with school-ground culture.
2 Naomi Miller once visited a school in Saskatoon. Of this visit she wrote: 'There were over a hundred students playing in the schoolyard, but there was no roar.

Some were swinging and sliding on slides, some were skipping, some playing catch or football. The only sounds were the slap, slap, slap of skipping ropes, or the thud of a football being kicked with different degrees of strength. The children were happy, even laughing without a sound. It was an amazing silence that I observed at the School for the Deaf': Letter to the author, 23 May 1989.

3 Sylvia Fraser, *My Father's House: A Memoir of Incest and Healing* (Toronto, 1987), 149.

4 For more recent American examples of the study of children's play patterns, based on direct observation, see Janet Lever, 'Sex Differences in the Games Children Play,' *Social Problems* 23 (1976), 478–87; Janet Lever, 'Sex Differences in the Complexity of Children's Play and Games,' *American Sociological Review* 43 (1978), 471–83; and Barrie Thorne, 'Girls and Boys Together ... But Mostly Apart: Gender Arrangements in Elementary Schools,' in *Relationships and Development* ed. Willard W. Hartup and Zick Rubin, 167–84 (Hillsdale, NJ, 1986).

5 Charles A. Dougan, *My Daughter's Request: Spotlight on the Yesterday of Country Folk* (Duncan, BC, 1991), 12.

6 Thorne asks whether American children have separate girls' and boys' cultures. On the basis of her own research and that of others, she concludes that they do not. I do not think the question would have arisen at all if she and others looked more systematically at children when they were away from school: *Gender Play*, ch. 6.

7 From the point of view of the transmission of the folklore of childhood, Edith Fowke notes that 'there is a complete turn-over [of children] every five years': Edith Fowke, *Sally Go Round the Sun: 300 Songs, Rhymes and Games of Canadian Children* (Toronto, 1969), 6.

8 Elizabeth Brewster, *The Invention of Truth* (n. p., 1991), 9–10.

9 A survey conducted in 1948 concluded that only about 5 per cent of the preschool population of British Columbia attended any kindergarten or other preschool group: E.J.M. Church, 'An Evaluation of Preschool Institutions in Canada,' *Canadian Education* 5 (June 1950), 20; see also Gillian M. Weiss, 'The Development of Public School Kindergartens in British Columbia,' unpublished MA thesis, University of British Columbia, 1979, 135.

10 Willard W. Hartup, 'Peer Interaction and Social Organization,' in *Carmichael's Manual of Child Psychology*, ed P.H. Mussen (New York, 1970), vol. 2, 392–3.

11 See T. Berntd, 'The Nature and Significance of Children's Friendships,' *Annals of Child Development* 5 (1988), 156–86, for a survey of research on the topic. In addition to the examples used in this chapter, Canadian recollections are full of descriptions of youthful friendships. Two of my favourites are Pete Loudon's affectionate description of his grade-school friendship with Frank, and Leila Carroll's of her friend Jean: Pete Loudon, *The Town That Got Lost: A Story of*

Anyox, British Columbia (Sidney, BC, 1973), 36–43; Leila Carroll, *Wild Roses and Rail Fences* (Courteney, BC, 1975), 63–7.

12 See Hartup, 'Peer Interaction,' 396; see also Lilian B. Rubin, *Just Friends: The Role of Friendship in Our Lives* (New York, 1985), esp. ch. 9.

13 Harry Stack Sullivan, *The Interpersonal Theory of Psychiatry* (New York, 1953), 245. Some research supports this notion. Thus David Rosenham explains that 'evidence is accumulating that kindness is pervasive in the behaviour of young children; it can easily be elicited in a variety of experimental or natural settings': 'Prosocial Behavior in Children,' in *The Young Child: Reviews of Research*, ed. Willard W. Hartup, vol. 2 (Washington, DC, 1972), 357.

14 Willard W. Hartup, 'Children and Their Friends,' in *Issues in Child Development* ed. Harry McGurk (London, 1978), 157–8; D. Eder and M. Hallinan, 'Sex Differences in Children's Friendships,' *American Sociological Review* 43 (1978), 273–350; Rubin, *Just Friends*, ch. 4.

15 This definition is looser than that employed by psychologists. David R.Shaffer, for example, says that 'the "peer group" consists mainly of same-sex playmates of different ages. Indeed, developmentalists define peers as "those who interact at similar levels of behavioural complexity" because only a small percentage of the child's associates are actual age mates': *Developmental Psychology: Theory, Research, and Applications* (Monterey, CA, 1985), 688.

16 See Hartup, 'Peer Interaction,' 369–73.

17 Joseph Kett, 'The History of Age Grouping in America,' in *Rethinking Childhood: Perspectives on Development and Society* ed. Arlene Skolnick (Boston, 1976), 216; see also Melvin Konner, 'Relations among Infants and Juveniles in Comparative Perspective,' in *Friendship and Peer Relations*, ed. Michael Lewis and Leonard A. Rosenblum (New York, 1975), 123.

18 Dorothy Livesay, *Journey with My Selves: A Memoir, 1909–1963* (Vancouver, 1991), 121.

19 Irene Brown, 'In and Around South Vancouver,' Vancouver Historical Society, *Newsletter* 14 (January 1975), n.p.

20 Merna Summers's short story 'Hooking Things' provides a fine acccount of a girl who slipped into shoplifting over part of her childhood: *North of the Battle* (Vancouver, 1988), 56–77.

21 See, for example, Section 3.04, 'Rules of the Council of Public Instruction,' *Manual of the School Law* (Victoria, BC, 1958), 114.

22 Edith Fowke has made invaluable collections of the games and pastimes of Canadian children. See her *Red Rover, Red Rover: Children's Games Played in Canada* (Toronto, 1988) and *Sally Go Round the Sun*.

23 Margaret Atwood, *Cat's Eye* (Toronto, 1988), 94.

24 *Vancouver Sun* 29 August 1981, A5. With slight variations in wording, girls employed this verse in many places in Canada and elsewhere: Fowke, *Sally*, 59, 151.

25 The rules governing marbles as they were played in southern Alberta in the 1930s are carefully described in Alvin Harms, *Prairie Sunset: A Boyhood Remembered* (Calgary, 1994), 67–86.

26 'Ships and sailors' is described in Loudon, *Anyox*, 39.

27 William C. Macklon, *The Fledgling Years* (Saskatoon, 1990), 32–3.

28 *Vancouver Sun*, 15 September 1995, A3.

29 A Greater Vancouver Yo-Yo contest is described in *Vancouver Sun*, 27 March 1958. Stuart McLean tells of his own experience with Yo-Yos, and of their history and supposed Canadian origins in, 'A Short History of the Yo-Yo,' *The Morning Side World of Stuart McLean* (Toronto, 1989), 179–85.

30 See, for example, *Vancouver Sun*, 29 April 1944, 28; 16 June 1944, 14; 19 June 1944, 10.

31 Marjory Helen Munro, 'A General Survey and Evaluation of an Institution for the Observation and Treatment of Problem Children,' unpublished MA thesis, University Of British Columbia, 1946, 71.

32 *Vancouver Sun*, 31 October 1994, A3.

33 Gerald Paul, 'Hope's Poor Cousin,' *United Church Observer*, October 1992, 42.

34 Victoria *Times-Colonist*, 17 September 1993, C1.

35 Opie and Opie also noticed that neighbourhood play in Britain was less aggressive than that of the schoolyard: see Iona and Peter Opie, *Children's Games in Street and Playground* (Oxford, 1969), 13.

36 For a discussion of 'bush' in Vancouver, see James M. Sandison, 'City Bush,' Vancouver Historical Society, *Newsletter*, 13 (February 1974), n.p.; and Rolf Knight, *Along the No. 20 Line: Reminiscences of the Vancouver Waterfront* (Vancouver 1980), 60–6. Going 'up the bush' in Toronto is described by Robert Thomas Allen, *My Childhood and Yours: Happy Memories of Growing Up* (Toronto, 1977), 19–31.

37 See Lee Bacchus, 'Heard It on the Grapevine,' *Vancouver Sun*, 25 August 1984, E5.

38 Nadine Jones quoted from a number of autograph albums from these years in her *Vancouver Sun* column, 11 July 1994, C5, and 29 August 1994, C5.

39 In 1994, the thirty-fifth anniversary of Barbie's entry on the market stimulated many newspaper stories and recollections. See, for example, *Vancouver Sun*, 9 March 1994, B1; ibid., 10 March 1994, A19; ibid., 16 April 1994, D6–7; ibid., 30 April 1994, D20.

40 Farley Mowat, *Born Naked* (Toronto, 1993), 45.

41 *Vancouver Sun*, 9 January 1992, A 13.

42 I did not understand oblique references to this case that came up in at least three interviews until I read Howard White, 'Duchaume: Anatomy of a Legend,' *Raincoast Chronicles* 9 (1979), 51–7.

43 Kerry Banks, 'Summer's Game,' *Western Living*, August 1984, 62.

44 Eric Stofer, *Growing Up in Victoria* (Victoria, BC, 1994), 37.

45 Gary Saunders, 'Bonfire Night,' *The Atlantic Advocate*, November 1978, 48.

46 E.A. Harris, *Spokeshute: Skeena River Memory* (Victoria, BC, 1990), 120.

47 Robert H. Thompson, *Penny Candy, Bobskates and Frozen Roadapples: Growing Up in the Thirties and Forties* (Victoria, BC, 1990), 3. F.G. Paci's novel *Black Madonna* (Toronto, 1982), 126–30, provides a fine description of the role that the skating rink and rink 'shack' played in many Canadian youngsters' lives.

48 *Vancouver Sun*, 28 October 1995, D9.

49 John A. Charters, *Over My Shoulder: Reflections and Recollections of a Newspaper Columnist* (Robson, BC, 1988), 64. See also Grant Buday, 'Halloween Was One Big Pig Out,' *Vancouver Sun*, 29 October 1994, D4–5.

50 See Joe Rosenblatt, *Escape from the Glue Factory: A Memoir of a Paranormal Toronto Childhood in the Late Forties* (Toronto, 1985), 33–5, for an account of this form of harassment.

51 Ebbitt Cutler, *I Once Knew an Indian Woman* (Montreal, 1967), 7.

52 'Dolls, Rollerskates and Dockyards,' in Knight, *Along the No. 20 Line*, 192.

53 For the wide-ranging reading of a sometimes sickly and often lonely child, see Earle Birney, 'Child Addict in Alberta,' *Canadian Literature* 90 (Autumn 1981), 6–12.

54 'Books,' Toronto *Globe and Mail*, 17 November 1984, 1.

55 *Vancouver Sun*, 5 June 1993, C9.

56 Mordecai Richler, 'The Great Comic Book Heroes,' in *Hunting Tigers Under Glass: Essays and Reports* (London, 1971), 78–89.

57 *Vancouver Province*, 22 November 1935, 29.

58 Lloyd H. Person, *No Foot in Heaven* (Saskatoon, 1978), 5–6.

59 Geiri Johnson, *My Compass Points North* (Arnes, MN, 1994), 111.

60 My subjective evaluation is confirmed, at least for American children, by an extensive investigation into the role of motion pictures in the lives of young people conducted by social scientists under the auspices of the Payne Foundation. The research, conducted between 1929 and 1933, is summarized in Henry James Forman, *Our Movie-Made Children* (New York, 1933). I am indebted to film historian Aristides Gazetas for drawing these studies to my attention.

61 See, for example, Rosenblatt, *Escape*, 47–8.

62 Marion Engel, 'The Smell of Sulphur,' in *The Tattooed Woman* (Toronto, 1985), 114.

63 Many children died in a theatre fire in Montreal in 1927.

64 In *Cat's Eye*, Margaret Atwood provides a fascinating fictional account of the role that power played in the lives of some girls after the Second World War.

65 Lawrence Freiman, *Don't Fall Off the Rocking Horse: An Autobiography* (Toronto, 1978), 20.

66 Michael Enright, 'Notes of a Native Son,' *Quest*, March 1984, 24.

67 *Vancouver Sun*, 20 December 1993, A3.

68 Allen, *My Childhood*, 33.

69 Ted Ashlee, *Gabby, Ernie and Me: A Vancouver Boyhood* (Vancouver, 1976), 127.

Chapter 11: Conclusion: Continuity and Change in the Lives of Children

1 *The Family and the Socialization of Children: Report of the October 1979 Workshop Directed by David Radcliffe ... [at] the University of Western Ontario* (Ottawa, 1980), 1.

2 John F. Conway, *The Canadian Family in Crisis*, rev. ed. (Toronto 1993), vii. See also part II: 'Victims of the Crisis: Children,' 41–88.

3 A thorough statistical analysis of the current state of Canadian families is laid out in *Profiling Canada's Families* (Ottawa, 1994).

4 Canadian Institute of Child Health, *The Health of Canada's Children: A CICH Profile* (Ottawa, 1989), ch. 2.

5 For a vigorous articulation of this point, see William A. Hynes, 'Lies, Damned Lies and Statistics,' *Our Schools/Our Selves* 33 (February 1994), 93–103; 'A Good Idea and Its Enemies: Part 2: The Best Kept Secrets of North American Education,' ibid. (July 1994), 95–107.

6 Viviana A. Zelizer, *Pricing the Priceless Child: The Changing Social Value of Children* (New York, 1985), 11. In my view, the change has been more of degree than of kind. As recent work on the history of childhood makes clear, in both the near and distant past most families viewed their children as affective as well as economic assets. On the other hand, children still play a major if not necessarily monetary role in their family's economy. They are also seen as a bulwark against neglect, loneliness, and hardship in old age.

7 British Columbia, *A Report on the Health of British Columbians: Provincial Health Officer's Annual Report, 1992*, 26.

8 See, for example, Bruce Curtis, D.W. Livingstone, and Harry Smaller, *Stacking the Deck: The Streaming of Working-Class Kids in Ontario Schools* (Toronto, 1992).

9 While I generally agree with Jean Barman that the public funds provided independent schools in British Columbia have to some extent 'deprivatized' many of them, the élitist schools in their ranks have changed very little. Indeed, one could argue that public assistance has enabled such schools to increase the social if not intellectual distance between them and public schools: Barman, 'Depriva-

tizing Private Education: The British Columbia Experience,' *The Canadian Journal of Education*, 16/1 (1991), 12–31.

10 *Health of Canada's Children*, ch. 6. See also the Vancouver School Board's brief, 'Canada's Challenge? Canada's Legacy? 1.4 Million Children Living in Poverty,' to the House of Commons Standing Committee on Human Resources Development, December 1994.

11 Sheila Baxter, *A Child Is Not a Toy: Voices of Children in Poverty* (Vancouver, 1993), especially 'Interviews with Children,' 42–77.

12 Ibid., 48.

13 *Vancouver Sun*, 7 May 1994, B12.

14 In nineteenth-century working-class families, wives and children who worked for wages outside the home often had greater control over their lives than their absolute legal dependence might suggest. In turn, the 'family wage' that made husbands and fathers the sole supporters of their families, and became increasingly prevalent from the late nineteenth century until the 1960s, may actually have increased paternal authority. The complexities of family dynamics, however, suggest that one should generalize on this topic with great caution. For the nineteenth-century working-class family, see Bettina Bradbury, *Working Families: Age, Gender, and Daily Survival in Industrializing Montreal* (Toronto, 1993).

15 See the 'Children in Distress' series, *Vancouver Sun*, 22 April 1995, A1, B4; 24 April 1995, A1, A13, A15, D4.

16 *Winnipeg Free Press*, 30 September 1994, B1.

17 *Vancouver Sun*, 9 April 1994, D20.

18 Professor Anthony Davis and members of his Conflict, War, and Violence class, Simon Fraser University, 'After Dunblane, What Can Be Done?' ibid., 29 March 1996, A9.

19 Canada, Statistics Canada, 1981 Census, *Canada's Lone Parent Families* (Ottawa, 1984), table 1.

20 See Alvin Finkel, '"Even the Little Children Cooperated": Family Strategies, Childcare Discourse, and Social Welfare Debates, 1945–1975,' an unpublished paper presented to the Canadian Historical Association, Calgary, June 1994.

21 See, however, Donald J. Weeren, *Educating Religiously in the Multi-Faith School* (Calgary, 1986), for some Canadian examples of efforts to add an explicitly religious dimension to such courses.

22 Reginald W. Bibby and Donald C. Posterski, *Teen Trends: A Nation in Motion* (Toronto, 1992), ch. 7. See also Reginald W. Bibby and Donald C. Posterski, *The Emerging Generation: An Inside Look at Canada's Teenagers* (Toronto, 1985). Some related American literature is much more alarmist. See, for example, Ken Magrid and Carole A. McKelvey, *High Risk: Children without a Conscience* (New York, 1988).

23 The most vigorous attack on the twentieth century's 'relativized and subjectified' morality under which 'virtues ceased to be "virtues" and became "values"' is made in Gertrude Himmelfarb, *The De-Moralization of Society: From Victorian Virtues to Modern Values* (New York, 1995).

24 A.J.C. King, A.S. Robertson, and W.K Warren, *Canada Health Attitudes and Behaviours Survey – 9, 12 and 15 year olds, 1984–85*, (Kingston, ON, 1985), quoted in *Health of Canada's Children*, 64.

25 Gabrielle Roy, *The Fragile Lights of Earth: Articles and Memoirs, 1942-1970*, trans. Alan Brown (Toronto, 1982), 149.

26 Baxter, *A Child Is Not a Toy*, 73.

27 Richard S. Cardinal, 'I Was a Victim of Child Neglect,' *Edmonton Journal*, 4 August 1984; reprinted as 'Alone and Very Scared,' in *Native American Testimony: A Chronicle of Indian–White Relations from Prophecy to the Present, 1492–1992*, ed. Peter Nabokov, 413–18 (Harmondsworth, 1991). I am grateful to Rebecca Priegert Coulter for drawing this diary to my attention.

28 Mary McKenzie, *When I Was Thirteen* (Aylmer, ON, 1979), 112. Mary McKenzie was the pseudonym Christina Young employed when she first published her diary some twenty years after writing it. She was the fifth of nine children of an Ontario farm family of very modest means.

29 The words are those of pioneer Canadian child-saver J.J. Kelso, quoted in *Children in English-Canadian Society*, 17.

30 See Penelope Leach, *Children First: What Our Society Must Do – and Is Not Doing – for Our Children Today* (New York, 1994).

31 Ellen Key, *Century of the Child* (New York, 1909).

32 'Declaration of the Rights of the Child,' adopted by the General Assembly of the United Nations, 20 November 1959; 'The Convention on the Rights of the Child,' adopted by the General Assembly of the United Nations, 20 November 1989.

33 The full texts of the 'World Declaration on the Survival, Protection and Development of Children,' the 'Plan of Action for Implementing the Declaration in the 1990s,' and the 'Convention on the Rights of the Child' are contained in James P. Grant, *The State of the World's Children 1991* (New York, 1991), 53–96.

34 'Convention,' Article 19.

Photo Credits

Index